MIRABEAU

MIRABEAU

MIRABEAU

A STUDY
OF A
DEMOCRATIC MONARCHIST

by

OLIVER J. G. WELCH

JONATHAN CAPE
THIRTY BEDFORD SQUARE
LONDON

FIRST PUBLISHED 1951

Dewey Classification

923.244

PRINTED IN GREAT BRITAIN IN THE CITY OF OXFORD
AT THE ALDEN PRESS
BOUND BY A. W. BAIN & CO. LTD., LONDON

CONTENTS

ILLUSTRATIONS

PREFACE

THOUGH cast in biographical form, this book is not intended to be a full biography of Mirabeau. Such an undertaking would not only require a much larger work, for his life is very fully documented, but it would also be superfluous, for the job has been done already. My aim has rather been to make a study of a man who was sufficiently remarkable in himself and who is perennially fascinating because of his relation to his times. Mirabeau is, as it were, a great question-mark in the margin of modern history, a man whose career forces us to pause and ask 'Need it have been so?' He is one of history's great failures, but his failure is more interesting than most men's successes; which is the reason why there have been so many books about him, and my excuse for adding one more to the number.

The materials for the study of Mirabeau's career are immense, and I make no pretence to have exhausted them. For the convenience, however, of serious students I have indicated the principal sources on which I have relied. These notes are placed together at the end of the volume, where they will not bother the general reader, while, for ease of reference, their numbers run in a single series throughout the text.

My thanks are due to Mr. J. M. Thompson of Magdalen College, Oxford, for reading a large part of my manuscript. How great has been the benefit of his criticism and encouragement will be readily appreciated by all English students of the French Revolution. I am also indebted to him and to Mr. Basil Blackwell for kind permission to reproduce from *Leaders of the French Revolution* the line drawing of Layfayette.

O. J. G. W.

Roselands
Bucklebury
1950

MIRABEAU

CHAPTER I

FORMATION

I N 1747 the only son of Victor de Riqueti, Marquis de Mirabeau, died of drinking ink. The father, though blessed with three daughters, and himself rising to renown in the world of writers, was anxious for a male heir. His friend, the Duc de Nivernois, communicated to him a secret which, he assured him, could not fail to result in the begetting of a boy, and when, on March 9th, 1749, the efficacy of the advice became manifest, the delighted Marquis wrote to the Duke: 'You know now that I have a son who owes his existence to you.'

The new infant Comte de Mirabeau was neither beautiful nor perfect. One ankle was slightly twisted and he was tongue-tied, but he was an exceptionally lusty baby, with two teeth already formed at birth. They christened him Gabriel Honoré.

The estate of Mirabeau was situated in Provence, and in successive generations of Riquetis the hot and extravagant temper of the south was sufficiently pronounced. The family had been merchants of Marseilles in the sixteenth century, and before its close Jean Riqueti had made a fortune, married a Provençal noblewoman and bought the château and estate of Mirabeau on the Durance. There his grandson entertained the young Louis XIV, and in 1685 letters patent raised the *seigneurie* to the dignity of Marquisate.

Ambitious and self-important, Victor, the present Marquis, had in 1740 added to his Provençal patrimony the modest Renaissance château and charming lands of Le Bignon, between Nemours and Montargis, and it was here that Gabriel Honoré was born.

This 'little basket of grassland', as the Marquis lovingly called it, 'so quaintly variegated with trees, coppices, water and tillage', was a welcome retreat from the scorched, rocky landscape that quivered in the glare as one surveyed its sparse mulberries and ilexes from the squat towers of Mirabeau in summer. Le Bignon was also convenient for Paris, a matter of importance to the Marquis, a man of the pen, who needed easy contacts with his kind.

He was a disciple of Quesnay, the physiocrat, who taught that agriculture was the only source of wealth, and Le Bignon became his chosen plot for the application of his philosophy. Here as the philanthropic farmer-squire watching the ripening of the crops, directing the irrigation of the water-meadows, seeing to the repair of buildings, chatting familiarly with his village folk, receiving their homage on feast-days when he would be with them at Mass in the morning, and in the evening with them again for the singing and dancing — in all this he was at his happiest and best. He was least happy in his family relations.[1]

A spell of military service was in the normal course of a young noble, but Victor Riqueti had little liking for the life, and as he came into his inheritance at twenty-five he was ready to quit the army at twenty-eight and give himself to his chosen part of *seigneur philosophe*. This was in 1743, and in the same year he married Marie Geneviève de Vassan, a girl of sixteen whom he had never seen, but whom he understood to be heiress to important fiefs in Poitou, Périgord and Limousin. Though the girl had nothing to commend her beyond the expectation of her mother's rent-rolls, and though marriage had, of course, nothing to do with romance, a certain minimum of compatibility was needed for even such a cold-blooded alliance as this to succeed. If that minimum was wanting between the Marquis and his bride, he had only himself to blame; he had found his prospective father-in-law detestable and his future mother-in-law scarcely sane, and should not have been unduly surprised when his wife turned out to be slatternly, moody, malicious and indiscreet. Yet he could not have married more rashly if he had been madly in love; he allowed himself to be gulled by the Marquis de Vassan, who gave his daughter a beggarly 4000 *livres* a year, while the rich mother reserved absolute freedom to dispose as she pleased of the fortune, expectation of which was the bride's solitary attraction.

A third son, Boniface, Vicomte de Mirabeau, born in 1754, completed the propagation of a husband and wife whose discord made a wretched home for their children to grow up in. The Marquise showed little affection for them, and their father sent the girls at an early age to the Dominican convent at Montargis. There were few subjects on which the Marquis was unwilling to theorize, and he had written a pamphlet on the education of girls, warmly advocating a sound home upbringing; but the case of his own daughters was, of course, a special one, so the three of them were packed off to their convent school, like the daughters of less enlightened noblemen, and saw their father only at intervals of several years, despite his interest in the education of girls.

2

Belonging to the last generation of European children to live without the protection of Dr. Jenner's vaccine, Gabriel Honoré fell a victim to the common scourge of small-pox before his fourth birthday. It left its permanent mark on a face destined to develop power but not beauty, a face whose features came from his mother's side and stirred in his father a secret resentment against him. His younger brother, Boniface, was more of a Riqueti in appearance, and the Marquis did not hide his preference for him. Neither did the Dowager Marquise, a formidable old lady of strict principles and steady piety of whom her children and grand-children stood in some awe. Awe was not, however, a feeling natural to her elder grandson, who, at the age of eight, shocked her by a pert remark on miracles. At her death she left a special legacy to Boniface, but Gabriel Honoré was passed over.

In 1753, when Gabriel was fully recovered from the small-pox, a tutor was installed for him. His name was Poisson, and he was a barrister who had come down in the world. He arrived with his own two sons who were educated along with the Count. The choice of this man for a tutor was one of the few paternal acts in which the Marquis was not mistaken. The grandees of the *ancien régime* were often astonishingly casual in the early upbringing of the sons whose procreation was to them such a source of pride and concern, and the Comte de Mirabeau should have been grateful that, at what we should call the kindergarten and preparatory-school age, he was not left, like so many of his kind, to the care of valets and chambermaids. For Poisson, in his way, did a good job. The regimen was over-strict, but that was the Marquis's fault; in this matter Poisson had no choice but to con-

13

form to the many and considered opinions of his employer. But he certainly gave his pupil an exceptionally good grounding and, what was more important, a taste for study which was to be the chief constructive influence on his career. An astounding gift for rapid assimilation of the writings of others, and a marked histrionic talent — these were Gabriel's distinctive abilities; and Poisson appears to have made something of both, for he introduced amateur theatricals into his curriculum and the Marquis was much struck by his son's gifts as a comedian. He had his moments of paternal optimism. 'Your nephew', he told his brother when the child was five, 'has suddenly become roguish, is for ever asking questions and is always on the go. He is rather a handful, but we keep a watch on him, and he is in excellent hands.'

It was on the moral, not the intellectual, side that the young Count's education left much to be desired. There was hot and rebellious blood in his veins, much obstinacy and much vanity; there was also an impulsive generosity. A woman of sense, humour and tenderness could have done much with him, but there was no such woman to sweeten his boyhood with her care: only his grandmother with her frigid rectitude, his mother alternating neglect with moods of conspiratorial affection, and his elder sisters whom he scarcely ever saw.

Meanwhile he received precepts from his father and mental training from his tutor, but no liberty. Under this unremitting pressure the boy became sullen and difficult, and the normal phase of childish lying was prolonged into a habit of deceit. Each peccadillo discovered had only the effect of bringing a further turn to the screw of supervision, and each turn made the young Count more ungovernable, till soon the good Poisson's grip began to fail. But the Marquis was not without his remedies. 'Since the strange passions and vices of this child', he wrote to the Secretary of State at a later date when invoking royal authority to supplement his own, 'seemed to come from an eccentricity of the spirit, I was advised to try geometry for him. A master undertook to look after him and reform him. He was taken to him morning and evening and brought back for his meals. He soon gave it up and declared like the others that his character was incurable. Wishing to give him polish and experience of comrades, I introduced him to a distinguished fencing master. This man, flattered by my confidence, did his best, but gave it up in like manner after the whole class had risen in rebellion.'

By the time Gabriel Honoré was adolescent his father had abandoned himself to irritation and disappointment with his heir. 'The elder of my boys', he wrote to his brother in 1763, 'might very well be called in plain French an ill-bred youngster, and seems to me, so far at least, likely to be nothing but an incurably perverse idiot, without taking into account all the vile qualities he seems to inherit. Education and, above all, the fear he has of me mask many of these qualities from the outside; but I see the nature of the beast, and I don't believe we shall ever make anything of him.' The Marquis's hatred of the Vassan strain is terribly apparent, and in other letters of this time we see reflected in the father's complaints the son's sullen resentment.[2]

3

In 1762 the Marquis's married life had ended in an agreed separation, his wife retiring to Limoges to live with her mother. Separation, however, failed to bring peace. His wife's departure from his roof was followed by the discovery of a moral lapse on her part which mortified him deeply, and now, living very much at her ease, she gambled herself so quickly into debt that her husband was forced to do what he could to check her wildness by financial controls. There thus began between them a long and embittered wrangling which lasted for eighteen years, in which their children became involved as partisans on either side, and in which neither parent hesitated to destroy any respect the children might have for the other.

On the separation of the parents a new personality entered the Mirabeau ménage. Madame de Pailly, wife of an elderly officer of the Swiss Guard from whom she was separated on terms of complete amity, had intelligence, beauty and charm. Meeting the Marquis at a time when his wife's impossible character was beginning to pass his endurance, she graduated decorously from friendship to relations of full intimacy and real tenderness. A not infrequent visitor before the departure of the Marquise, kind' a likely disciple, Quesnay asked him to come and see him, and after their second meeting the Marquis acknowledged the Doctor for master. Physiocracy became his ruling passion, and when Quesnay died in 1774 it fell to the Marquis, as his leading disciple, to pronounce his funeral oration.

The physiocratic system rested on the proposition that all things useful to mankind are the product of the soil; industry may transform and commerce distribute them, but agriculture alone creates wealth. This created wealth is to be found in what remains over when the farmer's livelihood has been supplied, his repairs and renewals paid for and any interest-charges met. In the case of the tenant this surplus takes the form of rent, and it is on this surplus alone that taxation should fall. In plain language the peasant (unless a freeholder) should pay no taxes and the landlord should pay all, and since in eighteenth-century France an almost exactly opposite arrangement existed, the revolutionary potentialities of physiocracy were considerable.

Flushed with a convert's enthusiasm, the *Ami des hommes* published, in 1760, his *Théorie de l'impôt*. He expected it to cause a stir, and it did. The treatise opened with a direct appeal to the King: 'Sire, you have roughly twenty million subjects. These people have all of them a certain amount of money, and they are practically all capable of the services you require from them; nevertheless you can have neither their services without money, nor money to pay for their services.' People and monarch were drifting apart, to the unhappiness of the former and the impotence of the latter. Such was the evil, and drastic remedies were then proposed. Taxation must be a tribute freely granted, not loot torn from the subject; it should fall on the produce of the soil and be assessed and collected by Assemblies of Estates; above all, tax-farming must go: 'Everywhere tax-farmers have bought the nation from the ruler, and, in the end, have destroyed the ruler, the nation and themselves.' The farmers-general were big game to shoot at, and they promptly obtained the arrest of the Marquis and his imprisonment in the not unpleasant if rather dilapidated château of Vincennes. He was not there long. Bourbon despotism in its decline was a beast of uncertain temper, vexatious rather than terrible, incapable of system whether in its severities or in its administration. So eight days after the tax-farmers had got the

Marquis de Mirabeau shut up, his friends at court got him out again. His further punishment was 'exile' during the royal pleasure to Le Bignon, and this, since it involved the inescapable company of his wife, may have been harsher than was intended. It was mitigated, however, by the presence of Madame de Pailly, who came on a visit for a month and delighted him with her quick and understanding conversation by the fire after supper, while the Marquise, slumped in her chair, with knees apart, snored. [4]

5

By 1767 young Mirabeau was eighteen, and the custom of his class and the tradition of his family dictated a period of military service. His father chose for him the regiment of Berri-Cavalerie, then stationed at Saintes, a choice determined by the qualifications of the colonel, the Marquis de Lambert. That he was related to the Vassan family was perhaps scarcely a recommendation; more in his favour was his connection by marriage with the Comtesse de Rochefort, the Marquis's loyal and life-long friend; better still was his high reputation as an officer and disciplinarian, but the decisive consideration was probably that Lambert was a physiocrat and disciple of the Friend of Mankind. So to the light cavalry at Saintes the Baron de Pierre-Buffière went, accompanied by a family servant called Grévin, charged with the equivocal duty of attending to his master's needs and reporting on his behaviour. Spying, Lambert explained, was not encouraged in the regiment, but he agreed with the Marquis that for Pierre-Buffière special arrangements might be desirable.

Mirabeau relished everything in the military life except the discipline. He was soon at loggerheads with his colonel and spent part of his first year at Saintes in the regimental prison. He gambled himself into debt at the card-table to the tune of 80 *louis**, got involved with a girl of the town, and, in July 1768, just a year after joining his regiment, fled without leave to Paris. On arriving he wrote hastily to that old friend of the family, the Duc de Nivernois. It was a vague effusion; he had been forced to

* The *louis* was worth 24 *livres* and roughly equivalent to the English gold sovereign.

desert the post of duty to escape intolerable humiliations put upon him by Lambert; he would be able to explain everything, but would the Duke please say nothing to his father for the present? Nivernois can hardly have been impressed. As for the Marquis, Gabriel need not have worried: Lambert had informed him at once of the desertion. For desertion it was, and a serious matter.

The first thing was to get Pierre-Buffière back to Saintes at once, and this task was assigned to his brother-in-law, Du Saillant, whose steady good sense was now for the first time enlisted for the liquidation of one of Gabriel's escapades. The Marquis's second daughter and her dependable husband were the only members of his family whom he found consistently satisfactory. His eldest daughter became a Dominican nun at Montargis and ended by going off her head; his youngest daughter, Madame de Cabris, was a scourge for his sins.

A certain mystery surrounded the trouble at Saintes. Mirabeau accused his colonel of vindictive persecution due to bitterness at his subaltern's greater success with women, a version probably truer of Mirabeau's conduct than of Lambert's motives. Mirabeau seems to have made some sort of promise of marriage to his Saintes girl, and Lambert intercepted a compromising letter. On his return the colonel confronted him with it, threw it into the fire and then demanded if Mirabeau still believed him bent on his ruin. The posture of victimization collapsed, and there was a gesture of penitence; the deserter would willingly go to prison and his chief hope would be to return to the corps to which he had so much to make good.

He was sent to the island fortress of Ré, and it would be pleasant to record that the incident now terminated in a manner befitting an officer and a gentleman. The less savoury truth is that in a few months Mirabeau was writing to his mother that Lambert was unworthy to hold command and had done everything in his power to ruin her son; and later on he was again in correspondence with the Saintes girl, his sister, Madame de Cabris, acting as go-between.

The alluring and oddly devilish Madame de Cabris was on her mother's side in the family schism, and Mirabeau naturally gravitated to their camp at this time. For the Marquis, it need hardly be said, was furious at the whole affair. He talked of sending Gabriel to the Dutch Indies and of making the as-yet blameless Boniface his heir, and wrote to D'Aulan, the commandant of Ré, warning him that his prisoner was 'hot-tempered, perverse and a born liar'. D'Aulan, however, was quickly bewitched by him and proved an easy jailer; Mirabeau was free in the citadel and able to sup with friends in La Rochelle. After six months the commandant supported his request to be allowed to join the expedition which was about to sail to Corsica, where the patriots were in revolt against the French government which had purchased the island from the Republic of Genoa in 1768. The Marquis yielded and obtained the revocation of the royal order of imprisonment, a faintly curious procedure since Mirabeau had been jailed for a military, not a filial, offence.

He was attached as a sub-lieutenant to a mixed expeditionary corps called the Legion of Lorraine, and marked his first day of freedom by fighting a duel in La Rochelle, after which, the worried Grévin reported, 'he went around swearing and fighting and giving vent to such wickedness as you never saw'. The Marquis had also become aware of a still more disquieting feature of his son's temperament — a conscienceless prodigality with money. 'He has cost me more than ten thousand *livres* in eighteen months during most of which he has been in prison,' he groaned. 'The fellow's dishonoured notes have upset me terribly. On top of his other good qualities he has the knack of borrowing on all sides: sergeants, common soldiers, it's all the same to him.'

Pierre-Buffière embarked with his unit at Toulon in April, 1769. The expedition made short work of the Corsican patriots and the young baron acquitted himself well and won praise from his superiors. Active service and the study of war suited him as garrison duty had not. He believed himself born for the service, and gloried to find himself the possessor of a steady nerve and an excellent eye for ground. According to his own account, there was not a book on war in any language living or dead that he did not read, nor any department of the military profession upon which he did not make voluminous notes. He returned to France mighty pleased with himself and with the manuscript of an unfinished history of Corsica in his luggage.[5]

Not sure of the welcome to be expected from his father, and having disembarked at Toulon, Mirabeau went at once to his uncle, the Bailli, at Aix-en-Provence.

The Chevalier Jean Antoine de Mirabeau was at this time the only surviving brother of the Marquis. At thirteen he had entered the Navy, where he served with the Mediterranean galleys. His youth was wild after the Riqueti fashion, brandy-drinking being his variant of the family excess; but he possessed also the Riqueti will-power, and at eighteen cured himself completely of the bottle. Thenceforth his career was that of a valiant and dependable naval officer, 'little liked, sufficiently respected and still more feared', as he put it. In the war of 1742-48 he was twice wounded and taken prisoner by the English, and though he had a hearty professional hatred of these 'enemies of the human race' he was very near in spirit to Anson, Boscawen and Hawke. In the short peace which followed he was appointed Governor of Guadeloupe, but his health forced him back to France in 1755; he cannot have been sorry, for everyone knew that war was coming again; it was no time for a fighting sailor to be pegged to a land governorship, and in 1756 the Bailli was once more at sea, taking part in La Galissonnière's disconcerting swoop on ill-garrisoned Minorca. His ship, *Orphée*, was in the thick of the fight with Byng's squadron, and if his account of the action had been available at the famous court-martial it would have done nothing to mitigate the severity of the judges.

A return of ill-health prevented further service at sea, and the highest office ashore might now perhaps have been his if capacity and honesty had been sufficient recommendation at the court of Louis XV. As it was, the Ministry of Marine eluded him, despite his brother's assiduous canvassing, and they made him inspector-general of coastal defences in the Channel, a sufficiently anxious job in the years which saw the annihilation of France's home fleets.

In 1761 he went to Malta. Like his brother, he had become a Knight of Malta in childhood, and the Grand Master now invited him to be General of the Maltese Galleys. It was at this period that he rose from Chevalier to Bailli of the Order of St. John.

He and his elder brother were the closest of friends and kept up an incessant correspondence in which the perplexities provided by the latter's family were an inexhaustible theme. After the Bailli's return from Malta in 1767 the Marquis was pleased that he should live in Provence and keep an eye on the family interests there, and so the Bailli, having become the perfect officer in the first half of his life, devoted the second to being the perfect uncle. Born in 1717, he outlived his brother and his nephews; in 1792, when the France he knew passed finally away, he retired to Malta, and there, four years before Malta of the Knights followed France of the Kings, he died.

7

The Bailli received his nephew with warmth. 'I was delighted to see him,' he wrote to the Marquis the next day, 'I found him ugly, but not unpleasant in appearance.' But it was the young man's intellectual fireworks which astonished him. 'If he is not worse than Nero he'll be better than Marcus Aurelius, for I don't believe I've ever met so much brilliance of mind. My poor head was bursting. He seemed to be as afraid of you as of the provost-marshal, but he swore to me that there was nothing he wouldn't do to please you.' The Bailli did not fully appreciate that he was, for the moment, the target for a battery of quite exceptional power, his nephew's magnetic charm; it was a weapon which seldom failed to demolish the fortifications of distrust or reserve with which people sought to protect themselves from the assault of his personality. The uncle listened with delight to racy anecdotes of the campaign and much solid information about Corsica; the young man was a sparkling companion for an old sailor with a stiff leg, and he seemed sensible, too, for he had half a mind, he hinted, to quit the army for the navy. The history of Corsica, some of which he read aloud, impressed the Bailli considerably; it was all very well, he reflected, for Victor to grumble at the boy, but at twenty-one *he* had not done anything so good. The nephew added to this favourable impression by sometimes taking down notes when his uncle was holding forth,

23

and by agreeing readily with his belief in the value of a feudal aristocracy. . . . ⁶

·The aristocracy of the *ancien régime* has often been condemned as a decadent society; to affix this label is easier than to define its meaning, and if it be true that in some matters their morals indicate the *fin de siècle*, it is equally true that in others their customs were of a primitive severity. In nothing is this more evident than in the unquestioned authority allowed to the head of the family. The Bailli was now his nephew's warm advocate, and was quite prepared to warn his elder brother that he was treating the boy unwisely. But Victor was, when all was said, head of the family and must be obeyed; his permission was necessary even for Gabriel to go to the château of Mirabeau. 'You will give me the greatest pleasure by granting him this permission,' the Bailli writes. 'I can assure you I found him very penitent for his past faults, and he seems to me to have a tender heart. He told me, with an expression which I am sure was sincere, that he didn't dare to hope that you would be willing to see him there, but that he would try to deserve it.'

Permission was granted, but the Marquis remained sceptical of his son's change of heart and attached a condition: 'It must be clearly understood that he won't be at Mirabeau when I arrive there, for the more he fears me the less ought I to allow myself to come near him until I am certain that he is capable of conducting himself properly. When he is, I'll allow him to go to Versailles, but not Paris.' To gain his father by capturing his uncle had seemed a promising policy, but progress was slow, though the uncle's advocacy was sustained in letter after letter. 'If he isn't a fraud, he's the stuff of which popes, generals, ministers *and perhaps agriculturalists* are made.' On Gabriel's return from Mirabeau the Bailli reported him deeply interested in problems of estate-management and full of plans for dealing with the flooding of the Durance. It was not difficult for such a nephew to persuade such an uncle to give him money for settling old debts, or to proceed at once to contract new ones.

The severity of the patriarch was quaintly blended with pedantry. 'I was never', he writes to his brother, 'one of those who believe in father-and-son comradeships,' and a few days later he proposes a test of Gabriel's sincerity: the boy must start the

serious study of political economy; 'It is indispensable, if he wishes
to bear my name, that he should have a thorough grasp of my
science. His ignorance would either disgrace me or shame him.
Order him to apply himself to this science and to master it
thoroughly; you can have no idea how it calms the heart and sets
the mind at ease.' When, with this letter, the post brought an
'Economic Catechism' fresh from the pen of the Friend of Mankind, as well as a copy of a little exercise set for his married
daughter, Madame du Saillant, it may have been the Bailli's
turn to be sceptical.

This was in the beginning of June 1770. Two months later the
Marquis took the serious step of summoning his son to his presence.
The meeting took place at the château of Aigueperse, seigniorial
residence of the barony of Pierre-Buffière. The Friend of Mankind
received his son, he records, 'with kindness and even tenderness'.
He had not set eyes on him for three years.'

CHAPTER II

RESPONSIBILITIES

THE meeting of father and son in August 1770 was followed by the restoration to the latter of the right to use his proper title — Count Gabriel Honoré Riqueti de Mirabeau. For a season the Marquis indulged those feelings of paternal pride and hope which he had for long so carefully controlled. There was no getting over the fact that the boy was, when all was said, a Mirabeau and his heir. Best to give him some responsible task — something to do with the family estates — and later to see about getting him further military employment, since he had done so well on active service. Yet even now, in the first confidence of his good resolutions, the Marquis found his son's temperament difficult to support. 'What the devil is one to do with this hot-blooded exuberance?' he asks the Bailli. 'What land is big enough for him? I can think of no one he'd be fit to marry except the Empress of Russia.' He returned to Paris after a month, leaving Gabriel to stay in Limousin with the watchful Du Saillants.

The Marquis had a further and very practical motive for cultivating his son at this moment: his mother-in-law, that 'everlasting mother-in-law' as Madame de Rochefort called her, was dying. On her decease her property would, at last, pass to her hitherto ill-dowered daughter. This was the event whose expectation had been the Marquis's original and solitary motive for marriage, but now, after twenty-seven years, his need of the long-awaited financial relief was enormously increased while his hopes of gaining it were diminished.

We have already noticed the Marquis's distress at Gabriel's spendthrift habits, and the latter's recklessness with money was soon to be a real nightmare to his father. Yet Victor was hardly in a position to adopt an attitude of intolerant severity in this matter, since he was himself an almost unbelievably bad businessman.

The income which he inherited from his father amounted, after deduction of all pensions and charges, to a modest 16,000 *livres*;*

* Equivalent roughly to £730 sterling at the same period.

yet in the early years of his independence he had undertaken capital expenditure amounting to not less that 141,800. Little of this investment was profitable. The Le Bignon estate, which accounted for 112,000, was in a sad state of dilapidation when purchased, and was for years a cause of expense, not a source of income. The rest went on a house in Paris and on a canal at Mirabeau which was never finished. In 1744 he found that his net income had dwindled to 5900 *livres*, and in an attempt to economize he moved his family from Mirabeau to Saulvebœuf, an estate of his wife's in Périgord. This move would, he thought, have the added advantage of making him known in a province where he would 'one day have great possessions'; always the expectation of Madame de Vassan's manors was the *ignis fatuus* on his road to ruin. Two years later the family moved again, this time to Le Bignon, though residence there was broken by spells in Paris. But again, no economy. Elaborate estate-improvements were undertaken, but philosophic enthusiasm for agriculture proved no substitute for a knowledge of practical farming, and the Friend of Mankind was later forced sorrowfully to admit that he had neither aptitude nor experience in such practical matters as building and crop-management. 'It is,' he added, 'a great disservice to the head of a house to educate him solely for the profession of arms.' It would have been well if such realistic reflections had come to him earlier and more often, for the one thing he never did — the one thing which might have made him solvent — was to sell the properties which he had not the working capital to manage profitably. But it was not in him to do so unambitious a thing; he was an optimist, for ever expecting salvation round the corner, repeatedly throwing good money after bad, obstinately convinced that it was the destiny of the House of Mirabeau to be one of the great families of France. This obsession with the status of the House contributed to the ill-feeling in the family circle. His wife resented wearing shabby clothes, but he insisted that she should have two chambermaids and a carriage and coachman of her own. There were many economies in the household which wife and children resented, but he would always pretend that he was economical on principle, not from necessity, with the result that his children, instead of sympathizing with his difficulties, thought him stingy and looked forward to an inheritance which could never be theirs.

In 1763 he borrowed 80,000 *livres* to make a dowry for his second daughter, Caroline, on her marriage to the Marquis du Saillant. True, he had recently sold the Saulvebœuf estate for the same sum, but as he had at about the same time made a dead loss of 50,000 on the sale of another property his downward course continued unchecked. This latter speculation is a fair sample of the enterprises which gradually ruined him. In 1752 the Duchy of Roquelaure, a property of the Rohans with seignorial juris-diction over thirteen parishes, came on to the market. The Marquis was after it at once. The price was a trifle of 450,000 *livres* and the yield, even on the seller's showing, not above three per cent. But the Marquis was sure he could increase this, and consulted his mother, who advised him at least to see the place before buying. The Duke, however, was, or pretended to be, in a hurry; he could not possibly wait for the Marquis to make the journey of inspection to Gascony; he must take it or leave it, and, incredible to relate, the Marquis took it *unseen*, borrowing the money at *five* per cent. One is reminded a little of the circum-stances in which he acquired his wife. He was fortunate, however, in being able to sell the Roquelaure land, though at a loss of 50,000 *livres*.

In 1763, undaunted by this experience, he invested money in a lead mine in Limousin. Finding he had not enough capital to work it, he proceeded to form a joint-stock company, and his reputation as an economist, now at its height, induced his titled friends to subscribe. Turgot, at this time *intendant* of the *généralité* of Limoges, put himself down for one share in this venture of his brother economist. But after thirteen years the best that the Marquis could say of the mine was that it 'promised to be profitable'.

By 1770 he was so encumbered with debts that to get control of his mother-in-law's wealth was his only hope of salvation. But the ructions with his wife since their separation seven years earlier had made it far from certain that he would in fact enjoy her long-awaited inheritance. This long-distance warfare was mainly due to Madame de Mirabeau's gambling debts; when her creditors dunned him for payment he stopped the amount out of her allowance, whereupon she raised shrill cries that he was breaking the agreement he had made. Then, when he heard she was compromising herself with an officer of the *Garde du Corps*, he obtained from the government a *lettre de cachet* confining her to the convent at Limoges where she had recently been living, since even 'Maman' had found her scarcely supportable in the same house. This was his first invocation of the royal authority to supplement his own in family matters, and it was not his last. Fortified with the royal order, he was able to bring his wife to one of their 'amicable' agreements: he would get the *lettre de cachet* revoked if she undertook to stay at her convent and not to travel from Limoges without his permission. He did not wish her unbridled tongue to go a-wagging about France, or her sluttish behaviour to disgrace him in Paris. So, for a while, she stayed at her convent, causing great mischief in that narrower society and nursing her grievances.

In 1769 their youngest daughter, Louise, was to be married to the Marquis de Cabris. She was seventeen, lovely and intelligent; he nineteen and bordering on imbecility. Her father had once more to strain his groaning credit for a dowry, but managed somehow to borrow 80,000 *livres*, the same sum as he had given to her sister. He also tried to persuade old Madame de Vassan to add something to this, as she had done to the dowry of her elder granddaughter. The old lady refused. This was not a good omen for the contents of her will, and the Marquis was the more disappointed since Louise was his favourite child.

Then, in November 1770, three months after Gabriel's homecoming, Madame de Vassan died. The will might have been worse, but it reserved land worth 8000 *livres* per annum to be her daughter's *exclusively*, whereas her son-in-law had based his calculations on the assumption that the whole of her estate would be at his disposal. In this expectation he had, in one of the 'amicable agreements', promised to raise his wife's allowance to 10,000 *livres* on her mother's death, and he was now exasperated to find that she was demanding to have it both ways, to receive, that is, a personal income of 18,000 while contributing nothing to the support or advancement of their children.

In his anger he turned to Gabriel. With a candour surprising in one who had never believed in father-and-son comradeships, he exposed for his son's instruction all the disgust, contempt and shame he felt towards his wife; still, the will had created a new situation, a reasonable arrangement must be made, and Gabriel, so far unembroiled, would be the best envoy. So the Count, charged with a mission of peace, went off to visit his mother. Their first minutes together showed that it was to be not peace but a sword. To be more exact, Madame de Mirabeau's reply to her son's conciliatory opening was to fire a pistol at him.* Thereafter she parleyed, at least sufficiently to put her own grievances before her son and to complain that his father had bastards. On returning from his embassy Gabriel urged the Marquis to refute this charge 'short of recriminations', and the two men laughed together.

This is not the place to pursue the subsequent expansion of Madame de Mirabeau's campaign against her husband. From this time forward, however, she pressed her claims and advertised her grievances with unremitting animosty, and found her chief ally in her daughter, Madame de Cabris. For the latter, resentful against her father for not having got for her from Madame de Vassan the same marriage gift as had gone to her elder sister, proceeded, out of the 80,000 her father had borrowed in order to dower her, to advance 20,000 to her mother as a war-chest.

The family was now in two camps, one consisting of the Marquise and Louise de Cabris, the other of the Marquis, Caroline du Saillant and her husband, and, at the moment, Gabriel. But Gabriel's partisanship was uncertain: he had a weakness for Louise, enjoying her vivacity and as yet unhurt by her malice, and he looked with a jaundiced eye on Du Saillant, remembering the Saintes affair; it is not always easy to forgive people their virtues, and Du Saillant was so evidently trusted by the head of the house. At this juncture, however, Mirabeau was not denied opportunities of securing his rightful position in his father's esteem. Though the embassy to Limoges had proved vain, the Marquis was still pleased to have 'a son who was a man' at his side and was ready to give him responsibilities of a more seemly description.

* This, at least, is Mirabeau's own account of what happened, written eight years later. Objective truthfulness about his own affairs was not one of his virtues, but it is difficult to see why he should have invented so unplausible a story.

2

The hard lot of the peasantry of pre-Revolution France is a commonplace of the textbooks, but it is well to dismiss from the mind the idea that the tenants on noble estates were mute and helpless victims of feudal oppression, paying monstrous dues to their landlords with bitterness but without complaint. Equally untrue is it to picture the *seigneur* of the *ancien régime* as an idle man of fashion living on his rents without ever needing to give his attention to the men and the soil which yielded them. In reality the noble landlord before the Revolution was often less detached from the sources of his income than the middle-class *rentier* who replaced him.

In the first place, the specific nature of the peasant's dues to his feudal lord rendered effortless rent-consumption difficult. Manorial dues were payable in kind and in services as well as in money. A peasant-holding might owe to the lord of the manor a composite rent — part cash, part produce and (less commonly) part manual labour. Precise quantities were specified — 2s. 6d. and a couple of chicken, for instance, or 8d., three smoked hams and a gallon of oats. Dues varied from manor to manor and from holding to holding with a multiplicity which exercised the vigilance and also the patience of the lord's steward. But these heterogeneous dues were usually attached not to the peasant but to his land; and when a holding was divided the question of rightful apportionment of dues became acutely difficult; how apportion among five tenants the obligation to render three dressed chickens and a hog's carcase? The attempt to settle these matters sometimes necessitated the use of such fractions as sixteenths of a chicken, quarters of a ham, and the like. In general, peasant cunning was presented with considerable opportunities for evasion of manorial dues by the very nature of the payments required, and it behoved the *seigneur* to review and scrutinize his rights at regular intervals if he was not to suffer a gradual loss of income. Some landlords were tempted to convert these feudal tenures into straight money-leases, but, as the Marquis de Mirabeau observed, farm produce was tending to rise in value, money to fall, so that such a solution lost the landlord in real income what it saved him in worry. That the survival of ancient manorial dues was a heavy burden to the peasantry is true; but it is almost equally true that these rights were considerable botheration to landlords who were involved in countless petty prosecutions of smallholders for the recovery of trifling amounts.

Nor was sly evasion of indisputable obligations the peasant's only resource, for by no means all manorial dues were undisputed. Where a specific due was set down in black and white in a document there was usually no help for it; but *seigneurs* often claimed rights of a more general sort, basing their claims on the alleged custom of the manor, or even of the province, and these rights the peasants might sometimes call in question. In such cases the matter would go before the royal courts, where, in the eighteenth century, there was a distinct bias against any seigniorial rights for which written evidence could not be produced. This readiness of peasants to challenge the lord's pretentions was much greater in the southern provinces of France than in the centre and north, for whereas the latter were regions of customary (feudal) law where the maxim *Nulle terre sans seigneur* prevailed, the southern third of the kingdom was the land of written (Roman) law where the maxim was *Nul seigneur sans titre*. Freehold was common, and the attempt to establish it perhaps commoner still.

With the exception of Le Bignon, practically all the estates of the Marquis de Mirabeau, including those brought to him by his wife, lay in *pays de droit écrit*, and the problem of peaceful relations with his tenants was seldom absent from his mind. He had high ideas as to the social value of a healthy and functioning feudalism, a deep-rooted dislike of centralization and of its agents, the King's *intendants*, and strong disapproval of those nobles, unfortunately so numerous, who allowed their feudal rights of jurisdiction, by no means contemptible even in the eighteenth century, to fall into disuse.

3

The year 1770 had been a famine year in the poor province of Limousin, and the Marquis had bought thirty quintals of rice for his famished peasantry at Pierre-Buffière. This paternal gesture was now to be followed up by the execution of a plan whereby his vassals might learn to regard their lord as their common friend and protector, a just father of them all. There was to be set up on the estate a 'tribunal of conciliation' for settling disputes. It was to be less a manorial court than an employers' and workers' board, and its purpose was to settle disputes out of court. Eight arbitrators were to be elected from the eight parishes within the barony, and if either party to a quarrel refused to accept their finding the Marquis undertook to pay the other party's legal expenses.

The honour of formally inaugurating this humane experiment was given to Mirabeau, who in February 1771 arrived at the château of Aigueperse as his father's representative. At least one familiar face was there to greet him, that of old Poisson, now steward of the family domains in Limousin. Mirabeau had taken up his father's project with enthusiasm, and found the attitude of the good folk of Pierre-Buffière, particularly the parish priests, friendly, co-operative and respectful.

The inauguration began with a solemn Mass of the Holy Ghost in the chapel of the château. Then to the great hall where the Count was to receive the members of the tribunal. Round a large table spread with a great green cloth the rustic elders, a little stiff in their Sunday clothes, took their places, bowing to right and to left, while in the background a crowd of the local inhabitants looked on. Then amid a respectful hush M. le Comte rose to speak. He first read an address from the Marquis to 'his dear friends, relations, vassals and countrymen', but he was soon making his own speech and warming to it, and he ended with a peroration which brought tears to his hearers' eyes. A reply by Poisson thanking his patron and complimenting his old pupil, a few further words from Mirabeau, and the proceedings terminated with *un bon repas*, a drinking of healths and a general loosening of tongues and waistcoat-buttons.

The value of the new conciliation board is shown by two facts: in its first year it settled no less than one hundred cases; but after 1781, when by legal separation *de corps et de biens* the Vassan lands passed from the Marquis's control, the tribunal came to an end and the Marquise was soon involved in sixty lawsuits with her tenants.[8]

4

More than ever pleased with his son, the Marquis wrote to Choiseul and obtained for him a captaincy in the dragoons of the Legion of Lorraine, and, as no service was for the moment required, he summoned him to be presented at Court. 'When they ask why I let him go to Versailles so young', he wrote to his brother, 'I answer "There at least he will not get into trouble except in so-called good company". For the rest, people have put up with Mirabeaus being different from other folk for five centuries, so they'll put up with this one too.' *Two* centuries would have been nearer the mark, and the exaggeration is characteristic, but the father's mood of proud indulgence is a pleasing change from his norm. Mirabeau's complete lack of respect for persons at court, his audacious familiarity (he button-holed that elder statesman, Maurepas, at his first introduction) considerably amused his father — for a while. But by midsummer he was beginning to doubt whether this life divided between Paris and Versailles should continue; the young man had touches of kidney-trouble and would be better if he could get regular hours and discipline; moreover, he was again finding Gabriel's company something of a trial; his bumptious cocksureness was reviving the old irritation; yes, decidedly the barracks was the place. The difficulty was that his regiment was in no hurry for him to report for duty, and even when he did so he would not have to stay more than four months in the year with his unit, and that on garrison-duty. Memories of the Saintes interlude were not reassuring. Efforts to find him some more active form of service were, however, unavailing, for the country was at peace, so the Marquis decided to send him to Provence in the hope that he might repeat there the success he had scored in Limousin.

5

But Provence was not Limousin. There existed in the southern county a strong spirit of local independence, and the inhabitants, a Mediterranean people, with a language and a temper alien to the French, looked less to Paris, northern and remote, than to their own Marseilles, with its strident busyness and Levantine contacts, or their own Aix with its sovereign law-courts or *parlement*. In country parts a jealous and egalitarian spirit was widespread. Each village community elected its 'consul', and the consuls of each district met regularly and elected representatives to go to the *Assemblée des Communautés* at Aix. This provincial assembly consisted of the municipality of Aix plus these representatives of the rural districts, and it exercised considerable administrative powers; as for the privileged orders, they sent two proctors each, no more.

Conscious of being well-organized throughout the province, stimulated by the sight of many freeholders in their community calling no man lord, the tenant-farmers of Provence were a stiff-necked tribe; 'republicans', the Bailli de Mirabeau called them. Provençal *seigneurs* were chronically at loggerheads with their vassals, nor was it a mere boorish obstinacy which they had to meet, for the peasants had educated leaders. Town had penetrated country, for substantial bourgeois, formed by the civic idea, had bought properties in rural areas. Here, excluded by the noblesse, they eased the resentment of the parvenu by lending their experience of affairs and their influence among the advocates and judges of the *parlement* to the cause of the rural commons. Men of this sort were glad of any chance of a smack at those whom they thought to be distinguished from them by privilege alone.

The Riqueti estates (Mirabeau itself and the neighbouring manor of Beaumont) were no exception to the general rule of bad relations between lord and vassal, and the Marquis's most stubborn adversary was one Mottet, an attorney of Aix. The fact that the Friend of Mankind was an improving landlord, far from gaining his tenants' respect, was a main cause of the trouble. This was largely due to the lack of definition of the rights of lord and tenants to the use of common land, particularly woodland and waste. The commoners claimed unlimited use for grazing their goats and for charcoal-burning; the *seigneur* saw in these two practices the best known formula for deforestation and soil-erosion. Claiming all the land as legally his own, he had sought to save it from ruin by a policy of enclosures in which he and his vassals would share. Unable, however, to bring them to his way

35

of thinking, he had resorted to more drastic action: he had made his seigniorial judge draw up an order that the common land was to come under the police regulations of a royal ordinance of 1669 for checking deforestation. The immediate result of this was defiance of his authority by the whole community, and it was this situation that his son had to deal with on his arrival at Mirabeau in December 1771.

The Count's behaviour at his first meeting with the Mirabeau community was not conciliatory. He lectured them for abusing his father's goodness; his grandfather had stood no nonsense, however, and neither would he; he had come to end all disputes: let them go now and return on the morrow when he would hear everyone and do justice. The meeting then broke up — in silence.

The next day only the consul appears; the Count, scarcely controlling his anger, orders him to go and collect the others, but even after some waiting only a handful of villagers put in an appearance. Mirabeau, a stranger to this people, twenty-two, touchy and inexperienced, boils over: let the consul warn the whole village that he will not tolerate their behaviour, that he is giving orders for the seizure of all beasts found in the woods and the imprisonment of those minding them, that he will show them — but what would he show them? For at this point that gathering of vassals turned their backs on him and, without a word, walked out of the hall.

Mirabeau went next to Beaumont. Here not a single villager answered his summons, and those who held manorial offices resigned them and stood solid with their neighbours under the leadership of a man called Boyer. That evening — it was two days before Christmas — Mirabeau, taking a walk, fell foul of a peasant going home, lost his temper and beat the man with his cane.

At Beaumont it was the custom on the evening of the Epiphany to have a bonfire. Mirabeau, as deputy-squire, was present with the crowd. Seeing Boyer standing next to him with his hat on, and taking it as a deliberate incivility, he knocked the hat off with his cane. When the man explained that he had meant no offence, had not even seen the Count, the anger of a fortnight burst over him, but his answer was to jam his hat defiantly on his head, shouting that he didn't acknowledge the Count as his lord, that he owed him no sort of deference and that he'd better not try knocking his hat off again unless he wanted trouble; at which, it appears, Mirabeau, perhaps feeling he had made himself a shade ridiculous before a hostile audience, saw fit to retire.[9]

The campaign, however, was not over. Soon afterwards Mottet of Aix was elected consul both at Mirabeau and at Beaumont to reinforce the people's cause, while the Count, on his side, prosecuted peasants, impounded animals, and even invoked the police of nearby Manosque to remove two troublesome persons, one of whom was called Boyer . . . But in the end and on the main issue — that of the woodlands — it was the community that prevailed, for the Marquis's ordinance was quashed by the Chamber of Waters and Forests of the *parlement* of Aix.

6

Mirabeau's conduct since his coming south is not hard to explain. The situation he had been given to handle was beyond his resources of prudence and knowledge, and his reaction into a humourless and impatient violence should have been foreseen; where the mature and dependable Bailli had failed, how should his callow and erratic nephew succeed? But there was more in it than this. Gabriel's volcanic temperament was in the eruptive phase of early manhood, unbiddable and extravagant. He was fighting the curb of the short money-allowance which was all that his father seemed willing to grant him. He was also straining against his father's pedantic control, against being an extension of the Friend of Mankind, and he resented the fault-finding note which had crept back into his father's letters of late. Suddenly he must make his own position, assert his own manhood, and an inordinate virility conspired with an almost psychopathic craving for spending-power to hurry him into the pursuit of an heiress.

Marie-Marguerite-Emilie de Covet de Marignane was the chief heiress of Provence. Aged nineteen, she was the only daughter of the Marquis de Marignane, an idle, wealthy man of pleasure who lived, separated from his wife, in a dissolute circle of kindred spirits. Emilie lived under the supervision of her grandmother, and was very ready to escape from it. The Bailli had already had his eye on her for his nephew, but Madame de Cabris wrote to warn her brother that Emilie de Marignane was already promised: 'You are too late. However, don't worry; she is hide-ously ugly and very small.' This was less than justice. Emilie's face was not ugly but it was commonplace; with her sallow complexion, her dark hair and eyes, she would have been quite unnoticeable in any group of Provençal girls, though one who looked closely might have detected a hint of hardness in the small bright eyes, of meanness in the small mouth. Her accomplishments were two: a gift for comedy — she had a fund of broad Provençal stories which she told in dialect — and a fine singing voice.

Though Mirabeau himself sang delightfully, it was not of a musical companion that he was thinking when he set out to capture his heiress in the spring of 1772. She was half-promised to a certain M. de la Valette and had two marquises among her other suitors, but these obstacles acted only as a spur, as did the nagging and ill-timed letters he was receiving from his father.

Recognizing the wealthy grandmother as the key-position to be gained, Mirabeau laid immediate siege to her, directing a fusillade of denigration against La Valette to which the latter (though well-enough munitioned) made no adequate reply. Still Mirabeau was a late-comer, La Valette had the support of Emilie's father and she herself remained undecided, so he determined to bring matters to a conclusion. He drove a coach to the Hôtel Marignane late one night, gained admittance from a maidservant whom he had bribed, left the coach standing conspicuous in the street for some hours and emerged early in the morning. This story comes to us at second hand, but whatever the exact details of Mirabeau's beau stratagem, one thing is certain: Marie-Marguerite-Emilie de Covet de Marignane was compromised.[10]

The wedding took place at Aix on June 23rd, 1772, and the festivites lasted a week. The most notable things about the occasion were the enormous expenses which fell upon the bridegroom (an amount which, added to his existing debts, far exceeded the first year's income of the young couple) and the absence of his parents. His mother's failure to attend the wedding was not surprising, though her refusal to sign the marriage contract, or even to answer Mirabeau's letter announcing his betrothal, was. But the absence of the Marquis and the Bailli is hard to account for. They had in no way opposed the match; even the father had gone no further than to disclaim responsibility; whatever the explanation, it seems clear that their absence from an event so important to their precious House was not unresented by its eldest son.

In the marriage-settlement the Marquis gave Mirabeau an income of 5500 *livres*, rising to 8500 by six annual increments; he presented his daughter-in-law with jewellery worth 12,000, and the pair were to have Mirabeau rent-free to live in. It was more than he could afford. From her much richer father Emilie received 3000 *livres* a year and a trousseau costing 8000. Thus Gabriel, like his father before him, acquired by marriage the expectation of wealth but not the present command of money, and the temptation to anticipate future fortune, was, to one of his temperament, inevitably disastrous. Bankruptcy, an overhanging cloud to the father, soon burst upon the son in a deluge.

CHAPTER III

ABERRATION

AFTER some visits and a spell in fashionable Aix Mirabeau took his bride home to the castle of his ancestors. 'This castle, seat of my fathers for four centuries', he once wrote, ignoring the fact that it had been in the family for two.

Neither Gabriel nor Emilie was in love, but for a honeymoon span they were both sufficiently pleased with their situation. Emilie, regaining her breath after the whirlwind courtship of her ugly, virile, voluble husband, enjoyed her entry into the ranks of the great ladies of the province, and relished being mistress of a high, turreted château with a village at its feet, for she had long desired to looked down on her neighbours from above.[11]

Gabriel had the sense of a situation which goes with the actor's temperament. He saw himself as the young and masterful bridegroom, present master and future lord of the estate from which he took his name, winner of the most coveted heiress in Provence, begetter of the next generation of Riquetis de Mirabeau. His marriage intensified the extravagance and pugnacious pride which had marked his first coming south.

Intoxicated by a delusive sense of financial independence, he launched forth upon a wild course of expenditure. In two years his own wardrobe contained at least thirteen complete suits, of costly materials and brilliant colours, while bills mounted up and up for dresses and jewellery for his Countess; she protested and even scolded, but was overborne by Gabriel, who acted like the most adoring lover, for such were the demands of the situation. The castle needed doing up, too, and the Countess's *salon* was to be redecorated throughout at a cost of 20,000 *livres*. 'The folly of this maniac,' growled the Bailli when later he saw the result, 'to panel and redecorate the only room which suits me! I'll never have the courage to live in a room which looks like the salon of the Duc de Nivernois and which can't be finished under 2000 *ecus*.' But this was not the Count's greatest extravagance. The approaches to the castle dissatisfied him. There existed two paths up the hill, but both of them were steep, stony and difficult for carriages, and Mirabeau wished to be able to drive his Countess with some speed and dignity within their castle walls. Between the crossing of the Durance and the castle hill there lay a desolation of rocks and boulders; what finer than to drive through this a smooth carriage-way with a gentle gradient? What matter that there would need to be some 500 metres of it, with at least fifty bends, or that much of it would have to be hewn out of the living rock?

These megalomaniac enterprises clearly sprang from the same source as his father's unhappy ventures — the procreative temperament to which the very splendour of an end is a guarantee that the means to achieve it will become available. Gabriel's present folly was, however, cut short by realities. Emilie was soon expecting a child, which probably sobered him a little. His creditors — Jewish moneylenders and local tradesmen chiefly, but also the *curé* of Mirabeau, the vicar of neighbouring Pertuis and sundry humble folk — were becoming impatient, which sobered him still more. A quick resource was to pawn Emilie's jewels; she would not be needing them for the next few months anyhow. A wiser step was to approach his father-in-law, who had so far done so much less than might have been expected for the young couple. Marignane offered to advance the sum which would come to Mirabeau on the death of Emilie's grandmother, but on one condition: he must have the Marquis de Mirabeau's discharge for the amount, since under the terms of the marriage contract all payments of Emilie's dowry had to be made in the first place to her father-in-law. His signature, however, could not be obtained, and Gabriel's best hope of getting square vanished. It was a bitter blow. He had been wildly extravagant, admittedly, but he had not gambled nor done anything criminal; yet his father, asked to do so small a thing to put him right again, refused on the ground that if cleared this time he would be sure to fall into debt again. The father's hesitation is understandable, but the son's reaction to such blank unhelpfulness might have been foretold. Seeing the dry land of solvency now hopelessly beyond his reach, he simply allowed himself to be swept on by the racing current of unchecked expenditure.

An extraordinary irascibility and pugnacity marked his behaviour to those who crossed his path at this time. Peasants and domestics kept out of his way if they could. An Aix creditor who presented bills which Mirabeau had given before his marriage got a thrashing on account. Peaceable lawyers who valued their skins showed reluctance to act on behalf of the Count's creditors, and the *parlement* of Aix had to appoint an attorney to handle their claims. Mirabeau insulted and threatened the wretched man in his own house.

2

If the Count's violence was beyond measure where lawyers were concerned, this was partly because his private mood was in tune with the feelings of the public towards the law-courts as constituted at that moment.

In 1771, the year in which Mirabeau came south, the government of Louis XV, having come into conflict with the *parlements*, those close corporations in which the legal profession had for centuries been organized, concluded the matter by abolishing them and 'exiling' their principal officials to out-of-the-way places. The Chancellor, Maupeou, then set up new courts in place of the old, hoping that the new, nominated magistrates would be obedient servants of the executive.

The old *parlements* had been the one institution in France which, in the atrophy of the States-General after 1614, had retained some vestige of right to resist the will of the monarch. Their weight as a counterpoise to despotism lay less in their formal right to refuse to register royal edicts (a card which could always be over-trumped if the King chose to hold a *lit de justice*) than in the fact that the families from which the *parlements* (or law-courts) recruited their staffs formed a firm and cohesive lump in the tissue of the nation. This lawyer-class, identifiable in French society since the fourteenth century, was a curious phenomenon. Bourgeois in origin, it was distinguished from the ruck of the middle class by its narrowly professional tone, by the pomp and circumstance of a virtually hereditary monopoly of bar and bench, and by the fact that many of its families, raised in serving the crown, had won titles of nobility. On the other hand they remained largely distinct from the feudal *noblesse d'épée* who despised them as mere *nobles de robe*. Standing astride the cleft which separated the territorial *noblesse* and the bourgeoisie this class of inter-married and all but hereditary lawyers and administrators formed an unacknowledged estate of the realm, with privileges, prejudices and an ethos all its own. Its class-solidarity and corporate opinion was a force which wise monarchs would not ignore.

When, therefore, Louis XV and Maupeou struck at the *parlements*, trouble might have been expected. France at once suffered one of the sharp fissions to which she is prone, splitting into self-styled patriots (who championed the *parlements*) and the supporters of the minister. Maupeou was not without friends, for most disinterested observers agreed that the encrusted privileges of the *parlementaires*, especially the buying, selling and bequeathing of judicial offices, amounted to a conspiracy in restraint of justice. Voltaire and most of the *philosophes* were of this opinion.

On the side of the *parlements* was a much larger part of the nation. In the forefront, of course, stood the whole lawyer-class except for a blackleg element which consented to staff Maupeou's new courts. A compact and influential group in the capital, in provincial centres which boasted *parlements* of their own, such as Rennes, Dijon and Aix, the *noblesse de robe* were the leaders of civic society, and the court risked much in making them into popular martyrs. Indeed it is a measure of the discredit into which Louis XV's government had sunk that such exemplars of unpopular privilege as the old lawyer-class should, by the very fact of being attacked by the court, have appeared as victims of tyranny to the people at large.

The *parlementaires* also had the sympathy of the *noblesse d'épée*. These naturally asked themselves how long feudal privileges would remain secure if the ancient rights and perquisites of the *parlementaires* were to be swept away like this. The alliance of Sword and Gown was more natural in Provence than elsewhere, for here the line between the two kinds of nobles was indistinct, and *gentils hommes* did not scorn to be magistrates. When, therefore, members of the old *parlement* of Aix were 'exiled' to the little town of Manosque, their many sympathizers included most of the nobility.

To their resistance, however, there was an important exception.

The Marquis d'Albertas, First President of the *Chambre des Comptes*, agreed to co-operate with the ministry, and his court became one of Maupeou's newfangled *parlements*. D'Albertas was a man of standing in Provençal society, and the magnificent public balls which he gave threatened the united front with which the 'patriots' had hoped to face the government. D'Albertas became a controversial figure.[12]

From the moment of his arrival in Provence Mirabeau, in conformity with his father and his uncle, had been a partisan of the old *parlements*. Among the first to pay a formal call on the Count, however, had been the Marquis d'Albertas. Mirabeau did not consider that his political alignment demanded the rejection of a sociable overture, and he became a fairly frequent visitor to the Albertas home. But the President's son seemed anxious for a friendship more intimate than Mirabeau thought consonant with his family's place in the anti-Maupeou, anti-Albertas camp, and a coolness developed. The temperature fell further as a result of Mirabeau's matrimonial triumph, for young D'Albertas was among Emilie's disappointed suitors. Polite appearances, however, were kept up; Madame d'Albertas came over to call on the new Countess, and there were reciprocal courtesies. When winter came fashionable people moved to their town houses in Aix, and the ceremony of paying and returning calls began afresh. Madame d'Albertas considered that she, as the First President's lady, was entitled to receive the first call; to admit this claim, however, might be taken as a recognition of Maupeou's upstart *parlement*, and the little world of Aix became sharply divided on the matter. Most of the wives, valuing political purity less than the favour of the chief hostess of the season, called. Those who stood aloof were the ladies of former *parlementaires* — and the Comtesse de Mirabeau. Supported by her father and her husband, she ostentatiously stayed away from the Albertas's entertainments during the carnival season, while Marignane and his son-in-law took the lead in the Assembly of the Nobles of the province in attacking the new '*parlement-Maupeou*'.

Then an incident occurred. One day Madame de Mirabeau, now with child, was being carried to the theatre in a sedan chair, her husband following on foot. At the top of a slope, almost at the theatre door, a coach cut in before them and pulled up so sharply that the bearers of the litter, finding their way blocked, placed it on the ground; then the ill-driven coach began to roll backwards. Realizing in the same flash that Emilie was in real danger and that the coach's occupants were D'Albertas and his brother and son, Mirabeau bellowed to the coachman to check the roll. The man did nothing, his rear wheel crunched over one handle of the chair and was like to crush the struggling porter when Mirabeau, just in time, snatched his wife up and out of harm's way. Then anger followed fright, and the Albertas's coachman and footman received a violent and very public dressing-down in front of their master before he had time to offer any sort of apology.[13]

3

Emilie's child was born on October 8th, 1773; it was a boy, and they christened him Victor. Gabriel's intense delight was clouded, however, by financial worries which could no longer be put aside. In desperation he wrote to a family lawyer saying that since neither his father nor his father-in-law seemed prepared to settle with his creditors, he was prepared to beg his father to obtain a *lettre de cachet* confining him to Château d'If, the island fortress opposite Marseilles, and putting him beyond their reach. As a matter of fact much the same idea had been forming in his father's mind, though he inclined to think that a royal order confining the young man to the Mirabeau estate would meet the case: in this way he would continue his domestic life but be 'under the King's hand' and so beyond the range of any judicial proceedings.

At the beginning of December Mirabeau *Père* received from Marignane a letter which ended all hesitation: all Emilie's diamonds, bar two bracelets, had disappeared, and her allowance was pledged three years in advance; worse still, several of the Count's notes-of-hand had already been dishonoured; if he was to be saved from a debtor's prison there was not a moment to lose. D'Albertas, doubtless glad to see young Mirabeau put down a peg, endorsed this view. The Marquis acted with commendable alacrity, and the order placing his son under house-arrest was issued within a fortnight.

Mirabeau had got off lightly. Beyond his creditors' reach yet not a declared bankrupt, he could lead a tolerable life within his estate boundaries, shooting every day as was his custom. But this did not last. Reports reached the Marquis that the young man was at it again, selling furniture and timber to raise the wind, and the Friend of Mankind, ready as ever to believe ill of his son yet unwilling to make the journey south and see things for himself, obtained a new order exiling the spendthrift to Manosque. Even this could not be called harsh treatment; Manosque was only some twenty miles from Mirabeau, and what actually happened was that Gabriel and Emilie went to stay there with some old friends of the name of De Gassaud.[14]

Gabriel's sense of his situation as a husband seems to have put little check upon his indulgence in casual amours; this he as good as admits in a letter to his sister, Caroline du Saillant, barely three months after his marriage. How did Emilie conduct herself? What were her feelings towards the wayward, irascible, amorous man at her side? Self-revelation was not her habit, and we can only conjecture; but it seems that while Gabriel had taken by assault the lightly defended outworks of her being, she never surrendered to him her inner citadel. Amazed and amused by her husband's attentions, her response was a bright rippling of the surface, the water beneath remaining unmoved and cold.

In the Gassaud home was the son of the house, a young musketeer on leave, and with him Emilie began an intrigue. Her husband's suspicions were confirmed when, after young De Gassaud had rejoined his regiment, a letter between the lovers fell into his hands. Deeply mortified, Gabriel wrote for advice to the Comtesse de Vence, a lady whom he treated with affectionate respect as a sort of adopted aunt and who had known Emilie from infancy. She replied with cooling sense: 'Since the day she was born your wife has had before her nothing but bad example, and you yourself have sought to destroy the little religion they taught her at the convent . . . Consider a moment, I beg you, how little equality there is between husband and wife in the eyes of society, and how little reason there is in the nature of things that what is permitted to the man should be so harshly punished in the woman, who often does no more than follow the example her husband has given her.' Returning the fatal letter, she begged him to destroy it.

The appeal to his sense of justice and to his vanity as a man of enlightenment was well aimed. Indeed, without waiting for Mme de Vence's reply, Mirabeau forgave his wife in an emotional scene before the assembled De Gassauds; her guilt and his magnanimity were fully explained, and she had to agree to write her lover a letter of dismissal which was to be returned when read to her injured husband. Then he himself wrote the young musketeer a letter of reproach; Mirabeau's sense of a situation was not always equalled by his taste in handling it, and the note of self-righteousness was ludicrously overdone. As for Mme de Vence's advice, he took it so far as to burn De Gassaud's letter in his wife's presence, but when Emilie's letter came back to him in due course he put it carefully away, for there were limits to the magnanimity even of the enlightened.[15]

It was just after this that he heard the humiliating news that the Châtelet of Paris, at the suit of his father, supported by Marignane and certain others including (unkind cut) Albertas, had declared him bankrupt. One-third of his income was left to himself and his family; the rest was to be reserved to pay off his debts. Though he felt his legal incapacity keenly at first he soon became used to it, and in the end he never bothered to have it removed. At the height of his popularity and renown in the morning of the Revolution he was still an undischarged bankrupt, and he died with his wedding suit unpaid for.

4

Mirabeau's self-righteous indignation with young De Gassaud had a special justification. At the moment when he discovered his wife's intrigue he had been helping forward negotiations for the young man to marry the daughter of the Marquis de Tourettes. It so happened that, just when Mirabeau was grandly forgiving his wife and reproaching his false friend, a hitch occurred in the negotiations. Very anxious lest it should seem that this was due to any spite on his own part, Mirabeau broke his bounds, rode over to Tourettes and generously put matters right again.

To leave Manosque was an act of disobedience to the royal order, though if Mirabeau had returned quietly and at once it might have been overlooked; the *parlementaires* exiled there enjoyed a certain freedom to come and go discreetly. But Tourettes, on the frontier of the County of Nice, was no distance from Grasse, and at Grasse lived Louise de Cabris. The temptation to see his wicked, delightful sister was too much for him.

Louise, now twenty-two, had been married for five years. Her imbecile of a husband had been selected for her by her father and Madame de Pailly with even less regard to personal preferences than was customary. Louise, as a matter of fact, did not see her betrothed till the day before the wedding, so if her marriage was a heartless and disgusting farce it seems unnecessary to blame this entirely upon what her father called 'the congenital irreligion of all his children'.

Half fury, half siren, Louise was the terror, the scandal and the entertainment of Grasse. In fits of fiendish temper she sometimes half strangled people, and once, at least, she challenged another woman to a pistol duel. Her blatant liaison with the Seigneur de Briançon shocked society perhaps less than her habit of going about with him in man's clothes. Over Gabriel she exercised at this time a wicked fascination, and there existed between them a mischievous and rather sinister entente; yet in him there was no demon of malice such as raved in her soul. Their father was to recognize this; deep as was to be his angry disgust with his elder son, he would admit in him a fundamental goodness of heart and the possibility of forgiveness; but to forgive Louise — that, he wrote, would be to forgive the devil.

At the moment of Mirabeau's illicit visit to Grasse the chief object of her anger was a certain Baron de Villeneuve-Mouans, who had attributed to her some obscene libels which had been pasted up about the town. On August 5th, this elderly gentleman was taking the air under the shade of a parasol when he encountered Madame de Cabris, her paramour and her brother, who had dined. Mirabeau promptly picked a quarrel, seized the sunshade and broke it over Villeneuve's head; then they clinched and in a moment were rolling on the ground, Mirabeau still whacking the Baron with the broken parasol as, struggling and kicking, they disappeared together over the edge of the low terrace on which the battle had begun and on which Louise and Briançon stood, splitting their sides with laughter.

A challenge in form from Villeneuve was now of course to be expected. Whether the formalities of a duel could be observed without advertising Mirabeau's breach of bounds was doubtful; for the moment, though, there was nothing to do but hurry back to Manosque, await the challenge and hope for the best. But the challenge never came. To the surprise and dismay even of Villeneuve's relations, that gentleman, having, in Mirabeau's words, been thrashed like a lackey, proceeded to act like one, and brought against his assailant a legal action for murderous assault.

This threw the fat into the fire. Mirabeau's disobedience in having left Manosque stood exposed to the eyes of authority. His best hope was intervention by the Friend of Mankind, and Emilie hastened north to Le Bignon to mollify him. His anger at his son's latest escapade was increased by the part the abominable Louise had played in it, but Emilie quickly established excellent relations with her father-in-law, and agreed with him that the best thing would be for her to stay comfortably at Le Bignon while he pulled the familiar ministerial strings to obtain yet another *lettre de cachet* to hoist her husband out of harm's way. The new order — the third on Gabriel's account — was obtained with expedition, and on September 20th, 1774, he was arrested and taken to imprisonment at Château d'If, the island in Marseilles roads.[16]

5

It was during his six months at Manosque that Mirabeau wrote his first serious work, the *Essai sur le despotisme*. Four years later he declared: 'I repent of having mutilated so fine a subject', and called the Essay 'a tissue of scraps put together without order, marked with all the faults of the age at which I was writing'. The book is certainly long-winded and pretentious, though here and there an epigram or phrase flashes like a rapier; but the Essay is important not for what it says of despotism but for what it tells us of Mirabeau.

It is strewn with allusions to Tacitus, and it is clear that the mordant historian of Roman despots is the author's master-mind. He calls him 'a great practical philosopher', and his admiration discloses a peculiarity of his own mind in that age of ideologues — a sense of history. For him historical facts are the only basis for a philosophy of politics. Though he writes with the mannerisms of the *philosophes*, Mirabeau at twenty-five is basically as impatient of un-anchored theories as Burke. While gladly recognizing Rousseau as 'the most elegant of French writers without any exception', he rejects the theory of the social contract. He will not have it that man is even logically anterior to society: the duration of infantile dependence requires the family, and there, albeit in embryonic form, society exists. 'Society is the natural state of man, as it is of the ant and the bee', and that, for Mirabeau, is that.

He is sceptical as to man's natural goodness. Every man has the germ of despotism in him in the cradle, as anyone who watches a howling infant can see for himself. Desire for power is the most active passion of the human heart, and statesmanship consists in controlling and distributing this explosive force. Free countries like Holland and England have mastered the power-impulse in their internal organization, yet even they yield to it in handling subject peoples. Most countries, however, simply oscillate between despotism and anarchy. 'Man, degraded by servitude, easily becomes the most ferocious of animals if he escapes for a moment from oppression. From despot to slave and from slave to despot is but one step, and it is easily crossed by the sword.'

When we remember how unsettled Mirabeau's life had been hitherto, the extent of his reading is remarkable. Its content is more remarkable still. In most cultivated minds of the eighteenth century there existed a vast, unrealized hiatus, a comfortable unawareness that anything worthy of serious study had happened in the interval between the fall of Rome and the Renaissance. Lycurgus, Pericles, Cincinnatus, Cato, Brutus and the rest were the objects of incessant allusion by political writers; antiquity was their neat store-cupboard of examples, and they thought it stocked to meet all requirements, the philosopher's complete historical outfit. Yet the subjects with which they had to deal and whose disorder was the cause of their discontents — the national state, hereditary monarchy, aristocratic privileges, ecclesiastical establishments, serfdom and the rest — were things for the understanding of which ancient history provided little guidance. They were legacies from the Middle Ages, from precisely those centuries which the intellectuals of the Enlightenment were inclined to lump together as ages of barbarism, unworthy of serious attention.

Mirabeau's Essay shows an awareness of this. Alongside the stock classical allusions there is a notably free citation of medieval and early modern examples, and it is evident that he is looking to the past not for glass-case specimens of political conduct but for the roots of the present. He seizes eagerly the vital truth that medieval kingship was in essence limited and conditional, and that absolutism is a morbid modern growth. He sees the greatest medieval monarchs, Louis IX in France or Edward I in England, freely admitting the contractual nature of their office, and he quotes with delight the famous coronation formula of Aragon. Charles VII and Louis XI are the sinister innovators who first perverted the monarchy in France; they it was who first levied arbitrary taxes and maintained a standing army with corps of foreign mercenaries; Louis XI was also 'the first King of France who bribed the States-General, and so destroyed the most venerable bulwark of public liberty'. Despotism rests upon the tripod of arbitrary taxation, a standing army and bureaucracy, 'this mania for the pen, which dates from Louis XI but to which Colbert gave a new impulse', and it was France's misfortune that Richelieu, Louvois and Colbert were men of genius. In this immature essay Mirabeau is feeling his way towards a political faith; the monarchy has been perverted for a century and a half but can still be restored to its true nature, and for this restoration Elizabeth of England, the Valois Charles V and the Bourbon Henry IV, 'that adorable man', are the models. A monarchy powerful because popular, and popular because responsive to the nation's heart and will — such is Mirabeau's ideal in 1774, the year of the accession of Louis XVI.

At Château d'If Mirabeau was a prisoner. His father was determined that he should now have a taste of real punishment. He was to be isolated and have communication with no one but his wife, who, if she wished, might visit or join him there. At this moment the hardest thing was to be taken away from his baby son. His paternal feelings were very strong, and he adored this infant; the child was unwell at this time, and on his prison-island Mirabeau would have nothing but his wife's letters to assuage his anxiety. But Emilie, having left her son in Provence with the De Gassauds, was dividing her time very agreeably between Le Bignon and Paris, far from her husband's clamouring creditors. For a while she wrote frequently and affectionately, but to his entreaties that she should return to Provence or, better still, join him on his island, she opposed elaborate excuses. He began to suspect her of alliance with his father, of preferring the comforts of Le Bignon and the gaieties of the capital to her duty. He began with less justice, to suspect her of other forms of disloyalty as well. Finally he tortured himself into writing a letter of reproach so violent that their fragile concord never recovered from the blow, and *vous* replaced *tu* in the rare letters they still exchanged.[17]

Meanwhile Mirabeau was having an inside view of the human realities resulting from the practice of arbitrary imprisonment. This practice, which, by denying liberty of the person, renders meaningless all other liberties, as of speech, printing or assembly, is the master-key of every tyranny in every age; but in France under the old régime it had a peculiarly infamous feature, since it was possible for private persons, by applying to the Secretary of State of the King's Household, to obtain sealed orders (*lettres de cachet*) for the imprisonment during the King's pleasure of relations whom, for good reasons or bad, they wished out of the way. Once arrested under a *lettre de cachet*, the victim was quite helpless: no appeal could be lodged in any court in the realm; the prisoner could neither sue nor be sued; he was 'under the King's hand' and lived suspended, as it were, in a legal vacuum without rights and without liabilities. A *lettre de cachet* did not necessarily mean being put in a prison, nor was its issue always unwelcome to one who had got himself into a scrape; Mirabeau's previous experiences illustrate this. But the instrument was, by its very nature, open to the most shocking abuse in the hands of spiteful, envious or embittered people who knew which ropes to pull.

According to Mirabeau's later account there were thirty prisoners at Château d'If while he was there, and of these only one could be classed as a criminal and only six had bad records. Of the rest three were men whose only crime was to have pretty wives 'protected by some of those base flunkeys whom people call *grand seigneurs*'. Then there was the case of the old privateer captain. This pathetic old salt had been under the Bailli in Guadeloupe, twenty years earlier. Now he was seventy-two, crippled with wounds and rheumatism, and a prisoner at Château d'If. Why? Because his daughter had represented that her father's drunkenness was a scandal to the public and a danger to himself, whereas the truth of the matter was that the old fellow, while fond enough of his liquor, could not abide a trollop, and on finding that his daughter was the kept miss of a local bureaucrat, had been so rash as to use threatening language to that official.

The Governor of Château d'If soon became indulgent to Mirabeau, who was able to correspond secretly with his mother and with Louise. The canteen-woman to the garrison became indulgent to him too. 'She was', he later explained, 'the only woman at the château who looked like one, and I was twenty-six.' Then one day the Chevalier de Mirabeau, being in Marseilles on his way back from Malta, hired a boat over to the island and was allowed to see his brother. Boniface, with his good-fellow air, was already coarsening with drink — 'Barrel' Mirabeau he was later called — and he had a loose and wagging tongue. When he got to Paris he let out something about Gabriel and the *cantinière* to Emilie. The news was perhaps not unwelcome to her, and the Marquis would have been less vexed at Gabriel's talent for relieving the monotony of prison than at Boniface's disobedience in visiting him had it not been for the sequel. The *cantinière* persuaded Mirabeau that her life was in danger from her brutal husband in Marseilles and begged his help. He gave her a letter of recommendation to Briançon, armed with which and a lot of her husband's cash she made her escape and took refuge with

Madame de Cabris at Grasse, whereupon her husband raised a storm in Marseilles and named Mirabeau as his wife's seducer.

Once more the Marquis saw the hand of the accursed Louise in Gabriel's misbehaviour; Boniface had blabbed out the fact of their secret correspondence, and now the Governor of Château d'If was writing to say how agreeable and well-conducted the Count was and to suggest that he be restored to liberty. Clearly the governor was just one more gullible victim of Gabriel's fatal fascination. Nothing for it but to have the fellow moved somewhere far away from Provence and its associations and, if possible, beyond the reach of the baleful machinations of Louise.

So Mirabeau was moved from Château d'If to the fortress of Joux, near Pontarlier, in the bleak Jura country near the Swiss frontier. He arrived there on May 25th, 1775, with the snow still lying on the ground and scarce a leaf upon a tree.

CHAPTER IV

SOPHIE

Marie-Thérèse-Sophie Richard de Ruffey was the youngest of the six children of a president of the *Chambre des comptes* of Dijon. The De Ruffeys were one of the most respected families of the *noblesse de robe* of Burgundy, substantial, cultured and circumspect. A conservative, bourgeois propriety pervaded their lives, but they had contacts with men of letters and with spirits more adventurous than themselves.

Early marriage to a steady husband was the aim of M. and Mme de Ruffey for their youngest child, and when she was fifteen they brought her home from her convent, being not without hope of wedding her to the widowed naturalist, Buffon; he, however, declined the match, for he was sixty-two, and Sophie had to wait apprehensively while her parents continued their search for a reliable gentleman.

They soon found what they wanted. The Marquis de Monnier, First President of the *Chambre des comptes* of Dôle, son of a Councillor of State and First President of the *Chambre des comptes, aides, domaines et finances* of the County of Burgundy, had lately lost his wife, daughter of a president of the *Chambre des comptes* of Dôle. His only daughter had married against his wish, and this had so embittered him that a desire to spite her conspired with other feelings to tempt him into a second marriage. When he heard that Mlle de Ruffey, plump, nubile and impeccably brought up, was his for the asking, he did not hesitate, and in 1771 Sophie de Ruffey, aged seventeen, became Marquise de Monnier. 'My dear President', Voltaire wrote to the bride's father, 'I did not know that M. de Monnier was a marriageable young man; I congratulate him, and think him very lucky to marry your daughter. I wish the two of them all possible prosperity.' The bridegroom's age was sixty-five.

Just after the marriage Maupeou's attack on the *parlements* deprived De Monnier of his office, and he retired to live quietly at Pontarlier. There Sophie lived with her pious, careful, not unkindly husband for two years, without evident dissatisfaction with the humdrum routine of a house where the most frequent visitors were the local clergy. Then M. de Saint-Mauris, commandant of the neighbouring garrison of Joux, began to pay frequent visits to the house and unmistakable attentions to its lady. But as a diversion from the slippered affection of her husband Sophie found M. de Saint-Mauris somewhat less than satisfying, for the commandant was in his sixties, too.

It could only be a matter of time before her own generation provided the variation which nature demanded, and there was a first flirtation, a timid, butterfly affair. There followed a second, rather more serious, with a young gunner officer, and Mme de Monnier's reputation began to be blown upon in the little town.

In June 1775 the De Monniers were entertained to a dinner given by M. de Saint-Mauris in honour of the coronation of Louis XVI, and their host introduced to them his prisoner and guest, the Comte de Mirabeau.

2

Mirabeau's life at Fort de Joux was tolerable enough. His father believed that in this remote spot he might safely be allowed more relaxation, and Saint-Mauris, who found his prisoner an amusing companion in a dull place, gave him considerable liberty. He encouraged his voracious reading while the Friend of Mankind sent him regularly *Ephémerides*, the periodical organ of the physiocrats, to assist his reformation. Now that physiocracy, in the person of Turgot, had captured the seat of power, who could say what brilliant career might not await the younger Mirabeau, if only he would be converted to the doctrine? At Saint-Mauris's suggestion and partly to please his father, Mirabeau began a treatise on the salt-mines of the Franche-Comté, and journeys of investigation were permitted. He was also free to hunt in the neighbourhood and to visit friends in Pontarlier. The only serious limitation of his movements was the necessity of returning to the fort each night, and even this rule was not strictly enforced, for he made trips into Switzerland with the commandant's connivance.

The principality of Neuchâtel, which lay just across the frontier, was one of the many anomalous polities which diversified the rich pattern of eighteenth-century Europe. It was under the protection of the Swiss Confederation to which geography attached it, but its suzerain was a dynast whose territorial interests could scarcely have been more remote — the King of Prussia. The French censorship had driven abroad many progressive publishers, and here at Neuchâtel the firm of Fauche, secure as Booksellers to the King of Prussia, operated beyond its reach. It was in order to place with them his *Essay on Despotism* that Mirabeau visited Neuchâtel. Fauche accepted the manuscript for anonymous publication and agreed, as part of the bargain, to advance a sum of money to the author against his note-of-hand.

3

Madame de Monnier was away from Pontarlier for a while after her first meetings with Mirabeau, and it was not till her return in the autumn that his dynamic masculinity began to disturb her senses, while the range and energy of his conversation, the music of his speaking voice, the compulsion of his luminous eyes and his jutting aggressive features invaded her mind. He was a prodigy beyond her little experience and her pale imaginings, and when, very soon, she knew that he was making love to her, the ground slipped away from under her feet.

Mirabeau had been a little puzzled by his sudden transference to Fort de Joux. Why, out of all France, this place? It occurred to him that the choice of this frontier post might be a tacit hint from his father to leave the country till time and paternal diplomacy should arrange his affairs. His father refused to communicate with him but the liberties permitted by Saint-Mauris, who was in direct touch with the Marquis, seemed to point in the same direction. It was some time since his wife, the only correspondent he was officially allowed, had bothered to write to him, but he now sent her a warm letter of appeal: let her join him at once that they might escape together to Switzerland and live there on what income they had left supplemented by his literary earnings. In mid-October he received her reply. It was a cold little note rejecting the plan with weak excuses. 'This proposal was too noble for her spirit,' he wrote; 'it was foolish of me to look for fruit on a tree which bore only flowers.' Fruit, however, was already offering itself on another tree. [18]

Mirabeau had fallen in love with Sophie. It was inevitable. 'I was most unhappy, and unhappiness doubles susceptibility.' The shock of contrast was too great. In other circumstances Sophie would probably have made no deep impression. She was not very beautiful and not very clever. But the qualities that were in her, sweetness and a certain exciting roguishness, beneath which lay a passionate generosity, were those which Emilie lacked and for which he was hungry. The heartless affairs in which he indulged left him undisgusted but quite unsatisfied. Mere animal relief could never meet the needs of a nature in which great warmth of heart and a capacity for tenderness existed together with a tyrannous sensuality.

If Sophie's difference from Emilie drew him straight towards her, the contrast between the intensity of her first great passion and the trivial loves which were the rest of his experience checked momentarily his onward rush. Sophie had a position of honour to lose through him, and her senile husband had been a welcoming host. Mirabeau, knowing well enough whither he and she were headed, felt some twinge of conscience and even took one firm step against his inclination. Through a friendly official he sent to his father an appeal that he would send Emilie to him at Pontarlier. But the Friend of Mankind would not press his daughter-in-law in the matter and hinted that the best thing his son could do was to leave the country. This answer removed the brake from the slipping wheel, and Gabriel received it with a secret satisfaction. Had he not done all he could? Was he not disowned and cast out by all but Sophie?

'Sophie,' he wrote later when disaster had severed them, 'do you remember the blissful, glorious day when Gabriel said to you "Shall I dare to be happy?" "Will you keep love's promises?" you asked, and I was your husband before we regained the power of speech. Ah, Sophie! I have kept those sacred promises, and the ardour with which Gabriel burns will last as long as life.' Love, he once admitted, is a dangerous sophist.

The blissful and glorious day was December 13th, 1775, and it was not long before the relations between Mirabeau and Madame de Monnier were the talk of Pontarlier. M. de Saint-Mauris was not likely to connive. Less the Count's jailer than his supervisor, he had to answer for his security to the government and for his behaviour to the Marquis. Gallantries entailing legal consequences would reflect upon his performance as custodian, and a scandal involving the young wife of one of Pontarlier's most venerable residents could scarcely be ignored. Memories of his own ill-success in the same quarter may have added personal envy to official anxiety, but there is no reason to accept Mirabeau's later accusation that Saint-Mauris maliciously organized a campaign of scandal and slander against the young woman who had scorned him and the young man she had preferred. Mirabeau was altogether too fond of posing as the young man of promise whom envious elders and superiors were for ever conspiring to crush, and the accusations he was soon to make against Saint-Mauris resemble unpleasingly those he made against Lambert, his colonel at Saintes. His readiness to complain of victimization is perhaps the least forgivable fault in his character.

It was not, as a matter of fact, the affair of Mme de Monnier which caused the first trouble between Mirabeau and the commandant, but something quite separate. In January 1776 a promissory note for 1500 *livres* drawn by Mirabeau in favour of his Neuchâtel publishers came into the hands of a Pontarlier tradesman. It had not yet fallen due, but the tradesman, uneasy as to the drawer's solvency, took it to the commandant. Saint-Mauris became agitated. Here was proof that Mirabeau, despite his legal bankruptcy, was abusing the liberty allowed him to incur fresh debts. Furthermore, the circulation of this bill made public the prisoner's trips into Switzerland, for which his custodian might get into trouble. Finally, the anonymous *Essay on Despotism* had recently appeared in France and had attracted the hostile attention of the authorities; should they connect its publication with the irregular excursions to Neuchâtel of a prisoner from Fort de Joux, Saint-Mauris would be in serious trouble indeed.

He taxed the Count sharply with the business and told him that henceforth he would be confined to the fortress. Mirabeau

begged for just four further days of freedom — just enough to
enable him to attend a ball which De Monnier was giving in
his honour — and the small part personal resentments played
with the commandant is shown by the fact that he granted the
extension. Mirabeau, however, failed to report at the end of his
four days. Defending himself later, he made much of the fact
that Saint-Mauris had never received his formal parole; it was a
defence which exposed him to the more damaging accusation of
having violated a gentlemen's understanding, and it must have
been his bad conscience over this which caused him, after his
default, to write a letter to Saint-Mauris announcing his intention of withdrawing himself from that officer's 'tyrannical
authority'. Mirabeau was not much encumbered by 'that chastity
of honour' which for Burke redeemed the nobility of the sword.

He passed part of the night of the ball in a cupboard adjoining his hostess's bedroom, and the next day hid himself in Pontarlier. The day after that he was caught by De Monnier's
servants in the act of stealing to his mistress's room; not for a
moment abashed, he asked to see their master, and proceeded to
explain to the old gentleman how he had been in Switzerland
and was even now on his way to Paris to see a minister; how,
passing through Pontarlier he had felt he really must drop in
on his dear friends to thank them for all their kindness; he had
come surreptitiously so as not to attract notice; would M. de
Monnier be so kind as to summon all the servants and swear them
to secrecy?

The plot continued to develop in an atmosphere of *opéra-bouffe*.
De Monnier was not quite deaf to the talk about his wife, for
M. le Curé had called and spoken to him of the matter; when,
therefore, she asked him to let her go for a while to her parents
at Dijon to let malicious rumours die down, he thought the idea
was a good one. It was. It was Mirabeau's. Sophie reached
Dijon on February 25th, and four days later Mirabeau was there
too. That night the De Ruffeys were attending a ball given by
M. de Montherot, Grand Provost of Burgundy, chief of police
of the province. With crazy audacity Mirabeau took it into his
head to present himself at the ball as the 'Marquis de Lance-
foudras'. Sophie, who had not expected him, was off her guard,
and her mother did not fail to notice her flutter of emotion.

Apologies were made, wraps were fetched and Madame de Ruffey led her party from the assembly in some agitation.

Not deceived for a moment as to the identity of the stranger, Madame de Ruffey at once exposed him to the Grand Provost as an escaped prisoner set on her daughter's ruin. Montherot was disinclined to act on the word of this fussy hen, but he had to do something. Accepting Mirabeau's promise not to leave Dijon, he left him at liberty, and meanwhile wrote to the Secretary of State, Malesherbes, for further instructions.

Malesherbes, a humane man who, as First President of the *Cour des Aides*, had been prominent in withstanding the autocracy in 1771, and who had lately appointed a commission to look into the whole question of *lettres de cachet*, may have smiled a little wearily on receiving this inquiry, for the House of Mirabeau had of late taken up a good deal more of his department's time than was reasonable for a single family. There had been letters from the Count after his escape from Joux, attacking his father in unmeasured terms. There had been copious letters from the Marquise, whose suit for judicial separation was now in progress, accusing her husband of the most unmentionable behaviour, and, of late, further outpourings on behalf of her son. 'It is well known', she wrote with an unwonted touch of diplomacy, 'with what disastrous facility the liberty of the subject was fettered under the late King. If the Comte de Mirabeau has not recovered this precious boon under a citizen-king and a citizen-minister, it is because it has fallen to him to make public a father's injustice, because he has had to demonstrate that a man who has taken the solemn title of Friend of Mankind is the sworn enemy of his wife and children.' There had also, of course, been letters from the Marquis rebutting these accusations and soliciting the support of the royal prerogative to quell family rebellion; in particular, would the minister be so good as to provide for the secure incarceration of the Count from henceforth? Malesherbes tried to impose a measure of calm. Towards the end of March he sent to Dijon instructions that Mirabeau should be interned in the castle there, but be allowed reasonable liberty to come and go. In the meantime he appointed a special commission to review the Count's by now somewhat tangled case, refusing to do anything more drastic till it had reported.

The commission reported at the end of April: the Count's breach of bounds at Manosque might be regarded as paid for by his detention at Château d'If and Fort de Joux, but he should not be released just yet because of his second evasion; apart from this, detention for a further six months was desirable to give time for the settlement of his debts and of the damages being claimed by M. de Villeneuve-Mouans for murderous assault. On the strength of this report Malesherbes made an order for the Count's transfer to Doullens in Picardy; it was his last act before quitting the ministry, and it seems that he earlier conveyed a hint to Mirabeau as to what was coming, and a veiled suggestion that he should get out of the country while the going was good. It was M. de Changey, Mirabeau's new warden and latest friend, who passed on the hint, underlining it by handing back his prisoner's parole.

4

Since the night of the Grand Provost's ball Sophie had been guarded by her family. The De Ruffeys kept watch and ward against the wicked Comte de Mirabeau during the anxious three weeks when he was at large in the town, though, for all their vigilance, the lovers contrived to spend most of one night together at the local Vauxhall. Meeting Sophie's brothers in the street, the seducer told them that their mother was acting idiotically in underrating her daughter's strength of character, that she would drive her to desperation by intercepting her letters and spying on her like this, and that she might well drive him to do something desperate too. When, on March 21st, Mirabeau was placed in detention at the castle, Madame de Ruffey must have felt easier, and when Sophie spoke of going back to her husband it was hard to find good reasons for hindering her. Three days later, accordingly, Sophie left Dijon to return home. It was Gabriel's idea: Pontarlier on the frontier was better than Dijon for what he now had in mind, and the doting credulity of old De Monnier was preferable to the vigilance of the Ruffeys.

But Madame de Ruffey was not leaving anything to chance. Convinced of De Monnier's gullibility, she dispatched her elder daughter, a canoness, to Pontarlier to maintain the watch, and the reverend lady installed herself hard by the Monnier house, noting all movements and even questioning Sophie's servants and intercepting her correspondence.

Then, on May 25th, it became known in Dijon that Mirabeau had escaped in the night, and Madame de Ruffey instantly reinforced the canoness, sending one of her sons to resist the abduction of Sophie, if necessary by force. Desperately anxious, she followed this up with letters urging her son-in-law to get a *lettre de cachet* confining his wife to some suitable convent.

Mirabeau had slipped away from Dijon accompanied by a couple of friends. While he made straight for Les Verrières, just over the frontier, these two went to Pontarlier to 'rescue' his *chère amie*. Twice Sophie, dressed for the journey on horseback, was on the point of joining them, but each time the canoness was on guard; and when her brother arrived, bristling with pistols, they lost courage and returned to Mirabeau to report failure. He, meanwhile, was in new difficulties, for the Verrières authorities were beginning to suspect the false name he had given and might discover his identity and arrange his extradition. Feeling he had better be moving, he went to Thonon, on the Lake of Geneva.

In this, his greatest adventure, he naturally turned to his old confederate, Louise de Cabris. Since the assault and battery of M. de Villeneuve, Grasse had become too hot even for her, and she was now living at a convent at Lyons, an arrangement which did not prevent regular meetings with her lover, Briançon. Gabriel wrote in haste to his sister: 'Do your utmost to see that the enclosed note reaches Sophie. It's only a line, but essential in order to keep her courage up. Write to me, write to me! I never had such need of you!'

Louise, who was already *en rapport* with the whole affair, responded instantly. It was an escapade after her own heart. Wearing her breeches and accompanied by Briançon she rode in haste to Geneva and on to Thonon, giving out that she was Mlle Raucourt of the *Comédie française*. Picking up Gabriel, she doubled back to the frontier. There the party split up for safety, for they realized that they were now being followed by police agents; Gabriel and Briançon went back to Lyons, hoping to throw off the pursuit of the two sleuths whom the Friend of Mankind, who had sworn to have his son locked up for good this time in the Mont St. Michel, was employing at thirty-one *livres* a day plus expenses. When Louise rejoined the men at Lyons she had a new plan. Gabriel was to go with Briançon to Provence and lie up in the latter's manor at Lorgues until the coast should be clear and Sophie's rescue could be again attempted; no harm in the delay; it would give Sophie more time in which to send the furtive packets of jewellery and cash which Louise was holding as a sort of escape-fund for the lovers.

Gabriel took a boat down the Rhône — just in time. The police-agents, reaching Lyons after a wild-goose chase around Geneva and the upper Rhône, had to be satisfied with arresting Briançon's valet, but they got out of him nothing more definite than that his master and Mirabeau were headed for Lorgues and had spoken of going on to Nice. So off they went again. After following a hot scent through Avignon and losing it in the fair-crowds at Beaucaire, they made for Lorgues. Cunningly pretending to be Lyons merchants, they scraped acquaintance with Briançon and contrived to sup with him; but all they got from their wary host was that the Count had indeed travelled south with him but had gone on by himself — to Nice, he rather thought. So off they went again (at thirty-one *livres* a day plus expenses) to Nice, where, after investigating several reports of 'gentlemen answering the description' and riding up perilous mountain paths on mules, they again drew blank. They returned to Lyons sore, tired and so discouraged that they appealed to Madame de Cabris for advice. She was all helpfulness and solicitude: she was deeply worried at the Count's escapade and only anxious to see him safely under lock and key; yes, to her certain knowledge he *was* at Lorgues; a pity they hadn't searched properly. So off the agents went again. When they reached Lorgues Briançon made no difficulties about a search, for while they had been making their dash to Nice Mirabeau had been speeding across Piedmont, and now, when they were searching for him again in Provence, he was back at his starting-base, having doubled north again through the Great St. Bernard and Switzerland to Les Verrières, the original rendezvous with Sophie.

She, meanwhile, had been busy collecting portable valuables, her own and her husband's, disarming his suspicions and watching for her chance. So long, however, as her brother and sister remained on guard there was no chance. Sophie acted the demure and repentant little wife, busy and happy in her home, attending to her husband's comfort, playing cards with him in the evening, devout at household prayers, going to the sacraments. Would he not send her brother and sister away? How could she hold up her head in Pontarlier when spied on like this? Why, she was watched and followed when she went out, yes, even when she went to church. Did he not trust her?

Yes, he trusted her, and at his request the canoness and her brother took themselves off.

During the morning of August 24th, Sophie received a smuggled note: tonight was to be the night; all was ready, every detail planned. That afternoon De Monnier looked at his wife's pretty, slightly babyish face, and said 'I trust you'. At nightfall, when the servants were all at evening prayers with their master, she put on men's clothes, hurried down the garden, climbed the wall, found the expected horse saddled and waiting, crossed the mountains with a guide by a little-known path, and, before midnight, reached the frontier, Gabriel and rapture.[19]

5

The lovers stayed three weeks at Les Verrières and then went to Amsterdam. This city was a great centre of the book-trade, and Mirabeau had now to think about earning a living, for the money and jewels Sophie had carried away would not last long. She attempted to justify taking her husband's property by saying that whereas her parents had married her 'at sixteen', when she was unable to dispose of herself, she was now 'marrying' by her own choice and 'recovering her portion'. It is easier to condemn this as sentimental sophistry than to defend the arrangements made by the De Ruffey parents for their daughter's future. What, one wonders, did they expect? Scarcely conjugal fidelity. For all Madame de Ruffey's lamentations that Sophie had only gone wrong through becoming careless about her prayers, that pious

lady was a realist, and knew perfectly well that for most girls of
the leisured class the arranged marriage was not only the gateway
out of the convent-school but also the sliding panel into a dis-
creet course of extra-conjugal amusements. To marry a daughter
in her teens to a sexagenarian was, therefore, to make it humanly
certain that she would commit adultery unless her husband should
predecease her before she could deceive him. Evidently the
financial benefit to be expected from the former alternative was
felt to outweigh the moral harm in the latter, and it was not the
peril to her daughter's soul which agitated Madame de Ruffey
but the damage to her reputation; it was the scandal, not the sin,
which worried her.

She worked up her aged son-in-law, who seems for his part to
have been inclined to a dignified passivity, to bring an action for
abduction and seduction against Mirabeau; at the same time
Madame de Valdhaon, De Monnier's married daughter, seeing
her chance to recover her position in his will, urged him to have
Sophie prosecuted for adultery, a proposal less pleasing to Madame
de Ruffey.

In Amsterdam Gabriel and Sophie, calling themselves the
Comte and Comtesse de Saint-Mathieu, lived in cheap lodgings
over a tailor's shop. They worked hard. 'From six in the morning
till nine in the evening I was at work,' he wrote. 'An hour's music
was my relaxation; and my adorable companion made life
beautiful — she who, brought up in opulence, was never so gay,
so courageous, so attentive, so sweet-tempered nor so tender as
in poverty. She made my extracts; she worked, painted and read
proofs. Her invariable sweetness and unfailing tact were disclosed in all their fullness.' We have his admission that his own
sweetness and tact were not unfailing. Sophie gave Italian lessons,
and he suffered such jealousy that he had to force himself to
go out to avoid scolding her for her grammatical slips. His
jealousy could make him unreasonable and harsh; it had been
torture to him to see Sophie and her most intimate friend at
home exchanging girlish caresses, and there were moods
when he would even throw her silly affair with the artillery
officer in her face. He was also overworked, for when, after a
few weeks, he obtained employment, it was hard and poorly
rewarded. He became a hack for the publishing house of Rey,

doing translations chiefly from English, which he learnt, in some measure, as he went along. It was a cramped and assiduous life, especially for Sophie, for Gabriel did not like to take her into the raffish and shabby company which was all that he could afford. When he went to masonic meetings he would get back very late, and she would feel neglected and hurt. Orchestral concerts in Amsterdam and the Hague were their one escape into the life of culture and fashion.

In addition to hack-work of various sorts Mirabeau wrote on subjects of his own choice. Music had always been his hobby, and he now wrote an article on orchestral composition, *Le lecteur y mettra le titre*,* in which he raised the question whether counterpoint and harmony had not been over-elaborated at the expense of melody; the purpose of music was to appeal to the heart, and one could have too much cleverness and scholarship. The essay was a little mirror reflecting the romantic dawn.

The revolt of the English-American colonies, just begun, moved him like the other young liberals. Resuming a theme touched on in his *Essay on Despotism* — that the mercenary soldier is the tool of the tyrant — he wrote an impassioned 'Warning to the Hessians and to other peoples of Germany sold by their princes to England'.

This *Avis aux Hessois*† is a work of pure rhetoric, the first clear demonstration that Mirabeau was above all things an orator. 'Intrepid Germans,' it begins, 'what is this stigma which you suffer to be branded on your generous brows? To think that at the end of the eighteenth century the peoples of central Europe should be the mercenary instruments of a hateful tyranny . . . that they should suffer the trade in men to be carried on in their midst, depopulating their cities and exhausting their countryside, in order to help insolent rulers ravage another hemisphere! How long will you continue to share the crass blindness of your masters? You honest soldiers, the faithful and redoubtable support of their power — of that power which was only entrusted to them for the protection of their subjects — you have been sold, and sold, ye gods, for what a purpose!' Yet was it, in part at least, because they were Germans that they had been so sold? 'This fidelity to your leaders . . . this habit of obeying without reflecting that there are duties more sacred than obedience and anterior to any

* Published London, 1777. † Published Cleves, 1777.

oath, this credulity which makes you follow the lead of a small number of ambitious madmen — these are your faults.' Such a criticism was no commonplace in an age which had no premonition of the Second Reich or the Third, and in a France more disposed to admire than to fear its interesting contemporary, the Prussia of Frederick the Great.

6

For seven months Mirabeau and Sophie lived together in Holland. They were in the glory of their passion, and they thought themselves secure. Their confidence was based at first on the belief that their whereabouts was unknown. In this they were mistaken. Mirabeau had introduced himself to Rey as the author of the anonymous *Essay on Despotism* and suggested that Rey should bring out a fresh edition. Rey naturally demanded corroboration of the stranger's claim from the original publisher, and Fauche of Neuchâtel was so annoyed that he promptly informed De Monnier where the fugitives were living. The lovers also believed that De Monnier would take no action any way; and indeed that lonely old man showed at first little inclination to seek revenge against Mirabeau at the cost of hurting his wife. He might have resigned himself to his wrongs had it not been for Madame de Ruffey. She had two objects not easily compatible — to save her daughter from final ruin, and to punish her seducer.

Urged on by her, De Monnier started proceedings against Mirabeau, but he sent a confidential servant to Sophie with money and an appeal that she would return to him. She refused both: 'Gabriel or death' was her attitude, and the proceedings went ahead. So long, however, as they remained abroad a judicial sentence could do little beyond making their return impossible, and that was what worried Sophie's mother, who saw visions of her daughter deserted in a foreign land by the heartless philanderer who had abducted her. Madame de Ruffey's object, therefore, was to get both lovers brought back to France, Sophie for correction, Mirabeau for the gallows. For this, however, the ordinary machinery of justice would not serve; the arrest and extradition of the fugitives would require political action at a high level; only the co-operation of the Minister of Foreign Affairs, the Lieutenant of Police, the ambassador at the Hague and the government of the United Provinces would suffice to do the trick, and these were wheels which only influence could set in motion. Madame de Ruffey therefore approached the Marquis de Mirabeau, hoping much from his evident facility in obtaining royal orders for private purposes. She found him, however, rather unhelpful. His first reaction to his son's flight abroad had been, if anything, one of relief: Sophie was no business of his, and there was much to be said for having Gabriel out of the country just when his wife's separation suit was reaching the moment of decision.

Then something happened which changed his attitude abruptly. There appeared a printed attack on his character as a husband and a father. Published in France, Holland and England, it was violent and scurrilous in the extreme, and consisted partly of the letters which Gabriel had written to Malesherbes. Whether or not Gabriel was the author of the libel, he alone could have supplied this material, and it was at once clear to the Marquis that exile was little obstacle to that combination of his wife's anger, Louise's malice and Gabriel's reckless literary flair which he dreaded. Then a second libel appeared. Published in the *Gazette littéraire* in the form of a letter from London (this to conceal residence in Holland) it was entitled *An Anecdote to add to the voluminous collection of Philosophic Hypocrisies*. It touched the Friend of Mankind on his most sensitive spot, for it not only attacked him as a fraud who preached virtue and benevolence 'while he was at once the worst of husbands and the most harsh and irresponsible of fathers', but it also ridiculed his economic theories. The article was signed 'S. M.' and the Marquis was able to guess at 'Saint-Mathieu', the name of one of his wife's estates.

Mirabeau was later to regret his 'accursed facility for writing', which had tempted him to answer his mother's appeal for support by dashing off these ill-considered libels. It was, indeed, the blunder which ruined him for it stung his father into action. In concert with the De Ruffeys he set to work once more, and the wheels of officialdom began to rotate.

Early in May 1777 Mirabeau noticed in a tavern he frequented a compatriot dressed as a cavalry officer. Something about the man aroused his suspicion. His companions picked a quarrel with the stranger in the hope of unmasking him, but without success. It was, in fact, Des Brugnières, the senior police agent whom Mirabeau had led on such a wild-goose chase seven months before, and to whom the Marquis was now giving a second chance to prove his skill. But even had Mirabeau known this for certain he would not have been seriously alarmed. He had had himself received as a citizen of Amsterdam, and he felt further confidence that the debts which he had incurred since his arrival, some 200 *louis*, would prevent the Dutch authorities agreeing to his extradition. Des Brugnières, however, was only waiting for the ambassador to obtain from the Hague the order for an arrest; the debts would be no obstacle, since the ambassador was ready to advance the amount himself.

Then, on the fourteenth, a friend tipped Mirabeau that his arrest was fixed for the next day, and the fugitives at last realized their danger. Their few belongings were packed in desperate haste and with what secrecy was possible, for they owed their landlord for the rent. There was not a moment to lose, but to leave the house together would look suspicious. Gabriel, therefore, went first, Sophie to follow and join him. He waited; no sign of her. Then they brought him word that she had been arrested; he went straight back to their lodging, walking openeyed into the hands of the city police and of Des Brugnières, who was in charge of a sobbing Sophie and the phial of poison which he had taken from her just in time.

CHAPTER V

VINCENNES

DES BRUGNIÈRES showed consideration for his prisoners. When he learnt that Madame de Monnier was two months gone with child, the pathos of her situation and the eloquence of her lover touched him. When Sophie, for her part, realized what was in store for her — separation from Gabriel and imprisonment in the Sainte Pélagie among the lowest women of Paris — she swore she would kill herself, and we may be as certain as were the two men that she meant it. In the end they persuaded her to put such thoughts aside, in return for a promise by Des Brugnières to use his opportunities as inspector of police to carry letters between the lovers after their separation.

A few days later Des Brugnières, writing to the Lieutenant of Police to report that the extradition permit had come through, ventured a suggestion. Was it decent for a lady of rank like the Marquise de Monnier to be sent to Sainte Pélagie? It was not her husband, after all, who had asked for the present order; might he not be very angry at her being put in a house of correction for harlots? Des Brugnières would take it upon himself, therefore, not to take the Marquise to Sainte Pélagie without further orders.

For Mirabeau the outlook was only a little less grim. He was destined for Vincennes; not for the fairly commodious château where his father had once spent a week, but for the grim keep adjoining it. It was one of the great State Prisons for victims of *lettres de cachet*, with a reputation second only to that of the Bastille. There he would stay 'during the King's pleasure', and nobody but the Friend of Mankind could guess how many months, or how many years, that might mean.

One reflection, however, might help to reconcile Gabriel and Sophie to their fates. Four days before their arrest the criminal judge of the *bailliage* of Pontarlier had given judgment against them at the suit of M. de Monnier. Mirabeau, for abduction and seduction, was sentenced *in absentia* to be beheaded in effigy, to pay a fine of 5000 *livres* and damages amounting to 40,000 *livres*. Mme de Monnier, for adultery, was condemned to be shaved and

71

branded and to be imprisoned for life in a house of correction.
To have fallen 'under the King's hand' was not the worst that
could have happened to them.

During the ten days' journey back to Paris Des Brugnières let
them be together when the party halted for the night, saving, of
course, his own presence, which security necessitated but which does
not seem to have bothered them unduly. Their last day, June 7th,
was spent in Des Brugnières's house. The Lieutenant of Police, Le
Noir, looked in, was touched by Sophie's misery and decided to
adopt his subordinate's suggestion and spare her Sainte Pélagie.
She would go instead to the less notorious institution kept by
Mlle Douay, Rue de Charonne.

When the moment of separation arrived there was a harrowing
scene, Gabriel at the end more overwrought than Sophie, and
blaming himself for that to which he had brought her; then, for
him, the drive through the darkening suburbs eastwards to Vincennes.

2

The keep of Vincennes was begun in 1337 and completed by
Charles V. The core of the fortress was the Great Tower, a building of immense solidity rising cliff-like from the ground, bare
and grimly functional. Around it ran a quadrangular machi-
colated curtain-wall overhanging a deep moat, the corners being
formed by four pepper-pot turrets. This *enceinte* was a formidable
fortification by itself, with galleries in its thickness running the
whole of its length, but it was dwarfed by the mass and height of
the Great Tower within. Enclosed between this central tower
and the curtain-wall there lay gardens and sundry sheds.

The prisoners' cells were in the Great Tower, excepting three,
which were in the outer wall. It was in one of these, in the western
corner, that Mirabeau was locked.

The cell was ten feet square. It was furnished with a truckle-
bed, two hard chairs, a greasy table and a chipped chamber-pot.
It was lit by one very small, heavily-barred window, and this
was to dominate his new life more than any other physical circumstance. It was something, he admitted, that it opened onto

the outside world, for at least the sounds of free people about their business drifted through; but the view it gave was a narrow patch of sky, no more, for outside there was fixed a projecting hopper, designed to prevent the prisoner seeing the ground below or signalling to friends outside.[20] Lack of light, however, rather than lack of view was Mirabeau's worst deprivation, for only when the westering sun shone directly on his little window was it possible to read or write without eye-strain.

The discipline of the prison was severe and the routine crazingly monotonous. The prisoner was left in utter solitude except for three daily visits by his turnkey, who brought the dreary and ill-cooked meals and performed the most essential offices, but was strictly forbidden to linger and chat; only a deaf-mute could have evaded conversation with Mirabeau, who soon knew his turnkey's family affairs, but such was the rule. The prisoner was forbidden to communicate not only with the outside world but even with other inmates. There was no regular provision for exercise; for some a walk in the garden was a rare favour; others were permitted to pace up and down for an hour each day in silence, with a warder for sole companion. On Sundays and Holy Days there was Mass in the prison chapel.

If there is one thing upon which all who knew Mirabeau were agreed, one thing which all who have studied him have recognized, it is the sulphurous, volcanic energy of the man. Energy was the principle of his being, and he puts one in mind of a great boiler for ever blowing its escape-valves. He had always to be doing, fighting, making love, writing or talking; for tranquillity he had no gift, and he burnt himself out in forty-two years by his manifold excesses.

And now this fiery, restless, amative creature was penned between four walls, ten feet by ten, in a dim light, without company or occupation, alone. The shock of sudden isolation was made agony by the parting from the first woman whom he had loved with passion, and who carried that which stirred in him the father-instinct whereby nature would have balanced his inordinate virility.

Yet while there was so much in Mirabeau to make this prison especially intolerable to him, he had certain compensating resources. He had a temperamental resilience which would not

73

allow depression to sit upon him for long. When it became clear that France was about to enter the American war, his spirits rose with the hope of expiatory military service. He had, also, the priceless resource of letters. Books were an absorbing passion, and books meant pens, ink and copious paper for notes and extracts. He was a predatory reader, whose perusal of any work partook of the nature of a slave raid. But his greatest resource was his expert skill in turning jailers into friends and advocates.

With the Governor of Vincennes, M. de Rougemont, he had, it is true, less than his usual success. De Rougemont, though not unkindly, was a somewhat fussy and self-important little man. 'It is contrary to the regulations' was for him usually the last word, and for this limitation Mirabeau could not forgive him. He would have obtained few ameliorations of his lot had he not in some measure circumvented the Governor's authority.[21]

One way to do this was already open. Des Brugnières, as good as his word, had obtained from the Lieutenant of Police, Le Noir, permission to visit Mirabeau from time to time. Des Brugnières's duties kept him moving about the provinces so much that his visits to Paris were irregular and infrequent; still, he was a link with the world of living men and, above all, with the Rue de Charonne. Convinced that if Sophie was to face life and motherhood in her present situation she must have cheer and comfort, Des Brugnières carried letters between her and Mirabeau as occasion offered. It was flatly against regulations and very risky for him, but the sole condition he imposed was that the letters should be returned to him after being read. It was thus that the beginnings of a famous correspondence came to be preserved.

Though Des Brugnières's rare and unpredictable visits were priceless, though the first letter in Sophie's bad handwriting gave Gabriel inexpressible delight, he was determined to secure more solid and dependable benefits. He judged that for this his best hope lay in the personality of the Lieutenant of Police.

A man in the middle forties, Le Noir was the type of public servant who, by adding prudence to authority and humanity to legality, enables government to operate more smoothly than might be expected. In 1771 it had fallen to him to be sent to Aix with the invidious task of assuring law and order during the setting-up of the new-fangled *parlement-Maupeou*

under D'Albertas, and of supervising the exile of the old magis-
strates. A less popular mission it would have been hard to find,
yet the general verdict of the Provençals was that this Parisian
had discharged his unpleasant duty with tact and moderation.

In 1774 he became Lieutenant of Police, but in the next year
he was removed from this post for a while for alleged weakness in
handling the grain-riots against Turgot's ill-fated reforms.
Attributing his disgrace to Turgot and Dupont de Nemours,
'Economists' both and friends of the Friend of Mankind, he might
be expected to harbour resentment against the whole sect, and to
be ready with sympathy for the younger Mirabeau, whose
published scorn for physiocracy was certainly one cause of his
imprisonment. To Le Noir, therefore, Mirabeau wrote soon after
his arrival at Vincennes.

Messages to the Lieutenant of Police had, however, to pass
through the hands of the Governor, and the first letters remained
unanswered. But an interview with De Rougemont put the matter
in order, though it came near to betraying the secret correspondence. On a Sunday in mid-August Gabriel wrote to Sophie:

I've a horrible fear. I was at Mass this morning. I had left
in a sheet of my rationed paper your letter to which I was
replying. I had no fear of being surprised in any way, since
M. de Rougemont was busy today arranging the fête.
[Sunday after the Assumption was a gala day at Vincennes.] When they came to take me from my stall they
told me that he was going to visit me, and, when I got back
to my room, there he was. My heart missed a beat. Nothing
had been moved on my table. I had left a fat book on my
papers which was still there, but it seemed to me that it
had been moved forward. Nevertheless I found the Governor
smiling and open-mannered, though he didn't sit down. 'I
found your room open,' he said; 'I waited for you here so
that you wouldn't have to come down stairs.' Then he went
on to talk of my health, which I told him was not good . . . I
asked his permission to write to M. Le Noir . . . He said
'Write to him about your affairs but don't speak to him again
about your clothes. Your father has asked me for an appointment, as I told you. I've been so busy that I've not been
able to see him. I've no doubt that this is the subject about
which he wishes to see me, so he'll blame me for this delay.

I promise you I'll speak very firmly to him, and, if he turns a deaf ear, I shall complain about it to M. Le Noir and you shall write to him as strongly as you wish' . . . He ended by saying that, to distract me a little, he would have me taken up to the lantern of the Keep this afternoon to have a look at the fair, at which all Paris will be, and to see the superb view.

Had De Rougemont spotted the letter? If he had, it would be the end of everything.

As he went out I said to him, 'Sir, if you see Brugnières, remind him, I beg you, that his month is nearly up. He promised me to come every month at least.' 'I see him rarely,' he replied, 'but if I do, I'll remind him.' Either he conceals his thoughts well, or else he suspects nothing.

He suspected nothing. The Marquis turned the deaf ear, communication with Le Noir was established, and a stream of letters, which the prisoner was permitted to seal up, began to flow from one who had too much leisure to one who had too little.

Much of it consists of the prisoner's complaints and requests. His grievance is always against his father; the general suggestion, growing more open as he gains confidence, is that Le Noir and he are brothers in misfortune, victims in turn of the sectarian bigotry of the Economists. He has been locked in Vincennes at the request of the Friend of Mankind; his father is chargeable for his keep; only in the most technical sense is he a state prisoner; yet his father, by refusing him necessities, above all clothes, has reduced him to a state of sordid misery worse than that of the criminal prisoners for whom His Majesty assumes total responsibility. His health is suffering also; prison life has brought on the old nephritic trouble, which is causing him increasing misery; worst of all, his eyes are suffering.

The damage to his eyes was itself the result of a concession early obtained, and without which his years in prison could scarcely have been borne. This was books. The prison-library, a meagre collection of what he called 'privileged ineptitudes', was quite insufficient for his needs. But he had an annual 600 *livres* of pocket-money from his father, there were the Paris booksellers, there were lending libraries and there were the periodicals. One by one these resources were made available by the understanding Chief of Police, and Mirabeau's long imprisonment became a unique opportunity for the stocking of his mind. But the physical cost was heavy. 'As to my eyes,' he tells Sophie after a year, 'it is too much work which is enfeebling them. From daybreak, when I get up, till ten in the evening I read or write without any interruption, not even for meal-times; for, apart from the fact that I spend barely five minutes over my meals, I read as I eat; you know it's an old habit of mine when I eat alone. The best eyes in the world would not stand this régime.' Some months later he writes: 'Certainly it is hard to be forced to take to spectacles before the age of twenty-nine; but it is harder still not to see with glasses except through a rain of black spots, the immediate and unmistakable forerunners of blindness.'

In time Le Noir granted Mirabeau other favours. He was allowed more time for exercise, and was free at certain hours to walk about the galleries in the curtain-wall. Here there were real windows which gave on to the world outside. 'One day,' he writes to Sophie in mid-winter of 1778-79, 'absent-mindedly and without knowing what I was doing, I started singing the beautiful monologue from Tom Jones . . . Well, I noticed that four or five people were standing and listening. I stopped pretty quickly for fear of breaking the rule.' But he sang from the windows again, and was even able to exchange words with the officers in the château, and with the ladies.[22] Little by little life became more supportable. He was allowed to employ the son of a turnkey as a copyist, which saved his eyes. He was permitted (actually at his father's request) to ride a horse in the narrow garden for his kidneys' sake; better still, after two years Le Noir accorded him the quite exceptional privilege of sitting and working in the garden.

But far the greatest boon was permission to write to Sophie. Mirabeau begged Le Noir for this in a letter of November 29th, 1777, repeating his fears for Sophie's mental state as her time drew near with no word from him. The heart of the Lieutenant of Police was moved, and he granted permission for the lovers to exchange letters on the condition that these should be read by him or his deputy and be returned by the recipients to his office. On December 28th, the first letter to Sophie of the new, authorized correspondence began: 'After a silence of more than six months, to have news of the one who is a thousand times dearer than oneself . . .'

3

The letters of Gabriel to Sophie[23] are our best windows into Mirabeau's mind. If they had been love-letters and nothing more their interest would be less. Simple love-letters are often as unprofitable to third parties as they are enchanting to their recipients. But the authorized letters are aimed quite as much at a third party as at the beloved; for Gabriel writing to Sophie is also Mirabeau impressing Le Noir and, later on, Boucher, the deputy who was given the correspondence to read when it became too voluminous for his chief. These men, notably Boucher, were highly cultured and intelligent, so that the 'Letters to Sophie' contain their writer's opinions, sufficiently considered but uninhibited by any prospect of publication, on a range of subjects wider than the entertainment of Sophie alone would have demanded. We have in this curious correspondence the views of Mirabeau on topics ranging from George III's system of government and the justice of the American cause to the nature of true love (that is, Mirabeau's love) and the destiny of man.

'The English government', he informs the patient Sophie in December 1778, 'seems to be crazy; but let it take care: those proud Britons will not meekly submit to being reduced to slavery; and it is that which is the sole object of the *Scottish junta*.' 'The Bostonians', he adds, 'are my heroes, and the majority of the Frenchmen who are with them are not.' (This was surely mere envy; when, in 1780 Boniface sailed west with Guichen and covered himself with glory, Gabriel found it very hard to bear.) His beloved must not, however, imagine that he had meant that it was to France's interest to *crush* England: 'Until such time as you shall see England and France joined by a reciprocal treaty of commerce which removes all causes of division, one of the two nations, and perhaps both, will be badly governed. It was necessary to uphold the American Colonies in order to force these proud and spirited Britons to renounce their mad ambition, and that is the way to save them. But we, we too need to take the way of salvation.' World affairs come a little nearer home in the tail of the letter: 'What a pity we are not at Boston! You would be at peace, I useful and esteemed, our daughter an American — born, that is, into the most worthy nation in the world!'

Sophie may have preferred him in another vein. 'I have said it to you a hundred times,' he writes, 'I am more in love with your virtues than with your charms, and a single word which depicts your soul is to me more delicious than those ravishing favours the mere thought of which fills me with madness ... I could never have loved greatly a woman without intelligence, for I must be able to reason with my companion ... I have so few ordinary prejudices, I think so little as other folk do, that a silly woman, steeped in pettiness and a slave to conventions, would never have suited me.' His need was the clever man's need for an agreeable listener of the opposite sex. As didactic in his way as his father, he perhaps felt the need more than most clever men, and Sophie's response to his correspondence-course in philosophy, literature and world affairs was sometimes a little disappointing. She made few pretences. · 'Go on with you!' she writes; 'I know too well the distance there is between my brain and yours to wish you not to feel it, so you've no need to make excuses for me on that point; on the contrary, it's right that you should feel it a little; you'll be all the more indulgent to your Sophie; and anyhow, who can be compared to Gabriel?'

Mirabeau's scorn of conventions did not save his passages on love and virtue from being turgid and rather tasteless imitations of Rousseau, though it should be recorded that no one was readier than he to admit the inferiority of his prose to that of the master.

'True virtue', he assures Sophie, 'in no way depends on the whim of mortals, on the diverse speculations of moralists, on dogmas, rites, times, places or sexes; it consists in a heart which is true, sensitive and sincere, and in the exercise of all one's faculties. Honour requires a woman to have but one lover, to respect herself in him, to be faithful to her oath and incapable of light conduct. But it is my opinion that when an honest woman has said

79

to a man "I love you", and has given him a kiss, she owes him all her favours.'

Sophie received pages and pages of this sort of thing. A little surprisingly, he denies that disregard of the marriage-bond can ever be justified, but, less surprisingly, hastens to ask the question, Is Sophie really married? Marriage is the union of man and woman guaranteed by society, since society is interested in its essential purpose, children. De Monnier had not, nor could have, given Sophie children; therefore Sophie was not married to him at all in the sight of Mirabeau. Society, unfortunately for the argument, persisted in thinking otherwise.

But there is more honest stuff in these letters than these modish sophistries. There is, especially in the early secret letters, the simple pain of separation: 'When bedtime comes I never fail to make your place for you; I press myself right against the wall and leave a great emptiness in my little bed.' This is worth pages on True Virtue. Sophie had kindled gratitude and tenderness, and his anxiety as her time drew near was no mere show to affect Le Noir. 'Where are you? What are you doing?' he asks in one of the secret letters. 'Can you endure life in the midst of those women? . . . Your description has left me so much to worry about! I shudder so often to think of the hateful company which surrounds you!'

He loads her with advice for her confinement. She must not fret if the child has not quickened: 'Can you believe that Gabriel and Sophie can have produced *an insensible being*?' She must not have the room too hot, whatever the midwife says; she must beware of eating too much ripe fruit; she must wear loose clothes and take regular, though not excessive, exercise; she must consult a reliable doctor and, above all, she must on no account pay any attention to old wives' tales or remedies.

The baby, a daughter, was born January 7th, 1778, and christened Sophie-Gabrielle the next day. The day after that Gabriel writes: 'Your letter, I can see, was written during your pains; you added but one word, one little word, after the event. Such a trembling little word! How its feeble letters tore at my heart!'

Tender solicitude for their love-child fills his letters henceforth. He writes about her present care and future prospects not only to Sophie but also to Le Noir and to his mother, who, if only to spite her husband, was inclined to look indulgently on Sophie and her child. The baby was put to nurse, and her mother, five months later, was removed to the convent of the Saintes-Claires at Gien, where she lived henceforth. Yet she continued to receive pages of advice, much of it most enlightened, on the care of infants and the education of the very young. When, however, she ventured to advise him in his turn on the ill-health of which he often complained, he laughed at her for a walking encyclopaedia of *récits de bonnes femmes*, adding 'as a consultant physician you are no use. When you were in practice, Ah! that was another matter altogether.'

4

One of the most constant themes in the letters from Vincennes is hatred of religion. This is a matter of capital importance, whether we think of Mirabeau as an individual, as a type of his generation, or as one who helped to shape later events.

His hatred of religion and its devotees is bitter and aggressive. Writing to Sophie one Sunday he says, 'I have passed from one hole to another hole, where they gabbled that tissue of solecisms which is called the Mass; but, for all that, I have not been raised from profane to divine love, for I am, I admit, of the earth earthy.' On another occasion he writes: ' "Alas!" I said this morning, during that senseless ceremony whose formulae were droning in my ears, "if only I were the man to persuade myself of the truth of the dreams of the devout, I would convince Sophie that we ought both to make haste and die. Then our separation would be over"; but we have not the good fortune to harbour such illusions; at the moment when we die our whole being will die with us.'

The anti-clericalism of the Freemason is developed in another passage:

I hate and fear pious people (*les dévots*), and I prize tolera-tion as the one thing which can give the civil authority a real and firm control over the whole ecclesiastical body, and maintain social tranquillity in spite of fanaticism, hypocrisy and superstition . . . As a general rule, have no sort of confidence nor even, so far as you can avoid them, social relations with anybody infected with religious zeal. One can never depend in anything upon people who sanctify perfidy, and refer all moral questions to a system which, even were it not false, absurd and pernicious, incessantly contradicts the passions, interests and general course of human life . . . I am deeply convinced that *true believers* are . . . either credulous ignoramuses or interested hypocrites or artful rogues or dangerous enthusiasts.

In so far as this anti-religious animus was personal to Mirabeau, one must wonder a little where it came from. Such anti-religious bigotry is usually a reaction against religious bigotry encountered in the home or the school. But Mirabeau's education was less formally religious than was common for boys of his class and generation. He missed the discipline of the Jesuit College from which so many benefited or suffered according to their temperaments. We hear, in fact, singularly little of any distinct religious influence on his youth; a shadowy Jesuit appears to have taught him for a while before he went to school, but the Abbé Choquard's Academy was as secular in general tone as were so many of those sophisticated and unbeneficed priests, the abbés of eighteenth-century France. The one influence against which Mirabeau did react with violence was that of his father, but the Marquis, though not anti-Christian, personified philosophic pedantry, not religious bigotry.

Mirabeau had, of course, the libertine's motives for discrediting a religion by which his works stood reproved, but this, taken by itself, seems scarcely sufficient cause for a hostility so pronounced and sustained. The key to the matter is perhaps that he was irrepressibly didactic. An immoral man who cannot leave the subject of Virtue alone is likely to become either a hypocrite or a rebel, and Mirabeau was not a hypocrite.

But to a very great extent he took his attitude to religion from his age, and this raises the further question, why was the fashionable eighteenth-century attitude to religion one of indifference, hostility and contempt? How did the church of Bossuet and Fénelon change in a lifetime into the church of Talleyrand and Loménie de Brienne?

The explanation is largely political. The Church in France was, in the vital matter of appointments, almost as dependent on the state as the Church of England. Bishoprics, abbeys and the like were either the perquisite of great families or the rewards of court favourites. Louis XIV during his last thirty years had been inclined to piety, and some good church appointments were the result. But since 1715 the State had meant, first, the godless Regent Orleans and, thereafter, the debauched and feebly superstitious Louis XV. A system at best radically corrupt had worked as badly as possible, so that the church in which Mirabeau and his generation grew up had a set of prelates none of whom was very inspiring, most of whom were worldly, and a notorious handful of whom were unbelievers or evil-livers. Nor was this rottenness confined to the highest levels. Despite the presence of thousands of parish priests whose integrity was one day to stand the test of persecution, the general tone of the clergy was profoundly secular.

Louis XIV was not only pious but also bigoted, and his gratuitous and inexcusable persecution of his Protestant subjects did incalculable damage to religion in France. Most obviously, it took from the national religion the healthy stimulus of competition, and turned the French Church into a state-monopoly. But the Huguenots who managed to flee the country against the royal decree were, it should be remembered, a minority; of the remainder, the majority made a sullen show of conformity to Catholicism, while nursing in their hearts, and bequeathing to their children, a smouldering hatred of the established church. The second generation grew up in a spiritual void, where Calvinism had been expelled but Catholicism had not entered, and the void was readily filled by a secular philosophy antagonistic to the whole Throne-and-Altar scheme upon which churchmen had been taught to rely, and which, when Mirabeau was sixteen, was capable of condemning the eighteen-year-old La Barre to have his tongue torn out and his head cut off for having insulted a crucifix.

If the grace and example of the priesthood was not such as to keep the faith alive in the laymen's hearts, its intellectual formation was ill-adapted to meet the challenge of the age. The education of priests was still substantially what the Counter-Reformation had made it. The Church of the eighteenth century was organized and equipped to fight with the forces of Protestantism, to fight, that is, a battle which was, in reality, over; it still stood, at ease in its old entrenchments, facing an enemy from whom no further attack was in the least degree probable. When, therefore, an enemy of a different kind, using new weapons, began to develop an attack from a quite different quarter, the Catholic Church found herself at a grave disadvantage, equipped with obsolete weapons and facing the wrong way.

The rationalist spirit of the eighteenth century met with astonishingly little effective resistance when it challenged revealed religion for possession of men's minds. In France, especially, Catholic apologetics, adapted to the confutation of the Calvinist, Jansenist and the Quietist, failed to meet the challenge squarely, and the name of Rationalist was, by a strange default, filched by a set of sentimental humanists from the intellectual heirs of Saint Thomas Aquinas.

Christianity is the religion of redemption or it is nothing. If Original Sin is not a fact the Church has no message and no function. But as the vast heresy of humanism penetrated the organism of Christian Europe like a tasteless toxic gas, progressive thinkers relaxed their hold on all transcendental truths, and the reality of Original Sin became less and less credible. A vague, anthropo-centric optimism was the agreeable climate in which these philoso-phers lived; they disdained to state their heresy in outmoded theological terms, and so, while Synod and Curia remained mute, prelates and abbés circulated at ease in fashionable salons, gaily exchanging sceptical witticisms with eminent unbelievers, and in the circles where opinion was formed the case for dogmatic Christianity simply went by default.

Mirabeau shared his generation's vast indifference to religion. He had more than his share of the prevalent disgust with the obscurantism, hypocrisy and complacency which smothered the church he knew like a slime. He committed himself to materialistic and atheistic opinions of the most downright sort. How deep did his apostasy really go?

Among his writings at Vincennes was found a sealed packet, undated, which was entrusted to Boucher and was not to be opened till after the prisoner's death.[24] This Mirabeau some-times felt to be near at hand, and the packet contained letters of farewell to his mother, father and brother, to Le Noir and Boucher, and to Sophie. To each of his next-of-kin he commends his daughter, particularly begging Boniface to prevent her being adopted by a strange family or left dependent on a religious order. The letter to Sophie contains this passage:

> Oh God! Mighty God! Give me back my love! Forgive me as the reward of her virtues! If, indeed, I have denied your providence, it was lest I should be tempted to believe you to be the accomplice of the wicked. You know that I was in good faith; your feeble creature cannot have offended you. Could you be angry with him and punish him for the weakness of his understanding? Look, at least, with mercy upon her whom my error has led astray: enlighten her, protect her and give her the strength to bear the pain of my loss, to discover truth, to show it to my daughter, and to deserve to be an object of your pity.

5

The voluminous correspondence of Mirabeau in prison did not suffice to fill the interminable days. He read omnivorously; notes and extracts piled up, became disordered and reappeared in his own writings without acknowledgments. But his plagiarism sometimes went further than mere carelessness could excuse, for he was guilty of deliberate piracy. 'Listen, dearest one,' he wrote to Sophie, 'I am going to pour my heart into yours', and he proceeds to pour out an article from *Mercure de France* verbatim.

He wrote a French grammar for Sophie, who needed it. He wrote her a book on mythology, and a treatise on inoculation. He translated Tacitus, Ovid, Boccaccio and Pope's version of the Iliad, which he thought better than the original. He translated Tibullus, and designed engravings for the book as well; he planned to do into French Fielding and the 'divine' Richardson. These things filled up time and might amuse Sophie, but translation was tedious work. 'Only the pleasure of working for you keeps me to it, all the more as I have a great project which absorbs me completely.' To raise quick money for the books he needed he wrote two lamentable pieces of cheap pornography, *Errotika Biblion* [sic] and *Ma conversion*, in which vice lost none of its evil while retaining all its grossness. That the fermentations of his imagination drove him to write these things is unlikely; the licence of his secret letters to Sophie — and of her replies — must have brought as much relief to the libido of the imprisoned as written words could produce. He had the effrontery to suggest that Boucher might connive at the sale of these books to the traffickers in such stuff: 'I'll have done my business in selling them, they'll do theirs in deceiving you, and you'll do yours in pinching them, if you can.' [25]

The 'great project' to which he alludes is his book *Des lettres de cachet et des prisons d'état.*

The book opens with a sketch of the historical background to the practice of arbitrary imprisonment in France. Despotism and this, its indispensable instrument, are represented as growths of the last three centuries, as things abhorrent to the laws of the Franks. Louis XI, 'this Tiberius of France', was the originator of the evil; he was 'one of the most ingenious jailers and executioners to be found in the over-lengthy list of tyrants who have disgraced humanity'. The cancer of tyranny, introduced by him into the body of France, grew from that time forth, though slowly until the advent of Richelieu. Under the Cardinal, however, the malignant growth swelled dangerously, and under Louis XIV it strangulated the national organism.

This historical theme is presented with cogency and is supported by a citation of documents and authorities so copious as to command admiration when we remember how little access to materials the author enjoyed. In succeeding chapters there is a rather diffuse dissertation on the origins and nature of tyranny. It adds nothing significant to the *Essay on Despotism* except for a chapter devoted to demonstrating the contribution of priestcraft to the enslavement of mankind.

Yet, despite the dissipation of literary force by these needless elaborations, the great central theme, the iniquity of arbitrary imprisonment, is worthily, and, in places, splendidly handled. It was natural, indeed, that those biographers of Mirabeau who wrote during the long liberal summer between the Fall of the Bastille and the Reichstag Fire should accord to this book a faintly patronizing pat of approval. '*Lettres de cachet* appear to us so monstrous a violation of justice and individual rights, it is so hard for us nowadays not only to accept them in principle but even to imagine them existing in practice, that a demonstration of their iniquity either bores us or surprises us as being something superfluous.' These words were written by the scholar and statesman, Louis Barthou and were published in 1913. They could not be written today.

Liberty of the person, Mirabeau insists, is not just one of many desirable liberties; it is *the* liberty, the precondition of all others, and no short-term necessity of state may ever be pleaded against it. *Lettres de cachet* and similar devices are, he further points out, evil in two ways: firstly they are unjust to the innocent man who is denied open trial according to law; secondly they injure the law itself by shortening its arm. 'The essence and force of law invariably consist in this, that it applies equally to all citizens.' From this principle, drawn from Cicero *De Legibus,* he will allow no departure. The *lettre de cachet* withdraws the individual from the action of a general law, the English attainder makes a law bearing on one individual, and both are wrong. The law of Habeas Corpus, on the other hand, is 'the true palladium of English liberty'.

The book is in two parts, and it is a pity that Part II was added. Here there is an abrupt descent from the grand theme of arbitrary imprisonment, with all its attendant evils poisoning public and private life, to the particular grievances and petty vexations of the inmates of Vincennes. Matter of this sort would have been proper and useful if placed in an appendix, but, solemnly entitled 'Part II', it is a trivial sequel to the much weightier chapters of Part I, while the decent dignity of the whole work is ruined by a spiteful attack, recurring on page after page, upon the professional rectitude and personal character of M. de Rougemont. This was the more inexcusable since the latter had been a party to the favours Mirabeau had obtained from Le Noir, and had even permitted his very young wife to show the prisoner various kindnesses.[26]

6

Much of Mirabeau's writing in prison was aimed simply at getting himself out of it. He wrote at great length to Le Noir.

He wrote penitently to his uncle, but the Bailli disbelieved in his repentance. 'If he had less talent for persuasion,' he observed, 'he would be more persuasive.' He wrote to his mother's kinsman, Marshal de Noailles. He wrote to the old Minister, Maurepas, reproaching him for listening only to his father's side of the case. He wrote to Amelot, the Secretary of State. He addressed a noble appeal to the King: 'I am a Frenchman, young and unfortunate;' it begins, 'these are claims enough to your Majesty's interest.'

One demand recurs throughout these appeals: that he may have either freedom or the chance to stand his trial before a court of law. If his father thinks to have done him a favour by putting him beyond the reach of the courts, he is mistaken. Writing to Le Noir, Mirabeau gives his anger against his father full rein. Wildly accusing him of having imperilled his wife's health by his pro-fligacy, he goes on, more justifiably, 'The tender-hearted Friend of Mankind, whose soul, too lofty to stoop to vulgar affections, disdains his family and loves only the human race, has persecuted his wife and his children . . . with the exception of one daughter, who has found favour with him because she has accepted his mistress (Mme de Pailly) and because her wily husband (Du Saillant) is an enthusiast for *economic mills*.' In a another letter he reminds Le Noir that there is an easy way out for him: 'I have only to write to Mme de Pailly base and suppliant letters, to beg M. du Saillant to act as my mediator . . . But may I be held in abhorrence by all decent people, the day when I shall beg favours of a woman whom I must reproach for all the sufferings of my mother and my family. I should despise myself were I to ask anything of a man so base as M. du Saillant.'[27] The thought of Caroline's fat husband and children living snugly with the De Pailly under his father's roof was bitter, and he believed them leagued in sinister cabal against him. He would not eat humble pie, not yet, at any rate. On the contrary, he composed for his father a massive Memoir, reviewing the tangled, unhappy story of their relations over the last ten years.

It is a superb piece of advocacy. The rhetorical style, which often mars his prose, is here in place, while his tendency to ver-bosity disappears in the urgency of his pleading. All the great forensic faculties are here: the masterly organization of a multi-tude of facts around a central and unifying thesis, the persuasive

manipulation of the less favourable elements in the case, the irony
to sting the obdurate conscience, the passionate appeal to move
the apathetic heart.

But the Marquis was unmoved. He continued to growl to the
Bailli about his son's pride, self-conceit and continual lying, and
if Mirabeau's liberation had depended upon the power of his
pen to insinuate into that closed mind any doubts of its own rectitude, he would in all likelihood have remained in Vincennes till
1789. But the old man harboured one feeling stronger than his
own self-righteousness, and this was his passion for his House, his
'posteromania', as his brother called it. His finances were now so
dilapidated that it was scarcely possible to set up the drunken
Boniface as a family man. With Gabriel in prison, therefore, the
future of the House of Mirabeau hung upon the life of little
Victor, Gabriel's son. But in October 1778 the child died.

'God has willed,' wrote the grandfather, 'by this latest blow,
to detach me from the world; and I venture to say that, for a long
while, I have clung to it only in order to try to do good, and to
perform my duty to the end.' His duty: duty to the House;
another grandson to his name; no way, perhaps, but to bring
poor, wronged Emilie and Gabriel together again.

Very tentatively and with extreme care lest he should appear
to be taking any initiative, the Marquis began to seek for a way
down from his pedestal.

7

The Comtesse de Mirabeau had long since accustomed herself
to grass-widowhood among agreeable and admiring friends. The
social round in her father's circle, where she enjoyed the amateur
theatricals, exactly suited her. She was busy on the stage when the
news of her little son's death was brought to her, and she grieved
according to her capacity. For the loss of her husband she had
never made any pretence of grieving at all.

This attitude was, however, no obstacle to cordial relations with
her father-in-law. Like him she held herself to have been deeply
injured by remarks written to Malesherbes by her husband, and
published by his mother in her disastrous memoir. While he was

in Vincennes she had informed him of their son's health only in the rarest bulletins, written in the third person. It was not from her that he heard of the child's death, nor, as far as is known, did she write a word of condolence. That was left to Sophie to do.[28]

Early in 1779 Mirabeau received a visitor. It was Pierre-Samuel Dupont.* An intelligent bourgeois of philosophical inclinations, Dupont owned a country place, Le Bois des Fossés, near Le Bignon, had been the first disciple of his neighbour, the Friend of Mankind, and had edited *Ephémerides* till its suppression by Maupeou in 1772.† With the opening of the new reign his physiocracy stood him in good stead, for he became a sort of *éminence grise* to Turgot. He shared that minister's fall in 1776, and was constantly at his bedside in his last illness. Turning to foreign affairs, he took part in the peace-making of 1783 and deserved and attracted the notice of the great, whose names had a way of recurring in his conversation.[29] A very honest man, he was, like most Economists, a bit of a prig, and, like most men, a bit of a snob.

Mirabeau was glad enough to see him, and excited at this first hint of possible liberation; for though Dupont was caution itself, he did not hide that he was in some sort an envoy. He was certainly a friend. He visited the prisoner most Sundays, talked to him of politics and books, and gladly lent him reading matter of various kinds, including some of his own works. Among these was the manuscript of an article on provincial and municipal assemblies with which he was particularly pleased. Mirabeau returned the paper in due course, but did not mention that he had made a copy of it. It was to be heard of again.[30]

Dupont explained that two things must be done before Mirabeau could have any hope of freedom. One was that he must apologize without reservation for the printed attacks on his father; the other, the vital condition, was that he must become reconciled with his wife; his father would never relent unless it could be made to appear that he was yielding to his daughter-in-law's request.

This second condition was the harder. For his father, despite everything, Mirabeau retained a vestigial respect, a dull ember of affection; from his wife's mean conduct he recoiled in simple and

* Known later as Dupont de Nemours.
† It was revived in 1775 under the editorship of the Abbé Baudeau.

uncomprehending disgust. To Sophie, Boucher and Le Noir he had called her 'a monster' and 'his most bitter and perfidious enemy', against whom he had evidence enough to ruin ten women.[31] There was, further, the question of loyalty to Sophie. On the strength of his promises she had refused overtures from old De Monnier, who, even now, was holding the door open for her return. If she were to consent to this, he told Boucher, he would never see her again. 'I may die,' he added, 'but I cannot change.'

Yet light was showing at last at the end of the long tunnel. Dupont was sympathetic, but gently insistent. What could he do even for Sophie and her daughter until he was free? Just a few words to Mme de Mirabeau, that was all; here was his pen, there was the paper, 'and I resolved', wrote Gabriel, reporting the interview to Sophie, 'to see, by making the attempt, if it was possible for me to say to this woman something which should be dignified without being cold, and make her understand what she ought to do without asking her to do it. So I wrote the following:

> Two people who have been joined in intimacy cannot, Madam, have become absolute strangers to one another ... If you remember the man you loved, you cannot be unaware that, even in his most ungovernable moods, a kindness is for him a sacred bond ... If, in this situation, you feel called upon to do nothing, I have nothing to say to you; but if you should act, you would certainly put me under an obligation which I should always recognize with gratitude.'

He hastens to assure Sophie that he has not yet done anything irrevocable, that he will not dream of doing so without her consent, her absolutely free consent.[32]

Sophie did not make difficulties. Her only fear, she explained to Boucher, was lest Gabriel should be worried by her consent seeming to be the fruit of generosity rather than of love, 'as if this were not the best proof of it which I can give him in the present circumstances'. She need not have feared for her proofs. When Gabriel sent her a draft of a second letter to his wife she returned it, urging him to write in warmer terms. She wrote to Mme de Vence, who, as ever, was supporting Gabriel's cause, explaining that the elopement had really been all her own fault. She wrote to the Comtesse de Mirabeau.[33]

The negotiations went at a snail's pace. Emilie, who had recently spoken to her father-in-law of obtaining a separation from Gabriel, was in no kind of hurry. Her reply to his first letter was glacial: 'Although I am unable to co-operate towards your welfare, I should be charmed to know that you are happy.'[34] He, on his part, was not yet ready for the act of grovelling that seemed to be required. 'All would be for the best,' he said, 'if Mme de Mirabeau and I could lose our memories.' Still, the light at the tunnel's end was widening and beckoning, and he began to hint to Sophie that perhaps, after all, a reconciliation with her husband, on certain terms, of course, had something to be said for it.

Then, in May 1780, after a year of these manœuvrings, Sophie-Gabrielle died of convulsions. Though the mother had known her baby for five months only, and though the father had never seen her at all, their grief was real. Parenthood was for both the welcomed crown of love's delight. When Gabriel spoke of future children they might have, Sophie answered, 'How gladly would I indeed! But who knows if we shall have that happiness again? And besides, will they make good this loss? This one cost us so dear; the others would be mere children of happiness.'

Yet each knew that the strongest link between them was gone, and Sophie, pressed by her mother, resolved at last to write her husband a humble, penitent letter. But her step-daughter had lately regained a hold over the old man, and the door, so long held open, was shut at last. Her letter was unanswered.

The loss of his daughter eased Gabriel's position appreciably. Things at length began to move, and Emilie, assured most solemnly that no forced reunion was intended, consented to express a wish that her husband might regain his freedom.[35] In July 1780 she received from him these words: 'I shall belong to you doubly, by your old rights and your new claims, as my wife and as my benefactress. You used to be my companion; you now become my Sovereign . . . Adieu, Madam; I cannot tell you how sweet it is to me, after such long unhappiness, to esteem you, to love you, to be indebted to you, to be again your husband.'[36]

The Friend of Mankind was pleased. 'It is the first time I have seen something of his which looks like genuine feeling,' he wrote. 'In this letter his pride unbends and is no more than dignity.'

In the final negotiations Caroline du Saillant acted as intermediary. Gabriel was willing to treat with his sister, whom he described as *une bonne bête*, though his jealousy of her husband remained. In the end Caroline, Mme de Pailly, the Baillie and Dupont broke down the Marquis's hesitations, though even now he would not agree to liberation pure and simple. Maurepas, old and ailing, was by this time weary of his importunities, remarking that there ought to be a special Secretary of State for Mirabeau family affairs, but Nivernois, his brother-in-law and the Marquis's oldest friend, used his influence, and in due course a *lettre de cachet*, in an unusual form, was issued:

> On behalf of the King, the *sieur comte de Mirabeau* is ordered to betake himself to such places as his father shall appoint to him, His Majesty forbidding the said *sieur comte de Mirabeau* to depart therefrom on any pretext whatsoever, and this until further order on his part, under pain of disobedience.

Versailles, the 13th of December, 1780

Signed
LOUIS

On behalf of the King: AMELOT.

CHAPTER VI

FOUNDATIONS OF FAME

I F the Marquis felt impatience or curiosity to see his son on his
release from prison, he mastered it. Gabriel, who was to be
known for the time being simply as 'M. Honoré', was domiciled
for a few weeks in the agreeable Château de Vincennes, after
which he went, with his father's consent, to lodge a while with
Boucher, whom he and Sophie had so often called their Good Angel.

Here there was a modest but cultured circle of artists, writers
and minor officials to whom the brilliant if notorious Count was
an exciting addition, and among whom he was welcome till his
attentions to their wives and his requisitions on their pockets
changed their mood. Three and a half years of reflection had
failed to refine his ethics regarding either women or money, and
a few days after his liberation he stole Caroline's watch to pawn
it. Boucher, a poor man, could ill afford to finance the friend
for whom he had already done so much, but when he asked for
repayment he received reproaches instead of his money in reply.
He was not, however, condemned to meditate upon man's ingratitude for very long, for in February 1782 he died.[37]

The moment of Gabriel's release coincided, not entirely acci-
dentally, with the last stage of the lawsuit brought by his mother
against his father for separation *de corps et de biens*. He at once
became active on his father's side, and corresponded with him
daily. But when, one day in January, the two met by chance at
the lawyer's, each got away as quickly as possible. The Count
went to Versailles to importune the ministers, but Maurepas said
that he was tired of being treated as the Marquis de Mirabeau's
man of business, that the family's endless scandals were a disgrace
and that the King wished to hear no more of them.

Though the Marquis wrote to his brother of the good reports
he was receiving of Gabriel, of how his prison-years had matured
him and enriched his mind without impairing his vivacity or his
peculiar talent for familiarity, nevertheless he still put off receiving
him; and when at last he judged it fitting to welcome home the
son whom, except for their recent accidental encounter, he had

not set eyes on for ten years, he was himself a shaken and impoverished man. For on May 17th, the *Grand' Chambre* granted his wife her long-sought decree of separation both as to her person, which did not matter, and as to her possessions, which did.

Two days later Boucher and Dupont brought Gabriel to the rather grand Hôtel de Mirabeau, Rue de Seine, which the Friend of Mankind had bought a few years back in a mood of confidence in the future of his science and of his House. We have the patriarch's account of the return of the prodigal: 'I said to Honoré, as I offered him my hand, that I offered it to the friend, and that I hoped one day to be able to bless the son.' A Roman gravity indeed.

Gravity, however, the son had neither inherited nor acquired, and eight days after returning to his father's house he suddenly vanished from Paris. There were already new creditors to avoid, for he had emerged from Vincennes 'naked as a worm', as his father put it without apparently seeking to supply his needs. But his chief motive for this new rashness was his desire to see Sophie.

How much of the substance of that old passion remained? This, after four years of writing about it, he may have been curious to discover. But the meeting with Sophie had a practical purpose. His father and he were anxious that the old Pontarlier sentence for abduction and seduction should be annulled, that he should, in the old man's phrase, 'have his head on his shoulders again'. But this was a matter in which Sophie was involved, and he knew he would be able to count on her for any assistance that was in her power to give. He meant to do all he could to restore his mistress's fortunes as well as his own, but it was a winding-up of their adventure which was in his mind as he took the road southwards to Gien.

She was expecting him. She had made secret arrangements that he might come to her in her room in the convent. A lay-sister, the porter and Dr. Ysabeau, the convent's physician, had all been drawn into her little plot. 'Come in the dark!' she had written. 'It is better at night. It would be good, dearest, if there were a moon!' That was in February. In March she wrote: 'I do not know if I love you always more and more, but what I know for sure is that I have never felt my love so much.' She had still two months to wait for 'her husband', and when at last he came, when her little plot had succeeded and he was safe in her apartment with the great wardrobe in which he was to hide in case they were surprised, she began to understand that this reunion, for which she had planned and longed, was to be a leave-taking. She had known, of course, that nothing like their first adventure was to be expected. Caution and a preservation of appearances would have to limit their happy days in the future. But she had thought of that future as a future with Gabriel in it, whatever the difficulties, even if he should have to be formally reconciled with his Countess.

He, meanwhile, had been thinking in another way. For him the future was beckoning with the promise of adventures fit to stretch and test his matured talents. 'I need fifteen to twenty more years,' he wrote at this time, 'and with any luck I ought to have them. When I am no longer fit for love, there will be nothing more for me to do here short of being a minister.' Apart from the eternal debts, he was all but free in a society stirring restlessly with novel ferments and almost sentient of the advent of portentous things. Paris and France, opportunity and perhaps fame lay before him, while the mean room in Amsterdam and the cell in Vincennes and the love-child he had adored in imagination and — it had to be admitted — Sophie herself lay behind. He would be kind, he would cheer her, he would use his persuasions. He knew that there was in her a capacity for tragic determination, and that on her lips 'Gabriel or death' was not a figure of speech. So she must be comforted. But she must be brought gently to see that it was foolish to try to prolong a relationship which had grown up out of a vanished situation, and whose unique perfume was irrecoverable. If she could be persuaded to seek again for a full reconciliation with her husband it might be for the best; he was not likely to live much longer.

For five days he remained concealed with Sophie in the convent. They were lovers, once again, after a fashion. But it is probable that, with his departure on June 2nd, she guessed that he was going out of her life. 'Adieu! My very dear Love,' she wrote four days later; 'I love you as I used to love you!' For a little while yet they exchanged letters, but there was death in her heart, and when Gabriel had satisfactorily concluded his business at Pontarlier she heard from him no more. In her desolation and in the illness which followed she owed everything to the care and friendship of Dr. Ysabeau. [38]

When Gabriel returned to Paris his father decided to overlook the escapade. It had been, of course, a breach of the conditions of his liberation, but the customary paternal thunderbolt did not fall. His wife's successful separation suit had humiliated and nearly ruined the Friend of Mankind, but it had made him distinctly more friendly. Judging that the unfortunate affair with Mme de Monnier was dying a natural death, he dispensed with explanations and granted his pardon on condition that Gabriel should give him a full account of his debts. As he was now quite unable to pay them, it was but a token gesture of the *patria potestas*.

Desiring peace and quiet he went down to Le Bignon, taking his son with him. It was the second occasion since his childhood that Gabriel had shared with his father the intimacies of daily life, and he did his best to make it a success. He was helpful about the estate, studiously considerate and deferential. Cards bored him, but he joined in the Marquis's little lotso parties in the evenings, partnering his father and struggling against sleep. Hunting he enjoyed, but, as the Marquis gladly reported to the Bailli, since he knew how his father hated meals being upset, he would get up at four on hunting days so as not to be late for lunch. For St. Victor's Day, the old man's feast, he composed a little arietta in dialogue to be sung by himself and Caroline, who came down for the occasion, and he planned that in one of the meadows a monument should be raised to the Friend of Mankind.

The Marquis wrote of his pleasure and his hopes to his brother in Provence. As was invariably the way with whichever brother was removed from the young man's physical presence, the Bailli was sceptical; yet the Marquis made some acute observations. 'Never was a man so blind about himself and so clear-sighted about others,' he noted, and there was a touch of the old asperity when he wrote: 'This man has a mirror in place of a soul; everything appears in it and vanishes immediately. If he had an intelligent wife, or merely an unspoiled one, she would do what she liked with him.' Sometimes he would answer his son's observations by pulling out his watch and reminding him just how many hours previously he had himself made the same remark. The father had the narrower understanding, the smaller gift of imaginative insight, but his was the more strictly original mind. The rude vigour and salty terseness of his writing are better than the florid and conventional verbosity which flowed too often from the Count's pen, and he found it difficult to pardon his son's plagiarisms. 'He is the magpie of all men of wit, the jay of every street-crossing,' he declared, for he did not see that with Gabriel the talent for plagiarism was raised to the power of genius.[39]

3

With the new year, 1782, it was time for Mirabeau to be leaving Le Bignon. His father and he agreed that a reconciliation with his wife was desirable on many grounds. Both were anxious for posterity, and Mirabeau was anxious about his income. His mother's separation had hit him as well as his father, since the chances were that she would leave the whole of her fortune to Louise de Cabris, who had never wavered in her support. Emilie, it is true, had secured the legal protection of her fortune from her husband's liabilities, but if she would live with him again his financial position would surely be easier. But the greatest advantage to be expected from a return to settled married life was the restoration of his social standing, so dilapidated by the escapades and imprisonments of the last nine years.

The Marquis wrote to his daughter-in-law, and the Bailli made cautious approaches in person. Emilie was non-committal, and the Bailli reported from Aix that she was completely absorbed in the pleasures of her father's worthless set, and much influenced by designing relations anxious to keep her wealth within the family by preventing her again becoming mother of the heir of Mirabeau. Chief comedienne and reigning divinity of the Comte de Galliffet's 'Court of Love' at Le Tholonet, 'Madame du Tholonet' would not easily be tempted to accept again the hazards of life with her husband. The most that she would suggest was that he should win some credit, possibly in the American War; then, perhaps, she would see.

For him, clearly, the indispensable preliminary was the removal of existing discredit, the replacing, that is, of his head upon his shoulders. In 1777 he had been sentenced at Pontarlier, for abduction and seduction, to a fine of 5000 *livres* and to damages to De Monnier amounting to 40,000. He had also been sentenced to decapitation in effigy for his contumacy, which meant simply that he was 'dead in the eyes of the law' unless, within five years, he purged his contumacy by appearing to answer the charge. Mirabeau's five years' grace would be up on May 10th, 1782, which is why, early in February, he presented himself to the criminal court at Pontarlier.

Submission to the court 'put his head on his shoulders again' and left him free to choose one of two courses. On the one hand he might accept the original sentence; but this would mean either paying over 45,000 *livres* or else going to prison, and he most certainly could not find 45,000 *livres*. On the other hand he was entitled to defend himself against the original charge, and this is what he meant to do, as he journeyed to Franche-Comté with his lawyer and his valet, Legrain.

Legrain was a recent acquisition. He had been in the service of a lady of rank but had given her notice, finding that he was not cut out for a lady's manservant. Then, in the Comte de Mirabeau, just out from Vincennes, he found the master he had been looking for. The Marquis warned him that if he had any savings he had better not let his master know of them, but Legrain wanted life and movement more than wages and security, and he had found in his new employer a man after his heart. He was made to sit at table with his master at the inns where they halted. [40]

On reporting at Pontarlier Mirabeau was put in prison. The ground which he took up was fundamentally simple. The charge was one of *rapt et séduction*. The charge of adultery might have been made; so might the charge of theft of De Monnier's money by Sophie and himself. In fact, however, the plaintiff had chosen to institute criminal proceedings for abduction and seduction, and the defendant's object was to confine the case to this chosen ground. For he was prepared to prove that the charge of abduction was false, since Sophie had run away of her own free will; and he was prepared to maintain that the crime of seduction could not, by its nature, be committed against a married woman. The prosecution, however, disputed this point of law and, furthermore, pressed the fact of adultery. Mirabeau's answer was to deny (what was true but difficult to prove) that adultery had taken place *in France*, and also to deny that a French court could, in a criminal suit, take cognizance of acts committed beyond the frontier. It was not at all certain, however, that this objection would be sustained, so Legrain, fortified with quarts of Arbois wine and very little else, rode off through the deep snow to Neuchâtel to persuade the Council of State there to refuse to let witnesses from Les Verrières testify in France to acts committed in the Principality. The amazing valet obtained the ear of the Chancellor, contrived to make the most happy impression and returned to Pontarlier having obtained all that was required.

The little criminal court at Pontarlier was no match for its prisoner, who lectured and browbeat his judges with astounding audacity till, in May, the case was removed to the *parlement* at Besançon while the prisoner remained locked up at Pontarlier, which put an end to these tactics. Legrain was again indefatigable in long rides between the two towns, and upheld his master's cause against all and sundry. On one occasion he made use of a horse-whip, with which he was rather handy. The victim in this case was one of the prosecuting counsel.

Mirabeau, from prison, managed to publish pamphlets on his case which won public admiration and seriously shook the confidence of his opponents. The interested party on the other side was not De Monnier, who would gladly have let the whole thing be, but that daughter of his, Mme de Valdhaon, who was out to ruin Sophie. Mirabeau's *mémoires* had the desired effect, for they made the De Valdhaons more ready to consider an accommodation.

When the Marquis heard of the stormy and litigious course which things were taking he was angry. He had a horror of Gabriel's *mémoires*, and the old distrust of his son when out of his sight was at once reawakened. He had expected that Gabriel, after purging his contumacy, would seek an amicable settlement with De Monnier, so he promptly dispatched the inevitable Du Saillant to Franche-Comté to arrange a pacification. Mirabeau blustered angrily for a while, but ended by allowing his brother-in-law to arrange terms. For himself these were satisfactory: De Monnier withdrew his charges and the criminal prosecution was in effect, if not in strict law, annulled. For Sophie the terms were not so good. She had been charged with adultery, as to the fact of which there was no doubt; nor was the locale of the misconduct a relevant issue in her case. She and her family were not sorry, therefore, to agree that she should remain at Gien during her husband's lifetime and forfeit all rights under her marriage settlement; but — and this she owed largely to her lover's audacious tactics — she was to recover her dowry.[41]

4

Being at Pontarlier with his head on his shoulders and his mistress off his hands, Mirabeau decided to pay a visit to Fauche at Neuchâtel. He had owed the firm money since 1776. His father, having no cash to spare, had sent a manuscript of his own to be used in part-payment; apparently it could not be placed, but when his father asked for it back, Gabriel kept a copy. Six years later he published part of it as his own work.

Now, in August 1782, he sold Fauche his *Des lettres de cachet*, the chief fruit of his lucubrations in Vincennes. He sold him, too, a naughty trifle of court scandal called *L'Espion dévalisé*, also written in Vincennes, by one of his fellow prisoners. Published at once under a pseudonym which deceived few informed readers, *Des lettres de cachet* caused an immediate sensation. Vergennes asked the Prussian government to do something about the book, since it came from the Prussian King's publisher. Fauche's offices were duly raided, some copies were confiscated and Fauche himself was imprisoned for a while. But the book was a success and its publisher could be philosophical; to its author, already used to notoriety, it brought a first instalment of renown.

In Neuchâtel at this time there were some political refugees from Geneva. The latter city-state existed under the triple guarantee of Savoy, of the Swiss Confederation and of France, and it was a narrowly oligarchic republic, in which full citizenship was restricted to members of certain old families. But the liberal ferments of the age had been active in the city of Rousseau, and in 1782 a party calling themselves Representatives took up arms, overthrew the oligarchy and set up a reforming and democratic government. The deposed oligarchs promptly appealed to the guarantor powers, and Vergennes, busy assisting the cause of democracy in America, hastened, to the disgust of many Frenchmen, to crush it in Geneva. A mixed force of Swiss, Savoyard and French troops easily restored the old oligarchy, and, in July 1782, the Genevese democrats were driven into exile. Some went as far as Ireland, with the faintly bizarre idea of founding a New Geneva in the neighbourhood of Waterford; others found a more natural refuge in neighbouring Neuchâtel, and with two of these Mirabeau formed a friendship which was to be important in the lives of all three. They were Clavière and Duroveray.[42]

Clavière was a business man and financier with connections and resources enabling him to bear his exile with equanimity. He had a capacious and fertile mind, and was generous both with his money and with his ideas. Personally rather diffident and unassuming, he had great powers of work and an ambitious wife. His chief handicap was an inability to express himself with clarity and force, and in Mirabeau he recognized a man who had precisely the facility which he lacked. Brissot, who knew them both, later wrote that 'Clavière was an inexhaustible mine of rough diamonds, but he needed a stone-setter. Mirabeau was nearly always a setter of stones. He had, as he himself used to say, a special talent for acting as *accoucheur* to Clavière'. The two men liked each other at once, and when they parted, the one to Provence and the other to Ireland, they remained in touch by post.[43]

Duroveray, formerly Attorney-General of Geneva, possessed great knowledge of jurisprudence and had drawn up the Genevese legal code. He was a great student of constitutional procedure, and added to a thorough knowledge of the routine of popular assemblies considerable skill in the art of debate. An ardent and eloquent champion of liberty, he had played a bold part among the democrats of his native city, and would gravitate, as by the law of his nature, towards liberal-revolutionary movements anywhere else.[44]

Both men were bitter against the triumphant party in Geneva, though perhaps even more resentful against the French government for its intervention. Mirabeau, for his part, was sympathetically indignant at his country's alliance with the forces of reaction, and he saw, at the same time, a possible means of inducing his government to take notice of him. Vergennes soon received a weighty memorandum on the recent history of Geneva: his department, it was suggested, had perhaps been misled into its recent action by the inadequacy of its information service; might it not be well for the Minister to employ the services of a confidential agent? And who would be better qualified for this task, whether by his abilities or by the fortunate accident of his presence so near to Geneva, than the Comte de Mirabeau? But the Minister of Foreign Affairs remained unconvinced of the advantages of utilizing the services of the author of *Des lettres de cachet*, and it is even uncertain whether he bothered to read his memorandum.

Mirabeau lingered two months at Neuchâtel, uncertain whether to expect punishment as an author or employment as an agent. He was uncertain, too, what attitude his father would adopt towards his latest skirmishes, for it was not to be forgotten that the old man held a general-purposes *lettre de cachet* of which he might at any time make unpleasant use. As there was time to kill he recalled that a considerable relief to the tedium of his recent imprisonment at Pontarlier had been the attentions of Mlle Babet, his jailer's daughter. It would be amusing to see something more of the girl, so he gave her an assignation: let her meet him at Les Verrières, at the inn of Dame Lisette. Legrain, too, deserved relaxation after his arduous campaigning, and his master told him to come and bring a local girl to whom, it seemed, the rascal had promised marriage. On the appointed evening, unfortunately, Babet had the migraine and could not come, so that the *partie carrée* was spoiled. Somewhat ruefully Legrain learned that there are situations in which the first duty of a confidential valet is self-effacement.

It was at the inn of Dame Lisette that Mirabeau had once waited for his Sophie; but that was six years ago.[45]

5

As soon as he learned that his father was not meditating punitive action but was, on the contrary, impatient that he should proceed to the business for which Pontarlier had only been a preliminary, to a reunion, that is, with his wife, Mirabeau left Neuchâtel. He presented himself to his uncle at the château of their House on October 10th.

The Bailli had received with reserve his brother's reports of his nephew's reformation, and, on hearing that he was coming to Provence, had protested at being made responsible for him. But he assembled the tenantry and had the bells rung and provided fireworks to welcome him, and when he arrived he fell under his spell just as he had fallen twelve years earlier, when the young fellow had come back from Corsica. History repeated itself in another detail, for Gabriel's first act was to persuade his uncle to pledge 5000 *livres* to satisfy his most pressing creditors. A disadvantage of the very public return of the Heir of Mirabeau was that it awakened the swarm of people to whom he had owed money since his last residence, so that the moment he showed himself in Aix they descended upon him like flies. He was still, of course, technically 'under the King's hand' and able to disregard their claims, but to have exploited this advantage would have been very unwise; the goodwill of society was important to one who wished to induce his wife to return to him, or, failing that, to represent himself as an injured husband.

Legrain took his master's debts seriously. Many of the creditors he sent away soothed only with promises, but he took the Count to task over the petty sums owed to little men; it was, he explained, the number of creditors satisfied which mattered, not the total amount of debt paid off; and when, one day, the Count won 150 *louis* at play, his valet persuaded him to hand it over so that he might pay those creditors who were likely to talk and spread the impression that M. le Comte was solvent. Mirabeau had come across a bundle of clothes left behind in 1774 and had pawned it to a Jew for three *louis*. Shocked that he had done no better than this, Legrain browbeat the Jew into returning the bundle, took some of the garments for himself and re-pawned the rest for eight *louis*. Then, with fine clothes and a full pocket, he booked a private box at the theatre and went to the play with a woman companion. It was a full house, and the manager asked if Monsieur would be so good as to share his box with another lady and gentleman. On his consenting, the Comte de Mirabeau and a lady were ushered in. 'Don't you blush?' asked his master. 'No, Sir,' replied Legrain, 'you should be only too pleased that I am letting you have half my box. At the theatre all are equal provided they pay — as in paradise!'[46]

The Marquis de Mirabeau persistently underrated the diffi-culties of reuniting his son with his daughter-in-law, and this despite the Bailli's warnings. He was convinced that Gabriel, with his confounded charm, would quickly 'arrange things' with Emilie, and he shut his eyes to the true situation. For it was not just a question of the Count gently overcoming the fears and appeasing the resentment of his Countess, but something more like a contest between rival clans, with the House of Mirabeau seeking to penetrate the locked defences of the House of Marignane, and with Emilie out of sight behind its walls. Nor did the Marquis appreciate the strength of the Marignane position, how they had drawn into their party most of the important people in and around Aix, so that the Bailli and the Count, popular enough with the common people, found themselves cold-shouldered in influential quarters.[47] Yet, deeply interested as he was in the whole matter, it does not seem to have occurred to him that his own presence in Provence might be a valuable, perhaps an indispensable, rein-forcement of the Riqueti cause, or that the persistent absence of the head of the House from the land of his ancestors was a mistake which was not to be repaired by letters of admonition, protest and complaint posted southwards by every courier. His dread lest the affair should end up in another lawsuit was natural enough. Far too much family linen had been washed in public during the last ten years, and the old man craved for a span of peace in which the gashes and bruises on the family's reputation might have a chance to heal under the bandage of obscurity. But why, then, did he do nothing to control in person the course of events in Provence? Why did he leave the actual conduct of the affair to his brother, who was showing signs of a fighting mood, and to his son, whose love of a fight he knew so well?

As a matter of fact the Count showed unusual patience and modesty in the opening stages of his campaign. On arriving in Provence he wrote his wife a polite little note announcing the fact, but nothing more. She replied to the Bailli, explaining that her father would never hear of having her husband under his roof, and that she was resolved to stay with her father: 'I have, I flatter myself, been instrumental in obtaining the liberty which M. de Mirabeau now enjoys, so it would be strange indeed if he were to use it to threaten mine.' Further letters passed to and fro, and Mirabeau did not blush to remind his father-in-law of the nature of conjugal duty; he was compensating his pride for the abject insincerities which had been forced out of him in Vincennes. But when it became clear that these stiff, diplomatic exchanges were achieving nothing, he decided to write Emilie a real letter.

> Mirabeau
> 13 November, 1782.

Emilie, listen to me, for it is a matter of your happiness and of mine. When the whole of life is at stake, nothing must be left to chance, there must be no rashness and no weakness.

You have loved me, my dear Emilie; you have loved me greatly; and the first man whom a woman has loved always means something to her heart. It would be easier for you to hate me than to feel for me nothing at all.

But why should you hate me? Because I have been hot-headed and bankrupt and jealous. Hot-headed you say? But that you knew before you were married, and remember, too, that your husband was never more imperious than when he was your lover. I went bankrupt? My Dear, have I not been more punished for it than you? And was not a very great part of my extravagance on your account, albeit against your wishes? And as for my jealousy, would it have been there if I had not loved you? . . . You do not hate me; you love me even, and yet you write me the harshest and most insulting letters — and you talk of divorce!

Divorce indeed! What means have you of obtaining it? Harsh letters that I have written you? What jealous husband has not written the like? Cruelties, maybe? Let your family suborn all the witnesses in creation, yet will this fact always remain: that since 1774 I have not seen you, and that since 1774 you have written me the tenderest letters. . . .

Certain parasites and persons interested in our separation are luring you on with this hope of divorce. It is an absurdity and they will never succeed in it. But where they will try to succeed is in this: you know what slander-mongers there are among barristers; they will choose one of the most violent as your counsel, and he will outrage me and do all he can to make it impossible for me to live with you henceforth. . . .

That is not all. Do you not know, my Dear, that a wife should live either in a convent or with her husband? I am not the man to impose this rule on you unless I am driven to it; but suppose they force me to it! Suppose they involve my honour in this fatal litigation! Little do those who are pushing you into it care whether you win or lose, whether you are in a convent or not, so long as you have no more children! . . .

Ponder well, Emilie. This moment can decide your whole life. I certainly do not wish for an unwilling wife, but, just as certainly, I owe it to myself not to let my house die out in order to allow my wife the barren pleasure of being, thanks to her pretty voice, the leading lady of a troupe of comedians. . . . .

I repeat, I do not want you against your will. But you are not a free agent and your will is not independent. Come and join me! I give you my word of honour that I shall not exercise my marital rights without your consent, your glad consent. I give you my word of honour that if, a month after our reunion, you persist with ideas of separation, I will let you return to your worthy father and I will never demand you back as long as I live. But I have a right to know your true opinion, and to break the chains of the obsession which holds it captive. . . . [48]

Two days after receiving this Emilie wrote to Caroline du Saillant, with whom she was always friendly:

We are quite resolved, my father and I, to go through with the separation suit if M. de Mirabeau attacks us; Papa will spare neither his fortune nor any other means to save me from a man who is so little master of himself. I feel quite confident that my father-in-law will not uphold him in the steps which he threatens to take against me. . . .

Though he got no reply to his letter, Mirabeau took no further step till after the new year. In January 1783 the Bailli obtained an interview with Marignane and his daughter, but they were not thinking of any sort of accommodation. Then Mirabeau himself proposed a tête-à-tête with Emilie, his uncle and her father to be in an adjoining room; she demanded twenty-four hours to consider the suggestion, and then turned it down. Not yet despairing of the personal touch, Mirabeau called at the Hôtel Marignane. Madame was not at home; Monsieur therefore announced that he would call again the next day; but when he did so there was a guard posted before the door with orders to raise the alarm if an attempt were made to pass. Finally, on

February 28th, Mirabeau wrote his wife one more letter; it was returned unopened, and he proceeded to action. [49]

He applied to the lieutenant of the *sénéchaussée* for an injunction to his wife to return to him within three days. He had to plead his case in open court, and obtained his order after a speech which amazed his hearers. They followed him from the court with cheers which were a foretaste of things to come. The reply of the Countess was to institute an action for separation before the high court of the *parlement* of Aix. Battle was joined.

In the law of old France separation of a wife from her husband was of two kinds: *séparation de biens*, the separation of her property from his, and *séparation de corps* which, if absolute, freed her from all personal conjugal duties, but which might be provisional, in which case she was permitted to retire to a convent for a while. The demand now made by the Countess was for absolute and unconditional bodily separation. The separation of her fortune had already been accomplished, nor would any court have reversed this position in view of her husband's record of insolvency and present condition of bankruptcy. But his bankruptcy was not, by itself, a ground upon which his wife could plead for bodily separation. Neither, it should be noted, was his adultery. Adultery by the husband was not sufficient ground for legal separation unless it could be proved that it had been accompanied by cruelty or by conduct publicly humiliating to the wife. Thus the two counts against Mirabeau which were indisputable — bankruptcy and adultery — were, for the purposes of his wife's case, irrelevant, which explains why, in the lawsuit which now opened, he was able to put up a skilful and prolonged defence. It also explains the tactics of the other side.

Mirabeau's case was simple. He had been apart from his wife since the day when she had left him to plead his cause with his father after the Villeneuve-Mouans episode at Grasse, nine years previously. At that moment and for some time afterwards their relations had been affectionate. The prolongation of their separation had not been of his choosing; far from it, for at Château d'If and at Fort de Joux he had repeatedly asked his wife to join him and even to escape with him abroad. She had firmly refused both proposals, and in so doing she had been within her rights; but she could not claim that his subsequent elopement with Mme de

Monnier constituted a personal humiliation to herself. Nor could she claim that occasional outbursts of temper before their separation constituted cruelty, since she had subsequently written him fond and wifely letters.

One of her oldest grievances was the publication of letters he had written to Malesherbes in which she was defamed. But the publication had been his mother's work, done without his authorization. Furthermore, the alleged defamation consisted of certain phrases hinting broadly at her lapse from conjugal fidelity and his magnanimous pardon. Could she press this point of libel when to do so might cause its foundation in fact to be disclosed — when he held, and she knew that he held, that letter written to break off her relations with young De Gassaud?

One of Mirabeau's first acts after proceedings had been opened was to publish *Observations* in which Emilie's affectionate letters featured prominently. Since their effect was to represent her as a naturally loving wife alienated from her husband by her family's influence, she could not reasonably object to their publication. But the retort from her side was a counter-memorandum which at once degraded the whole dispute to a level of vilification which had the effect which Mirabeau had foreseen — the effect of rendering a re-union morally impossible. For Marignane, urged on and assisted by De Galliffet, his daughter's over-intimate friend, now published old letters written to him by the Marquis de Mirabeau in all the heat and bitterness caused by the Count's earlier aberrations. This publication by a father-in-law of the epistolary excesses of a father, written in confidence and under privilege, written to him as a friend and ally with a common interest in the welfare of their children, was a peculiarly base action, and when old Mirabeau heard of it he was so angry as almost to support his heir in the wretched lawsuit in which he had become involved.[50]

The Marignane strategy was becoming clear. Mirabeau's neat system of defence was to be overwhelmed, to be swept clean away by a vast flood of personal denigration. Everything that could be alleged against his personal character was to be used; no discreditable episode was to be passed over in the effort to convince the court that no woman should be bound in conscience or required by law to live with such a monster.

Seldom, it must be admitted, has prosecuting counsel had such a wealth of material to draw on for this kind of attack as was presented by the career of the defendant. Seldom, too, has a court been more manifestly biased. Practically the whole class of *parlementaires* of Aix was knit to the Marignane interest. The family's influence ramified throughout that close society, and, with the exception of Mme de Vence, it turned its back upon the intrusive, impudent, scapegrace heir of the absentee lord of Mirabeau, and anticipated with pleasure his public humiliation. For Marignane had briefed Portalis, a man destined to collaborate with Napoleon on the Codes, and already the most brilliant ornament of the Aix bar. As three other distinguished advocates had been engaged, and as the remainder had been given to understand that to counsel the defence would not help their careers, the professional assistance at Mirabeau's disposal was unimpressive. He could offer no pecuniary inducements, and his opponents had made things worse by stirring up his creditors so as to remind the public of his bankrupt condition. So serious, indeed, did this pressure become that the Bailli had to pawn his diamond Cross of Malta to ease it for the moment.[51]

Mirabeau secured the services of a certain Jaubert, a young barrister of mediocre parts. Another young lawyer, a Marseillais of real ability but questionable reputation, also helped. This was Jean-Joachim Pellenc, and he appears to have given his services spontaneously. He was drawn, it would seem, by a sort of sympathy for this lone adversary of secure and opulent pride, by some instinct that here was a career for the clever but unendowed to follow.

But Mirabeau was not relying principally on these men, for he had determined to plead his case in person. The Marignane publication had made the whole affair so brutally personal that there remained no longer any reason of prudence why he should stand back, leaving the cut-and-thrust in open court to his representatives. The Marignanes had chosen to proceed by way of personal attack: very good: he would meet it in person, and perhaps they would have cause to regret their methods by the time judgment was given. They had asked for a fight and they had, presumably, measured the spirit of their adversary; but only he, as yet, guessed the full measure of his talent.

The case came before the *parlement* at the end of May 1783, and Portalis opened with the utmost violence of personal abuse, not only of Mirabeau but also of his father. He accused the latter of having broken his solemn promise to his daughter-in-law that she would not be called upon to rejoin her husband after his release from Vincennes, and of having incited his son to demand her return in order to repair the ruin of the House caused by his own lawsuit with the Marquise. Was it mere coincidence that in two generations the wives of the Riquetis had been driven to demand the protection of the law?

A few days later, on May 23rd, Mirabeau replied. His speech had been prepared with the help of Jaubert and Pellenc, and it lasted nearly five hours.

He has been represented as unfit for the rights and responsibilities of a husband. His riposte is to demand that, while the case is *sub judice*, his wife shall dwell in some suitable convent, since her father's house is too uncertain a protection for the reputation of the Comtesse de Mirabeau. So long as she remains there 'we shall see her, as we have seen her, walking in company without her father, moving in society without her father, at public entertainments without her father. We have seen her running the amusements of the social set of an unmarried man; we have seen her in that man's house, enjoying the pleasures of a private theatre. On her father's estate we have seen her, and shall see her once again, doing the honours of a house which is the known resort of men of pleasure, and living there in a numerous company — a company in which the men are a good deal more numerous than the women. . . .'

This was but a beginning. Portalis had spoken on two successive days, and there was a mountain of abuse and insinuation to demolish. Mirabeau warmed to his work, and soon, as the superb periods rolled forward, the listeners in that crowded courtroom knew, and the speaker, feeling their rapt attention, also knew that the Muse had descended and that an Orator was beating on the portals of fame.

Yet at this charmed moment it was in him to overstep the bounds of prudence and also of decency. Portalis had accused him of libelling his wife in those published letters to Malesherbes; Mirabeau had warned Emilie of the danger of mentioning this delicate matter, but his warning had been disregarded. Very good: the veil which her advocate had partially lifted in order to discredit him — that veil he would himself tear clean away to reveal his wife as an adulteress, once pardoned and hitherto shielded by her husband's generosity. He proceeded to read in court that last letter from Emilie to De Gassaud.

The act, of course, rendered the reunion for which he was ostensibly pleading quite impossible, but what matter? Had not the other side done as much already by their whole approach to the case? It was not his marriage which was now at stake, but his honour and his reputation. He had pardoned her fall; he had hidden it; for years he had endured imprisonment and humiliations which she, free to enjoy the estimation of good society, had done nothing either to shorten or to mitigate; yet all the while he had kept her secret. 'So long as the breath of life is in me I shall have the satisfaction of thinking that an action worthy of a better man than I, worthy of a truly virtuous man, is the immediate cause of my misfortunes. Is a man who, looking back over his life, can recall the behaviour I have mentioned, either able or bound to call by the name of wife a woman capable of such ingratitude?'

Then he turned from the unhappy Countess to direct his fire at Portalis himself:

And you, who have questioned me at such length throughout two sessions, answer me in your turn! Were you not the first to arm Mme de Mirabeau against me? Are you not the person really responsible for this lawsuit? You talk of courage. Did you have the courage to tell your client that she could not, without dishonouring herself, adopt the methods which you have been pursuing? Was it not your flattering compliance which deterred you from contradicting M. de Marignane when, without asking your opinion, he declared that this suit was necessary? You will deny it, of course; deny then also, if you can, that you have prevented Mme de Mirabeau from receiving my visits and from agreeing to conferences. Deny that it is you who have been the prime cause of all the misfortunes which have ensued and of those which are yet to come... Deny that you are the author of the infamous libel which you have had the baseness to write but not the courage to sign. . . .[52]

Portalis, enjoying the easy assurance of the professional challenged by the amateur, had forgotten that the amateur would be uninhibited by professional etiquette, so that he was quite unprepared for this furious assault on himself in his professional capacity. He left the court visibly shaken, and, it is said, took to his bed for several days. Indeed the Marignane camp was utterly disconcerted by this terrific speech. They had thought that they alone would be the attackers and they had been contemptuously confident. Now they had reason to regret that their offensive had driven their adversary to throw to the winds his chances of winning his case in the gratifying fury of hitting back and hitting where it hurt most. They had overestimated the element of material interest in Mirabeau's motives, and underestimated his personal and family pride. They would get their decree of separation sure enough, but they would emerge from the contest battered and bespattered. It was evident, on the other hand, that Mirabeau was winning the respect which the public pays to a bonny fighter. Even among the lawyers he was gaining admirers, and when his opponents thought of protesting that their profession had been insulted in the attack on Portalis they received little support.

Emilie herself was acutely alarmed, for her husband's speech had stirred up a most unpleasant curiosity about the details of her private life. It was particularly embarrassing to have such tittering and malicious talk at this moment, for it so happened that the Archduke Ferdinand of Austria was in Aix and intended, it was rumoured, to be present at the next hearing. The Archduke was the Queen's brother, and Emilie had often toyed with hopes of obtaining a position at court; the Bailli, indeed, believed that if only her father-in-law could help in this matter she would show a new readiness to put her matrimonial affairs in order; however, that might be, it certainly would not do for the scandal which her lawsuit had stirred up to percolate from Aix to Versailles.[53]

Portalis resumed his pleading on June 13th. His tone was noticeably less aggressive, though he made good use of the defendant's production of his client's letter to De Gassaud. He suggested that it had been written under duress and insisted that a husband who could dictate such a letter and subsequently read it in open court was one to whom his wife should never be restored.

Mirabeau was due to reply on the seventeenth. The day before, Emilie learnt that the Archduke would be in court. Scared lest her husband's second speech should be anything like his first, she hurriedly suggested a compromise: she would be content with a separation of two years only, during which time she would live in a convent, on condition that he should clear her publicly of the worst imputations arising from his reading of the De Gassaud letter.

This proposal reached him two hours before he was due in court. Though it would mean recasting his prepared speech and even appearing to eat some of his own words, he nevertheless agreed. In court he proceeded to explain that he had read the letter not to besmirch his wife, but to rebut the charge of cruelty against himself, by showing how magnanimous he had been to pardon behaviour which, to say the least, had been injurious to his pride. The speech continued. The terrible, angry gladiator of the former occasion was invisible today; instead it was a strong man, patient, gentle and forgiving, that held the court's attention:

No, I am no longer the passionate lover who sighed for you, who wished you back for love as much as for duty; but I am still merciful, I am still generous; I am, and would remain, an austere but tender friend, mournfully compelled to snatch you away from the enchantments which have led your youth astray, from the seductions which have been your undoing. . . .

There were, it is said, tears in many eyes when he finished. But if there were any in the eyes of Emilie they were tears of rage. Was this the way he fulfilled his part of the bargain — this hypocritical effusion which, with its insufferable tone of pity and condescension, had added insult to the injury he had promised to undo? The humiliation of being treated as a sort of Magdalen by that reprobate in front of all her acquaintances, in front of the Archduke!

She reverted immediately to the demand for a full and permanent separation, and her husband went back to his original position, to a simple demand, that is, for her unconditional return. This, of course, necessitated a third speech and a third change of tactics, but he was equal to it. He read extracts from Emilie's kindest letters in an attempt to prove that only the sinister pressure of her *entourage* prevented her from obeying the secret dictates of her heart, and he ended with a plea that the court would 're-open to him the way of domestic virtue' which he pledged himself very solemnly to tread thenceforth.

Again it was a moving speech. But three moving speeches in succession, each of which moved in a direction different from the other two, while they might establish the reputation of an orator, could scarcely win the case for an advocate, and there could be little doubt what the judgment of the court would be. On July 5th it was pronounced: Madame de Mirabeau was granted her unconditional decree of bodily separation. The judges believed that after such bitter and public mutual recriminations, more particularly after the Count's production of the De Gassaud letter, the resumption of normal married life was a moral impossibility. It was substantially the same conclusion as Mirabeau had foretold to Emilie before the lawsuit started.

It had long been evident to Mirabeau that his bitterest opponent was the Comte de Galliffet; that it was he who had closed Emilie's heart to any thoughts of reconciliation, who had incited her and her feckless father to publish their fatal memorandum, and who had, above all, exposed the name of the Comtesse de Mirabeau to the winks and insinuations of the county's gossips. Mirabeau had lost his case in court, but there were gentlemen's affairs beyond the competence of courts and lawyers to settle, and he took the first opportunity of challenging De Galliffet to a duel.

They fought with rapiers. At one agonizing moment the devoted Legrain thought his master run through the body, but De Galliffet's point had been turned and the blade had passed under his opponent's arm. Renewed ring, clash and slither of steel: Mirabeau pinks De Galliffet in his sword-arm; it is nothing, says De Galliffet, who wishes to go on, but Mirabeau will on no account fight with a wounded man; courtesies, explanations: Mirabeau makes it clear, so he thinks, that there will be another meeting unless M. de Galliffet avoids the society of Mme la Comtesse. De Galliffet either does not understand or does not care. Renewed challenge: M. de Mirabeau will await M. de Galliffet at the fountain of Vaucluse; their quarrel is becoming known and Papal territory is to be preferred. But De Galliffet does not present himself.

Many years later Legrain told how his dear, dead master fished some crayfish from the fountain and sent them to his adversary 'because they walk backwards'. Legrain, especially in old age, had a gift for anecdote.[54]

The lawsuit was for Mirabeau both a defeat and a victory. He had missed what he had set out to gain, his restoration to the best society of his ancestral province. Victorious, he would have been accepted everywhere; defeated, he must expect in many circles the cold shoulder and the averted glance. Had he succeeded, his later career would have been affected, for, when the elections of 1789 arrived, he would presumably have been chosen to represent the class to which he belonged by birth. Furthermore, his career in the intervening period might well have been more regular, and he might have sat in the States-General with a reputation untarnished by six years of dubious shifts and equivocal adventures. His background would have been different from the political demi-monde which was his antechamber to the Hall of the National Assembly.

But much had been gained. The court's judgment had been received with derisive whistles, and, while De Galliffet became a target for brickbats and a subject for ribald songs, Mirabeau received ovations. It was he, furthermore, who remained in possession of the field. The victorious Marignanes found Aix so uncomfortable that they retired to their country house, while their vanquished opponent lingered some two months in the town, very much at his ease, a popular and increasingly familiar figure among the admirers of the Saint-Huberti, who was singing at Aix and at Marseilles that season.[55]

In losing his lawsuit he had, it is true, become unseated from his appropriate niche among the grandees of his ancestral province; but he had come to ground to stand on his own feet, an aristocrat by birth, a man of the people by adoption. For unexpectedly and rather mysteriously, while defending his private interest he had captured the public imagination. The Provençal Nation, with its appetite for equality, saw in Marignanes and Galliffets representatives of what they found offensive, and when they saw a lone combatant, impudent, versatile and audacious, fronting the battlements of privilege and hurling bolts that made them tremble, they fastened upon him as their champion and representative man. When next he came among his compatriots they would remember that courtroom at Aix, and return him to the north with their acclamations ringing in his ears.

CHAPTER VII

THE FRINGES OF POLITICS

UNWILLING to accept as final the Aix judgment, in which, after all, only five of the nine judges had concurred, Mirabeau went to Paris in the autumn to lodge an appeal with the King's Council. In the new year Marignane and his daughter came north to resist it. She even had the nerve to present herself at her father-in-law's house. Bitterly disappointed at the course things had taken in Provence, the Marquis thought the appeal nothing but an expensive folly. Groaning at his son's apparent inability to handle a situation without making himself the hero of a crisis, he washed his hands of him by handing back to the minister the royal order he had held for controlling him. Since the Count was now thirty-four the abdication was scarcely premature. But if Emilie thought that she could again come purring to his side she was mistaken, and when she called she was refused admission. The old man was through with them both.

The campaign of libels was resumed. The Countess opened and the Count replied. Marignane, however, had influence with Miroménil, Keeper of the Seals, who ordered the Count's *mémoire* to be suppressed.

Angry at this partial intervention of authority, Mirabeau protested to Miroménil in a letter, and then in an interview in which high words passed. Then, losing patience, he had an edition of his suppressed *mémoire*, with an account of this conversation added as a preface, printed in Holland and smuggled into France.

The folly of this action is the more inexplicable since his appeal would, in all probability, come before the *Conseil des parties* of which Miroménil was president. In the event, it is true, the appeal was dismissed by a subsidiary committee of the Council; Miroménil, furthermore, proved so anxious not to appear actuated by personal feelings that, as it turned out, he took no steps against the contraband reprint. But Mirabeau was not to know this and fully expected a *lettre de cachet* to be issued against him. Men had been clapped in prison for a tenth of his offence.

This episode is one of the least accountable things in his career. It was such a gratuitous invitation of trouble. What conceivable purpose, apart from the venting of spleen, was the contraband reprint, with its preface libelling a minister of state, supposed to serve? How can its author have failed to see that it could only ruin his chances of a successful appeal, while exposing him to the anger of the government which he had so lately been soliciting for a job?

We have here one of those unpredictable and explosive aberrations which repeatedly interrupted his career, making impossible a steady course towards a chosen goal. He suffered, there can be no doubt, from a grave temperamental instability, and this may be easier to understand when we recall that insanity appeared not only in his maternal grandmother but also in his father's mother, for that severe and pious lady had, at the end of her life, collapsed into a shocking and terrible dementia. Mirabeau's instability was intermittent in its effects. He was not incapable of foresighted self-control. But on many occasions he would react to stimuli with an unreflecting violence and a disregard of remoter consequences capable of doing irreparable damage to his reputation and his fortunes.

So it was now, in 1784. At a time when every consideration of prudence and ambition required him to be in France, in Paris, his own heady recklessness drove him into exile. Realizing too late the consequences to be expected from his behaviour, he decided to escape them by passing to the land which exercised so potent a mixture of attraction and repulsion upon thinking Frenchmen in the last years of Bourbon absolutism.

2

He crossed to England in August, but he did not travel alone.

Earlier that year he had been pursuing one of his transient intrigues with a lady whose husband was absent. Anxious to provide cover for the Count's visits, this woman invited a friend, a Madame de Nehra, to leave the convent where she had been dwelling and come to live with her.

Madame de Nehra was repelled by Mirabeau the first time she

met him. A virginal instinct recoiled from the brutal masculinity of the heavy frame, the massive head, the craggy features and the cratered skin. But soon, as she saw how the granite of that face could melt in the most engaging smiles of humour and sympathy, she found herself oddly attracted. She saw him daily, and every day her pleasure in his company increased. The force and point of his conversation, the way he had of expressing ideas only half-formed in her own mind, the strange vital warmth of the man — these things began to encompass her. There was no kind of infatuation; only a growing delight in his company, a deepening admiration for his mind, and, in the way of sentiment, the quickening of a feeling that was fundamentally maternal.

Soon Madame de Nehra's friend became jealous, whereupon she returned to the convent; she had no wish to steal her friend's lover. But it made no difference. The Count visited her regularly, content with the rigidities of the convent parlour provided he could be with her for an hour or two each day; for he was discovering something he had not known before, the nature of love for a woman as a complete human person.

Henriette-Amélie de Nehra was the natural child of the Dutch poet and statesman, William van Haren, and the name she used was an anagram of his. She had been orphaned at an early age and, on the death of the uncle who had then cared for her, had been sent to this convent in Paris with a small annuity to support her. Here she had lived demurely since the age of fourteen. Brought up originally as a Protestant, she had come to share her generation's distaste for theological truths, but she was to die a Catholic. She was only nineteen when her meeting with Mirabeau altered the course of her life so strangely.

Her beauty was fairy-like and uncommon. With her slight figure, the delicate features of her little almond-shaped face, her rose-petal complexion, her wide-set blue eyes and her mass of ash-blonde hair, she could scarcely have presented a greater contrast to the burly male in whose company she was now seen. 'All who have seen her', wrote the Marquis, 'say that she is charming and touchingly open-hearted.' Freshness combined with poise and innocence joined to wisdom were a rare endowment in the circle of Mirabeau's acquaintances, who wondered why this enchanting and unblemished creature should link herself to a hardened roué who was sixteen years her senior and looked more. They would have been more puzzled still had they known that she was not, at any time, in love with him. 'I knew well', she wrote in after years, 'that he was not really the man for my heart's need . . . I loved him tenderly; I preferred him to all other men; but I was not in love.'

When he paid his hurried and imprudent visit to Holland in May he asked her to accompany him. She hesitated. There was her friend's claim to consider; there was still a remote chance of Mirabeau's wife returning, and she would do nothing to hinder this. In the end she agreed to travel with him, but it was only at the end of the trip that they became lovers.

She saw that her refusal to be more than a friend was making him unhappy, and she believed that he needed her. Unmarried and without family ties, she thought she might bring into focus the blurred and unsteady life of this man who had been cast off by wife and father and had no devoted friends. It was with full deliberation, therefore, and a fair idea of what she was undertaking that she took a silent vow to live for him alone, to follow whithersoever he went and to stay by him in good fortune and in bad as long as he wanted her. From him she exacted no sort of promise at all, and it was thus that, when he fled to England in August 1784, 'Yet-Lie' (as he called her) went with him.[56]

3

Mirabeau was not without contacts with good English society. During the Aix lawsuit he had found a friend and warm partisan in Lord Peterborough, who happened to be there with two other Englishmen of rank. But there was an older contact than this.

At Choquard's academy he had made friends with two Scottish boys, Gilbert and Hugh Elliot. Since that time Gilbert, the elder, had married, succeeded to the baronetcy of Minto and entered Parliament, while Hugh had risen to be minister-plenipotentiary at Copenhagen. It happened that a copy of *Des lettres de cachet* fell into Hugh Elliot's hands, attracted his attention and roused his curiosity about his old school friend. A traveller in Copenhagen said he thought he could discover the Count's address and present circumstances through a French friend in London, and Elliot gave him a message to forward. The Frenchman in London was none other than Brissot, the future Girondin, and when Elliot's message reached him he took it to Clavière, whom he knew to be in touch with Mirabeau and who had just come to London from Dublin in connection with the Waterford scheme. Elliot's message offered the Count asylum in England if he needed it, and hinted vaguely at some sort of diplomatic employment. It reached Mirabeau in Provence, just after the judgment of his lawsuit.

'I recognize my dear Elliot from the account you give me of him,' he wrote to Brissot. 'There is no other nation which can show such marks of kindliness and generosity. . . .' He went on to give an account of his affairs and to complain with the old Vincennes bitterness of the way in which his father had left him to flounder in the quicksands of insolvency. Brissot was doubtless shocked at the tyranny of a patriarch who was, it seemed, pocketing the bulk of his son's annual allowance instead of using it to pay off the debts which were his justification for withholding it; but one wonders what Brissot thought of a son who was so ready to traduce his father in a letter to a total stranger.

Hugh Elliot himself may have felt somewhat swamped by the Gallic effusion which he shortly received: 'It was long ago, my dear Elliot, that my spirit divined yours, and that some instinct gave me foreknowledge of your virtues before age had developed them or made me capable of appreciating them. But when you were inspiring in me the first deep and lively sentiments I had known, when, in the springtime of our youth, I cherished you with so tender a friendship, who could have said that one day I would owe you all my gratitude and affection for the wishes for my welfare and happiness which you would send from one end of Europe to the other, after so many years of silence and separation? . . .' Mirabeau outlined his career during those years: 'Suffice it for you to know that my destiny has been a continual storm and my life a tale of romance; that, enslaved under the double despotism of my father and of the government he has provoked, I have made great mistakes and experienced great ills; that all these mistakes have left my honour intact, and that some have even improved my moral character . . .' It was not a very objective account, and the self-portrait reached heroic proportions as he wrote of the recent lawsuit: 'When I arrived everybody fled from me; I was anti-Christ . . . I spoke in public four times, my spirit aroused my genius and I had the greatest possible success. It was with good reason that the ancients made a god of the gift of speech. The public, always prone to extremes, sided with me to the point of idolatry . . . In the end I have become, as it were, the demagogue of Provence.'

Then he turns to Elliot's offer: 'You understand, my dear friend, that I cannot think of being a burden on anyone.' What he would welcome above all would be some diplomatic post, if his friend has enough influence in the northern courts to obtain it for him. The main thing, however, is to be sure of liberty and employment for one's energies, 'two advantages which I can never enjoy except far from my lamentable country'. [57]

Hugh Elliot took his time in replying, and then pointed out that it was Gilbert, not he, who had been the Count's special friend at school; furthermore, Mirabeau had over-estimated his power to help him, and it would be quite impossible for a post in the British service to be given to a foreigner. A post in the British service was not, however, quite what Mirabeau had hinted at, and the letter suggests that Elliot was having second thoughts. He wrote to Brissot that 'in view of certain circumstances' known to him, it was impossible for him 'to render the celebrated author' the services for which he asked. Was it, Brissot wondered, that, in addition to *Des lettres de cachet*, another anonymous work by the celebrated author had reached Copenhagen? Had the minister-plenipotentiary chanced upon the *Erotika Biblion* as well? [58]

Undiscouraged, however, by Hugh Elliot's sudden reserve, Mirabeau, on arriving in England ten months later, hastened to renew his acquaintance with Sir Gilbert. The latter's family were at Bath, and the baronet took his old schoolfellow down there with him. Henriette was left in London, for it was uncertain how the Elliot womenfolk would regard her. But her lover wrote back in glowing terms: 'Gilbert is goodness itself. He has all sorts of plans for my future and for bringing us closer together. For example, when he goes to Scotland he is going to arrange for us to lodge in a little house in his grounds, because he wants us to pass the summer with him, which will be very economical and agreeable. . . .'

Gilbert's impressions were posted to Hugh: 'I found him as ardent a friend as I left him, and as little altered as possible by twenty years of life, of which six have been consumed in prison . . . He is very much ripened in his abilities, which are really considerable, and has acquired a great store of knowledge . . . Mirabeau is as overbearing in his conversation, as awkward in his graces, as ugly and misshapen in face and person, as dirty in his dress, and withal as perfectly *suffisant*, as we remember him twenty years ago at school. I loved him however, then, and so did you . . . I brought him with me the other day to Bath, where he made such hasty love to Harriet [Gilbert's sister-in-law], whom he had little doubt of subduing in a week, and where he so totally silenced my John Bull wife, who understands a Frenchman no better than Molly housemaid, where he so scared my little boy by caressing him, and so completely disposed of me from breakfast to supper, and so astonished all our friends, that I could hardly keep the peace in his favour; and if he had not been called unexpectedly to town this morning, I am sure my wife's endurance, for I cannot call it civility, would not have held out another day.' [59]

It was Lady Minto, in fact, who had suggested the 'little house in the grounds'; if he really must come to Minto he must lodge, she insisted, with the gamekeeper; on no account would she have him again under the same roof.

The Scottish visit did not materialize, but Gilbert Elliot's kindness was constant none the less. He took the Count on a tour which included Windsor, Oxford and a visit to the astronomer Herschel, and he introduced him to Lord Lansdowne (Shelburne) and to Edmund Burke. Burke invited him down to Beaconsfield, and the absence of any record of their talk is one of history's most tantalizing silences. Had their contact been maintained Burke's *Reflections* might have been less inclined to blame the French Revolution for not being English, and the great conservative Whig might not have felt called upon jokingly to assure his later guest, the refugee Abbé Maury, that he had had his house 'purified' since Mirabeau's visit. [60]

Mirabeau also met the celebrated radical non-conformist, Dr. Price, whose sermon at the Old Jewry so incensed Burke six years later, and he picked Price's brains in the preparation of a work upon which he was at the moment engaged. This was entitled *Considerations on the Order of Cincinnatus* and it is an example of the truth that there was no subject in heaven or on earth upon which Mirabeau was not prepared to write. 'Had anyone offered him the elements of a Chinese grammar', wrote the rather unkind Dumont, 'he would, no doubt, have attempted a treatise on the Chinese language.' The present subject was, however, somewhat less remote. An hereditary order of chivalry had been started in America to consist of officers who had fought for independence, but it had been hotly criticized, particularly in a pamphlet by a South Carolina judge. Mirabeau had annexed this paper and enlarged its argument that to make an hereditary order of those who had fought for American independence would be to betray the principles for which they had fought. He had shown his work to Franklin before leaving France, and he now borrowed material from Price (including a letter from Turgot) to plump out a sizable essay on the subject. It was his first signed publication, for his pen looked like being henceforth his only source of income and he wished to make a literary name. One thing clearly appears — Mirabeau's growing contempt for hereditary nobility as such; another motive may be suspected — envy of Boniface who, as a participant in the triumph of Yorktown, would qualify for membership of the new order.

Perhaps the most valued friend made during his stay in England was the wise and good Sir Samuel Romilly. Romilly had read *Des lettres de cachet* with qualified approval the previous year, but he was keenly interested in the Irish project of the Genevese exiles, and it was through these that he met Mirabeau. The latter read him the Cincinnatus tract, and, wishing for an English edition to appear at the same time as the French, persuaded Romilly to undertake the translation. This work brought the two men into very close association and, though Romilly found the author by no means easy to please, a friendship grew between them. 'I think his character was well known to me,' Romilly afterwards wrote. 'I doubt whether it has been as well known to the world . . . His vanity was, certainly, excessive; but I have no doubt that, in his public conduct as well as in his writings, he was desirous of doing good, that his ambition was of the noblest kind . . . He was, however, like many of his countrymen, who were active in

the calamitous revolution which afterwards took place, not sufficiently scrupulous about the means by which those ends were to
be accomplished . . . More than once I have heard him say that
there were occasions upon which *la petite morale était ennemie de
la grande.*' [61]

Before the moralist yields to the temptation to pass judgment
on Mirabeau's peculiarly assailable character he should remember
two things: the first is that Mirabeau was attracted to men of
virtue; the second is that, for all his ill-repute, men of outstanding
integrity were attracted to him. The man who, while so far from
personal respectability, won and retained the warm regard of
Samuel Romilly, of the future Lord Minto and, later, of the Count
of La Marck, is easy neither to classify nor to condemn. [62]

Lady Minto was not alone, however, in finding the opinionated
and overbearing Gaul somewhat difficult in society. Romilly
tells of a dinner at which he was present, and during which
Mirabeau fell into an argument with John Wilkes on the English
penal code. Wilkes chose to defend its irrational severities, attributing the Englishman's well-known contempt for death to the
frequency with which he witnessed public hangings. Mirabeau was
not at all amused. Missing the briny irony of this very English
piece of extravagance, he launched into a voluble and impassioned
attack on the immorality not only of the opinion but also of its
defender, and Romilly was thankful that Wilkes's cynicism, which
had provoked the outburst, was cool enough to prevent the consequences which must otherwise have ensued. Mirabeau's readiness to dispute with eminent men in a language of which he had a
most imperfect command was displayed again a little later. Writing
to Romilly, who had gone on circuit, he described how, at Lord
Lansdowne's table, he had become over-heated in controversy
with the author of *The Decline and Fall of the Roman Empire*, upbraid-
ing him for his approval of despotism. Perhaps the Count failed
to catch the name of the gentleman whom he surprised with these
reproaches, for Mr. Gibbon, the historian, was, as a matter of fact,
at Lausanne. [63]

Mirabeau was repelled by the dreariness of the English sabbath
and by the colourless solemnity of English protestantism, which he
thought must be very bad for children. He was amazed at the
riotous proclivities of the London masses and at the licence of

the press, the theatre and the political cartoons. He found the people as a whole purposeful and serious but too commercially minded; they had a civic sense and a national pride which was greatly to be envied, but he deplored the Francophobia assiduously fostered in many quarters. It seemed to him that every citizen was a politician, and he was surprised at the interest women took in public affairs. As for the secret of the country's greatness, it lay, he thought, in one thing — the inviolability of her civil liberties; for her political liberty he had no respect, and he found her administration atrocious. 'If the Englishman is the freest social being on earth, the English people is one of the least free that exist,' he wrote to Chamfort. 'I think that, man for man, we are worth more than they, and that the land of the vine has it over the land of the coal-mine, even in its influence on moral character . . . What a thing, then, must liberty be, when the little bit which is contained in one or two good laws can place in the front rank a people so little favoured by nature!'

He was surprised and delighted by the loveliness of English farmland and of English gardens, but he found London a dour and tasteless city which had neglected the scenic possibilities of its river banks, and in which shutterless houses frowned uninvitingly behind unnecessary iron railings painted in depressing colours. But it was cleaner than Paris and much better paved. In one respect, however, he found England incomparable, and that was in its horses. Whether on Epsom Downs, where he watched the races, or in London streets, the horses of England were superb; there seemed to be as many horses in London as there were men, and they were so well groomed that one might well wonder which served which. English stables, he declared, were positively cleaner than most Paris hotels.

Though he met some eminent men, though he saw everything he could from Westminster Abbey and the opening of Parliament to the London hospitals, though he sampled English life at levels ranging from a visit to 'the local' to the banquet of a city company (where he was impressed to see the greatest nobles present as the guests of fishmongers) he and Henriette were almost without resources, and lived very simply in lodgings in Hatton Street, Holborn. She fortunately, was a careful manager as well as a sweet and understanding companion. 'I swear to you', her lover wrote to Chamfort, 'with all the sincerity of my heart that I am not worthy of her, and that her soul is quite above the ordinary in its tenderness, its delicacy and its goodness.' They both had need of her qualities, for Mirabeau was finding it harder to live by his pen than he had expected.

4

A Frenchman in England might write as he pleased, but, partly for that reason, the French journalistic colony in London had a singularly unsavoury reputation. In the 'seventies and 'eighties London had become the resort of a set of French journalists who lived largely by blackmailing influential people and even the very government of their native land. It was part of the price which Bourbon despotism paid for its muzzle on the press. Unable to use the *lettre de cachet* and the prison cell to control this expatriated literary demi-monde, the government was constrained to adopt its methods for fear of worse indignities, and between Paris and London there was a furtive coming and going of secret agents armed with money, promises and threats, with which to buy up an impending libel or to hire a venal pen or even to decoy the less wary scribbler into returning within arm's reach of his paternal government.

In this reeking journalistic backwater probably the most slippery fish was Morande. He was well known to the French police. A thief before he was old enough to be a libertine, he had, at fifteen, narrowly escaped hanging. After two years in a house of correction he had fled to England, where he plunged with gusto into a career of journalistic blackmail. His first big work in this line appeared in 1772 and was entitled *Le Gazetier cuirassé, ou Anecdotes scandaleuses sur la cour de France*. Brissot, one of his victims, hints that he was paid to write it by a very important person, but, however that may be, the Du Barry, after an attempt to kidnap him had failed, paid him handsomely to suppress it. Beaumarchais was empowered by the government to offer 500 guineas down and a pension of 4000 *livres* for life, and Morande's first big literary deal was thus satisfactorily concluded. His luck was in and it remained in, since two years later the disappearance of Louis XV from this world and of Madame du Barry from Versailles made it safe to publish *Anecdotes sur la comtesse Du Barry*. This appeared in 1776, but Morande had not been idle in the meantime. It was perhaps natural that he should write against Beaumarchais, but it was more audacious of him to turn his pen against Voltaire. During the American war he was suspected of being in the pay of the British government, but he afterwards acted as a spy for Vergennes and earned permission to return to France. While not availing himself of the permission to put himself within the reach of Le Noir's police, Morande undertook to serve the Minister of Foreign Affairs in a new way. Vergennes was so worried by the stream of libels from London that he conceived the chimerical idea of inducing the British government to stop it, and Morande assured him that a stiff bribe to a leading parliamentarian — Sheridan for instance — would do his business. He had even, it seems, drafted a bill for that orator to introduce. That a shrewd and experienced statesman like Vergennes should have toyed with such a fantastic proposal is some measure of the insinuating plausibility of Morande.[64]

A recent recruit to the London colony of French journalists was Linguet. A disbarred lawyer and a writer of flashy talent, he founded a periodical called *Annales politiques et littéraires*, the only paper, it was said, which Louis XVI read with pleasure. But Linguet's soul was twisted and misshapen by envy and malice, and his pen was so venomous that in due course it earned him a spell in the Bastille. He emerged in 1782 and retired to London where he continued his *Annales* and where, in 1783, he published his *Memoires sur la Bastille*. Romilly read it and thought the style pretentious, and Mirabeau, seeing a rival to his own *Des lettres de cachet*, agreed with him.[65]

Linguet, though venal, was not a literary criminal like Morande, and his genuine ability combined with his lack of scruple and his vitriolic temper to make him formidable. He seems to have gained an ascendancy over the other French writers in London, and his enmity was not a thing to be disregarded. It was an enmity, however, which Mirabeau had the ill-fortune to incur.

Their relations were friendly at first, but Linguet seems to have behaved towards Henriette with the freedom of manner which he thought that her position would permit, whereupon

Mirabeau showed him the door. From that moment he could be sure that if Linguet could thwart his literary career he would do so.

In 1784 journalists and politicians were much agitated by the evident intention of the Emperor Joseph II to defy Europe in general and Holland in particular by opening to navigation the Scheldt and the port of Antwerp, closed by treaties dating back to 1648. Joseph ordered a vessel to sail up the river to Antwerp; the Dutch, accepting the challenge, fired on it, and both sides prepared for immediate war. Holland appealed for help to Britain and France, but Joseph II appealed to France too, and Vergennes was in a dilemma. 'Remember always, Monsieur,' the Queen said to him, 'that the Emperor is my brother.' 'I shall always remember that, Madame,' replied the Minister, 'but I shall consider above all that His Highness the Dauphin is your son.' To support the Emperor would, he knew, infuriate the nation; to support the Dutch might not be forgiven by the Queen. In the end he contrived, with some adroitness, a middle course; France came forward as a mediator, the Scheldt remained closed and the Emperor received a money indemnity, part of which was paid by France — an item which was at once debited by public opinion to Marie Antoinette's account.

Before this solution was reached England had made clear her support of Holland, and Mirabeau had gone into print with a pamphlet called *Doutes sur la liberté de l'Escaut*. Romilly says the true author was Benjamin Vaughan, but though Mirabeau probably used another's work as a foundation, the 'doubts' he expressed were specifically French. Their keynote was an Austrophobia which seems today excessive, but was in line with average French opinion in 1784. Joseph II was represented as the ambitious disturber of the peace, and behind Joseph was Catherine of Russia; working hand in hand, they were threatening nothing less than the partition of Holland and her colonies, and if Joseph were not stopped the Scheldt might well become an anchorage for Russian warships. France should give the Dutch all support, not stopping short of war, and it would be well if the Belgian provinces should follow the sixteenth-century example of their northern brethren and throw off the Habsburg yoke.

Linguet in his *Annales politiques* had taken the other side, and Mirabeau contemptuously accused him of trying to cover up a total ignorance of the subject by a screen of pompous verbiage and a shameless abuse of metaphor. So Linguet now had a double score to pay off against one whose pen might make him a formidable rival if he should establish himself among the French journalists in London.

5

Mirabeau had brought from France a servant, Jacques-Philippe Hardy to act as valet-cum-secretary. He had nothing with which to pay Hardy's wages and borrowed six *louis* from him on arriving in London. But, in place of a stock of cash, he had intended to bring with him, in addition to the Cincinnatus manuscript, two works which might prove saleable. One was a small printed book of court scandal entitled *Journal de Monsieur*, whose sale could only have filled his pocket at the price of lowering him to the level of Morande. The other was a transcript of some unpublished correspondence between Voltaire and D'Alembert, and it had been obtained by distinctly shady means.

The original letters belonged to the Prince de Condé, who had entrusted them to Chamfort, his private secretary. Yielding to Mirabeau's entreaties, Chamfort had put friendship before secretarial punctilio and lent him the letters to read, whereupon Mirabeau had hurried off with them, divided the bundles among certain assistants and proceeded thus, in the course of a single night, to obtain copies of the whole lot. One of the accomplices in this little job had been Hardy, newly engaged.

In the haste of his departure Mirabeau had left it to Hardy to pack these two works, but when he later came to look for them they were nowhere to be found. At first he was merely furious with his servant's negligence, but later he and Henriette began to miss personal belongings and to wonder whether the disappearance of the book and the transcript was quite the simple accident it had at first seemed. Some of Hardy's comings and goings were suspicious, and one day Henriette examined his box while he was out and found in it some of the Count's linen. Advised by Sir Gilbert Elliot, they decided to prosecute, and when Hardy was arrested certain other articles were found in his possession, including the *Journal de Monsieur*. He on his side was preparing to sue his master for his arrears of wages, but the charge of larceny had to be dealt with first.

The case came on at the Old Bailey on February 23rd, 1785, Hardy being charged with having stolen *a book valued at 2s.*, twenty-seven shirts, two cotton nightcaps, six pairs of silk stockings and sundry other trifles. He pleaded not guilty. On the face of it as humdrum a case as ever there was, yet the court was crowded, and there were eminent persons in the crowd. Clustering round the plaintiff were such grandees as Lansdowne, Rutland and Richmond, as well as Edmund Burke, Dr. Price, the economist Benjamin Vaughan and, of course, Romilly and Sir Gilbert Elliot. Brissot and two or three other Frenchmen of repute were there too, ostentatiously separating themselves from another group, which stood round the defendant and in which Morande and Linguet were conspicuous.

The prosecution had to prove that Hardy had meant to steal the articles; that they had been found in his possession was insufficient proof of guilt against a valet and secretary. Cross-examination was principally concerned with such minutiae as laundry-marks, but the real interest of the trial centred on two matters which were deliberately kept out of focus. Mirabeau's counsel, recounting the motive for the prosecution, alluded to the vexing disappearance of the Voltaire-D'Alembert letters, but Hardy, reflecting on his own share in their transcription, resisted the temptation to tell the court how his master had come by them. On the other hand the plaintiff, when pressed for details about the 'book valued at 2s.', admitted that it was the *Journal de Monsieur*, but refused to give any further information as to its importance to himself — or to Hardy. His sudden discretion was noted, especially by Linguet.

After a hearing whose strict impartiality greatly impressed Mirabeau — he vowed he would see trial by jury introduced into his native land — Hardy was acquitted. The defence had done all they could to discredit the plaintiff by alluding to the suspicious haste with which he had left France and to the irregular nature of his relations with the witness 'Madame de Nara'. But Elliot solemnly vouched for the Count's honourable character, and the judge interposed to remind the jury that these attempts to discredit the plaintiff were quite improper.

But Hardy acquitted might well be more dangerous than Hardy in the dock, for now there was nothing to deter him from giving Linguet all the information he wanted as to the source of those transcripts or the purpose with which Mirabeau had brought to England that 'book valued at 2s.'. But the latter's friends were very staunch, and, to parry the first return-stroke of the scotched snake, Elliot, Burke and Romilly, immediately on leaving court, drew up an exact and truthful report of the proceedings and got it printed in next day's *Public Advertiser*. A Linguet-inspired version was thus prevented. Better still, Mirabeau contrived to persuaded Morande to print in his *Courrier de l'Europe* a translation of the correct report.[66]

It was check to Linguet, but not checkmate. Mirabeau's position remained most uncomfortable, for Linguet was not likely to forget his revenge, and Hardy's action for recovery of wages was still to be expected. On March 7th, Romilly received a letter from his friend Baynes: 'The Count', he wrote, 'called upon me today . . . Hardy has printed an English libel against him, apparently translated from the French of Linguet: this, I trust, will be of no great service to H. if he should bring his cause to a trial. The Count complains bitterly of his hard fate in losing Madame de ——— . . .'[67]

6

'Madame de ———' left London on March 2nd, 1785, for France. With Linguet on the warpath there were in England no journalistic prospects for her dear friend, but rather the probability of a deal of trouble. It was characteristic of her to hasten alone across the Channel to see if she could make straight the way for his return.

First impressions were not heartening. On all sides Henriette was warned that there would be a *lettre de cachet* for the Count the moment he came back, and Dupont de Nemours advised her that she was in some danger herself as his collaborator and had better look to her own safety. Instead she went straight out to Versailles, and somehow or other obtained an interview with Breteuil, the minister who issued arbitrary warrants. Breteuil was touched by the courage of this unimportant but beautiful little woman, but he said frankly that the King was displeased with Mirabeau and that the Queen resented his attack on the Emperor in the Scheldt pamphlet: let Madame return to her convent; he would see to it, he added kindly, that she was not troubled there. But Madame was not to be deflected, so the Minister told her that she might return that evening, and that in the meantime he would see the King. At the second interview he assured her that it would be safe for her friend to return; the government, he added with a smile, would consider the Count as being under her care.

'Bless you!' wrote Mirabeau. 'Bless you a thousand times for your courage in braving Versailles on my account. My whole life shall be devoted to blessing you. . . .'[68]

7

The money problem remained. After the separation of his wife Mirabeau's only regular income was the 3000 *livres* (about £132) allowed him under his bankruptcy out of the 8500 settled on him at the time of his marriage. He was still burdened with 112,000 *livres* of pre-bankruptcy debt. The Marquis and the Bailli had paid off 50,000, which was slightly less than the total deducted from the Count's income in the ten years which had elapsed, so that his accusation that his father had done nothing to put him right, while unjust, had some foundation. A father anxious to restore his son's credit could and would have done more. On the other hand Mirabeau had in the meantime added a fresh 50,000 *livres* to his liabilities. These new debts were not, of course, strictly legal, but they could not in practice be repudiated any more than those provided for under his *interdiction*. Mirabeau's problem, then, in 1784 was how to carry 50,000 *livres* of debt while living on 3000 a year.

Thrown off by his father, he had at least the consolation that this would be the best possible recommendation to his mother, and he actually coaxed that moody and unpredictable lady into borrowing from a moneylender, on wildly unfavourable terms, a nominal 30,000, out of which he was to receive in cash, and without liability, the sum of 19,000. Momentarily flush, and all creditors forgotten, Mirabeau set up in an expensive way in the Chaussée d'Antin, and he was living thus when, in 1784, Henriette de Nehra entered his life.

She assumed the office of controller-general of their finances. They moved to inexpensive furnished rooms, the horses were sold to pay the corn-merchant's bill, the coachman was dismissed and domestic staff cut to a minimum. 'Yet-Lie' watched the laundry-lists and mended the linen with her own hands. Accounts were kept, and Gabriel was even prevailed upon to report whenever he broke into a gold *louis*. When he made her presents he would hasten to assure her how cheap they were; when, later, she paid the bill, she would discover the price; in the case of trinkets the jeweller could sometimes be persuaded to take them back.

Henriette brought into Mirabeau's life something more than a measure of economic order. She divined that it was not as a lover but as a father that he might attain some degree of moral stability and she took it upon herself to provide for his need.

A sculptor called Montigny had repudiated the son to whom his wife gave birth in 1782, and Mirabeau, the real father, had adopted the infant in the following year. When, after the return from England, Henriette saw some hope of a settled home, she offered to take this three year, child to herself and be a mother to him. As once with little Victor and again with Sophie-Gabrielle, so now with 'Coco' (as they called him) Mirabeau was fondly absorbed. His adopted son was to have all the advantages which his own childhood had wanted, and of these the first was a mother's watchful care. 'I want him to be with you as much as possible,' he wrote to Henriette when away from home; 'otherwise people will get him into the habit of lying, of being polite as people are in society, of being a parrot — everything, in fact, which I dislike. I implore you, *chère amie*, watch over your foster-child.' When 'Coco' started childish lying his father explained that he must be punished but at the same time be given so much liberty that he would not be tempted, and he must be rewarded for increasing truthfulness. Hearing that 'Coco' had learnt a lesson well he wrote: 'Tell him that I don't intend to engage a secretary, since I'm counting on him when I come home.'[69]

Mirabeau did not live to have 'Coco' for his secretary, but the child, known to the world as Lucas de Montigny, lived to be the appointed guardian of his memory. Cared for in his later youth by Madame du Saillant, he devoted himself thereafter to the collection of material for a great vindication of his father's character and career. It appeared in 1834, a work in eight volumes entitled *Mémories, biographiques, littéraires et politiques de Mirabeau*. 'If this man', wrote Montigny in his introduction, 'who has been accused of having *sold* himself, had not died without fortune, poverty would not have forced his adopted son to put off the fulfilment of this most sacred duty, during more than thirty years spent in an obscure employment.'

8

In 1776 Turgot, the economist, had been dismissed from the ministry of finance, and had been replaced by Necker, a rich German-Swiss banker from Geneva, who had made an early fortune in association with the Paris bank of Thélusson and by some well-timed speculations in British funds during the Seven Years War. His appointment was an act of deference by declining monarchy to the rising power of international finance.

France was a rich country but the state was verging on bankruptcy; the King was an absolute despot, yet unable to draw on the principal resources of his kingdom. Such was the paradox of the *ancien régime*. The richest sources of revenue were beyond the government's reach, protected from the tax-gatherer by a high, thick, ornate and totally obsolete wall of privileges, personal, regional and corporate. The remedy — demolition of the wall — was as obvious in theory as it was difficult in practice, for the King was surrounded in his daily life by the *noblesse d'épée* whose first privilege was to attend him, and obstructed in his legislative acts by the privileged *noblesse de robe*. These were usually able to persuade the nation that their *parlements* were the one remaining barrier against tyranny, while the converse and equally valid proposition — that they were the chief obstacle to reform — was one which the government was never able to place before the nation at large. The Byzantinism with which Louis XIV had surrounded the monarchy had fatally weakened its power of popular appeal, so that Maupeou's suppression of the *parlements* had been misunderstood by an angry nation, and the first act of the well-intentioned Louis XVI had been to gratify an apparent popular demand by restoring those lawyers' corporations to their old privileged position. It was the first and not the least of his many mistakes.

Only a major surgical operation on French society could achieve justice for taxpayers and a sufficient revenue for the state. Turgot had prepared to operate and he had been dismissed. Necker never dared to suggest the knife at all. With loans and manipulations he masked the symptoms instead of treating the disease, but he won a reputation for ability and rectitude by publishing a national balance-sheet, his *Compte rendu* of 1781. That it was cooked was not visible to the majority, who were sufficiently impressed that the national accounts should have been rendered at all. But the King never really liked Necker, which is one reason why he fell in the same year.

After the short and embarrassed ministries of Fleury and D'Ormesson it was decided to entrust a minister of the wizard variety with the intriguing task of achieving national solvency without hurting anybody's feelings. The Queen's old tutor, the Abbé Vermont, favoured Loménie de Brienne, Archbishop of Toulouse, but the King had a prejudice against free-thinking prelates, and it was therefore upon the candidate favoured by the Queen's favourite, Madame de Polignac, that the election fell. Such were the auspices under which, at the beginning of October 1783, Charles-Alexandre, Comte de Calonne, became Controller-General of Finances. Handsome, bland and plausible, he had at least one qualification for handling the nation's creditors in an easy familiarity with the art of handling his own.

He hastened to convince the privileged that they had nothing to fear. D'Ormesson had ventured to cancel the patents whereby the tax-farmers sucked nourishment from the nation's fiscal arteries. Calonne restored them. Then he hastened to the rescue of the *Caisse d'escompte*, France's nearest approach to a national bank. D'Ormesson, having demanded a loan of 6 millions when the bank had already over-issued its notes, had been obliged to authorize a suspension of cash payments. Calonne repaid the 6 millions, and payments were resumed. Certain arrears of interest on government loans were paid up, public expenditure was increased and, by 1785, Calonne was presiding over a stock-market boom in which the shares of the *Caisse d'escompte* stood at a premium of 183 per cent.

This increased Calonne's popularity but also his difficulties. With such attractive investments to be had as the shares of the *Caisse d'escompte* and of its associate, Cabarrus's Spanish Bank of St. Charles, or of the new Paris Water Company with its novel steam-pumps, government securities were being left in the cold. Indeed, a boom which made it harder for the government to borrow was the last thing Calonne wanted, so he decided to promote bear activities against the market favourites in order to redress the balance, and to employ as his principal agent a Genevese rival of Necker, the financier Panchaud.

It was Panchaud who, at the instance of Turgot, had founded the *Caisse d'escompte*, but he was no longer directly concerned with it. With a gift for publicity and social intercourse, Panchaud had become banker to the Court, and had drawn round him a circle of intelligent and adventurous men which included the Abbé de Périgord (Talleyrand), the Duc de Lauzun (Mirabeau's comrade-in-arms in the Corsican expedition), the Comte de Narbonne, Dupont de Nemours, Chamfort and Clavière. It was Clavière who now introduced Mirabeau to Panchaud, and so placed him in Calonne's field of vision just when that minister was looking about for a man with a telling pen.

Faced with an annual deficit in the region of 80 million *livres*, Calonne had, since taking office, borrowed 225 millions. The decree authorizing his last loan had been registered, however, only after much hesitation and criticism by the *parlement*, and now, in 1785, his loans were sagging badly; which was alarming, for he foresaw the necessity of raising another 80 millions in the current year. Panchaud's bear dealings should help to improve the relative market value of the public funds, but Calonne thought a press campaign might help as well. In Mirabeau, whom Panchaud thought 'the first man in the world to speak on a question about which he knows nothing', he thought he saw the instrument he needed.

Mirabeau, who once said that all a man needed in order to be an eagle in finance was to know his four rules of arithmetic and how to conjugate *avoir*, had already done a piece of writing for Clavière and Panchaud. This was a tract on the *Caisse d'escompte* which had appeared in May. Banks, it maintained, should be under governmental control not only as to the extent of their note-issue, but also as to the size of their dividends, for a feature of the boom was a reckless speculation in these futures. On the other hand, direct government interference with the market, such as the Minister's recent decree cancelling retrospectively certain dealings, was unjust and pernicious.

Whatever Mirabeau now wrote was sure of a public, and the shares of the *Caisse d'escompte* fell. Calonne took note, and forthwith employed him against the Bank of St. Charles. As a matter of fact Clavière and Brissot had a pamphlet on that subject just ready for the press, but Calonne persuaded them to hand it over to Mirabeau, who touched it up and published it under his own name. Brissot was not pleased, but the St. Charles shares dropped from 800 to 420 and Calonne was — at first. Then he became nervous. The Spanish ambassador complained and so did the chief of the injured speculators, the great banker Le Couteulx de la Noraye. Yielding to their pressure Calonne proceeded coolly to suppress the pamphlet as 'being the work of one of those persons who dare to write on important matters in which they are insufficiently versed to give the public useful information'. Swallowing his fury, Mirabeau relieved his feelings a little by writing against Le Couteulx de la Noraye, chief bull in the bank-share market. Calonne suppressed that pamphlet too.

But he had come to realize that Mirabeau was no mere venal scribbler. The bulls had been so hard hit by the St. Charles pamphlet that they were in danger of defaulting, and Calonne, for the second time, was meditating a decree for the retrospective cancellation of dealings. Remembering Mirabeau's former attack on this kind of thing, he tried to win his silence by taking him into his confidence; but, though gratified by this approach, Mirabeau was not to be talked over. He found himself antagonistic to the juggling opportunism of this minister. It was scarcely a matter of principle, but rather one of innate prejudice. Gambling had never been one of his vices, and his personal fecklessness over money did not exclude from the basement of his mind a certain obstinate feeling that money ought to be earned, and that, as his father had taught, the soil, not the stock-market, was the source of honest wealth.[70]

For Calonne had now gone over to the bulls. His campaign against the bank shares had succeeded, but the prices of the public funds had fallen in sympathy, so that nothing had been gained. Besides, Calonne was himself a large shareholder in a concern which would infallibly suffer if bear operations went on. At his first interview with the King he had, with an air of candour suited to the man and the occasion, admitted private debts amounting to 220,000 *livres*, whereupon Louis had opened his desk and handed him shares worth 230,000 in the newly founded *Compagnie des Eaux de Paris*. Issued at 1200, the Water Company's shares stood in 1785 at well over 3000.[71]

In October Mirabeau's third financial pamphlet, a criticism of the Paris Water Company, appeared. It was, unlike the former two, mainly his own work. It objected to the project of handing over the total water supply of Paris to a private monopoly, and cast doubt on the practicability of pumping water to every house in Paris. The old system of public fountains and water-carriers was well enough, and the Water Company was promising more than it could, or should, perform. Clavière, anticipating this publication, had sold his Water shares and made a packet.

The water-carriers, very numerous and threatened with unemployment, were delighted, and Mirabeau enjoyed his first taste of popularity with the working class of Paris. But Calonne was much vexed. Clavière was hauled up and told sharply to stop writing on these topics, and Mirabeau was divided between indignation at this muzzling order and anger that his tract should have been attributed to Clavière, who, for once, had not written most of it. Calonne was not vindictive, but he was finding Mirabeau so unbiddable that he was considering locking him up for a spell when Lauzun and Talleyrand, who were on good terms with both, advised their threatened friend to leave the country till the dust had settled. Germany, where the reign of the great Frederick was clearly drawing to its close, might be worth a visit, and perhaps, if the Count specialized in the study of German politics, some sort of mission might be given him later.

Mirabeau took their advice, but with no indecent haste. For there had been a reply to his Water Company pamphlet, and it had come from Beaumarchais, better known as the author of that recent and resounding success, the *Mariage de Figaro*, than as a director of the *Compagnie des Eaux*. Mirabeau wrote a rejoinder. It was the charge of the fighting bull against the matador, for Beaumarchais had one gift which had been denied to his assailant — the rapier of wit. When Mirabeau put himself forward as the champion of decent family men in danger of losing their savings in the Water Company, there were those who asked if he had not also been denied a sense of the ridiculous. Yet as he reflected on the episode he had reason for self-satisfaction, for the water shares had come down from 3600 to 2000, and were staying down. Further, in his reply to Beaumarchais he had hit back at Calonne, explaining that his attacks on speculation had been written at the Minister's express wish.

It was after he had gone to Germany that he learnt that the St. Charles directors, reporting to their shareholders, had written: 'It is certain that, in order to discredit the Bank, use has been made of one of those unfortunate men whose lives are a long alternation of crimes and punishments, and who devote to speaking evil the few moments left to them by their habit of doing it.' That such words had been printed without Calonne's permission was scarcely to be believed, and Mirabeau at once wrote an open letter to the Minister which was as recklessly damning as it was justified. But the explosion was muffled. Lauzun and Talleyrand managed to prevent publication and told their friend that it would ruin him utterly. At the same time they suggested to Calonne that some sort of diplomatic mission might have the double advantage of keeping the unruly pamphleteer away from France yet beholden to the government.[72]

9

Mirabeau together with Henriette and 'Coco' reached Berlin on January 19th, 1786. He arrived full of eagerness to balance his education in theoretic politics by adding to his knowledge of England a study of the most perfected despotism in Europe. But except for a note from Vergennes introducing him to the ambassador, the Comte d'Esterno, and the acquaintance of a certain Marquis de Luchet who was attached to Prince Henry of Prussia, he had neither introductions nor resources. Within three days of his arrival, therefore, he wrote to the King direct. It was not particularly surprising that Frederick the Great should reply by return of post; his punctiliousness in these matters and his interest in foreign visitors were well known. But even Mirabeau may have rubbed his eyes when he opened the royal missive and read ' . . . I much appreciate the offer which you have made to present yourself here . . . If you would care to give me this pleasure the day after tomorrow . . .'[73]

It was a brief audience, to be sure. The visitor, moved by the sight of the soldier-despot, arbiter of peace and war in Europe for a lifetime, sitting shrivelled and weak before the fire, spoke little. But the next day he ventured to put in a letter something he had left unsaid because of the presence of others. Ill rewarded for his 'truly great services' to his country in the sphere of finance, and embroiled with M. de Calonne, he had, he explained, left France partly for safety and partly in search of employment. His immediate intention (this in strict confidence to His Majesty alone) was to push on to Russia, the country most ready to employ foreigners, since he could not, of course, hope to be of use to a government so perfectly staffed and organized as that of Prussia.

With this last opinion King Frederick tacitly agreed, though he sent back a courteous note telling the Count that he was welcome to stay in Berlin as long as he pleased, and that the King hoped to see him again one day.

In search of useful acquaintances and avid for information, Mirabeau proceeded to make contacts. He met Dohm and other savants, and made two friendships of special importance. One was that of Major Mauvillon, a military engineer of French extraction and professor at the Carolineum College at Brunswick. Deeply versed in the politico-economic structure of central Europe, he was attracted by the inquisitive and synthetizing vigour of Mirabeau's mind. He put his knowledge without reserve at the Frenchman's disposal, and the latter was more eager to make use of it than to acknowledge publicly the extent of his debt. But Mauvillon had no jealousy, and when, in 1788, there appeared under Mirabeau's name eight octavo volumes of a work entitled *The Prussian Monarchy under Frederick the Great, with an Appendix containing Researches on the present condition of the principal regions of Germany*, he resented so little the fact that, though the bulk of the work was his own, his name appeared but once in a rather cursory acknowledgment in the preface, that he continued in a warm and regular correspondence with the nominal author. He later declared that his share had been to rough-hew the work, and that without Mirabeau's power to impart finish it would never have been fit for the press. Mirabeau, if less than generous to his collaborator, had the considerable grace to dedicate *De la monarchie prussienne* to the Friend whom Mankind had begun to forget, 'not only as to one of the inventors of that noble science of political economy which should one day bring about the happiness of the world, but also, my Father, to atone a little by this worthy employment of my mature years for the troubles which my stormy youth may have caused you'. But the Marquis was only a little mollified. His son's physiocracy proved, on examination, none too sound, while his sneers at Catholicism were as offensive as they were uncalled for.

The other notable friendship made on this first visit to Berlin was that of Prince Henry, brother of the King. Frederick the Great had always had a predilection for things French, but there was now in Prussia a conscious movement in the opposite direction, a growing feeling that Prussia should be ethically and culturally the sun of Germany rather than a satellite of France. Those who wished to scrape the Gallic veneer off Prussia and reveal the honest German timber beneath reckoned among their number the future Frederick-William II, and the French Foreign Ministry, knowing that cultural preferences may be determinants in diplomacy, regarded the impending succession of old Frederick's impressionable nephew with disquiet, and pinned its hopes for the continuance of French influence upon Prince Henry, the most Francophil of the Hohenzollerns. Yet when Prince Henry took a sudden and impulsive liking to Mirabeau, D'Esterno was more vexed than pleased to see the scarcely presentable author of Fauche's banned publications hobnobbing with royalty at Potsdam, and making for himself a position which the Ministry at home might think it worth while to exploit.[74]

For the greater part, however, Mirabeau lived arduous days

in Berlin, picking men's brains, reading voluminously, practising his German, working late into the night and working again, wrapped in his dressing-gown by the cold ashes, before Henriette and 'Coco' were up in the morning. But by mid-April he judged that he had enough material in hand to make an impression in the right quarter at home, so he decided to return to Paris. His note of leave-taking to the King procured the second interview for which he had hoped.

Frederick, though much distressed in his breathing, kept him a whole hour. They talked of the emancipation of the Jews, a subject much in Mirabeau's mind since his coming to Germany. Then he asked the King why he had not, in addition to being the Caesar of Germany, become its Augustus and used his power and genius to foster the literary re-birth of his country. Perhaps those old eyes held for a flash the ironic gleam Voltaire had known, as Frederick asked in reply what boon he could have conferred on German letters half so precious as leaving them alone.

With a pamphlet on the Jews (cribbed from Dohm) in his valise, Mirabeau reached Paris on May 22nd, and called at once on Talleyrand. He had a scheme to put to him: Frederick the Great was dying; Potsdam politics might well be critical for France in the immediate future; the Ambassador, stiff, formal and slow, was not to be relied on to keep pace with the intrigues which would surround the new king; surely the government would see the advantage of sending on a secret mission to Berlin a man of first-rate abilities who enjoyed informal but cordial relations with the most influential personages?

Talleyrand may well have had doubts as to the entire suitability of his voluble friend for a diplomatic mission, but the scheme interested him none the less. Mirabeau was out to win the attention of the government, but so also was he. Agent-general to the Clergy of France, he had done pretty well already; but it was only a beginning. He was hungry for rank, office and wealth — especially wealth — his immediate aim being a bishopric, and in Mirabeau's scheme he saw certain possibilities. Suppose that he were to press the scheme on Calonne? Calonne, he knew, was envious of Vergennes and anxious to replace him at the Foreign Ministry; probably he would do better there than in the Ministry of Finance, and his translation would certainly create an interesting vacancy. It might well tickle his fancy to have his own information service working in Berlin alongside the official ambassadorial outfit, and it would surely be easy to find in that service a function for the Abbé de Périgord which would bring him closer than ever to Calonne. There were rumours of Vergennes retiring; a reshuffle of portfolios seemed likely; in the game of musical chairs one must keep close to the seats or else be left standing when the music stops.[75]

The good turn Talleyrand and Lauzun had done Mirabeau by suppressing his open letter to Calonne now made it possible for them to put forward his idea of a secret mission with hope of success, and Calonne, the least rancorous of men, invited Mirabeau to send him something in writing on the European situation. Leaping at the chance to show the Minister that, if he was an eagle in finance, he was a lion in foreign affairs, Mirabeau sent him an exceedingly able report *On the Present Situation in Europe*. Calonne was impressed and so was Talleyrand. Vergennes, not averse from the establishment of a second line of communication with Berlin so long as his department was not committed and Calonne's department paid, approved in principle of the secret mission though scarcely of the choice of Mirabeau, of whom he knew so little that was good and about whom D'Esterno had been sending him sufficiently acid comments.

Nevertheless it was arranged that the Count should return to Berlin and send home a series of confidential dispatches. These would go first to Talleyrand, who would decipher and edit them (and display, incidentally, his own talents hardly less than the Count's); the Abbé would then pass the letters to Calonne, who would pass them to Vergennes, who would show them to the King.

Mirabeau had reason to be pleased. He had got what he had wanted for the last four years, a diplomatic mission. That it was secret, that he had no official status, was a drawback of which he was soon to complain bitterly. For the moment, however, what mattered was that he had a salary and an opportunity in the service of France. Setting out on July 3rd, 1786, he stopped a few days at Brunswick as the guest of the Duke, and rejoined Henriette in Berlin on the twenty-first of the month.

His mission lasted six months, during which he sent back over sixty-five letters, many of considerable length. His superiors could not complain of his industry, and indeed, since he received a mere 300 *louis* in all, they were getting exceptional value for their money. Talleyrand, his 'dear master', sometimes had occasion not only to reduce the verbal bulk of his reports but also to remove indiscretions and errors of taste.

The letters from Berlin are of the greatest interest. Though much space was necessarily given to court gossip of merely momentary importance, the reading of these letters, together with the previous memorandum *On the Present Situation of Europe* and certain authentic passages in *The Prussian Monarchy*, obliges us to recognize in Mirabeau qualities of a very high order. Probably he would never have made even a passable diplomat; he was too impulsive, too indiscreet and, it has to be admitted, too thick-skinned. Prince Henry realized this, and became careful not to let him have autograph letters of any significance, a precaution for which he later had good reason to be thankful. But there is in these writings, nevertheless, a powerful sweep of the mind, an integration of multifarious details into a grand general scheme, which tempts one to guess that their author had it in him to be great in the Ministry of Foreign Affairs. There, at the centre, he would have been at home, giving to his country's policy a consistent impulse and direction, while leaving the delicacies of diplomatic intercourse to his agents. Mere surmise this, of course, but what at least is certain is that Mirabeau was supreme as a commentator on current affairs, and gifted with an almost uncanny prevision of the shape of many things to come.

As he looks at Europe he sees three powers which are, each in its way, a menace to the peace.

The first is the Austria of Joseph II. The Emperor is a menace because he is a restless spirit, always up to something. Will he, when the weak Frederick-William succeeds the victor of Leuthen, start a war of revenge against Prussia for the loss of Silesia? Will he set Europe in flames by renewing his designs on Bavaria? Or is Turkey to be his victim and Russia his ally? In either case France is directly concerned, for she can accept neither the destruction of the Central-European balance nor a threat to her special commercial privileges under the Sultan.

But Joseph II would be less of a menace were he not bound hand and foot to Catherine II of Russia. In that confederacy lies the real danger to the eastward. Mirabeau sees Russia projecting a great south-eastward expansion whither the Volga and the Caspian point the way, and, with a pretty anticipation of troubles that were to absorb Palmerston and Disraeli, he remarks that Britain had better be thinking of her security in India. 'What revolutions, what clashes of peoples and interests will result from the unrolling of the destinies of this great empire, which enslaves and dominates successively everything which surrounds and adjoins it! . . . What kind of head, then, must the Emperor have, if he cannot be persuaded that it is better for him to have the Turks and the Poles as neighbours rather than this strange nation, ready for everything, capable of anything, producing the best soldiers in the world and the most malleable people on earth?' Mirabeau foresees the end of truncated Poland: Prussia is up to no good in that quarter, but still it is Joseph who looks like being the prime mover: 'Think of Poland, I adjure you! What they have done there they will do again, and that even without the intervention of Russia, that sleeping giant whose awakening could change the face of the globe.'[76]

Still it is from Austria that he sees the immediate menace — the menace of a unification of Germany. His belief that Vienna, not Berlin, was likely to prove the cuckoo in the German nest is the one really big miscalculation in his long-range forecasts, but the meaning for France of such a unification he sees with the lucidity of a Clémenceau. 'Suppose Germany to be united under one sceptre,' he writes in *De la monarchie prussienne*. 'In that case the outcome of this conflict [between French and Germans] becomes, to say the least, very uncertain. The French nation is not so military as the German. We are better duellists, no doubt, but incontestably less good as soldiers; we are more active, more impetuous, more capable of the impossible, but less capable of calm, of subordination, of order and of discipline (and that is almost everything in war) . . . For the rest, we live under a pleasanter, richer and more abundant clime, and therefore, as possessors, we shall always live under constant threat of attack by those who wish to possess.'

The third country which Mirabeau sees as a potential disturber of the peace is Britain, sore after her defeat in the late war yet growing so rapidly in wealth that she may be tempted to a war of revenge against the Bourbon powers. Britain's policy, he thinks, is to encourage Prussia to resist Austrian pretensions even to the point of war; such a war, she calculates, will, under existing treaties, bring France in on Austria's side, and at once Britain has her chance of renewing her triumphs of the Seven Years War. But Britain alone will not *start* a war; neither will Prussia (except possibly over Poland) and neither, it goes without saying, will France. This, for Mirabeau, is the key to European peace; here, in these three states, is a triangle of fundamentally peace-loving powers, and French wisdom will consist in adding to the existing Anglo-Prussian understanding a Franco-Prussian alliance and a Franco-British treaty of commerce. [77]

Mirabeau's conception of this triangle of peace owed something to the Duke of Brunswick. This destined commander of the beaten side at Valmy was, in 1786, an advocate of the addition of France to that Anglo-Prussian entente which it was a function of his House to represent. But though Mirabeau at this time liked and admired the Duke, his own conviction that France and England ought to come together was no second-hand notion or novel fad, but the fruit of ruminations whose traces can be found at least as early as his letters from Vincennes.

It was a conviction which was shared by Talleyrand and Lauzun; and when, on September 26th, 1786, a commercial treaty was, with the blessing of Vergennes, signed by Lauzun (for Calonne) and by Eden (for Pitt), the three friends could congratulate each other that they had created around Calonne the climate of opinion in which he had performed the one wholly creditable act of his ministry.

Though he thought Prussia a power making for European stability, and securing for the German peoples 'the incalculable advantage of living in small states', Mirabeau was not blind to the nature of the Prussian thing. [78] He was impressed by the ceremony of the military oath to the new sovereign. 'Nevertheless,' he wrote, 'all this martial pomp . . . is in my opinion too purely and simply a display of military power; it seems to say: "I am, above all, king of the soldiers. I rely on my army because I am not sure of having a kingdom." I am convinced,' Mirabeau added, 'that these purely military forms will be modified under the new reign.' [79] So, it seemed, were many Prussians. Mirabeau was much struck by the public reaction to the great Frederick's death: 'Depression everywhere, but nowhere grief', he writes on the day of the decease. 'Business as usual and no lamentations. Not a face but expresses relief and hope; no regrets, no sighs, no words of praise; this, then, is the end of all those victorious battles, of all that glory. A reign of nearly half a century! Everyone wished for its end and everyone is glad of it'. A month later he adds: 'Today two-thirds of Berlin vie with each other in proving that Frederick II was an ordinary man, almost below the average. Ah! if only those great eyes which, at the bidding of his heroic spirit, could fascinate or terrify at will, could open again for one instant, would these flattering imbeciles have the courage to die of shame?' A slavish people fundamentally. When Mirabeau witnessed the new king's reception of the Estates of Prussia, he remarked that nothing was wanting to the solemnity of the occasion but rather more dignity on the part of the deputies and the appearance, at least, of free discussion.

Frederick-William II lacked all the great qualities of his predecessor as well as any of his own. Gone was the wonderful exactness and order which had reigned in the cabinet of the old king. The prey of designing mistresses and visionary quacks, sitting reluctantly at a desk littered thick with unread state papers in wild disorder — such was now the head of the Prussian state. Nor was the new king even soldierly. His attendance at reviews was perfunctory and brief, a change indeed from Frederick II, who 'covered with years and glory, regularly spent two hours, in the depth of winter, drilling, cursing, praising and incessantly driving the troops who, although tormented, were overjoyed to see The Old Man (as they called him) at their head'. [80]

Such a successor as Frederick-William II was clearly in need of advice, nor was Mirabeau the man to withhold it. There is, unfortunately, no record of the expression on Talleyrand's face when he read a letter dated August 22nd, five days, that is, after the death of Frederick the Great, in which his correspondent wrote: 'I have sent my great *mémoire* to the King; he has simply acknowledged the receipt, adding that I might be sure that what-

ever reached him from me would always give him pleasure.'
Frederick II might have been tickled; Frederick-William II
was not amused. As for Prince Henry, when he found that he
had been recommended to his nephew and sovereign by this French
adventurer, he told the Ambassador that it would be well if his
government were to send to Berlin in future none but officers
of rank and proven discretion; the Marquis de Lafayette, who
had made the most happy impression on a recent visit, would,
he suggested, be *persona grata*.

Yet, for all the *gaucherie* of its address, the letter to Frederick-
William is a remarkable document. Employing boldly the term
laisser-aller, the writer warns the King against governing too much.
More freedom is what Prussia and most other states chiefly need.
Let trade be freed from the restricting tangle of duties and imposts
which formed the protective system of Frederick II, and (the
physiocratic panacea) let the government draw its revenue from
one universal tax on land. Let the bourgeois be free to buy landed
estates, and so bring fresh capital and fresh brains to enhance the
value of the land. Let all subjects be free to emigrate, and so
demonstrate that loyalty and happiness, not compulsion, keep
them at home. Let the army be recruited by free enlistment;
its quality will improve, and the saving on the machinery of compulsion at home and enticement abroad will offset the cost of
higher pay. Let the King break down the social barrier separating
military from civil officials, a barrier which, should a weak king
ever come to the throne, must lead to pretorian government.
Above all, let the King be on his guard against aristocracy:

> The most absolute monarch's interests are coincident with
> the principles of popular government. It is not kings that the
> peoples fear and resent; it is their ministers, their courtiers,
> their nobles — in a word, aristocracy. *If the King only knew,*
> they say. They always invoke royal authority, and are always
> ready to give it a free hand against aristocracy. And who
> are the prince's enemies if not the grandees, the aristocrats,
> who would like the King to be among them no more than
> *the first amongst equals*?

Soon, very soon, there would be a time for such a word to the
King of France. But Mirabeau had scarcely improved what
chance he ever had of being in a position to speak it.

CHAPTER VIII

SCANDALS AND ELECTIONS

IN mid-summer, 1786, Jean Pierre Brissot was pursuing as usual the welfare of mankind. No official word had yet been spoken of any appeal by the government to the people, but the air was already vibrant with rumour that some sort of election and representation was imminent. As the last sands of the credit of the old régime ran out, anxiety, speculation and hope darted like sparks from mind to mind, and the head of Brissot coruscated with eagerness to publish something that would be of advantage to the commonwealth.

It happened that he had in his possession a copy of a work on provincial administration and assemblies. He had been given it by Clavière and understood it to have come originally from the pen of Turgot. Since that minister had now been dead for five years, and since this essay of his seemed especially applicable to the country's present needs, Brissot felt that to print it would only be to do what its great author would have wished. He was making the preliminary arrangements when, meeting Mirabeau, just back from his first visit to Berlin, he mentioned the matter to him as a matter of interest.

Somewhat to his surprise Mirabeau, instead of applauding the project with his customary enthusiasm, began to raise objections; but as he offered no solid reason against publication and as it was not exactly his business anyway, Brissot went ahead. Then it became apparent that Mirabeau's opposition was something more than a disinterested opinion, for he came to Brissot and pressed his objections with such insistence as even to hint darkly that publication might lead to a *lettre de cachet*; the implication seemed to be that the Count, being in close touch with Calonne, had inside knowledge of his disposition and that Brissot, who had not, had better be careful.

Then Mirabeau returned to Germany, but Brissot was not yet free from his odd and menacing gesticulations. He received a letter which, after a lot of elaborate courtesies, came to the point, to wit 'a manuscript which, by a piece of indiscreet thoughtless-

ness, M. Clavière has entrusted to you, and which, with an impru-
dence infinitely more serious, you have been on the point of printing . . . I cannot repeat too emphatically that the publication of
this manuscript would compromise me so completely that it
would do me an irreparable injury, for which it would be no
compensation to see myself forced to hand you over perhaps to the
judgment of the authorities, certainly to that of the public.
Finally, Sir — and this is the real consideration which I would
put to your conscience — you would hinder, not to say frustrate,
the most important operation ever planned for the regeneration
of France. . . .'

All this was both mystifying and vexatious, and even a little
shocking. What business was it of Mirabeau's? What was all
this about the publication of Turgot's paper 'compromising him'?
What was this 'important operation for the regeneration of France'?
Why this mystification, these veiled threats? What had so agitated
Mirabeau that he, of all men, should threaten a friend with a
lettre de cachet? Had he some sort of proprietary right over the
work? But if so, why not say so? If Brissot had had any inkling
of this, would he have mentioned his plan of publication so
casually in the first place?

Such were the queries and complaints which he put in a letter to
Talleyrand for him to forward to the Count. The Abbé forwarded
the letter and added some pretty sharp observations of his own;
for he knew, which Brissot did not, that Mirabeau had, the previous year, sold this same essay on provincial administration to
Calonne as his own work. Since Mirabeau's present income
depended on Calonne's favour, it was easy to see why he was
alarmed at the prospect of the essay which he had sold as his own
work for the Minister's private use being published to the world
as a work of Turgot.

Mirabeau, it would seem, had forgotten that Clavière had had a
copy in his possession for some time past; but what he can hardly
have forgotten was a fact known probably to only one other person
— that the essay in question was the work of neither Turgot, as
Clavière and Brissot believed, nor of himself, as Calonne had been
assured, but of Dupont de Nemours. It was the composition which
he had shown to Mirabeau to relieve his boredom in Vincennes, and
of which the studious prisoner had made and quietly kept a copy.

To raise money and to impress the Controller-General Mirabeau had sold him another man's property, and no scruple seems to have worried him till the deception looked like being discovered. Yet what did he expect? Dupont, whom Calonne had made Director of Commerce, was certain to take notice of the piracy, and even if it did not become a public scandal it was certain to become common knowledge to the whole circle to which Dupont as well as Mirabeau belonged. It was a circle which found many things easier to forgive than deliberate violation of a friend's copyright, yet a year later, after Calonne had gone, he coolly sold Dupont's essay again, this time to the public and, this time, as being the work of Turgot.[81]

2

Calonne had bought the essay on provincial administration partly to gratify a man whose pen could derange his financial contrivances and partly because he was genuinely on the look-out for ideas. He was intelligent enough to know that France was not to be saved by loans and stock-jobbing expedients alone, and that some programme of constitutional reform was necessary to restore the public confidence upon which everything ultimately depended. But his light mind carried no system of its own and his search for a constitutional policy was entirely opportunist. He snatched at ideas and projects in the spirit of a company promotor anxious above all for something which would look well in the prospectus.

Mirabeau, while obliged to keep in with the Minister upon whom his Berlin job depended, had no illusions about him and watched his rake's progress with intense interest. It was, indeed, worth watching. For in 1786, unable to raise the money he needed by further public loans, Calonne began to dabble on the bourse. But Calonne was the government and a certain circumspection had to be observed, so he proceeded in the following manner.

Treasury bills to the value of 11½ million *livres* and falling due at the end of 1787 were deposited with the *Caisse d'escompte*. The bank was instructed to treat these bills as collateral for loans it was to make to two groups of investors named by the Minister, and these loans were to be used by these 'investment trusts' for bulling the shares of the *Cie. des Eaux de Paris* and the *Cie. des Indes*. These were the principal objects of speculation on the bourse, and Calonne's hope was that if their quotations remained high prices in general would benefit — in particular the shares of the *Caisse d'escompte*; for (apart from his private interest in the Water Company) it was with the shares of the *Caisse d'escompte* that he was really concerned. He had brought about a revision of this bank's statutes so as to authorize an increase of its capital by 80 million new shares, and of these he had arranged that 70 millions should be alloted to the Treasury by the gratified directors. In plain words, since the public would no longer lend the government the money it required, the Controller-General had invented a mass of new shares in the state bank, had kept seven-eighths of them for the government and was now trying to keep up their value by employing secret agents to create a totally artificial boom on the strength of the government's own post-dated cheque.

The syndicate formed to bull the India shares consisted of three persons, Seneff, Pyron and Barroud, and they went to work with such reckless enterprise and such inadequate instructions that very soon they had bought up nearly all the India shares in existence, a number far in excess of what Calonne wished to hold or they could possibly pay for. They had overrun the mark and their problem was how to unload their colossal holding without breaking the market. Help of a kind was, however, at hand in the person of one who could scarcely have flourished in his special form and character in any other time and place. This was the Abbé d'Espagnac, aristocrat, canon of Paris and vicar-general of Sens, later fraudulent contractor to the armies of the Republic and companion of Danton on the scaffold. Now, in 1786, an ecclesiastic of thirty-three years, he was probably the most audacious speculator on the Paris bourse, and it was he who had sold (though not delivered) most of the India shares so avidly bought up (but not paid for) by Seneff & Co. Knowing well enough their difficulties he now bought back the *whole* of their holding for later settlement, and he then proceeded to buy India shares on the open market till he had acquired all the shares in existence and some 9000 more into the bargain. The result, of course, was a spectacular rise in India stock and sleepless nights for many who wondered how they were to get India shares for delivery by settling date at the end of March 1787. The Abbé d'Espagnac had placed Calonne's agents and a good many other people at his mercy, but he had also risked inducing a scandal which might bring down the Controller-General and heaven knew what else besides.[82]

3

While these things were happening in Paris Mirabeau, in Berlin, was feeling increasingly frustrated. Pleased enough at the outset with his secret mission, he soon began to resent the slights he received from the Ambassador, the apparent lack of interest shown by the government and the gross inadequacy of the fifty *louis* a month put at his disposal. 'I realize better than anyone', he writes to Lauzun in November 1786, 'how mediocre my harvest is, but it should not be forgotten that I have neither pecuniary means nor ministerial advantages.' Did not they realize that information came through contacts which meant entertainment which meant expense? To Talleyrand he complains: 'I have neither the cash nor the necessary means for discovering details,' and he adds with a touch of bitterness: 'I am acknowledged neither directly not indirectly. At any moment the authorities could dispose of me and my papers, and I should be ruined here and at home for having shown an incautious zeal.' At the end of December he writes: 'They are poor judges of men who think to make of me nothing but a reporter. . . .'

He was, in short, sick of it. But his impatience would have been less had he not known that France was big with new things, that Calonne had emptied his box of tricks and that the government had reached at last the point where it must borrow not simply money with which to pay but authority with which to act.

It was on December 29th, 1786, that Louis XVI announced that he intended to convoke an Assembly of Notables.

This hand-picked assembly of privileged or influential men, topped by the princes of the blood, would, Calonne hoped, accept the necessity for such curtailment of fiscal immunities as would make a balanced budget possible. There was, of course, no question of the Notables exercising any legislative power; the business was simply to coax them into lending the force of their eminence to reforms so far-reaching that they were beyond the government's moral, though not its legal, competence. In particular it was hoped that a vote of confidence by the Notables would stultify in advance the obstruction which might be confidently expected from the *parlements* when called upon to register drastic decrees.

Calonne's plan of action would not, indeed, have been a bad one had it not been for one factor in the situation — his own reputation. His personal charm and olympian self-assurance had sufficed to carry all before it in the early days of his ministry, but his gay personal extravagance, his fashionable vices and his debts, condoned by smart people so long as he seemed to be saving the state's solvency together with their privileges, told heavily against him as soon as he began to ask for assistance and sacrifices. The Notables, therefore, wasted little time in making clear their opinion that the levity of the Controller-General, not their own privileges, was the true cause of the crisis which had brought them together. Only an unimpeachable reputation could have given Calonne much chance of winning over this assembly of rank, wealth and brains which, a cool but desperate gambler, he had backed himself to dominate. But the failure of his gamble was made certain by the appearance during the second week of the Notables' sessions at Versailles of a little book entitled *Denunciation of Stock-Jobbery*. It was from the pen of Mirabeau.

He had left Berlin on January 20th, disgusted with his unprofitable mission, but he had invented another mission for his government to give him, one, moreover, in which he would be a diplomat and not a reporter. There was trouble afoot in Holland, where a republican party was in revolt against the Stadholder. Since the latter was Frederick-William II's brother-in-law it looked as if Prussian bayonets would put a swift end to Dutch republican aspirations, the more since Britain was intimating to France that if the latter upheld the republicans she would support Prussian intervention with her fleet. Mirabeau was wholeheartedly on the side of the Dutch 'patriots', and thought it disgraceful that France should let Prussia and England turn her old ally Holland into a satellite under a client House of Orange. He had for some time past been in touch with members of the republican party, while on the other hand he had, through the Dutch ambassador at Berlin, contrived, so he thought, to convince the Princess of Orange that he was the true representative of the mind of the French Foreign Office. The opportunity of a lifetime seemed therefore to be almost within his grasp. What other man possessed his special knowledge of the Prussian court together with the confidence of the Dutch democrats? Let the government send him to Holland specially charged to secure a settlement acceptable to the democrats yet dishonourable neither to the House of Orange nor to that of Hohenzollern; France had but to put a firm face on it and Prussia and England would quickly moderate their tone; Dutch liberty would be saved, an awkward obstacle to the formation of the Franco-Anglo-Prussian triangle of peace would be surmounted, French prestige as the champion of liberty would be restored, and Mirabeau would be a made man.[83]

A splendid dream, but no more. Vergennes, who had demurred at the choice of Mirabeau for the unofficial Berlin mission, would never dream of entrusting to this *soi-disant* authority on foreign affairs the forthcoming ticklish negotiations at Nymegen, while Calonne was not Foreign Minister, nor in any way anxious to make the reputation of the man whom he had sent to Prussia partly to oblige his cronies Lauzun and Talleyrand but chiefly because he had been such a nuisance in Paris. When, therefore, Mirabeau, full of himself and the salvation of Europe, returned to Paris he found that another man had been sent to Holland. His chagrin was intense. It was increased by Calonne's neglect to nominate him secretary to the forthcoming assembly. This was another post for which he had been angling, and he felt he had a claim to it since he believed that the minister owed the original idea of assembling the Notables to him. Calonne, however, oblivious of his debt to the vendor of the Essay on Provincial Administration, had given the post to its author, Dupont de Nemours.[84]

So Calonne had sent him to Berlin simply to stop his embarrassing irruptions into the sphere of finance, had he? The secret mission, to which Mirabeau had addressed his incomparable energies in the hope of a career to follow, had been a mere device to amuse him, had it? And now, it seemed, Calonne was saying that all Mirabeau needed to keep him quiet was money. Very well then! Denied honourable employment in the service of his government, he would carve his way to importance by an attack on the Minister's financial methods which would break over him just when he could least support it, when he was making his desperate bid for the confidence of the notabilities of the nation.

Mirabeau had got wind of the strange proceedings of Seneff & Co., and of the cynical audacities of the Abbé d'Espagnac; he had guessed that these pretty goings-on were not unconnected with the recent increase in the authorized capital of the *Caisse d'escompte*, and he had reached the brutal conclusion that his Majesty's Controller-General of Finances had turned his department into something not far removed from a bucketshop. Working with speed and fury he wrote, documented, saw through the press and published — all within five weeks of returning from Berlin — the 143 pages of his *Dénonciation de l'agiotage au roi et à l'assemblée des notables*.

The King read it and remarked sorrowfully that this time, at any rate, Mirabeau had told the truth; the national hero, Lafayette, read it and used it to attack the Minister before the Notables, and on April 8th, 1787, almost exactly a month after its appearance, Calonne was dismissed.

In retrospect Mirabeau's blow may seem to have been aimed at a minister already tottering to his fall. It should, however, be remembered that the *Dénonciation* was written before Calonne had faced the Notables; that Mirabeau had given Talleyrand the manuscript to show him, and that Calonne, though not actually mentioned in it by name, had recognized it as dynamite but had made the mistake of merely offering cash for its suppression. Furthermore, the outcome of Calonne's meeting with the Notables was quite unpredictable. If he were to succeed in bluffing that assembly and retaining office, then prison for Mirabeau was more than probable. In the event an order for his arrest was actually made, though it was never executed because Calonne, amiable even when in the toils, passed him a hint to slip across the frontier for the moment, and because the danger soon vanished with the Minister's fall. But on neither of these things could Mirabeau count when he printed his *Dénonciation*, and its publication must stand, therefore, as an act of courage. 'If I were to write a treatise on politics,' he once remarked, 'I would deal at length with *the art of daring*.'[85]

5

Multifarious activities and abortive projects crowded Mirabeau's days in 1787 and 1788. It was a time of hope deferred and of desperate financial stringency. It witnessed also in his intimate life an erotic storm which drove him out from that calm anchorage of the affections which Henriette had supplied, back into the bitter sea of sterile indulgences where he was to be tossed for his remaining years.

The supreme need of his nature — more essential to him than women's love or men's friendship, hugely as he demanded these — was full and high employment. He wanted money and he courted fame, but these were but means to his end, ways to that fountainhead of government which alone could slake his vital thirst. To say that he was exceedingly ambitious is to miss the peculiarity of his problem. High office was not for him, as for ordinary men of ability, simply the just and desired reward of meritorious years, a thing pleasing to vanity but not essential to sane and balanced living; it was the object of a raging thirst, of an unbearable craving. He wrote and wrote and won fame as a publicist — and that fame was about as much relief to his creative energies as an erotic novel would have been to his inordinate virility.

It was about this time, in these last two years of the old order, that he began perhaps to have his first flickering doubts of success. He was nearly forty, and how little he had to show! Yet what assurance could he have that his prodigious capacity for work and his remarkable gifts would ever receive official recognition? Disowned by his father, rejected by his wife, childless — what standing had he in a society where the fief and the family were the terms of men's thought? Bankrupt, adulterer, fugitive, prisoner, adventurer, controversial scribbler — what chance that authority would select such as he to fill a position of high trust? Two things only, it seemed, might work the miracle: either some sort of political revolution might open up new avenues to advancement in a changed society, or else he might by some remarkable achievement force those who dispensed promotion in the existing order to recognize his claims. Hitherto he had pinned his hopes on this second chance, and the Berlin mission had seemed a fore-taste of success till it ended in disappointment. Nevertheless he must persist with the policy of self-advertisement; not for one moment must either the ministers or the public be allowed to forget him. The secretaryship to the Notables is denied him: he publishes his *Denunciation of Stock-Jobbery* the mission to Holland is given to another: he reasserts himself with an *Adresse aux Bataves* exhorting the democrats to stand firm against the Orange-Hohenzollern plot to enslave them. This work has a decided success, to the considerable annoyance of a certain De Bourges who has written most of it. Then, turning to yet another field, he publishes *Observations d'un voyager anglais sur la maison de force appelée Bicêtre*.

The observant traveller was Romilly, who came to Paris for a holiday in the summer of 1788, accompanied by one of his many Genevese friends, Etienne Dumont. He did not hasten to renew his acquaintance with Mirabeau. The Old Bailey episode may have left in his mouth an after-taste not entirely agreeable to a lawyer of strict principles, and he was perhaps more than half prepared for the notable lack of enthusiasm shown when he mentioned the Count's name to such respectable reformers as the Duc de la Rochefoucauld, M. de Malesherbes and M. de Lafayette. But if he had actually decided to drop Mirabeau, as Dumont asserts, that proved something easier said than done, for Mirabeau discovered his address and looked him up forthwith.

Hearing a carriage draw up at the door Romilly fled to his room and left Dumont to explain to any visitor that he was out. M. de Mirabeau was then announced, and whatever intention Dumont had of getting rid of him melted into irresolution and then evaporated altogether in the genial warmth of this stranger's company. M. Dumont was from Geneva? How near to his heart was that oppressed republic whose misfortunes he knew so well from his good friends Duroveray and Clavière, M. Dumont's compatriots and fellow exiles! Never, he declared, would he be happy until he could liberate that city, nursery of so many famous men, from the fetters imposed upon it by the revolution of 1782. They talked for two hours, and to Dumont it seemed like a minute. Delighted by the Frenchman's impressive knowledge of Genevan politics and European affairs, Dumont's attempt to maintain a front of reserve collapsed so utterly that before the overwhelming visitor took his leave he had limply promised to dine with him that very day.

Thenceforth their holiday was filled with Mirabeau. 'I never saw a man', wrote Dumont, 'who, when he chose, could make himself so agreeable . . . It was impossible to maintain reserve with him; you were forced into familiarity, obliged to forego etiquette and the ordinary forms of society, and call him simply by his name . . . Intimate intercourse with him was attended with a sort of agreeable asperity, a pleasant crudity of expression, more apparent than real; for under the disguise of roughness was to be found all the reality of politeness and flattery.'

One day the travellers went to inspect the Bicêtre. Romilly was shocked at the conditions he found in the hospital and the prison, and spoke of them to Mirabeau the next day. The latter urged Romilly to write something on the matter and let him have it. Then, possessed of the English manuscript, he put it into French along with a tract Romilly had written on the administration of criminal law and published the two together. There was here no breach of confidence; indeed, when Romilly got home he very kindly published his observations on the Bicêtre as being a translation from Mirabeau. Questions of copyright were not to bother two men labouring in neighbouring countries in the common cause of humanity.[86]

It was the glory of England and France at this time to produce the pioneers of the humanitarian movement. Romilly's share in that noble effort is in no danger of oblivion, but the share of Mirabeau, if smaller, deserves to be recalled. He was a foundation member of the *Amis des Noirs*, the society organized by Brissot for the abolition of the Slave Trade, and when with the Revolution the prospect of French abolition became immediate, he was much concerned to concert the French campaign with that of Wilberforce. A real obstacle to abolition in either country was the fear that it would simply leave the profits of the trade to the other while availing the negroes little. One of the longest and certainly one of the most moving of Mirabeau's speeches is the oration on the Slave Trade which he delivered to the Jacobin Club in February 1790. His description of the middle passage of the slaver, 'this long floating coffin', is not easy to forget; nor is the mighty sarcasm with which, answering those who have excused the traffic and minimized its inhumanities, he sets forth the sickening catalogue of horrors: as period follows accusing period, each ends with the words '. . . and this commerce is not inhuman' till the accumulated effect becomes terrible as the voice of Judgment. [87]

In this summer of 1788, while Mirabeau was finding so much time to put at the disposal of his foreign friends, he was busy with the task of seeing through the press the formidable bulk of his (and Mauvillon's) *Monarchie prussienne*. It was a work by which he set great store, no ephemeral pamphlet or topical polemic but something massive which would, he hoped, establish him in the estimation of serious men. He had hoped to publish it under the aegis of the government, and had asked Montmorin, the amiable mediocrity who had just succeeded to the Foreign Ministry on the death of Vergennes, for authority to print it in France. Montmorin had hesitated and finally refused, so the work was printed in Paris with 'London' on the title page, a concession with which the government was apparently satisfied. The undertaking was financed, in the main, by a Paris publisher of the name of Le Jay.

In August Gabriel wrote to Yet-Lie: 'Four copies of my work have been printed on vellum for those who are dearest to me in the world — yourself, the Abbé de Périgord, the Duc de Lauzun and Panchaud.' Yet it was in this same August that Henriette at last and very sadly resolved to end her life with him. Physical faithfulness she had never expected from her friend, and she had accepted his many passing affairs with other women with resignation, even with a kind of compassionate indulgence. There had been times when she had been his confidante, when he had come to her for advice how best to wind up an amourette which had grown tedious or embarrassing. All this she had borne and would bear so long as his erotic escapades remained outside the walls which enclosed the loyalty and tenderness of their special relationship. So long as she possessed his heart and mind she was resigned to sharing his body. She did not yet admit that, even with his strange character, such bisection of the personality must some day prove an illusion, that sooner or later there would come to him some passion which would invade the ground she had hoped to keep inviolate.

It was the wife of the publisher Le Jay who arose swiftly to menace the home with which Henriette had contrived to surround her dearest friend. Sensual, alluring, intelligent and covetous, Madame Le Jay fastened upon Mirabeau with determined rapacity. Hers was the managing will behind her weak husband's unimportant business, and the handling of Mirabeau's material gave her all the opportunities she required. To yield to her at first must have been no matter for him, but once the casual and habitual surrender had been made he found himself unexpectedly, almost alarmingly, entangled, and then, when he had plunged and struggled awhile, held fast. For Mme Le Jay did not intend to be cast off in her turn, and she had the instruments with which to secure her hold — a carnal lure with which Henriette neither could nor would compete, and a smart kind of intellectuality which made her formidable in a field where Henriette had not yet feared a rival. She spotted, too, the innate extravagance of her new lover, and because this was the one excess to which his dearest friend had put a curb, it was pitifully easy to make for him a grievance of Henriette's devoted economies.

He was most horribly torn. 'Dearest one', he had written in the previous year, 'I have only had one lucky day in my life, that on which I came to know you and on which you gave me your friendship. The rest of my life is set amid all manner of vexations great and small, and if your presence softens them and makes everything bearable, I know for sure that your absence is a pain that eats up my life. Oh Henriette! If ever an infernal spirit should rise up between us, if you should abandon me to my fate, I might seek distraction in the vortex of pleasures, but I would find no happiness there and I should soon meet death on my way.' And now the infernal spirit had come and had demanded and received admission, and devoted and compassionate Henriette had not the power to exorcize it. She wrestled with it; she was made ill; there were atrocious scenes. His soul was never completely occupied by the enemy and he could rage and weep at the devastation of its advance. But he was helpless and Henriette, too, was helpless, because from the outset half his forces had gone over to the invader.

It was in mid-August, 1788, that Henriette kissed little 'Coco' goodbye and left the house of Mirabeau for ever.

6

On the fall of Calonne in April 1787, the Queen's favour secured the succession for Loménie de Brienne, the free-thinking Archbishop of Toulouse. Never came man to so lost a business, yet, though absolutism was now manifestly in its death agony, this capable prelate faced the rising clamour with a kind of arrogant courage. Lamoignon succeeded Miroménil as Keeper of the Seals, but Montmorin remained on at the Foreign Ministry. He had a certain gift for surviving the fall of colleagues.

Calonne had tried to win confidence by summoning the Notables. Brienne sought to revive it by an authoritarian display. Calonne had hoped to bluff the Notables into giving him a mandate which would have made obstruction by the *parlements* appear in its proper light as a defence of sectional privileges. Brienne sought to draw on the overdrawn account of absolutism one last cheque which, if honoured, might give the régime a few years of grace in which to underpin itself with new supports. That it must soon come to a national representation was, after Calonne's fall, generally agreed; but just what kind of representation — what sort of popular assembly and what manner of election — these were questions as yet unanswered. But on one point Brienne was clear: there must be no calling of the nation into council till an appearance at least of order had been given to the government's finances. The King must not seem to be calling in the people because he had no choice: the principle of authority must be saved.

It was a plausible policy but it had come too late. Brienne might draw up his edicts for loans and taxes with a swagger, but it rested with the *Parlement de Paris* and the provincial *parlements* to register them, to gear them to the machinery of the courts; and where Calonne's nominated assembly of the privileged had proved intractable it was fairly certain that the *noblesse de robe* in their ancient citadels would not prove more compliant. In constitutional theory these *parlements* were nothing but judicial and juristic committees of the ancient King's Council, and just as in the thirteenth century Saint Louis had sometimes done justice in person, so in the eighteenth Louis XVI could, by summoning the *parlement* to his presence, resume the plenitude of judicial and legislative authority and silence all objectors. This was the theory behind the ceremony known as a Bed of Justice. When, therefore, Brienne's edicts were resisted, all that might seem necessary was for a *lit de justice* to be held in order that resistance should collapse. That indeed was the position in constitutional law. But the legally permissible was no longer the politically possible. Already, in the Assembly of Notables, the demand for the States-General had been raised, and the public had begun to echo the demand. When, therefore, in July 1787 the *parlement* refused to register Brienne's tax-edict and declared the assent of the States-General — of the elected representatives of the Clergy, Nobility and Commons of the realm — necessary for new taxation, the King could (and did) hold a *lit de justice*; and when the *parlement* still protested he could (and did) 'exile' them to Troyes by an arbitrary order. But what he and Brienne could not do was to avoid a head-on collision with public opinion. From the summer of 1787 to the summer of 1788 the struggle between ministry and *parlements* raged, and with each episode in the crisis the political impotence of the government became more evident. The handsome playboy, the Duke of Orleans, put the weight of his riches and the prestige of his lineage behind the lawyers' cause, *noblesse d'epée* joined with *noblesse de robe* in aristocratic resistance to despotism, while the common people, as yet not fully engaged, applauded their natural enemies, so universal was the suspicion and distrust of the Archbishop, of his patroness the Queen and of the whole rickety system of 'ministerial despotism'. There were serious riots, and the troops and their noble officers proved unreliable. The Revolution had, in fact, begun with a revolt of the privileged against despotism.

7

The attitude of Mirabeau to these developments was, on the face of it, somewhat equivocal. With the revolt of the privileged he had only qualified sympathy. He was anxious to see the monarchy ruling powerfully and he was as convinced as ever that the oppressive devices of despotism must go. But he had no desire to see it make way for aristocracy. If the resistance of the noblesse were to lead to the reunion of the monarchy with the nation through a popular assembly he would support it, but if it were to stop short with the erection of an oligarchy he would have none of it. It was to a meeting — and an early meeting — of the States-General that he looked forward, but in the meantime he hoped that the government would govern and, incidentally, give him a job. 'The Archbishop of Toulouse', he writes to Mauvillon in May 1787, 'is a man of great talent and purpose; it is impossible for him not to realize sooner or later that it is better for him to employ me than to ignore me.' In October he writes to Montmorin to remind him how valuable and ill-rewarded have been his services in Berlin, and to warn the Foreign Minister not to listen to malicious tittle-tattle but to remember that his correspondent is a man as fit to serve a ministry as he is capable of hurting it; and, lest the Minister should imagine that he is seeking to hire only his pen, he says plainly that he would prefer to serve the government in some active way rather than 'to risk displeasing it in his capacity of instructor'. Finally, in case the Minister should still fail to take his meaning, he appends a list of posts he would be glad to accept: Warsaw, Petersburg, Constantinople — it is all one to him so long as he has an outlet for his energies.

Montmorin, while doubtless appreciating the anxiety of this unemployed gentleman to make no difficulties, did not trouble to reply, and a smile may have passed over his rather episcopal countenance when, a month later, he received the more modest request that he would give a measure of government support to the Count's latest project, a sort of periodical digest of the English newspapers for French readers.[88]

Two days later Mirabeau wrote to a young magistrate urging him to resist the arbitrary acts of the ministry and not to be fobbed off with promises of a States-General in the vague future;

if the government's needs were really so pressing, then the national assembly ought to be called for 1789 at the latest, and not in five years' time as Brienne was now suggesting.

It was timely, for the next day, November 19th, a crisis was reached. The King with his Keeper of the Seals came to the *parlement* and, without observing the formalities proper to a *lit de justice*, ordered the registration of Brienne's latest loan-edict. The councillors, ranged and robed in the majesty of the law, were reminded that 'the legislative power, absolute and undivided, belongs to the King alone'. Brave words, but the attempt to overawe opposition failed. Sabatier begged the King to summon the States-General without delay, the old Jansenist, Robert de Saint-Vincent, read His Majesty a lecture such as no Bourbon king had heard before, and finally the Duke of Orleans, present as a peer of the realm in full court, protested against the legality of the proceedings. Orleans cut a poor enough figure, to be sure; he had been coached by Sabatier, he nearly missed his cue and he spoke his protest with evident nervousness. But these details mattered nothing beside the rank of the spokesman and the fact that he spoke. The Head of the House of Orleans, second only to the House of France itself, had denounced the King's action in the presence and in full court. The effect was as great upon the people as their applause was fatal to the vain and ductile nature of the future *Citoyen Egalité*.[89]

Together with countless other congratulations the Duke received a rather fulsome letter from Mirabeau, of whom he had doubtless heard something from his very agreeable friend Lauzun. Mirabeau also wrote again to Montmorin urging the early summons of the States-General. When, however, the Foreign Minister, alarmed at the friendlessness of the government, suggested that if the Count really wished to serve he might take up his pen and write something against the *parlements* Mirabeau excused himself. The *parlements*, however undeservedly, were at the moment the mouthpiece, the only mouthpiece, of the people, and he replied proudly that he would never make war on them except 'in the presence of the nation'. A week or so later, somewhat less proudly, he wrote a pamphlet supporting the government and received cash for it. Yet it was hardly a prostitution of his pen. He had always been in two minds over the *parlements* as defenders of the nation's liberties, while on the necessity of the States-General he never compromised nor wavered.[90]

8

In the end, of course, the government gave way and summoned the Three Estates. What might have been an act of power and confidence carried all the marks of confusion and weakness, for not only did everybody know that the Estates had been summoned as a last resort by a ministry at its wit's end, but the actual announcement was accompanied by so much hesitation, so much self-contradiction, so many second thoughts as to the method of election and even the date of meeting, that France was fretted into a mood of criticism and doubt months before it had to address itself to the novel excitements of a general election. The first announcement, tentative and nebulous, was made in July 1788; the final regulations for the election were not issued till the end of January 1789. Meanwhile the date of meeting had first been fixed for May, then advanced to January and finally put back to May again; and it was not till the very end of December that the government took the quite capital decision to double the number of deputies to be elected by the Third Estate. If they had wished to convince everybody that they did not know what they were about they could scarcely have done so more effectively. Fortunately, however, the disgust and dismay of the public remained focused on Brienne, who fell in August, while its hopes were centred on Necker, who had succeeded him.

Mirabeau later described Necker as a good kind of man unjustly accused of possessing talent and depth of thought. That was in May 1789, when the financier's political ineptitude was beginning to worry perceptive men.[91] But Mirabeau never had any use for him at any time, and found his ostentatious rectitude insupportable. What claim, he now asked the public, had this man to be regarded, like Aristides, as the Just, when his qualifications for the key post in the government consisted solely in his alleged financial talent, whereas his methods were to be distinguished from those of the discredited Calonne only by their lack of audacity? Necker it was, he publicly insisted, who had first blinded the nation to its true position by financing the American war on loans, and the fact that, unlike Calonne, he had neither private debts nor mistresses was insufficient recommendation for his return to office. 'We are going to have this charlatan Necker,' he wrote a week before the appointment. 'Necker, the King and the mob — and the mob alone has courage. . . .'[92]

But the banker's popularity remained unassailable, and when, on December 27th, the government announced its decision to double the representation of the *Tiers*, the public gratitude to Necker, who had not in fact originated the measure and had only advocated it after much hesitation, rose to idolatry.[93]

The following day Mirabeau wrote to Montmorin:

> . . . The man of whom all are thinking, the *god* of the moment, has too many reasons to hate and perhaps to fear me for me not to realize that you might prefer not to see me during the first moments of public effervescence. It would be best to let him return to the stature of an ordinary mortal, which I am pretty sure will not take long . . . Meanwhile, M. le Comte, you love the King, and are bound to him as a man and as a minister. For my part, as a citizen I tremble for the royal authority, which is more necessary than ever at the moment when it is leaning towards its ruin. Never was there a more embarrassing crisis, nor one offering more pretexts for licence; never was the coalition of the privileged more daunting to the King or more redoubtable to the people; never did a national assembly threaten to be so stormy as that which is about to decide the fate of the monarchy. . . .
>
> Meanwhile, is the ministry considering what means there are of avoiding the danger of falling under the assembly's control, or rather of turning its assistance to good account? Has it a fixed and solid plan which the representatives of the nation will have only to sanction?
>
> I, at any rate, have just such a plan. It is linked to a constitutional scheme which would save us from aristocratic conspiracies, from democratic excesses and from the utter anarchy into which authority, through wishing to be absolute, has plunged itself and us. Do you wish to see it? Do you wish to show it to the King? Will you have the courage to appoint for once to his post of Citizen a faithful subject, a brave man and an intrepid defender of justice and truth? Without the

support — the secret support at least — of the government I cannot get into the States-General; I have already realized that one of your colleagues will shut all doors against me . . . Whereas, if we come to an understanding it would be very easy for me to avoid difficulties and overcome obstacles; and indeed there are no more than three months in which to get ready, to draw up one's policy and to show oneself a worthy and influential defender of the throne and of the common weal.[94]

Once more Montmorin did not deign to reply. If he gave the letter any thought at all he may well have asked himself why he should be expected to do so. Who was this Mirabeau after all? A *déclassé* noble with a shady record, a political *enfant terrible* who had done a bit of secret reporting for the government under the dubious auspices of Calonne and the Abbé de Périgord: a man forever touting for employment: a man who wrote ministers letters full of unwanted advice, indecent boasting, implied menaces and shameless solicitations: a man to fear? Possibly, in certain circumstances. A man to trust?

For answer to that question Montmorin had not long to wait, for early in January, just after the Count had left Paris for Provence to seek election, there crashed upon the public the enormous scandal of the *Secret History of the Court of Berlin*.

9

Talleyrand, who had just been made Bishop of Autun, had, it will be remembered, decoded and edited Mirabeau's letters from Germany, keeping the originals and presenting the edited version to Calonne. On returning to France Mirabeau had recovered the originals from him and made a copy. What his intentions were at this stage we do not know, but any copyright in this correspondence rested, of course, with the government which had commissioned it. It was certain that its publication would make a sensation, and it might well make money, for the letters combined serious reflections with picturesque and scandalous anecdotes in exactly the way to tickle the taste of a large public. It was equally certain that publication would utterly destroy what reputation for honour — not to mention delicacy — the author still enjoyed. If Mirabeau wished to convince Talleyrand and all that circle that he was no gentleman, the government that he was unfit for any sort of trust, foreign courts that he could never be *persona grata* and the world at large that he would do anything for money, it was in his power to achieve all four effects simultaneously by publishing the Berlin letters.

And yet, at the very time when he was advertising himself to the Foreign Minister as a man of whom the government had need, at the moment when he was presenting himself to the nobility of his province as a candidate for election — at this moment of all moments his confidential letters to the government were offered for sale to the public under the catchpenny title of *Histoire secrète de la cour de Berlin.*

Such an act of insanity is not lightly to be explained by the moral obtuseness he had already shown in matters of literary integrity. For the act was less a crime than a blunder, and a gross and obvious blunder at that. It so staggered people that numerous explanations, some plausible, all discreditable, were quickly forthcoming. Yet it is in the very enormity of the blunder that the key to the business is probably to be found.

Encouraged by Madame Le Jay, he had returned to all his old extravagant habits and had run up a formidable list of new debts. Never had he been more at his wit's end for money than at this moment when he was desperate to get into the States-General. Yet how conduct an election campaign when he had not even the ready money for his journey to Provence? He had tried to touch Montmorin but with no success; and all the time, here in his bureau, was this immensely saleable manuscript. *De la monarchie prussienne* had won him some praise, but as a business venture it had been a failure, and the production of its two editions (eight volumes in octavo, four in quarto) had nearly ruined the unfortunate Le Jay. But Madame Le Jay knew of the Berlin letters in her lover's keeping, and made it plain how she expected him to rescue both the firm and himself from bankruptcy. Mirabeau was tempted; he was horribly pressed where he had fewest defences. He gave the letters to his new secretary, Comps, with orders *not to part with them even to himself.* But he had underrated Madame Le Jay. He had not quite expected that she would take the matter into her own hands, burgle Comps's desk and whip the fatal manuscript off to the printers.[95]

Twenty thousand copies, without either author's or printer's name, were sold before the inevitable suppression. The scandal was immense. The King of Prussia, whose amours and superstitions were set forth in detail for the delectation of the reading public, was beside himself with fury, and Montmorin was especially embarrassed by the fact that France's one friend at Potsdam, Prince Henry of Prussia, not only featured largely and none too flatteringly in the letters, but also happened at this very moment to be visiting Paris. By order of the *parlement* the book was burned by the public executioner.

Mirabeau, writing from Provence, affected complete ignorance of the whole affair: if the correspondence had appeared in print it was none of his doing, and the unhappy Comps was repeatedly urged to make every kind of public disclaimer, and also to press Madame Le Jay to send southward some of the profits. But the attempt to carry the matter with a high hand was futile. His friends blushed for him; Talleyrand, whose cynical careerism had been given a publicity somewhat embarrassing to a bishop about to canvass the votes of his diocesan clergy, refused, for the time being, to have further relations with him; finally an acidulated note from Montmorin, written at the end of February, concluded with the words: 'I thank you for giving me your view on Provence, and for the offer you are so good as to make of a special conference on that subject; but it seems that, to say the least, no good purpose would be served were I to have henceforth the honour of receiving you.'[96]

Yet Mirabeau was not prosecuted; neither, which is more surprising, was Le Jay. Legal proceedings might have been a shade embarrassing for the government, which, after all, had chosen this indiscreet secret agent. In normal times, however, the government would not have needed to bother with legal proceedings, it being in cases of precisely this sort that *lettres de cachet* were so handy. But the times were far from normal; the first general election for 175 years was in full swing, and, while the government was a prey to every kind of hesitation, the author of

Des lettres de cachet and of the *Histoire secrète* was receiving remittances from Madame Le Jay and triumphing as the man of the people in Provence.

10

When he reached Aix in the middle of January Provence was already engaged in a local rehearsal of Act One of the Revolution. While the poor were suffering from the worst winter on record following the ruined harvest of 1788, the middle classes were noisily protesting against the form in which the Estates of Provence were preparing for the election. The Three Estates of the province had been convoked in 1787 after a century and a half of disuse. During this long intermission, however, the Third Estate had retained its regular *Assemblée des Communautés* together with considerable functions in local government. Such political life as Provence had retained was, therefore, bourgeois, and the middle classes were understandably indignant that the privileged orders should now insist on sitting and deliberating as separate bodies. They demanded that the clergy and nobility, having awoken to political life after their long sleep, should join with themselves in one general assembly and should carry henceforth their fair share of the taxes laid upon the province. The Estates of Provence were to be, in effect, a kind of local constituent assembly as well as an electoral college. The Commons went further still: they demanded that Provence should be represented in the States-General not as a bundle of constituencies, or *sénéchaussées*, mere administrative districts of the Paris-centred bureaucracy, but as a *nation*.

The government, which was not prepared to countenance such thorough-going federalism, refused these demands, and the clergy and nobility stood on their rights. The mood of the Commons was, therefore, already excited when the exciting personality of Mirabeau *fils* appeared in their midst. The lawsuit of six years ago was not forgotten, rumours coming in from France had enriched the local legend, and his arrival was, by his own account, like that of the spark in the powder barrel.

Yet it was by his own order, the nobility, that he was as a

matter of course seeking election; but they, too, remembered the lawsuit, and this renewal of enthusiasm by the common people whenever he showed himself was to them anything but a recommendation. As in 1783 so now, but with heightened expectation, the people swarmed round him and idolized him with a strange spontaneity; and he was not a little intoxicated with it. He took up the popular cause and criticized the present constitution of the Estates in a speech to his fellow nobles. He roundly denied the right of two orders who were not the nation to prevail over the nation. It was the theme of the Revolution in a nutshell, but it was not the way to win his hearers. He had, however, discounted their disapproval: 'I don't worry,' he wrote to his father, 'but I am making it sufficiently clear that if I am not a noble I shall have to be a commoner. My motto shall be this: Get into the States-General at all costs!'

When the news of the *Histoire secrète* reached Provence any hesitations the nobles may have had about rejecting him were at an end. His denials of authorship were not heeded and would not have cleared his character even if they had been, for the *Histoire secrète* was not his only offence of this kind. There had also been issued by the house of Le Jay a correspondence between Mirabeau and a friend, Ceretti. The topic was the incapacity of Necker, the letters were dangerously outspoken and they had been published without Ceretti's permission. A demagogue without the code of a gentleman, a man who had given the deepest offence to the two principal ministers of the crown — what chance had he of election by the gentlemen of Provence?

On February 8th, on the pretext that he did not actually possess a fief in the county, the noblesse refused him permission to sit among them any longer. He had anticipated the blow by printing an eloquent declaration of his position. He recalled how the last of the Gracchi, perishing at the hands of his fellow patricians, had hurled dust at the heavens and called upon the avenging gods: 'and out of the dust Marius was born — Marius, less great as the destroyer of the Cimbri than because he beat down in Rome the haughty sway of aristocracy'. Then, three days after his exclusion, he published his personal vindication *To the Provençal Nation*. Against the jealousy and fear which have led his own order to cast him out he appeals to the people at large: they shall be judges between him and his fellow-nobles; they shall decide what are the real motives of those who have discovered his technical disqualification only after his speeches have begun to alarm them and after he has participated as of right in six of their sessions.

It was as well that he was winning the Commons of Provence, for he had lost the good opinion of almost all who counted in Paris. His latest publications had scattered his friends in shame and confusion and left the field open to his enemies. Libels were being printed, and Comps posted to him a sample of these; it came from the pen of his sometime secretary and valet, Hardy. Linguet, it may be noted, was now in Paris. Mirabeau decided to make a hasty visit to the capital to repair, if possible, the worst of the damage, but he had little success and was soon headed southwards again. When, however, he re-entered Provence the bells were rung and the way was thronged as though it were the route of a returning conqueror.

On March 6th, he entered Aix as candidate for the Third Estate. There was the wildest enthusiasm. They paraded with music and torches, they let off fireworks, they crowned him, they read him addresses, they called him *Father of his Country*. That night the whole town was illuminated. Next day a deputation from Marseilles arrived, and a crowd went off to the Hôtel Marignane and demanded to speak to Madame la Comtesse. Emilie appeared and listened to an harangue in the provençal she loved: she ought to go to her husband, they shouted; a pity for such a fine race to die out.

Emilie remained with Papa; but she renewed her correspondence with Caroline du Saillant and began to show an interest in her husband's fortunes.[97]

Mirabeau was taking no chances about his election, so to provide a second string to his bow he went to Marseilles. Once again his reception was triumphal, though he thought it worth while all the same to publish an anonymous pamphlet in praise of his own character. Hardly had he left the city, however, when he was overtaken by news of serious riots there. They were not unheralded, for there had already been trouble at Toulon, at Manosque and in the villages. Caused partly by the rising price of food, these disturbances, which were not confined to Provence,

were really the opening of the second phase of the Revolution —
the attack by the masses on the privileged. In some instances the
rioters went into action with cries of *Vive le Roi!* In Marseilles
authority was helpless before the mob, and the military governor,
at his wit's end, begged the people's idol to return with speed and
use his influence to restore order. Back to Marseilles, therefore,
Mirabeau went. It was an act of some courage, for though the
primary election, conducted by virtual manhood suffrage, was
over, he was a candidate for the forthcoming and decisive secon-
dary and was exposing his precious popularity to all the hazards
attending definite action in a civil commotion.

He found that a sort of bourgeois militia had already been
formed by young men of good position, and that they had already
named a company after him. He took charge at once, put this
citizen guard into shape to police the city, and, by a modest show
of force and a lot of popular eloquence, contrived to restore order.
It was the victory of personality. But scarcely had it been won
when news came of disorders at Aix which had culminated in
bloodshed and pillage, and for a second time Mirabeau rushed
to the rescue. A citizen-militia on the Marseilles model was
hastily enlisted and took over control of the town from the small
regular force whose presence had merely angered the mob, while
the commandant practically handed over the town to Mirabeau's
care. The Archbishop of Aix showed resource and sense in devising
emergency measures to deal with the bread shortage, but it
was above all the actual presence of Mirabeau, riding proudly
and confidently about the streets and haranguing the people in
downright and homely terms, which, in an astonishingly short
time, restored the peace.

He was rewarded; for it was not merely as a grand orator and
a good fellow but also as a courageous and active citizen that, on
April 4th, the people of Marseilles elected him. Two days later
he was returned at the head of the poll as deputy for the Third
Estate of Aix, and it was for Aix, scene of his first forensic triumph,
that he chose to sit in the States-General of the Realm.

CHAPTER IX

TRIBUNE OF THE PEOPLE

WITH the meeting of the States-General at the beginning of May 1789, begins the most famous and least complicated phase of Mirabeau's political career. The phase is clearly marked and ends on a definite date, June 27th. It is the most famous part of his career because it is that in which, at a moment of crisis, he may well have determined the course of history. It is the particle of his life which secures the mention of his name in even the briefest accounts of the Revolution. It is also the least complicated part because it is that in which he pursues a simple object, understood and approved by the overwhelming majority of his associates. With his ruined reputation his way is not easy. He has to put up with calumny and hooting before he can win applause. But a hostile audience is no new thing to him, and in the eighth week he seems in a fair way to become their leader.[98]

By Saturday, May 2nd, the great majority of the elected deputies of the Clergy, Nobility and Third Estate of the Kingdom had reached Versailles. At eleven o'clock in the morning the King began the ceremony of welcoming them. There were nearly 1200 deputies, and as each made his separate reverence to the King the business became very tedious, especially for Louis. The clergy and nobility were received in a private room, and it was not till four o'clock that the King was ready for the Third Estate. To welcome them he went to the more public Hall of Mirrors. The magnificent clothes of prelates and nobles had already caused some offence to class-conscious commoners wearing the plain black prescribed for them, and it was a mistake of tact on the King's part further to mark class distinctions by giving a special and more intimate welcome to the privileged. This was Mirabeau's impression, and he vented it in Number 1 of a newspaper, *États-généraux*, which he brought out the same day.

This publication was itself a challenge to the régime. The censorship still stood, but Mirabeau, holding that it should rest in abeyance in the presence of the nation in council, sought no official approval of his proofs.

On Monday the Estates and the Court met for a solemn Mass in the church of Saint Louis. The Archbishop of Paris was celebrant, the choir of the Chapel Royal sang, and the Bishop of Nancy preached a sermon which lasted two hours. Mirabeau, regarding the Catholic Church as an obsolete institution with nothing to give to the new France, was bored by the service and critical of the sermon. 'After the gospel', he wrote in *États-généraux*, 'the Bishop of Nancy went up into the pulpit. *Religion is the strength of states; religion is the one and unfailing source of their prosperity*; such was the theme of his discourse. It seemed long, a patchwork without plan, ideas, style or purpose. It was for a different kind of lead, for a different inspiration, in a word, for another order of things that we looked in this august assembly. All the common-places, from the baptism of Clovis down to the illness of Louis the Well-beloved at Metz, and from declamations against luxury to abuse of philosophy, were duly worked in. It is quite evident that the orator was not at his ease, that he had neither plan nor decided opinions, and that he had misjudged his epoch.'

One sentence, however, caught Mirabeau's attention and earned his approval. 'France, your will suffices.' The pity he thought, was that the whole address was not a development of this theme, and when the Bishop, misjudging his epoch, said; 'Sire, accept the homage of the clergy, the respect of the nobility and the most humble petitions of the Third Estate,' there was a raising of eyebrows among the Commons.

'Never', Mirabeau's report concludes, 'was a finer opportunity more completely missed.' The next two years were to be a tale of fine opportunities missed, and it was to be his melancholy role to mark them as they slid into the irrecoverable past.

After Mass was finished the *Te Deum* was sung. Then, by rank and order, that unique congregation walked in procession out into the sunlit street and the crowd. There was fluctuating cheering. Of the deputies two, it was noticed, drew most cheers: Philippe, Duke of Orleans, who preferred to walk with the nobles as a deputy rather than take his place by the King with the Princes of the Blood; and Mirabeau, who walked with the Commons. The King was warmly greeted, but there was silence for the Queen.

On the following day, Tuesday, May 5th, the Estates assembled in the *Salle des menus plaisirs*, and the session began. The *Menus plaisirs* had been appointed as the meeting-hall for the Third Estate. It was used for this first combined meeting of the three Orders to hear the King's speech because it alone was large enough to take them all.

In the minds of the Commons and also of those priests and nobles who were set on big reforms, one question was at this moment uppermost — were the three Orders, after that day's meeting, going to continue to meet as one grand assembly, or were they to sit and vote as three separate houses? In the past the latter method had been used, but since no States-General had met for 175 years the argument from precedent was not very weighty. Against it was the government's innovation in doubling the number of deputies of the *Tiers*, making them equal to the privileged Orders put together. What could this mean, if not that the supporters of reform were to be enabled to out-vote the privileged? It was known that among the nobles there was a small minority for reform, and among the clergy a large minority of the same mind; these elements added to the solid phalanx of the Third Estate would ensure the triumph of the reform movement — provided the Estates sat together and voted *par tête*. On the other hand, if they sat separately and voted *par ordre*, it would be two-to-one against reform on every issue touching privilege. Such a situation would falsify all the confidence of the last few months and frustrate the will of the people expressed in countless *cahiers*, including that of the *Tiers État* of Aix. Such was surely not the intention of the good King. The Commons, therefore, awaited his speech with hope, though perhaps scarcely with confidence. They had noticed at Saturday's reception disturbing indications of the King's inclination to treat the privileged Orders as different from themselves, and now, as they assembled in the great hall, the distinction was once more made; the Clergy and Nobility entered by the main door, the Commons being ushered in by a side entrance.

The King read a short speech full of expressions of fatherly solicitude for his people which evoked applause. Then Barentin, the new Keeper of the Seals, spoke at some length. According to Mirabeau he was inaudible to three-quarters of those present; his speech, the first to give a hint of the government's intentions, was the first disappointment of the day. There were, it seemed, to be reforms — a more equal sharing of the tax burden by the privileged, perhaps a measure of freedom for the press, and a reform of the criminal code. But of a bold and imaginative programme of national reconstruction there was no hint. What, however, was far more depressing was that the question of immediate importance — vote *par tête* or *par ordre* — was not answered at all. The matter, declared the Keeper of the Seals, was to be left to the States-General to decide.

Just how unsatisfactory was this evasion of responsibility by the government was at once clear to the reformers. The two privileged orders had been provided with separate meeting-places; the first item on the agenda as soon as this Royal Session was over would be a routine verification of powers, that is, an examination of the credentials of each deputy. Without a clear directive from the government on this point, it was quite certain that the clergy and nobility would repair to their own halls and proceed with the verification as separate chambers, and, once established as separate chambers, it might be impossible to persuade them to sink their identities again in one united assembly. The vital object, the vote *par tête*, would only be attainable by means of a vote *par ordre* in which the majority was likely to be two-to-one against it.

Barentin was followed by Necker. The Director-General of Finance was the key minister. It was impending bankruptcy which had produced the present crisis, and Necker, it was generally understood, was the man who had persuaded the King to double the number of the Commons. Recalled to office after the failure of the successors to his first ministry, the reputation of the banker from Geneva stood high. Necker's voice was not strong and the latter part of his speech had to be read for him. When, after three hours, the speech was over, the Finance Minister's reputation had scarcely been enhanced. 'Insufferably long-winded, full of repetitions, pompous trivialities and things making no sense, while devoid of any guiding idea, any statesmanlike resource or even any brilliant financier's expedient'; such was

Mirabeau's verdict in his newspaper. He heaped scorn on Necker's characteristically weak suggestion that for discussing some matters it would be better for the assembly to sit as three chambers, for the discussion of others to sit as one; and he hastened to warn his readers of the immediate danger: 'Brought together at the Monarch's bidding, the deputies provide a representation of the nation . . . They, and they alone, have the right to regulate the form of their deliberations; but the King has the incontestable right to forbid this great question — should the Orders separate or remain united? — to be decided before it has been fairly considered; and it would be, if he allowed the deputies to begin by separating.'[99]

This was bold doctrine, but his intention had been bolder still; for he had written a speech imploring the King to let this vital question be debated and voted on there and then, in full session in the royal presence, and he had only been prevented from delivering it because, as he was on the point of rising, the King stood up and ended the session. What effect such an appeal at such a moment would have had is very doubtful. It would have been grossly out of order for a private deputy to rise without the King's permission, and Mirabeau was the last man in whom such a liberty would have been pardoned. On the other hand it might have provided the thing which the proceedings had so depressingly lacked — the note of leadership. At this moment the deputies, newly arrived from their provinces, mostly strangers to each other, but ready and eager to support the Monarchy in bold and constructive reforms, were a soft and pliable substance ready to take shape under the hand of any passable artist in government. The things they at present wanted — leadership and discipline — were the very things which the government, and, at this moment, probably the government alone, could have provided. The bulk of the deputies asked for nothing better, and Mirabeau writhed with contemptuous impatience at the Director-General's fumbling. 'If Necker had had an ounce of talent', he later wrote, 'he could have secured 60 millions' worth of taxes and 150 millions' worth of loans within a week, and the next day have dissolved the Assembly.'[100]

On the second day, May 6th, the three Orders met in separate chambers, and the weary struggle to re-unite them into one body began. The next day the government took a step which suggested that, while it lacked the courage to impose its views on the major issue of the method of voting, it was not above petty measures against its critics. It forbad the publication of *États-généraux*. Mirabeau at once began to publish under the unimpeachable form of open *Letters of the Count of Mirabeau to his Constituents*. The government lacked the nerve to cut communications between a deputy and the electors, and the battle for uncensored periodicals was thus in fact, if not in law, won.

Left alone in their great hall, the Third Estate took up the position that they were a mere collection of private individuals without corporate character until the powers of *all* deputies had been verified by the only authority they would recognize as sufficient for the purpose, that is, by the Three Estates forming one national assembly. On the other hand the privileged Orders in their separate chambers proceeded to verification. In both chambers, however, there were dissentients — 114 among the clergy and forty-seven among the nobles. It was the existence of these minorities which gave the Commons hope.

Their opening move was suggested by Malouet. A deputation was sent to the clergy and the nobles. The former showed an accommodating spirit and agreed to appoint commissioners to discuss re-union and, further, to invite the nobles to do likewise. They were as good as their word, in fact better, for they interrupted the verification of their powers pending the decision on the union of the chambers. Even the nobles, after six days' delay, agreed to appoint a committee to confer with the other Orders, but their attitude was more reserved and they went ahead with their separate verification. Their conduct was in marked contrast to the fraternal helpfulness of the clergy and Mirabeau began to wonder whether the best policy would not be to widen the difference between them, win the clergy over to the policy of union and leave the nobility to indulge their class prejudices in an isolation which would sooner or later become ridiculous if not dangerous.

It was not till May 13th that the nobles even agreed to elect their committee. By then the clergy's committee was elected and ready for discussions. In the Commons next day Rabaud-Saint-Étienne moved that sixteen commissioners should be appointed to confer with those of the other orders. Le Chapelier made a more daring suggestion, that the Commons should declare themselves in effect the national assembly and henceforth regard those priests and nobles who stood aloof as defaulters. On the sixteenth Robespierre vainly suggested what was perhaps already in Mirabeau's mind: that separate talks would be begun forthwith with the clergy. By the eighteenth patience was wearing thin. The nobles had still done nothing. It seemed high time for the Commons to adopt a decided attitude, if the project for re-union by agreement were not to peter out.

Two alternative proposals lay before them, Rabaud's and Le Chapelier's, and Mirabeau's first important speech to that assembly was a criticism of both. Chapelier's proposal he considered inopportune; it would involve, in effect, a solemn decree by the Commons, an act hardly consistent with the position they had taken up, which was, precisely, that they were not *yet* a corporate body; moreover it would involve lumping the nobles and clergy together as defaulters, which would be unfair to the latter who had, on the whole, shown some readiness to discuss union. Rabaud's motion, which was simply for tripartite conferences, suffered from much the same defect. It entirely disregarded the arrogant conduct of the *noblesse*, and suggested a suppliant attitude on the part of the Commons unbefitting the representatives of the people. Mirabeau then gave vent to his hatred of his own class: 'Can one, without wilful blindness, flatter oneself with hopes of conciliation with the members of the nobility, when they do not deign to indicate readiness to lend themselves thereto until they have dictated laws which will make all conciliation impossible? When they preface their consent to name commissioners with the haughty declaration that they are a legally constituted chamber? And once they have themselves stood in judgment on their own claims, how much true collaboration is to be expected of them? No, Gentlemen, if one compromises at all with such pride one soon becomes a slave.'

The right course, he then urged, was to approach the clergy.

They, at least, had not yet declared themselves legally constituted; they seemed anxious to act the part of mediators, they enjoyed the confidence of a large part of the nation, and it was for them, guardians of morality and Christian principles, to bring the nobility to a more fraternal frame of mind, or at least to encourage the reformers among the nobles, a group at present all too small. 'Send to the clergy, Gentlemen, do not send to the nobility; for the nobility lays down the law, the clergy negotiates.'

It was, however, the motion of Rabaud-Saint-Étienne, which had been in their minds for four days, which was passed.

Two days later the nobles appointed their commissioners, and on May 23rd the conferences began. It soon became clear that the nobles would make agreement impossible.

In the course of French history the *noblesse* had repeatedly shown a curious blindness to their own real interests. Pride, the sense of being of finer clay than common men, is the special failing of an aristocracy, but it may be corrected (as in England it was corrected) by a sense of the drift of events and an instinct for self-adjustment to novel conditions. But again and again in French history the *noblesse* were blind to political realities; drawing the cloak of their feudal rights about them, they repeatedly spurned foresighted co-operation either with the Monarchy above them or with the people below. This is well illustrated by their conduct in the last States-General before 1789, the meeting in 1614. Four years earlier the great Henry IV had been murdered, and the regency was in the weak hands of his widow. Some of the greatest nobles revolted and, accusing the government of squandering public money and oppressing the poor, demanded the summons of the States-General. The political situation was fluid. Like 1789, it was a moment when an impress might have been stamped upon the substance of French politics to shape it for centuries to come. It was the moment for the nobles, as the only possible leaders of the people, to found a constitution. What do we find? We find that when the president of the *Tiers État*, in the course of a speech, compared the Three Estates to three brothers, the nobles formally complained of his presumption to the government, some of them openly protesting that they had no wish to be called brothers by cobblers and cordwainers. This was not what Talleyrand would have called a political attitude. By their inveterate hugging of everything which separated them from the rest of the nation the nobility condemned themselves to political isolation. Absolutism instead of a constitution was the consequence of their stupidity, for after their last exhibition of irresponsibility in the Fronde, Louis XIV, with tacit national approval, deprived them of all but ornamental functions. Had they learnt their lesson, now in 1789?

It seemed that they had not. They stood out for three separate chambers and the vote *par ordre*. They took their stand upon precedent, a singularly unhelpful attitude, since not only had the long interval since the last States-General rendered such arguments excessively legalistic, but also the precedents themselves were not all in their favour. In the States-General of 1308 voting had been by heads, in those of 1346, 1384 and 1484 by provinces. On May 26th, the conferences broke down.

4

The following day Mirabeau made a second speech advocating the approach to the clergy alone. He repeated his former arguments, but with increased force, for the intransigence of the nobles and the breakdown of the tripartite talks had in the meanwhile shown the wisdom of his policy of dividing the privileged Orders. The *Tiers*, he argued, must be prepared for a trial of strength. They might soon have to assert themselves by summoning the nobles or by publicly protesting against their conduct; if this should come about, what a difference it would make to be already amalgamated with the clergy!

This time his motion was adopted. The clergy were 'invited in the name of the God of peace and the national interest to join themselves to the Commons in the hall of the General Assembly in order there to work together for union and concord'.

But the measure failed. Many of the clergy were deeply moved by the appeal, but they could not command a majority. The attitude of the Clerical chamber may well have been influenced by the fact that just at this time a proposal of a different sort was being mooted there. This was the Bishop of Langres's suggestion that the privileged Orders should be formed into *one* chamber. There was much to be said for this. It would remove the Commons' fear of always being outvoted by two to one, and it would provide the basis of a two-chamber parliamentary system, the advantages of which France, after bitter experience of single-chamber legislatures, was later to acknowledge. But Mirabeau's respect for the English constitution did not reconcile him to the idea of any sort of aristocratic senate, and he opposed the Bishop of Langres's suggestion in a long open letter.[101]

At this point the King intervened. He sent a letter expressing his concern at the way time was passing with nothing done because of the deadlock, and ordered (the actual word was 'invited') the conciliation committees of the three Orders to resume their talks forthwith under the presidency of the Keeper of the Seals.

This was a fresh turn of events, and Mirabeau was quick to perceive its possibilities. The coalition with the clergy for which he had hitherto worked was but a manœuvre to isolate the nobles and bring nearer the establishment of one chamber. But to Mirabeau the achievement of one chamber speaking for the nation was not the ultimate goal. He was a revolutionary, but also a monarchist, and with him monarchism was not, as with most of his colleagues, a vague matter of sentiment and traditional piety; it was a cold conviction that the executive must on no account be enfeebled, and that the progress of the nation could only be achieved by a strong executive working in close collaboration with a legislative assembly genuinely representing the nation; he was a monarchist because, at the moment, the only possible executive was the monarch. He hated the privileges of clergy and nobles as obstacles to the union of king and people. This was his political philosophy now, and he never departed from it. Before long the monarchical element in his thought would divide him from his colleagues; but that point had not yet been reached.

Mirabeau leapt at the apparent opportunity of direct collaboration with the King. 'To what end,' he asked the Commons, 'are the efforts of the privileged orders directed? To fill the King with distrust of our intentions and projects, because they well know that the power of a king united to his people is something which tyrannical prejudices, oppressive intentions and the pressure of private interests are unable to resist . . . We are mighty indeed if all we need to make the good cause triumph is to march hand-in-hand with the King.' He demanded that there should be presented to His Majesty 'a most humble address'; but audacity rather than humility would be its mark if Mirabeau could carry his audience with him. He would have the Commons declare that they 'have *authorized* their commissioners to take part in the conference to which His Majesty has deigned to *invite* them, and at the same time to inform him of their conviction that the deputies of the different Orders are deputies to one single and self-same assembly, the *National Assembly*, in which alone the verification of their powers can be definitely completed'.

On May 30th, the address was drawn up, and it bears Mirabeau's mark. It begins with an apology for the fact that the 'faithful Commons' had not long since formally expressed their gratitude for the convocation of the States-General. This they would have done if their powers had been verified, which they would have been if the nobles had ceased to raise difficulties. The responsibility for the breakdown of the first conferences between the Orders is placed squarely on the *noblesse*. Then follows a passage in which is evident something all too rare in the liberal manifestos of that time — a sense of history: 'Sire, your faithful Commons will never forget what they owe to their Kings; they will never forget the natural alliance of Throne and People against divers aristocracies, whose power could only be established upon the ruin of royal authority and of the common weal.' It was a stirring document, a noble appeal to Louis XVI to remember the wisdom of his ancestors and return to the old alliance of Crown and Commons by which Capets, Valois and Bourbons had, each in their way, prospered, which none of them had neglected with impunity, and which had been the making of France.

The joint conferences were resumed that same day, though there was delay in the presentation of the address. The Dauphin was seriously ill at Meudon where he died on June 4th. It was urged that at such a moment the King should not be troubled. The address was not presented till the sixth, when expressions of respectful sympathy were added. It was noted, however, that deputations from the other Orders had in the meanwhile been received by the King — a small matter, no doubt, but not without its effect.

The King's reply to the Commons' address was entirely evasive. More definite were his proposals made through the Keeper of the Seals to the joint conference. From these it was clear that the government intended the Orders to sit separately. They would, it was hoped, keep in close touch with each other, and, if disagreements arose, the King would act as referee, his decision being final.

The Commons now saw that patience was getting them nowhere but they made one last appeal to clergy and nobles, both as individuals and as orders, to join them. The appeal, however, ended as an ultimatum: the Commons announced that they were about to call the roll of all the *bailliages* of France and to proceed to verification 'with or without the presence of the deputies of the privileged classes'.

On June 12th, the ceremony began, and on the next day, when the roll-call came to the *bailliage* of Poitou, three country curés presented themselves with their credentials. There was wild enthusiasm, for it was recognized to be a portent. The ranks of privilege had broken, and precisely where Mirabeau had insisted they could be broken — on the clerical flank. Next day six more priests joined the Commons, and by June 16th, nineteen soutanes could be counted in the Hall of the Assembly. Within a week the Archbishops of Vienne and Bordeaux with 150 priests seceded *en bloc* from the Clerical Estate, leaving the framework of three chambers in ruins. But by that time the situation had changed profoundly.

5

Ever since the first disputes with the privileged Orders the *Tiers* had been feeling their way to the conception of themselves, with or without the others, as a truly national assembly. It was now time to embody this idea in a solemn resolution. After the accession of the priests they were no longer just the Third Estate. What, then, were they? The great debate to settle this question began on June 15th.

It was the Abbé Sieyès who made the first proposal. His reputation as a political philosopher was already established, for in January his pamphlet *Qu'est-ce que le Tiers État?* had won a widespread popularity, many candidates, including Mirabeau, making use of it in their election addresses. 'Politics,' the Abbé once confessed, 'are a science in which I think I am perfect.'[102] Sieyès now proposed that the assembly should call itself 'Assembly of the known and verified representatives of the French Nation'. As a title this lacked succinctness. The next formula, suggested Barère, was sixteen words long, less a title than a political manifesto. Then Mirabeau, though feverish and unwell, rose to speak. He considered that Sieyès's formula had certain defects. It pressed dangerously upon the bounds of legality. 'We are all of us here,' he reminded his audience, 'under the form of summons which the King has given us', and he argued that, as they were not *yet* legally constituted in any other form, it would be unwise to adopt Sieyès's proposal, since it implied an excommunication of the nobles and most of the clergy, who were assembled under the same royal summons as themselves. The King might well repudiate the title, and he would have legality — and the privileged classes — on his side. Was a conflict with the Monarch worth risking on such an issue? It was not even certain that they would have the support of the electorate: 'Do not imagine that the people is interested in the metaphysical discussions which have agitated us hitherto.'

He admitted that Sieyès's formula expressed the strictest and purest political principles such as were to be expected from such a philosopher-citizen, but the application of principles needed sometimes to be tempered by expediency: 'There is this essential difference between the metaphysician who, meditating in his study, seizes the truth in its impelling purity, and the statesman who is bound to take previous events, difficulties and obstacles into account. The one thinks only of *what is*, the other is concerned with *what is possible*. The metaphysician, travelling on a map of the world, passes effortlessly over everything, unimpeded by mountains, deserts, rivers or abysses; but when a journey has to be made in reality and a destination has to be reached, one must always remember that one is on the ground and no longer in the world of ideas.'

He moved that the assembly should call themselves simply *Representatives of the French People*. Such a title would be at once accurate and inoffensive: 'Who could challenge it or deprive us of it? Who could protest at innovation, at exorbitant pretensions or at the dangerous ambition of our assembly? Who can forbid us to be what we are? Yet this description, so inoffensive and unpretentious, will, in time, become great, imposing and majestic. It will be all-sufficient when the people, raised by our exertions, shall have assumed the rank to which the eternal nature of things destines them.'[103]

Men's capacity to misunderstand each other in debate is illimitable, and Mirabeau's proposal was attacked by following speakers on the grounds that it favoured the separate existence of the privileged Orders, and that the phrase 'representatives of the *people*' was too modest and humble a title. One speaker, the young and eloquent Barnave, accused him of undue concern that the assembly should choose a title acceptable to the King. What need of royal sanction, Barnave asked, when the people had spoken?

On the second day of the Great Debate, after Mounier had proposed a title which surpassed even Barère's in verbosity, Mirabeau rose for the second time to defend his formula.

Dealing first with the question of the royal sanction, he used words which must have shocked many present: 'I believe, Gentlemen, that the King's veto is so essential that I would prefer to live at Constantinople rather than in France if he were without it: yes, I declare, I can conceive nothing more terrible than the sovereign aristocracy of six hundred persons, who could make themselves irremovable tomorrow, hereditary the day after, and would end, like the aristocrats of every country in the world, by usurping everything.' It was a neat rebuttal of the ridiculous suggestion that he, of all men, had any weakness for aristocracy; it was also his first public avowal of that monarchism which lay, hitherto unsuspected, in the foundations of his thought.

Injecting some hard sense into a debate which had hitherto been singularly windy, he urged two practical points: first, the important thing was for them to constitute themselves promptly as an assembly *capable of action*; let them take a title sufficient for that, but not one which might appear to injure the other

Orders which, after all, did exist, even though the assembly denied their right to act in isolation. Secondly, the formulae suggested by previous speakers were too long, too legalistic and too pompous. What, he asked, would the average elector make of 'The Assembly formed by the majority of all the deputies sent to the States-General, duly summoned, deliberating in the absence of the minority, duly summoned'?

After careful criticism of the formulae proposed, Mirabeau wound up thunderously with one of his great passages: 'Representatives of the people, pray answer me this: are you going to tell your constituents that you have rejected this name "People", that, though you are not precisely ashamed of them, you have, nevertheless, sought to avoid this description because it does not sound grand enough . . . Wiser than you, the heroes who founded the liberty of Holland took the name of *beggars*; they were content with this title because their tyrant's scorn had meant to disgrace them with it; and this title, by attaching to them that huge class which aristocracy and despotism despised, was at once their strength, their glory and the guarantee of their success. The friends of liberty choose the name which serves them best, not that which flatters them most; they will call themselves Remonstrants in America, Shepherds in Switzerland and Beggars in Holland; they will make a boast of their enemies' insults, robbing these of their power to humiliate by adopting them as titles of honour.'[104]

He was greeted with a hubbub of abuse by those determined to label him an aristocrat in disguise, and it was not Mirabeau's formula which was adopted. Later in the debate a deputy from Berry, Legrand, proposed the title 'National Assembly'. It had the simplicity which Mirabeau had asked for, though it sounded a note of defiance such as he was at the moment anxious to avoid; but, above all, it had dignity. Sieyès gladly supported it and, on June 17th, it was adopted by a five-to-one majority. Mirabeau, in a third speech, had opposed it, but he abstained from voting.

He saw the likelihood of the adoption of the new name leading to a direct collision with the Crown. 'National Assembly' was no new term. It had been used in a loose way by everybody, including the King, to denote the States-General as a whole. When, therefore, the Third Estate plus a handful of priests took it as applying exclusively to themselves and to such churchmen or nobles as should thereafter join them — when, furthermore, they appended to their resolution a further one declaring all existing taxes illegal, though authorizing their collection during the life of the Assembly and afterwards only if freely granted by it — they were performing a revolutionary act. It was a challenge which the Monarch would be bound to accept. Mirabeau, though as determined as anyone to secure the legislative authority of the Assembly, was also anxious to preserve the executive authority of the Crown, and he saw ahead a conflict in which one or the other was likely to suffer. That was why he had spoken against the new title. A politic fear of losing his influence over the ardent majority, by becoming lumped with Mounier and the moderates, explains his abstention from the vote. 'I shouldn't be surprised,' he said to Dumont the next day, 'if civil war were the fruit of their beautiful decree.'

6

The government accepted the challenge. On June 19th, when the self-styled National Assembly was busy appointing committees, the Council met at Marly to consider measures to put the *Tiers* in their place and regain the initiative for the Crown. It was decided to hold a plenary Royal Session like that which had inaugurated the States-General, and to declare the royal will. In the meantime the Commons must be prevented from meeting. This attempt to shut the stable door after the horse had bolted led, as is well known, to the Tennis Court Oath on June 20th. The importance of this episode was less than its dramatic quality. It was little more than a re-affirmation of the decisive resolutions of June 17th. It raised the temperature but it left the situation substantially unchanged.

Even now, when at long last the court had been driven into action by the revolutionary initiative of an assembly which it could so easily have managed seven weeks earlier, there was division and hesitation. There was a tussle between Necker, Montmorin and others who advocated concessions to the Assembly, and the die-hards anxious for an uncompromising assertion of the prerogative; the Queen and the King's brother, Artois, were the strength of this party, and Louis wavered in between. In the end, after the Royal Session had been postponed a day to gain time, Necker drafted a king's speech which in its general tone reflected a victory for the advocates of authoritarianism.

On Tuesday, June 23rd, the Hall of the Assembly was surrounded by 4000 troops, a number significantly in excess of merely ceremonial requirements. When the Three Orders were assembled the King arrived. Necker, it was noticed, was not with him. Though the King's speech contained things which he had opposed in Council, he had not resigned; he had, on the contrary, been on the point of entering his carriage to go to the session when his wife and daughter persuaded him that this would be beneath his dignity; so he stayed at home in protest against a policy to which, as a minister, he stood committed. Not till that evening did he resign, and by then things had happened which might conceivably have been prevented had he resigned on Sunday, the day his policy was rejected in the Council. His popularity was still such that Louis might have shrunk from coupling the new action of the Crown with the departure of Necker from office.*

The King's speech outlined what was in itself a notable programme of reforms. No taxes were henceforth to be levied without the assent of the nation's representatives; there was to be an annual budget; clerical and noble exemption from national taxes was to be abolished; internal customs barriers were to go, and so was the hated *corvée*; press censorship and arbitrary arrest under *lettres de cachet* were to be abolished or at least restricted.

Had such a programme been presented on May 5th, it would have been received with raptures. Now, on June 23rd, it was spoken into a stony silence. For Louis had prefaced his list of reforms with this declaration: 'The King wishes the ancient distinction of the Three Orders of the State to be preserved in its entirety . . . that the deputies freely elected by each Order, forming three chambers, deliberating by orders and at liberty, with the Sovereign's approval, to agree to deliberate in common, should alone be considered as forming the body of the Nation's representatives. Consequently, the King has declared null the

---

* Necker, at the request of the King and Queen, immediately resumed office. His gesture of resignation was, therefore, of no effect.

SIGNATURES, INCLUDING MIRABEAU'S, ATTACHED TO THE TEXT OF THE TENNIS COURT OATH

resolutions taken by the deputies of the Third Estate on the seventeenth of this month, as well as any subsequent ones, as being illegal and unconstitutional.'

The royal voice droned on through fourteen articles on the procedure of the States-General and thirty-five on desirable reforms; but few of the Commons were paying much attention now; they were disappointed, angry and perhaps a little afraid. What would happen next? Would they have to accept these partial reforms conceded as of grace from the throne, and abandon their proud posture of a sovereign assembly? Dared they stand their ground and spurn the merely consultative role to which it was evidently intended to confine them? That would be defiance, rebellion almost, and these deputies had been conditioned by generations of obedience to kings. Then there were those troops outside — would Louis, in extremity, use them? What else were they there for? And apart from that, would defiance be understood in the country at large, when the King was in the very act of granting so much of what the electors had asked? What mandate had deputies received to resist a reforming monarch? And now at last the King was ending. 'I command you, Gentlemen,' they heard him say, 'to disperse at once, and to present your-selves tomorrow morning each in the chamber allotted to your order. . . .'

It was over. The King and his attendants left the hall. The majority of the nobles followed him; so did a minority of the clergy. The rest remained, fumbling with their hats, exchanging looks of anxious inquiry, hesitating.

The Marquis de Dreux Brézé, Master of the King's Household, entered the hall. As the King's representative he kept his plumed hat on; deputies shouted to him to uncover; he refused with an oath and spoke peremptorily: 'Gentlemen, you have heard the King's orders.'

Mirabeau was on his feet in a flash, his face convulsed: 'Yes, Sir, we have heard the wishes which have been put into the King's mind. As for you, who have no standing as his spokesman in the National Assembly, you who have here neither place nor voice nor right to speak, it is not for you to remind us of his words. However, to avoid any misunderstanding or delay, I tell you that if you have orders to make us move from here, you had better ask for authority to use force: for we shall not quit our places except at the point of the bayonet!'

There was a general shout: 'That is the Assembly's will!'

Dreux Brézé turned to the President, Bailly: 'I recognize M. de Mirabeau as the deputy for Aix,' he sneered, 'and not as the mouthpiece of the Assembly. You have heard, Sir, the King's order?'

Bailly replied that, since the Assembly had resolved to continue sitting after the Royal Session, he could not adjourn it without its free vote taken after discussion.

'Is that the reply which I am to take to the King?' asked the Grand Master.

'Yes, Sir,' answered Bailly, 'for I take it,' he continued, turning to the deputies, 'that the assembled nation cannot receive orders.'

Dreux Brézé retired, *backward*, some witnesses record, as if from the presence of majesty. Sieyès spoke: 'Today you are what you were yesterday: let us deliberate.'

But the danger was not over. Any minute now they might hear the beat of marching feet, the shouted command, the clink of firelocks announcing the end. One thing remained to be done, and Mirabeau did it: he proposed and carried a motion declaring that the person of every deputy was inviolable, and that whosoever should prosecute or arrest a deputy for words spoken in the Assembly would be guilty of a capital offence.[105]

The Assembly was now decked for sacrifice, its breast bared to the stroke which would destroy its visible existence. The stroke was never given. Whether from a real reluctance to use force against his people's representatives, or from fear that the soldiers might refuse to turn their bayonets against them (Louis had just heard of mutiny in the Paris garrison) or from simple and innate irresolution, the King did not order the soldiers in. In what had been essentially a trial of nerves the Commons had won. During the next three days some fifty nobles and nearly all the remaining clergy joined them.

On June 27th, Louis XVI ordered the amalgamation of the Three Orders, and absolute monarchy in France was at an end.

CHAPTER X

THE DELUGE

'IT remains only for them to form a Constitution,' Morris, the American, wrote on June 27th, adding 'as the King is extremely timid he will of course surrender at discretion. The existence of the Monarchy depends upon the moderation of this Assembly.'

It was, however, not about the continued existence of the monarchy but about the permanence of their own newly-won legislative status that the reforming deputies felt misgivings. Louis had made no free concession; he had surrendered from weakness a position he had explicitly declared he would hold; he must, therefore, be expected to try to recover it. The die-hards among the clergy and the nobles were making no secret of their disgust at the amalgamation of the Orders. The reformers, therefore, remained watchful for the first sign of reaction, and the Assembly worked in an atmosphere inimical to counsels of moderation.

Mirabeau now appeared to his colleagues, to the Court and to the Ministry as the incarnation of the revolutionary spirit. His aspect counted for much — the massive head with its great shock of hair, the patrician beak of a nose, the mouth, thin-lipped, curved and scornful, the large red-rimmed eyes, the pock-marked skin. 'His very ugliness', wrote Madame de Staël, 'lent expression to his face, and his whole person gave the impression of irregular power — just such a power as you would picture to yourself in a tribune of the people.' His defiant words to Dreux Brézé, putting in one white-hot sentence the central article of the nation's new faith, had singled him out for fear and hatred and adoration.

He could have been a supreme demagogue, perhaps the first modern dictator, had not his powerful intelligence closed to him a course of merely vulgar ambition. As sincere as any in his con-viction that there should be liberty in a civilized country, he knew, what so many then forgot, that civil liberty is always a relative condition, never an absolute state; that it cannot exist, either in logic or in practice, without order, and that in revolutionary times the price of order, no less than of liberty, is vigilance.

The scandals of his private life, coupled with his recent inflammatory courses, convinced many in all parties that he was simply the spendthrift profligate seeking to restore a private fortune out of public calamities. It was a natural conclusion, but unjust. Certainly he welcomed in the advent of the revolution a chance of displaying abilities which had remained ill-employed amid the respectabilities of a settled society, but he was no mere careerist. He knew what a testing time was at hand for government, he had measured the men in power, and he had measured himself.

Among those who were shocked at his conduct, seeing him as a bad man exploiting the passions of the hour for dubious purposes, was Pierre-Victor Malouet, deputy for Riom. Nearing fifty, grave, far-seeing, a judicious and moderate reformer who had in the last eight years gained administrative experience as *Intendant* of Toulon, Malouet had, even in the first days of the States-General, become perturbed at the drift of things. Deeply distrusting the motions of popular enthusiasm (his own election by acclamation had worried his legal soul) he was appalled by the planlessness of the ministers, and had warned Necker and Montmorin in April of the danger of meeting the Estates without a programme ready prepared. He deplored the preponderance in the Commons of opinionated little men 'quoting the *Contrat social*, declaiming vehemently against tyranny and abuses, and each of them proposing a constitution'.[106] Malouet had been friendly with the Comtesse de Mirabeau at the time of her lawsuit with her husband, and had conceived the worst opinion of his morals together with a grudging respect for his talents, which recent exchanges in debate had increased. It disgusted him that, in an assembly so lacking in the ballast of responsibility and experience, the formidable deputy for Aix should engage recklessly in rocking the boat.[107]

Malouet was surprised, therefore, when, at the end of May, Duroveray and Dumont, whom he had known at Geneva, told him that Mirabeau wanted to meet him. Preferring neutral ground for an encounter with the demagogue, he agreed to a rendezvous in Duroveray's apartment that evening.

Mirabeau came straight to the point.

'I come to you,' he began, 'because of your reputation. Your views, which are nearer to mine than you think, are the reason for the step I am taking. You are, I am convinced, one of the sane friends of liberty; so am I. You are alarmed at the storms which are gathering; I am no less alarmed. There are among us many hotheads, many dangerous men. Among the aristocrats in the first two orders the intelligent men all lack common sense, and as for the fools, I know many capable of setting a match to the powder. The question is, therefore, whether the monarchy and the monarch will survive the coming tempest, or whether the mistakes already made, and those others which infallibly will be made, are to engulf us all.'

This was certainly not the kind of thing Malouet had expected. What was the man getting at?

Mirabeau continued: 'What I have to add is quite simple. You are, I know, a friend of M. Necker and M. Montmorin, the two men who, in practice, count in the King's council. I like neither of them, and I don't suppose they care for me; but it matters little whether we like each other if we can come to an understanding. I am appealing to you to arrange a meeting with them.' The government, while putting aside the idea that this States-General could be treated like the assemblies of the past, must choose a consistent policy and stick to it: 'If the plan is sensible within a monarchical framework,' he concluded, 'I pledge myself to support it, and to use all my means and all my influence to halt the invasion of democracy which is advancing towards us.'

Almost as delighted as he was surprised, Malouet nevertheless answered guardedly that he was sure the ministers sincerely intended to do all they could to promote a régime of liberty. 'Very good, let them say it and prove it!' Mirabeau answered, 'It's not, however, vague words that I want, but a definite plan. If it's any good, I'll devote myself to it; if, on the other hand, they intend to trifle with us, they'll find that we are to be reckoned with.'

Malouet hurried off to Necker, whom he found with Montmorin. He told them excitedly what had passed, but his news fell flat. Montmorin recalled the disgraceful business of the Berlin Letters; what confidence, he asked, could be placed in such a man? Necker said nothing and gazed at the ceiling. But Malouet persisted: he had no brief for Mirabeau's character, but believed that a man with such influence, such skill in debate, such sheer lung power (an important asset in the vast Assembly Hall) ought to be enlisted for the government if he were willing. Necker said he thought the man's influence had been exaggerated, but in the end agreed to see him the next morning at eight o'clock.

Malouet let Mirabeau go to the interview alone. It was a mistake for which he later blamed himself bitterly: 'Instead of acting as an intermediary to two men who detested each other, but whom it was so vital to bring to an understanding, I waited like an awkward fool to hear the result of their conference.' As the deputies made for their seats for the morning session he saw Mirabeau coming towards him with an angry flush on his face. As he stepped over a bench next to Malouet he growled 'Your man is a fool. He shall hear more of me!' Then he passed on.[108]

2

A month later, a few days after the amalgamation of the Orders, Mirabeau encountered an acquaintance. 'Don't you recognize your old friends any more?' he bantered. 'You haven't spoken a word to me yet.'

The Comte de La Marck apologized: they had had so little occasion to meet of late, belonging, as they had, to separate chambers; but it would be different now, and they must see more of each other; would M. de Mirabeau do him the honour of dining with him?[109]

Among the foreign troops in the permanent service of France was the Regiment of La Marck, raised in the days of Louis XIV. Recruited from Germans, this infantry regiment was an hereditary property of the Counts of La Marck. In 1768 Count Louis, having no male heir, arranged to pass on the regiment to his daughter's second boy. Her husband, the Duke of Aremberg, a sovereign prince of the Holy Roman Empire, was attached to Belgium by residence and property and to the House of Austria by family tradition. Maria Theresa, whose good relations with Versailles were about to be confirmed by her daughter's marriage to the Dauphin, smiled on the proposal, and so it came about that Auguste Marie Raymond, Prince d'Aremberg, while still a youth, entered the service of France. Marie Antoinette, leaving all she loved and understood to meet her destiny among the critical and brilliant French, was advised by her mother, among many things, to befriend the young Prince d'Aremberg. She regarded him thenceforth as one upon whom she could rely, and he repaid her with his greatest virtue and her greatest need — loyalty.

When in 1773 old Count Louis died his regiment and title passed to young Prince Auguste, who had meanwhile served as a subaltern, and was thenceforth known as the Comte de La Marck. During the American War he took his regiment to India. A severe wound in the chest left him with lung trouble for the remainder of his eighty years. After the war he held the responsible post of Inspector-General of Infantry. A good Catholic and a man of singular integrity, he watched the beginning of the revolutionary drama with a detachment and understanding which were admirable in one whose instincts and sympathies were those of the *ancien régime.*[110]

It was in 1788, at a fashionable dinner at Versailles, that he first met Mirabeau, who had been invited to satisfy the curiosity of certain members of the *grand monde* concerning an outsider whose name was increasingly on men's lips. What first struck La Marck was the man's appearance — his square, burly figure, his great leonine head made still more striking by an excessive mass of curled and powdered hair, his clothes a shade too fashionable, his coloured buttons and shoe-buckles a shade too large. Nor were his manners quite right: he bowed a little too low and overdid his compliments when introduced. In that company, in fact, he appeared gauche, especially, La Marck noted, when he addressed ladies.

But when dinner and small-talk were over and the conversation turned to politics, the stranger at once and as by natural right took charge of it. La Marck became fascinated. He made a point of improving the acquaintance, and Mirabeau became a frequent guest at his table, meeting there a society to which he had hitherto had no entry. On one occasion the Duke of Orleans was, by his own request, the fellow-guest of Mirabeau, but that dinner was not a success. Mirabeau thanked his host for the honour of the introduction, but said emphatically that he neither liked the Duke nor trusted him.

With the elections La Marck and Mirabeau lost sight of each other; while the latter was conducting his stormy campaign in Provence, the former was securing election by the nobility of Quesnoy on the Belgian frontier, a district where he had valuable mining property. Their encounter at the end of June renewed their acquaintanceship.

They dined tête-à-tête.

'You're pretty displeased with me, aren't you?' said Mirabeau on entering.

'With you and a good many others,' his host replied.

'In that case, you ought to begin with those who live at the Château. The ship of state is being battered by the most violent tempest, and there is no one at the helm.' Mirabeau developed his theme with energy, blaming Necker above all; it was his criminal negligence in meeting the Estates without a plan which had been the cause of the trouble. France was rich enough, and it was an imbecility to suppose that the deficit could not be made good.

'But at what, then, are you yourself aiming, with the incendiary line you have adopted both inside and outside the Assembly?'

'France's lot is decided,' answered Mirabeau; 'the words "liberty" and "taxation by consent" have resounded throughout the kingdom. There is no solution now without a government more or less similar to that of England.' Was it his fault, he asked, if the ministers repulsed him and forced him to assume the leadership of the popular party? 'The time has come when men must be valued by what they carry *here*,' and he tapped his forehead.

Unwilling to admit the assumption that it was a law of nature that Mirabeau should be a leader, if not of good men then of bad, La Marck again chided him for using his eloquence to increase the government's difficulties.

'The day the King's ministers consent to talk sensibly with me,' his guest replied, 'they will find me devoted to the royal cause and to the salvation of the monarchy.'

This was interesting. Where, asked La Marck, did he think the present course would end?

'In the ruin of France,' came the emphatic reply, 'and if they wish to save her, there's no time to be lost in employing the only means to that end. The way they are going on is absurd, crazy. They leave the Assembly to its own devices, and flatter themselves either that they can suppress it by force, as the aristocratic party would like, or that they can bring it to heel by M. Necker's empty and redundant phrases; whereas what is needed is for the government to set about forming a party within it through the agency of men who have the power to influence it, lead it and calm it.'

Some days later Mirabeau was again La Marck's guest. His host's elder brother, Aremberg, was there, as well as Lauzun and several others. On a hint from La Marck, Mirabeau spoke little and guardedly on the events of the hour; but as he took his leave he whispered to his friend: 'Let them know at the Palace that I am more for them than against them.'[111]

3

Almost every day witnessed episodes justifying Mirabeau's dark prognostics. Repeated mutiny by the French Guards in the capital led to the imprisonment of fifteen ringleaders in the Abbaye, and on June 30th a mob broke open the prison and rescued these patriots. French troops failed badly to suppress this riot, and the next day the great-hearted Assembly persuaded the King to pardon the mutineers. Debauched by the gold of Orlean's agents, the drink they spent it on, the plaudits of the populace and their own impunity, the garrison troops of Paris became a menace to authority. The government fell back upon trying to overawe the capital from outside, and moved fifteen regiments, eleven of them foreign, into the country between Paris and Versailles. This was a remedy more dangerous than the disease, a selling of what was popular and national in the monarchy to purchase force for the momentary needs of the government. Even level-headed royalists were dismayed, while deputies who had made themselves conspicuous on the popular side were beginning to fear sudden arrest.[112]

By July 8th, the Assembly was thoroughly alarmed at this concentration of troops, and Mirabeau proposed an address to the King for their removal. 'Thirty-five thousand men are already deployed between Paris and Versailles. Twenty thousand more are expected. Artillery-trains are following, gun-sites have been chosen. All communications have been secured, all movement is intercepted; our highways, our bridges and our walks have been turned into military posts.' He recalled the sinister massing of troops around the Assembly in the previous month, but this was much more serious. 'Since it is free men that the King wishes to command, it is time to put away these odious appearances, these offensive proceedings, which only too easily persuade those who surround the monarch that the royal majesty consists in the degrading relationship of master to slave.' What excuse was there for these troops? Had not Paris settled down quietly at the King's mere request after his clemency over the Abbaye disturbance? 'Never has the people had such reason to be tranquil and confident; everything points to an end of its miseries, everything assures it that the kingdom will be regenerated, and it is upon us that it fixes its attention and its hopes. Should not we, therefore, standing at the King's side, be the best guarantee of the confidence, obedience and fidelity of the people?'[113]

This last was, of course, largely clap-trap. It was a speech to a sovereign assembly. La Marck would have disliked such phrases as 'enemies of the people' and 'apparatus of tyranny' with which the discourse was liberally peppered. Yet though Mirabeau spoke with his eye on the Left, his belief that King, Assembly and Nation must be fused together informs the whole oration. Though he delighted the hotheads, he was not being inconsistent with the monarchist convictions he had lately confessed in private. On the contrary, these remained axiomatic. He would strike with all his power at the enemies of the unity of the kingdom; he would strike to right or to left as the occasion demanded; and the present occasion, when Louis was so manifestly yielding to Artois and the intransigents, required that he should strike at the Right.

These troop movements were a menace for a variety of reasons. How, he asked, would the poor of Paris, struggling with rocket-

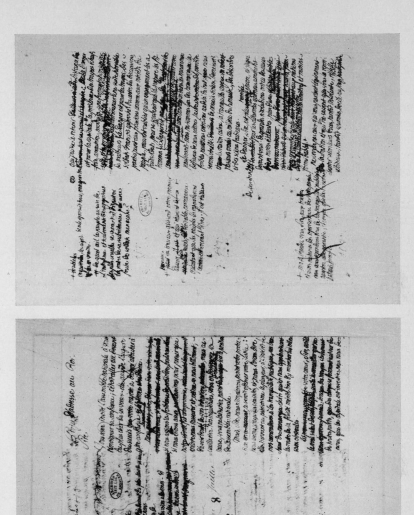

DRAFT IN MIRABEAU'S HANDWRITING OF THE ADDRESS TO THE KING, JULY 8TH, 1789

ing bread prices, regard these legions camped around them and eating a daily ration which might be relieving their own hunger? And what of the menace to military discipline? Some of the troops were foreigners, but others were Frenchmen, citizens, that is, who shared the feelings of the hour. Was it wise to draw these men into the magnetic field of political excitement between Versailles and the capital? Might not their presence outside Paris shake their discipline even while that of the foreign regiments alarmed the populace within? Had those responsible considered 'by what terrible impulsion a maddened people is driven on to excesses the very suggestion of which would at first have made it shudder?' Let the Assembly, therefore, present an address to the King requesting him to remove the troops, and suggesting, furthermore, that a citizen-militia be forthwith formed to guarantee order.

A committee was appointed to draw up the Address. Lameth, who was on the committee with Mirabeau, whom he disliked and distrusted, admitted that it was he who gave the Address its passionate eloquence. Mirabeau reported for the committee the next day. His proposal for a citizen-militia was rejected, though the logic of terrible events was, within a week, to create in the National Guard precisely what he had suggested. For the rest, the Address was adopted by 744 votes to 4, and presented to the King on the evening of July 10th. Mirabeau, with Robespierre, Barère, Pétion and others, was one of that deputation, and it is said that, though it was Clermont-Tonnerre who read aloud the long Address, Louis kept his dull and myopic gaze fixed the while on the deputy for Aix.[114]

The next day, Saturday, the King replied: the Assembly might move to Noyon or Soissons if they would feel safer; he would himself go to Compiègne to keep in touch with them; but he would not remove the troops.

'We have not asked permission to run away from the troops,' Mirabeau commented, 'but that the troops should be moved away from the capital.' The King's answer was, in fact, no answer; the Court was committed to reaction, and that same day Necker and other moderate ministers were dismissed.

It was notice to the nation that the government had abandoned collaboration with the Assembly for reform. What followed was the great Parisian insurrection which culminated in the capture of the Bastille on Tuesday, July the Fourteenth.

Mirabeau, by a strange fatality, was prevented from witnessing the crisis he had foretold. Just as it was about to break, news reached him that a neglected political philosopher was dead. He hurried away to attend his father's funeral.

The old man had of recent years been reduced to small account in reputation and estate, his opinions unheeded by a new generation, his Paris house made over to the Du Saillants who had sponged on him for years, beloved Le Bignon sold. As France moved towards transformations less orderly than the disciples of Quesnay had envisaged, the Friend of Mankind rented a house at Argenteuil, and there he lived his last years peacefully with his dear Madame de Pailly, a courtyard separating their quarters out of respect for the conventions. He deplored what he saw of the Revolution, and though he had his moments of pride at Gabriel's recent career, the old habit of depreciation remained. Profoundly an aristocrat, he had seen with weary irritation his elder son cast out from his order, and in his will ('I belong to the age', he had prefaced it, 'when all acts of this sort were begun by this formula of the Christian: In the name of the Father and of the Son and of the Holy Ghost') he had left all to Boniface who, a family man at last and deputy for the nobility of Limousin, gross, bibulous, disorderly, and in debt, but with a gift for the salty remark, was winning a certain position on the Right. Yet it was his elder son, with his conviction of the reformative power of a popularized monarchy, who was the lawful heir to his philosophic legacy. As Gabriel, with Boniface, followed the body to the graveside there were offences enough to regret and little enough of kindness to remember, though he had kept through all a certain regard for that obstinate, didactic and despotic old man. Indeed, as the later years loosened their relationship and put an easeful space between them, each in his way had acknowledged in the other the eminent originality of their race, and a sort of wry, mutual respect had begun to appear. It was at least with genuine pride that Gabriel declared to his constituents and to the public that this loss ought to put all citizens of the world into mourning.[115]

He was back in his place for the evening session of the Fourteenth. Nerves were badly frayed, for the Assembly, having declared its confidence in the dismissed ministers, had sat all the previous night. They had met again at nine that morning, and when, about five o'clock, they met once more, they were in no mood to receive with caution the tendentious report which two representative Parisians brought them of what had been done in the city that day.

They were convinced that the Court was resolved to arrest the Revolution by force. They had heard that Artois, the Duchesse de Polignac and others had, that very day, visited the German regiments and entertained the officers with refreshments. The sack of the Bastille seemed to them to be the capital's just reaction to an immediate threat. They sent a deputation to the King imploring him to order the troops away, but as Louis would still give no assurance on this vital point the Assembly decided on a second all-night session. It was a gesture in part theatrical. 'We resolved to prolong our session throughout the night,' wrote Mirabeau, 'partly to present ourselves to our enemies, like the Roman Senate to the Gauls of old, in the discharge of our sacred functions, partly to be ready at any moment to make a final effort to influence the Throne and to succour the Capital ... Never shall I forget that sad spectacle: the nation's deputies, whom the King had convoked, a prey to a consuming dread; old men seeking an hour's rest on tables or on the carpet; the weaker members lying on the benches; all seeing the sword hanging over them and over the fatherland, and all dreading a morrow more fearful still.'[116] Early on that morrow it was decided to send one more deputation to the King. Time might well be precious; nevertheless formal proposals were made as to what should be said, and the wearisome process of amendments would have followed, had not Mirabeau cut short the solemn verbiage.

'Tell him,' he shouted, 'that the alien hordes by which we are besieged received yesterday a visit from Princes and Princesses, from ladies and gentlemen in favour; that they received their endearments, their exhortations and their gifts. Tell him that all night long these hireling foreigners, gorged with gold and wine, have boasted in their impious songs of the coming enslavement of France, and called with brutal oaths for the destruction of the

National Assembly. Tell him that in his own palace courtiers have been dancing to the strains of this barbarous music, and that such was the overture to St. Bartholemew's Day.'

A regimental band playing under the Queen's windows was scant excuse for these wild words, yet even in his rage he recalled what the Kingship had once been and could again be. In the Address of July 9th, there had been a characteristic allusion to Saint Louis and Henri Quatre, and now he concluded: 'Tell him that the Great Henry of blessed memory, whom, of all his ancestors, he wished to take for model, let provisions pass into rebel Paris when he was besieging it in person, whereas his own savage advisers are turning back from loyal but famished Paris the flour which normal trade would bring it.'[117]

The deputation left the hall, but was stopped outside by the Duc de Liancourt, who had good news: in a final effort to free the King from disastrous advisers, he had used his privilege as Master of the Wardrobe to wake Louis early and had, at last, persuaded him that it was a revolution, not a revolt, with which he had to deal; His Majesty was even now on his way to the *Menus Plaisirs*. Immensely relieved, the deputies gave vent to rejoicings which Mirabeau thought undignified and premature.

The King arrived. Accompanied only by his brothers, Provence and the defeated Artois, he stood uncovered and spoke briefly. One sentence alone mattered: ' . . . counting on the love and fidelity of my subjects, I have given the order to the troops to move away from Paris and Versailles.' One other thing was noticed: the term 'National Assembly' on the King's lips for the first time.

He returned to the château on foot, accompanied by the deputies in a body. Their cries of 'Vive le Roi!' were taken up by the spectators, by the troops; it was a sort of triumph. That night Artois emigrated.

Next day the Council discussed a suggestion that the King should fly to Metz, but Louis was not easily persuaded to become a fugitive King, and the idea was dropped. Instead, while the Polignac set, quite routed, prepared to follow Artois, Louis signed an order for Necker's recall, and on the seventeenth he paid his memorable and not uncourageous visit to Paris. 'Whoever advised this step is a bold fellow,' Mirabeau observed. 'Without it Paris was lost to the King; two or three days later he might not have been able to enter it.' Louis's visit to Paris, from which he was by no means confident of returning alive, was probably his his own idea; it was, in the passive courage it demanded, a characteristic act.

Meanwhile the Assembly had demanded the dismissal of Breteuil and the other guilty ministers. This was an audacity which shocked some moderates like Mounier, but Mirabeau, in a powerful speech, carried the point. Why? It was a serious invasion of the prerogative, and he did not wish to weaken the Crown; still less did he wish to see Necker back. But he did wish for a parliamentary ministry, and he saw in the establishment of the legislative's right to censure ministers a step towards it, since necessity, he believed, would bring ministers into the Assembly to defend themselves, and a further necessity would require that only such men should be ministers as could convince the chamber. His speech shows that he had the English example in mind. Did he already see himself as the great minister, answering, coaxing, leading the Commons of France, trusted by the King and fortifying him in return with their votes? Perhaps. For the moment, he delivered a significant attack on the fashionable doctrine of the separation of powers.

4

In the orgasm of the Bastille insurrection Paris had reconstituted itself as something like an independent republic, and when Louis went to the Hôtel de Ville he encountered, and recognized, two institutions spontaneously generated — the Commune (or municipality) and the National Guard. Had Mirabeau's proposal of July 8th been accepted by the Assembly and by the King, Louis would, before the fatal fourteenth, have had a citizen force with leaders of his own choosing, a possibly valuable lever over the democracy of the capital. Now the King was faced with a citizen-militia which owed nothing to him for its foundation, and which had already chosen as its leader that famous comrade-in-arms of Washington, the Marquis de Lafayette.

The Parisians, furthermore, having murdered Flesselles, last of the ancient line of Provosts of the Merchants, had appointed a chief magistrate with the new title of Mayor, and their choice had fallen upon Bailly. His popularity was due to his staunch conduct in June, his election to the accident that, at the critical moment of popular enthusiasm on the fifteenth, he was on the spot.

Mirabeau regarded it as a major misfortune for France that Bailly, and not he, should have been elected Mayor. When the sometime prisoner of Vincennes visited the ruins of the Bastille a day or two later his reception by the people was such that he may well have thought that he would have swept Bailly aside had they been rival candidates. But we can dismiss his complaint to La Marck that the only reason why he missed the mayoralty was that decency forbad him standing in view of his father's death. Decency had nothing to do with it. Nobody on the fifteenth knew that a mayor was going to be acclaimed that day, so there was no question of candidatures; it was simply that, at the critical moment, Bailly was in Paris and Mirabeau at Versailles. But it was a misfortune. As mayor of Paris he would have commanded what otherwise he had to court and solicit — the attention of the King and ministers, of the National Assembly and of M. de Lafayette. As for the Parisian masses, though he could not be their mayor he might still be their idol, and he proceeded to woo them; when Necker, returning to office, made a noble appeal for an end of reprisals against those who had stood for order during the insurrection, Mirabeau, it must be recorded, showed an unworthy readiness to condone the acts of the mob. He began to patronize young Desmoulins, who had blazed suddenly like a meteor of insurrection in the capital but was enormously flattered by the Tribune's attentions.[118]

5

The terrifying spread of château-burning and anarchy in the provinces, fruit of the mysterious mass-suggestion known as the Great Fear, led to the delirious night session of August 4th, when the clergy and nobles renounced their privileges and the Assembly happily voted away much of the law and custom of the

French countryside. Mirabeau had an inkling of what was coming and, with the excuse of a family conclave, absented himself from proceedings whose extravagance he condemned but knew he would be unable to control.[119] Not that he had any tenderness for feudal privileges; he would have been the last to defend the seigneur's rabbit-warrens and dovecotes and other rights which vexed and impoverished the peasantry, and he spoke strongly on August 7th against the King's right of hunting outside his domain being excepted from the general abolition: 'The royal prerogative is in my eyes too precious for me to consent that it should consist in a futile and oppressive pastime.' Still less had he any love for the tithe. But the hysteria of August 4th was not the mood in which responsible legislators re-mould the land-law of an ancient country; such precipitancy could only excite a population which badly needed a sedative, and 'crush under a pile of ruins the rising edifice of liberty', as Mirabeau wrote to his uncle in October.

It was the same anxiety to avoid exciting a people whose temperature was already too high which made him question the opportuneness of a declaration of the rights of man. The nation should not be given such heady liquor on an empty stomach; only after a solid meal, in the form of a good constitution established and working, might it taste the wine of human rights without danger. But Mirabeau and those like Malouet and the Bishop of Langres who agreed with him were overwhelmed by the enthusiasts headed by Barnave, and it was voted that the Declaration should be drawn up and affixed as a preamble to the constitution. He bowed to the majority with sufficient alacrity to be made *rapporteur* to the committee on the Declaration.

He took the lead in hammering out a draft and presented it on August 17th; but, as it pleased neither Left nor Right (it was indeed something of a hotch-potch) he again urged that the Declaration should be postponed till after the articles of the constitution had been settled. Certain members of the Breton Club* angrily accused him of abusing his powers as an orator to lead the house into contradictory resolutions, and tried to discredit him by allusions to the scandals of his former life. It was an irrelevance which he treated with the scorn it deserved; as

---

* Better known as the Society of the Friends of the Constitution, and later as the Jacobins.

for inconsistency, thirty volumes from his pen, he declared, existed to disprove that accusation. But the contest between the realist and the ideologues for control of the Assembly had begun.

It was a warfare in which the realist had no advantage but his talents. His opponents' minds were unclouded by any doubt of the virtue and wisdom of the Sovereign People, or of the adequacy with which they represented it, while their hearts were so sour with suspicion of authority that they had no hesitation in suddenly weakening the executive of a country accustomed for generations to obey kings whose will was law. Furthermore, they were uninhibited by responsibility to facts from over-bidding the cautious for plaudits and votes. Mirabeau, on the other hand, though convinced of the mischievous stupidity of this conduct, was obliged to compete with them on their own ground. He dared not risk being labelled a man of the Right, for this, he judged, would be the end of his influence. There were men on the Right whom he respected — Malouet, Mounier, Clermont-Tonnerre for example — but they were not material of which a party could be made. Though men of liberal inclinations, there was about them a fastidious individualistic rectitude which fitted them ill for the shifts, the jobs, the compromises which practical politics demanded. The name this group soon adopted — *Les Impartiaux* — fairly expressed their personal merits and their collective ineffectualness. Somehow, then, Mirabeau must beat Barnave, the Lameths and their sort at their own game, and yet contrive to avoid appearing a mere scourge to the Court and the Ministry. It was not going to be easy.[120]

The first serious trial of strength took place over the question of the royal veto. Was the new constitution to allow the King an absolute veto on legislation, or a merely suspensive veto, or no veto at all? Mirabeau, consistent with the opinion which had shocked some of his hearers in June, was for an absolute veto. Its exercise, he believed, would be rare in practice, as the example of England suggested; but the veto, held in reserve, would be a salutary check on the extravagances of the Assembly, a check all the more necessary since the majority of deputies, scenting aristocracy, would not hear of a second chamber resembling the powerful English House of Lords. The absolute veto, furthermore, might bring with it the right of dissolution, as the obvious way of resolving deadlocks between executive and legislative. Mirabeau never lost sight of the transcendent importance of a workable elasticity in the constitution: the government must respond to the wishes of the Assembly, but, equally, the Assembly must remember its duty to the government and its responsibility to the people; anything likely to cause government and Assembly to defy each other or forget the third person of that trinity must be avoided at all costs. While sharing the general dislike for an upper house as a refuge for aristocracy (had he not been rejected by the nobility of Provence?) he was almost alone in grasping the unique merit of the English constitution — a government physically present in, and answerable to, the legislature; a legislature sobered by knowing that it must pay for thwarting the government by undergoing the trials of an election; a ministry fortified against merely factious opposition by holding the trump card of an appeal to the electorate.

Yet in the speech he delivered on this subject on September 1st, he failed completely to impress his hearers. This was perhaps partly the result of a carelessness on his part arising from his peculiar methods of work.

As is well known, Mirabeau wrote very few of his own speeches. He had collected round him team of talented and serviceable assistants who drafted the speeches which he delivered. His own contribution usually consisted of three elements: he provided the germinal idea, he touched up the draft, and he delivered it as a speech. The biographer of a dead orator works under the serious limitation of never having seen and heard the man in action, and Mirabeau's hearers were so emphatic as to the magical effect of his presence that we, who can at best only read what he spoke without knowing where inspiration carried him beyond his text, must believe that the cold print bears about the same relation to the living speech as a map does to a landscape.

Besides his secretary, Pellenc, his regular assistants were Etienne Dumont, Duroveray, Clavière and, a little later, Reybaz. Political exiles from Geneva, they had brought in their luggage a prejudice in favour of revolutions. Dumont and Duroveray had lately come to Paris hoping that their compatriot, the Director of Finances, would do something for Genevan liberty, and their disappointment with Necker over this matter accorded with

Mirabeau's comprehensive contempt. Dumont, once a protestant pastor, privately resented devilling for a man whose tainted reputation alarmed his delicacy, but he had oratorical gifts which combined with a singular understanding of Mirabeau's ideas to make him probably the most serviceable member of the team. Clavière, Brissot tells us, 'loved Mirabeau more than all his other friends' and their friendship was of some years standing. Duroveray, who, like Clavière, was particularly helpful on financial topics, was a busy and ubiquitous man much concerned for his master's popularity. The latter referred to these men as his *atelier*. We may think of them best as a brilliant editorial staff. Indeed, in relation to the nineteen Letters to his Constituents and the *Courrier de Provence* which succeeded them after July, that is exactly what, for a while, they were. But the unique feature of their collaboration was that their principal organ was the voice and person of their chief.[121]

For his speech on the veto, however, Mirabeau went outside his 'workshop' for assistance. The Marquis de Casaux, an estate-owner in Grenada, had become a British subject with that island's annexation in 1763. Mirabeau regarded him as an authority on the English constitution, and it was a paper of his which he took with him on September 1st. 'After being forced to listen to so many execrable speeches', wrote Dumont, 'Mirabeau's appearance in the tribune delighted everybody; but . . . the embarrassed constructions, the singularity of the words, the lengthy periods and the obscurity of the reasoning cooled the attention of the Assembly. It was at length made out that he supported the absolute veto, and this excited much disapprobation. Mirabeau, who had scarcely looked at this trash before he left home, threw himself immediately into digressions, inveighed against despotism, and by some smart things, which he had always at command, obtained the applause of the galleries; but the moment he reverted to his fatal manuscript, the tumult started again and he had much difficulty in getting to the end of his speech . . . The galleries never found out what side of the question he had taken, and the Palais Royal, who were in a frenzy against the supporters of the absolute veto, did not cease to regard Mirabeau as one of its most zealous opponents. That which would have destroyed the popularity of any other seemed to have no power over his . . . I never saw Mirabeau out of countenance but this once. He confessed to me that, as he proceeded with the manuscript, which he had not read before, he felt himself in a cold perspiration. . . .'[122]

Dumont, of course, was jealous. The speech was, it is true, more pedestrian in style than the products of the *atelier*, but it was neither involved nor obscure; on the contrary it was a lucid exposition of the case for trusting the executive not only with the right to withhold assent from legislation but also with the power to dissolve and appeal to the country. It is hard to believe that his hearers can have had any doubt as to where the orator stood. Further, in its thought it was as much his speech as any Dumont prepared for him. 'Nobody objects to the veto of the National Assembly, which in effect is nothing but a right of the people, entrusted *to its representatives*, to resist any proposal tending to re-establish ministerial tyranny. Why, then, object to the monarch's veto, which also is nothing but a right of the people *specially entrusted to the prince*, because the prince is as interested as the people in preventing the establishment of aristocracy.' Here is the very marrow of Mirabeau's creed. Monarchy was, for him, essentially a popular thing, and its opposite was not democracy but oligarchy. It is significant that, at a moment when aristocracy seemed to be in process of rapid disestablishment, he spoke of the danger of re-establishing it; but he knew that its essence is the oligarchic spirit, and that this would find for itself new forms as soon as privileged landlordism had disappeared.

Few of his speeches contained more wisdom than this one; none made less impression. But the explanation is to be found less in Casaux's text than in the circumstances of the moment. The first Constitutional Committee had consisted mainly of moderates and had reported in favour of a second chamber and an absolute veto. But it had been appointed on July 14th, and during the weeks of its labours the Bastille crisis, the abolition of feudal privileges and the Declaration of Rights had taken place and had completely changed the climate of opinion. Desmoulins and the other agitators of the Palais Royal had, in particular, made the veto into an enormous popular bogy, and, the very day before Mirabeau's speech, had nearly staged a march on

Versailles. Between the demagogues and the ideologues the veto question simply had no chance of being considered on its merits, and it is not surprising that Mirabeau felt a cold perspiration as he realized that he had misjudged his audience and his moment. His hearers failed to get his drift because, in a closely reasoned discourse, he was saying the opposite of what most of them, being frightened, hoped and expected to hear. As for the workers of Paris, the veto was the enemy, Mirabeau was their father, *argal* Mirabeau would defend them against the wicked veto. When a report that he had been killed in a duel proved to have been exaggerated, it was suggested that he should be given a bodyguard. Paris refused to be disabused; alighting from his coach at Mme Le Jay's door the orator was fairly mobbed by his grateful fellow-citizens, and Desmoulins for a while refused to credit that his idol, the Thunderer as he called him, had done other than oppose the veto. Accordingly when Necker announced that the King would be content with a veto that should be merely suspensive, Mirabeau, relieved that his precious popularity had taken so little hurt, was glad to drop the subject. He voted with the huge majority against the second chamber on September 10th, but abstained from voting for the suspensive veto on the following day.[123]

It was on this eleventh (or perhaps the twelfth) of September that Mirabeau saw a priest coming to him across the chamber. Recognizing him as Vallet, the Curé of Gien, he asked him what brought one of his sort over to the benches of the Left. For answer the priest handed him a letter, and watched with curiosity while he read it. The letter was from Dr. Ysabeau, and it concerned one whom the doctor had attended for some years past, and whom M. le Comte would doubtless remember — the Marquise de Monnier, widowed these six years. This lady, the letter explained, had been on the point of marrying an estimable gentleman of the district, a M. de Poterat, when, on September 8th, he had died very suddenly. But the tragedy, alas, had been a double one, for Madame de Monnier, yielding evidently to an access of despair, had, early in the morning of the ninth, taken her own life by asphyxiation, to the great distress of the writer and of her other friends at Gien.

Sophie. . . .

Memory, suddenly bright and sharp, leapt out across eight years to jab at what had seemed a deadened nerve. Gabriel, finding no words, took the priest's hand; then, all discomposed, he walked out of the Hall, nor did men see him in the Assembly the next day, nor the next.[124]

6

The States-General had met in May for one primary purpose: to help the government to save the credit of the state. Four months had now passed, and Necker and the Assembly had between them achieved less than nothing. The very real, if largely destructive, achievements of the Assembly in the political field had brought the fiscal machine nearly to a standstill. In the general uncertainty and expectancy engendered by the Assembly's generous resolutions and the government's evident incapacity to protect property, most Frenchmen had simply stopped paying their taxes, and Necker had found nothing better to do than try to tide over this unexpected moratorium by raising loans which were so under-subscribed that the national credit came near to vanishing. As Mirabeau reminded the Assembly in mid-August, the incomes of the state's creditors and employees were in immediate danger of ceasing. As a last expedient the Minister, in late September, proposed a special non-recurring 25 per cent tax on incomes; it was to be called a 'patriotic gift' and the tax-payers, in the absence of any appropriate machinery, were to assess themselves. Why this new tax should be expected to succeed when the old ones were not being paid was not very evident. 'Enthusiasm will do to vote it,' commented Dupont de Nemours, 'but only wealth can pay it'; and enthusiasm was notably absent. Deputies who had promised their constituents a reduction of taxes shrank from voting for the sacrifice now demanded, nor could Necker's personal contribution of 100,000 francs convince many that his capacity as a minister was equal to his virtue as a citizen.* On the twenty-sixth, however, Mirabeau threw his weight behind Necker's proposal.

He spoke three times and still the issue hung in the balance.

---

* Necker had resumed office on July 28th.

When he mounted the tribune a fourth time he had to speak extempore. He began in a tone of blistering irony. He supported the Minister's proposal, he said, because it *was* a proposal, because there was simply no time to amend it or find a better: 'I do not think M. Necker's plans the best possible, but heaven preserve me, in such a critical situation, from opposing to them my own. It would be vain for me to urge their superiority. One cannot in a moment compete with a prodigious popularity won by striking services, with long experience, or with the reputation of the greatest known talent in finance' ('Your man is a fool, but he shall hear more of me!'). Then, having scorched the Minister with sarcasm, he proceeded, by an astounding *tour de force*, to win acceptance for his proposal. He scared his hearers out of their wits, making the monster of bankruptcy seem almost visible in their midst. Did the rich, of whom the sacrifice was demanded, think to escape the consequences of hugging their possessions? 'Stoical spectators of the incalculable evils which this catastrophe will spew all over France — impassive egoists, who think that these convulsions of despair and misery will pass like so many others, and all the quicker for being more violent — are you quite sure that a multitude without bread will permit you quietly to relish the dishes whose number and delicacy you have refused to diminish?' To right and to left the deputies sat or stood, the spellbound audience of a great actor. 'Ah, M. le Comte!' cried Molé of the *Theatre français* when it was over, 'What a speech! Mon Dieu! How you have missed your vocation!' The great voice rasped pitilessly on. 'What a damned rascal!' gasped a noble, 'but what talent!' At last, at the precise moment of climax, a final sentence, taunting and terrible snapped the tension: 'Bankruptcy, hideous bankruptcy is at your gates; it threatens to swallow you up with your possessions and your honour — and you discuss things!'[125]

7

La Marck had pondered much over Mirabeau's hint that he wished to serve the King, and the more he thought of it the more convinced he became that this was the man the Court needed.

A doubt remained: was Mirabeau, as was commonly said,

venal? That he was hard up was certain. After his father's death he had told La Marck that he did not expect to touch a penny of his inheritance for a considerable time, and meanwhile he was hard put to it to pay his valet. Evidently, then, he was not, as many believed, in the pay of Orleans, not yet at any rate.

One day in September, he came to La Marck with a worried air. 'My friend,' he said, 'it is in your power to do me a great service.'

'Name it,' said La Marck.

'I don't know which way to turn. I haven't so much as a half-crown. Lend me something.'

La Marck handed him fifty *louis*, which was all his loose cash. Mirabeau was touched. 'I don't know when I shall repay you,' he said. 'I haven't yet been able to attend to my inheritance, and already my relations are going to law with me.'

La Marck told him not to worry, adding that he would always find it a pleasure to purchase independence for a man of his character and talents. Mirabeau was moved.

The immediate problem for La Marck was how to induce the Court to trust and employ him; a wall of prejudice would have to be broken down, their bitter anger with his conduct as a demagogue and their respectable distaste for his reputation as a profligate.

La Marck decided to start by sounding De Cicé, Archbishop of Bordeaux and Keeper of the Seals. A great prelate of liberal views, leader of the clergy who had seceded *en masse* to the Commons, lately brought into the ministry to please Lafayette and reputed to be an admirer of Necker, De Cicé appeared to be the one minister whom it might be useful to approach. He surprised La Marck by saying at the start that he had lost all confidence in Necker, that the man was quite hopeless and was ruining France. But, as the conversation proceeded, it became evident that the Archbishop's mind was running not on what Mirabeau might do for the government in the Assembly but on what he himself could do if only he had Necker's place.

The approach to the Ministry through De Cicé having proved a blind alley, La Marck next decided to approach the Court directly, to go to the Queen. He put the matter first to his old friend, the Comtesse d'Ossun, a Lady of the Bedchamber very simply devoted to her mistress. Would she, he asked, assure the Queen that his recent relations with Mirabeau meant no lessening of his devotion to their Majesties, that, far from it, the change was rather in the deputy for Aix, and that he seriously believed that the monarchy had need of this man's services?

A few days later he saw the Queen herself.

'I have never doubted your sentiments,' she said, 'and when I learnt that you were associated with Mirabeau, I felt sure that it was with good intentions; but you will never be able to control him, and as for your views as to what the King's ministers should do, I do not agree with you. We shall never, I think, be in such straits as to be reduced to the pitiful necessity of having recourse to Mirabeau.'

It was perhaps all that could be expected for the moment. 'You will never be able to control him'; there, certainly, lay the difficulty. He had already impressed on his friend how hard it would be to overcome royal aversion so long as he pursued his inflammatory course in public. 'But what position, then, am I to adopt?' the other had asked. 'The government rejects me, so I have either to place myself in the opposition, which is a revolutionary party, or risk losing the popularity which is my strength. The armies are face to face; it's necessary either to treat or to fight, and the government, by doing neither the one nor the other, is playing a very dangerous game.'

The two men were being drawn together not only by a similarity of purpose but also by the love of complementary characters. La Marck, the Belgian, was warmed by the Provençal's fire, heartened even when alarmed by his audacity, fascinated while perplexed by his devious activities; and to Mirabeau the other's steady singleness of mind was a strength and a refreshment; he respected a caution unalloyed with cowardice, an integrity free from the self-righteousness so common in the upright men of that day.

After the check with the Queen La Marck promised Mirabeau fifty *louis* a month if he would undertake to borrow from no one else. It was accepted with tears of gratitude, but the loan did not lose the friend; on this La Marck is explicit: 'Till the time of his death', he writes, 'his feelings for me never altered for one instant.'

They met almost daily during September. The air was once more heavy with political thunder. In Paris the price of bread was rising; rumours were current that the King intended to fly; a new and ominous impatience with the Assembly was to be noted. 'Opinions are changing fast,' wrote the observant Morris, 'and in a very little time, if the *Assemblée nationale* continue their present career, a majority of this nation will, I think, be opposed to them. Their adherents, however, are zealous, and if a civil war does not take place, it must be . . . that from the King's feebleness of character nobody can trust themselves to him or risk themselves in support of his authority; but if he escapes from Versailles and falls into different hands from those now about him, there must be a struggle.'

On the twenty-third the Flanders Regiment arrived at Versailles.

'What are these people thinking of?' Mirabeau asked his friend in exasperation. 'Don't they see the abyss which is opening under their feet?' And another time he exclaimed; 'All is lost! The King and Queen will perish, and you will see it; the mob will batter their corpses.' When La Marck looked horrified, 'Yes, yes!' he added, 'they'll batter their corpses. You don't sufficiently realize the dangers of their position. Meanwhile they ought to be made aware of them.'[126]

On October 1st, their blindness led them to a supreme act of political insanity. The banquet of welcome given by the Gardes du Corps to the Flanders officers — a normal inter-regimental courtesy which it would perhaps have been prudent to omit in these abnormal times — was converted into an outright royalist demonstration by the folly of the Queen. That she, carrying her baby Dauphin and accompanied by the King, came in when the ardours of wine and loyalty were reaching their height, that the band played the song of deathless fealty from Grétry's opera, that there was cheering and a drinking of loyal toasts — these things are certain; that those young blades showed their hearts in wine and trampled the national colours underfoot was widely reported. Mirabeau was furious at this mischievous parody of monarchism, and spoke of it with violence; for indeed a better pretext could not have been given to those eager to bring the force of Paris to bear on Versailles.

The belief that the Court was again plotting reaction was strengthened by the King's sudden stiffness over the constitutional resolutions. On October 5th, at the morning session, the

Assembly was informed that his acceptance of the Declaration of Rights, the Suspensive Veto and other laws was strictly conditional on the executive power remaining unimpaired in his hands.

The Left was instantly aroused, with Mirabeau in the van. Though the preservation of the royal executive was his aim, he would have nothing to do with the sabre-and-bayonet brand of royalism favoured by the Queen. Yet, though he spoke in anger, his political conceptions were evident even now. The executive must not be independent of the legislative, but that was not to say that it should be weak. He pointed out that the King's reply had not been counter-signed, a serious omission, since there must be no evading 'the salutary law of responsibility'. As for the recent banquet, the King must certainly forbid any repetition of such a scene.

Pétion had spoken violently of this episode, and a deputy of the Right challenged him to put his denunciation in writing. Suddenly irritated, Mirabeau said that, though he thought this would be unwise, he would, if it were insisted on, sign it himself, 'but first, I ask this Assembly to declare that the King's person *alone* is inviolable, and that all other individuals in the state, whosoever they may be, are equally subject and answerable to the law'.

The threat to the Queen was thinly veiled. The moderate Mounier, who was president, was horrified. A little before midday Mirabeau went up to him and spoke earnestly in an undertone: news had come in the last hour that Paris was on the march; let him bring this scandalous session to an end; let him make some excuse — pretend to be ill or something — and go and warn the royal family; let him say, if he liked, that he had it from Mirabeau, but above all let him act quickly as there was not a moment to lose. Mounier, in bitter distress, concluded that the monstrous tribune enjoyed some sort of collusive knowledge and was trying to stampede the Assembly. After some hesitation he compromised. He left the house in session, handing over his chair to the Bishop of Langres; then he went off to find the King — vainly, as it proved, for Louis XVI, at this crisis in the destiny of the monarchy, was out hunting.

The session continued, turning to other business, and Mirabeau left the hall.

Some four hours later the women of Paris arrived.[127]

CHAPTER XI

THE FIRST DEFEAT

THE events of the fifth and sixth of October transformed the situation morally as well as materially. They transformed it morally because the King and Queen had, for the first time, suffered insult and violence to their persons. Hereditary kingship is a symbol of the religious and instinctive forces which, more powerfully than common sense and self-interest, bind society together. For this reason monarchy must always be surrounded by a certain aura of majesty, expressed in ceremony. A king is set apart by his office, which he holds by the hazard of inheritance and not by election. The republican's faith is that every man should rule, the monarchist's that any man may rule; and because the odds are that the king, while standing in an extraordinary position, will be a very ordinary sort of fellow, the appearances of majesty must surround him. In particular, because he is the symbol of the unity and continuity of national life, his person must be inviolable.

This inviolability the October Days destroyed. The prestige of Louis XVI as a ruler had been gravely enough impaired by his wavering treatment of the Estates in June and the collapse of his irresolute experiment in reaction by force in July. But the King coming freely to the Hôtel de Ville and giving his retrospective sanction to a revolt of his capital was one thing: the King dragged to the capital from his palace and seat of government at Versailles by a screaming mob which had stuck on pikes the gory heads of bodyguards who had prevented by a matter of seconds the murder of the Queen — this was something of an altogether different kind. Majesty itself was violated.

We may perhaps doubt whether Mirabeau, a man of the rationalist enlightenment, fully appreciated the deepest significance of the event, but he saw quite clearly that the monarch had fallen into bondage and that the end of it must be anarchy.

Early on the seventh, when there were few about in the dishevelled palace, he came to La Marck. 'If you have any means of getting the ear of the King and Queen,' he said on entering, 'persuade them that France and they are lost unless the royal family leaves Paris. I'm busy with a plan to get them out. Will you be able to go and assure them that they can count on me?'

'Get on with your plan,' La Marck replied. 'When it's ready I'll be able to make it reach them all right.'

Whether the royal pair could be induced to count on Mirabeau was not so certain. That someone had planned the events of Monday and Tuesday was obvious. Who was it? Suspicion pointed to Orleans, known paymaster of the Paris revolutionaries; but it pointed also to Mirabeau. His real attitude to the monarchy was as yet understood by no one, whereas his thinly veiled threat against the Queen, spoken from the tribune even while the women were on the march from Paris, now echoed with sinister significance in the minds of all who shuddered as they recollected Monday night. And why should not he, like Desmoulins who had been his guest for the last fortnight at Versailles, have been in the pay of Orleans? Even La Marck was puzzled to explain his friend's reckless words, and taxed him bluntly with them. How could the man who had so recently shown such anxious foreboding of disaster to the royal pair have said even the least word to increase their mortal peril when the catastrophe was upon them? Mirabeau seemed penitent; he had been carried away by the torrent of his own words and his irritation with the extreme Right whose fantastic imprudences had brought about the whole ghastly situation; but he had, he admitted, done wrong. Such an explanation, feeble as it sounded, was enough for La Marck, for he knew sufficient on his own account to clear his friend. He had seen for himself that there was no understanding between the latter and Orleans. Only a few days before October 5th, the Duke and Mirabeau had met at his own table, 'and I saw clearly', he afterwards wrote, 'that there was a reserve between them which excluded all suspicion of a secret understanding'. Furthermore, a day or two later Orleans had asked him brusquely when Mirabeau would start serving the Court. And if this was not enough to clear Mirabeau of complicity in an Orleanist plot, was there not the plain fact of his poverty? Was it conceivable, he reflected, that Mirabeau should have been on the Duke's enormous payroll at the very time when he was, with evident embarrassment, soliciting La Marck for the loan of a few *louis*?[128]

There was another circumstance which aroused suspicion of Mirabeau. Where had he been throughout the afternoon of Monday? After his unfortunate speech he had left the Assembly, and disappeared. He was not seen again till his return to the hall about six in the evening. Then, finding there an inextricable confusion of sweaty and ribald fishwives and deputies as scared as they were ridiculous, he did later, by the mere authority of his voice and manner, restore a measure of order and decorum. But there were, nevertheless, something like six hours to be accounted for, since his absence at such a time had not passed unnoticed. What, people now asked, had he been up to? The answer was simple, but as yet only La Marck knew it: Mirabeau had spent the afternoon with him.

The Queen's contemptuous loathing of the renegade noble had been expressed forcibly enough in the interview in which La Marck had first hinted that it might be wise to enlist his help. The prospect was vastly worse now. Marie Antoinette regarded Mirabeau quite simply as her would-be assassin.

Meanwhile he got to work on his plan for her liberation. Within a week, two things became known. The first was the imminent departure of Orleans to England. It had been given the face-saving form of a diplomatic mission, but it was virtually exile and Lauzun assured Mirabeau and La Marck that it was Lafayette's doing. Secondly, they learned from Monsieur's captain of the guard that the pin-headed Count of Artois had been giving a first demonstration of what was to become standard *emigré* statesmanship by hatching in Savoy a conspiracy to gather an army which should burst into France and liberate the King. True, this fatuity had already been dropped by the Court and steps were being taken to countermand the preparations, but the news was important because it suggested two things: first, that the royal family were now seriously thinking of flight, and, second, that if they were not quickly provided with a sane scheme they would in all probability adopt an insane one.

On October 13th, the friends were already considering how 10,000 troops might be concentrated between Paris and Rouen without arousing general suspicion. La Marck was also able to give the other an encouraging bit of news: the Count of Provence and the Queen had expressed disappointment that Mirabeau was not attending the Assembly's military committee; they wanted him, it seemed, to keep an eye on matters of that sort. Though this was presumably Monsieur's idea rather than the Queen's, it did suggest that not all doors to the confidence of the Court were barred and bolted.[129]

By October 15th, Mirabeau had worked out his plan and embodied it in a memorandum which he at once sent to La Marck.

2

The memorandum began with a survey of the facts:

The King is virtually the prisoner of Paris. He cannot choose his personal bodyguard, nor has he any direct authority over the National Guard to whom his safety is entrusted. The Assembly will be as much the prisoner of Paris as the King.*

This state of things plays into the hands of all who wish to discredit the cause of reform by saying that neither King nor Assembly is a free agent. A tendency to repudiate their actions on this pretext is already evident in certain quarters.

Will even the King's personal safety be assured in Paris? It will be at the mercy of movements outside the capital and commotions within, leading in all likelihood to a violent collision between capital and provinces. The Parisian masses when aroused are irresistible. Winter is coming on; there may be a food shortage or a financial collapse; what will Paris be in three months? Certainly a hospital, perhaps a theatre of horrors.

The ministry is without authority. True, Necker is still popular, but he has admirers rather than a party and his resources are known; his financial expedients can delay but not avert ruin. Trade and industry are at a standstill. Law and order rest on two things, public opinion and the revenue. Public opinion is increasingly divided, and the taxes are being paid less and less.

The Assembly, which came into being by accident rather than by the mandate of the people and which was not originally elected to be what it is now, has made the regrettable error of

---

* The Assembly held its last meeting at Versailles on October 15th, after which it followed the King to Paris, sitting at first in the Archbishop's Palace, near Notre Dame, from which it moved to the Riding School, on the north of the Tuileries Gardens, on November 9th.

declaring its earlier decrees irrevocable, thus depriving itself of freedom to retrace its steps and correct its mistakes. This is the more unfortunate since, because of its inexperience, its work is necessarily somewhat experimental.

The only way to save the state and the constitution which is being born is to place the King where he will at once be able to join forces with his people, and that means leaving Paris.

'Paris has long swallowed up all the taxes of the Kingdom. Paris is the headquarters of the fiscal system which the provinces abhor. Paris has created the debt. Paris by its mischievous jobbery has ruined public credit and compromised the national honour. Must the National Assembly also see nothing but this city, and for her sake bring ruin to the whole kingdom? Many provinces are afraid that she will dominate the Assembly and direct its labours. Paris wants only financial operations; the provinces think only of agriculture and trade. Paris wants nothing but money; the provinces demand laws. The dissensions between Paris and the provinces are known; the smallest incident will cause an open collision.'

What is to be done then? First, three things which must at all costs *not* be done.

'To retire to Metz or any other frontier would be to declare war on the nation and to abdicate the throne . . . Who can foretell to what extremes fury might not carry the French people were they to see their King desert them to join their enemies and himself become one of them? How far might they not go in organizing resistance to the forces which he would be going to gather? Why, after such an event, I would denounce the King myself!'

Equally fatal would be a flight into the interior followed by an appeal to the loyalty of the *noblesse*. 'Justly or not, the entire nation . . . will for a long time regard the whole class of *gentils-hommes* as their most implacable enemies. The abolition of the feudal system was the expiation of ten centuries of folly. It might have been done in a more orderly fashion, but there is no going back on it. To join with the nobility would be worse than to throw oneself into the arms of a foreign and hostile army; it would be to opt not for a great nation but for a handful of individuals, not for peace but for civil war with utterly unequal forces.'

Hardly less perilous would be a third course — to escape in

order to denounce the Assembly and break off all relations with it. Like the second, it would start a civil war, because a great part of the nation supports the Assembly's decrees, feeling that, for all its mistakes, its general policy is sound, and that it must be upheld because without it there will never be a constitution at all.

There remains a fourth course: not without dangers, it is true, but it is idle to hope to escape from a great danger without running risks in doing so. This course is to leave Paris and go to Rouen, at the same time appealing to the nation as a whole against the Paris demagogues.

Speed and secrecy are essential. The ministers should not be let into the secret since their attitude is too uncertain. Only those who have a part to play should be informed, and that only when all is ready for action, and only such delay should be allowed as is necessary to make the present constrained position of King and Assembly so abundantly clear to the people as to justify the step in their eyes,

Meanwhile, on some pretext or other, a force of about 10,000 men, composed exclusively of national regiments, should be concentrated on a point as nearly as possible equidistant from Paris and Rouen. In the unlikely event of the provinces misunderstanding the manœuvre, reliable commanders should hold themselves ready to check any adverse move, and so gain time in which the position may be explained to the people.

If these precautions are taken, the King should be able to leave the Tuileries in broad daylight and make for Rouen.

The advantages of Rouen are that it is central, has access to the sea, and controls the main stream of supplies entering Paris; furthermore, going to Rouen will appear not as a flight but as a reunion with the provinces. Finally, Normandy is very populous, the Normans are more tenacious than other Frenchmen, and it would be easy to join Brittany and Anjou to Normandy, which would form an irresistible combination.

Before the King's departure there must be ready prepared a proclamation addressed to all the provinces. It should announce that the King is throwing himself into the arms of his people, that he has suffered violence at Versailles, that in Paris he is denied the ordinary citizen's right to come and go as he will, and that he is anxious lest this state of affairs should provide malcontents with an excuse for disobeying laws decreed by the National Assembly and sanctioned by himself, thereby endangering a revolution to which he is as attached as the most ardent friends of liberty. As for the laws themselves, some of them he accepts as they stand, without reserve; others seem to him to require reconsideration, and he is anxious that the nation shall have the chance of this. He is going to call the Assembly to join him, but he will later summon a new convention to confirm or modify the present Assembly's work.

He regards the national debt as sacred; on this point he is inflexible. He will submit to the greatest personal sacrifices, and live simply like a private person without the pomp and luxury of the old court. On the other hand he thinks it unjust and unwise to make a proportionate reduction in the salaries of the thousands of state employees.

Finally, he entrusts his honour and safety to the loyalty of Frenchmen, and wishes nothing but the happiness of all citizens and to be himself regarded as one of them.

There should be a second proclamation addressed to the Assembly, explaining the King's reasons for leaving Paris and inviting the Assembly to follow him. If the Assembly should find itself denied freedom to move, that fact would terminate the session in law if not in fact, in virtue of the decree whereby the Assembly has declared itself inseparable from the monarch.

'The one point on which the King ought to be inflexible is to reject every project which has not as its sole object the peace and safety of the state and the indivisibility of monarch and people. This indivisibility is in the hearts of all Frenchmen; it must be given reality in action.'[130]

If Mirabeau's reputation rested on this document alone he would rank as an unequalled judge of public affairs. His perception and his prescience are equally astonishing. Here he is, a man occupied and distracted by the day-to-day shifts of that passionate and uncertain time, yet writing in the fifth month of the revolution a survey of the present and the future which embodies the truths which are to be the commonplace reflections of later historians in their retrospective calm. 'The Parisian masses when aroused are irresistible . . . Who can foretell to what extremes fury might not carry the French people when they see their King desert them? . . .

How far might they not go in organizing resistance? . . .' Our minds race forward to Varennes, to Danton and the Commune of 1792, to Valmy and the September Massacres, to Carnot and the armies of the Republic.

We have in this memorandum a synopsis of Mirabeau's political convictions; his contemptuous repudiation of the nobility, those gentlemen of the sword whose separation from the general life of the nation was so largely of their own choosing; his impatience with the demagogues of the extreme Left, their invincible ideology and their narrow rancours; his fear of the explosive force of the Paris mob; his recognition of the quickening pulse of patriotism, shown in his care of such details as the employment of French troops only for covering the move to Rouen. He sees the kingship in deadly peril, placed between the rapier of reaction and the pike of revolution and likely to fall from a chance thrust at any moment, while all the while great France asks nothing but to possess her old monarchy and her new laws in peace.

3

Despite an Address to the Nation to popularize Necker's 'Patriotic Gift' — an address whose composition was entrusted to Mirabeau as the measure's victorious champion — the levy was as great a failure as he had secretly expected. The resources of the Banker were at an end, and only an operation of political surgery, cutting into the substance of established property, could now restore the credit of the state. Unable either to borrow or to tax, the government had one last resource: it could confiscate.

No one doubted who the victim would be. It would be the Church.

The Church was rich. She owned about one-sixth of the landed wealth of France. This endowment was not, in truth, excessive, for it had to support most of the country's educational and charitable institutions as well as its diocesan clergy. But it seemed excessive because Church property was absurdly ill-distributed. The great prelates were by no means all opulent voluptuaries, the country *curés* were by no means all strenuous under-fed pastors in shabby cassocks and leaky boots; but these extremes did exist, and it is extremes which attract attention. Indeed the maldistribution of the Church's income had become a burning grievance to the lower clergy which they had vented during the elections when, meeting their bishops for the first time as political equals, they had in some electoral assemblies made things pretty hot for them. It was clear that the Church would not be united in defending her possessions in their present form.

Again, Church property was a body of wealth conveniently separable from all other possessions. Since the revolutionaries had declared the sanctity of property, an attack on noble estates would have been hard to justify now that the pretext of feudal oppression had been removed; it would have been a capital levy bringing all property into question. Church property, on the other hand, was of its nature something set apart. It could be nationalized on a theory incapable of extension to the possessions of ordinary citizens, and speculating financiers could play with it without fear.

But what, even apart from such considerations, would have marked the Church for sacrifice on the altar of national solvency was the anti-clerical, even anti-Christian, bias of contemporary thought. The Church upheld ancient traditional practices; the intelligentsia inclined to think that mankind could be emancipated by burning its records. The Church taught man's need of divine grace; the intelligentsia believed that man was naturally perfectible. The Church preached submission to the King, her Eldest Son; the intelligentsia criticized and ridiculed the whole system of which he was the head.

Disbelieving in revelation, Mirabeau detested a church which claimed authority to teach and a privileged position from which to do so. Like most of his kind and generation, however, he was comfortably certain that Christianity was moribund. Since it had lost its hold on themselves they assumed that, with a little time and a little more enlightenment, it would lose its hold on everybody else. Meanwhile, therefore, they were willing to leave the clergy a diminished position as guardians of morality, much in the spirit of Gibbon when he wrote that all religions are equally true to the believer, equally untrue to the philosopher and equally useful to the magistrate. 'The liberty of the nation', wrote Mirabeau at the close of 1789, 'had three enemies, the clergy, the nobility and the *parlements*. The first does not belong any more to this century, and the sad state of our finances should have sufficed for us to kill it.'[131] With the excuse of the nation's need the clergy could be deprived of their property as they had already been of their tithes, receiving state-salaries in exchange; it would then be easy to impose further controls. To Mirabeau such treatment seemed both enlightened and generous. But so fixed was his determination to wreck the privileged position of Catholicism that, in the discussions on the rights of man, he had even objected to the word 'toleration' as implying that non-Catholics were to enjoy religious freedom on sufferance rather than of right;[132] while a month later his *Courrier* lamented that the Declaration reserved to the civil authorities the right to interfere with religious observances if they endangered public order, protesting that it was on just such principles that 'the Dominics and Torquemadas' had relied.

Was his fury for religious liberty impartial? Would he have denounced the atheistic intolerance of a Combes as roundly as the Catholic intolerance of a Louvois? We cannot be sure, though in 1784, in discussing Joseph II's decrees against religious orders, he had written: 'Despise monks as much as you like, but do not persecute them, and above all never rob them, for no one, from the most determined atheist to the most credulous capuchin, must ever be persecuted or robbed.' He actively disliked Joseph II, however, so this remark is not conclusive proof of an impartial hatred of religious intolerance. But his essential largeness was shocked by bigotry, and his disposition was to agree that it takes all sorts to make a world. 'Let us tolerate writers of whatever sort,' he wrote; 'Let us likewise tolerate even the gentlemen with rosaries.'[133]

The first proposal for secularization was made by Dupont de Nemours. Then Talleyrand moved that one-third of Church revenues should be appropriated by the nation. Mirabeau trumped the Bishop's card with the more drastic proposal that all the goods of the Church should belong to the nation save what was necessary to maintain worship and the care of the poor, and that every curé should have 1200 *livres* (about £60) a year and his house and garden, an arrangement by which many of them would be better off. The Assembly forthwith became involved in learned disputes over the nature of ecclesiastical endowments, the intentions of the original benefactors and the rights of corporations against the state. Mirabeau was only able to hold his place in the front of debate owing to the learning and acumen of the invaluable Pellenc, who provided him with the speech which, on October 30th, decided the issue. The nationalization of Church property was voted by 568 to 346 on November 2nd.

Could the matter have rested there, it might have been no great matter. But the nationalization of the Church's property inevitably involved the nationalization of a part of the Universal Church by a French state now under the impulse of men quite alienated from the Catholic idea. That would be a very great matter indeed.

But for Mirabeau it was gratifying to have snatched the initiative in this matter from such an acknowledged expert as Talleyrand, for behind the Bishop's feline countenance was an ironic spirit which could chuckle at the adroit audacity of the move, and be all the readier to forget an old quarrel at a time when Mirabeau was anxious that he should do so. It was about this time that the two men resumed friendly relations.

4

When, on October 15th, La Marck received Mirabeau's memorandum on the perilous position of the monarchy, he hastened to take it not to the Tuileries — that in view of the Queen's mood would have been useless — but to the Luxembourg, residence of Monsieur, the Comte de Provence. Comings and goings here were being watched only a degree less suspiciously than at the Tuileries, and a secret interview was arranged for midnight.

Monsieur (Louis XVIII in the changed world of 1815) was the elder and far the more intelligent of Louis XVI's brothers. A reader, thoughtful and well-informed, he had shown some understanding of the national crisis even before the breaking of the storm. Though inclined to be heavy and pedantic, he might have been a useful adviser to the King had not the Queen disastrously preferred the more agreeable manners of the younger brother, Artois.

Monsieur read the manuscript at once, throwing out comments. When he had finished he said he approved of the general plan, but was sure that the King could never be brought to adopt it. In that case, La Marck suggested, it might be best to persuade the Queen first, but Monsieur disagreed: it was quite a mistake, he said, to think that she could make up her husband's mind on so grave a matter. 'The King's weakness and indecision,' he added, 'are beyond description. To get an idea of his character imagine yourself struggling vainly to hold together oiled billiard balls.'[134]

It is clear from his memorandum that Mirabeau had already envisaged the possibility of civil war. His plan was not to provoke it but to place the King in such a position that if it came the monarch and the national interest should quickly prevail. Anybody inclined to regard the document as irresponsible should remember that Mirabeau was taking his life in his hands by writing it. If it became known he was ruined, and Comps, his secretary who copied it out, became so terrified of the lamp-post that he toyed with the idea of clearing himself by informing the Assembly.[135]

Nevertheless, the memorandum did not represent the sum total of Mirabeau's remedies. Closer to his heart was the desire to stabilize the country by giving authority to the government, and this meant doing two things: first, replacing the existing ministers by men able, resolute and true to the Revolution, and second, bringing the Ministry into the Assembly.

As things stood, the King's government was external to the legislative body. The ministers tended to be merged in the Court, and the record of the Court had not been such as to inspire liberals with confidence. When ministers did make their infrequent appearances before the Assembly they came as messengers to announce policies in which, as likely as not, the Austrian Woman had had a hand. Thus the mere fact that a certain course was recommended by the executive was a reason for the legislators to view it with suspicion. Furthermore, the fact that ministers were external to the legislative, that there were no government benches, 'left to ambition,' as Malouet observed, 'no outlet but that of demagogy'.[136]

The establishment of responsible parliamentary government had become a fixed idea in Mirabeau's mind. He had exposed his views privately to Malouet and La Marck, and publicly, though partially, in debate in mid-July. On August 4th, De Cicé, Archbishop of Bordeaux, and two others had been taken into the Ministry, but the value of this step had been neutralized by their ceasing to act as deputies. On September 14th an article appeared in the *Courrier de Provence*. It urged that the greatest cause of delay and discord in achieving order with liberty had been the absence of ministers from the Assembly, and it reproached 'narrow-minded and suspicious politicians' for fearing that the independence of the legislative would suffer from a union 'of which a neighbouring state provides an example and whose good effects are proved by experience . . . Until our constitution has stood the test of time wise men will always admire England for practical results superior to the sublime theories of our Utopians.'[137]

The allusion to England was perhaps inevitable but probably unfortunate. Frenchmen were little disposed to imitate the institutions of their ancient aristocratic enemy, and the House of Commons with its bought majorities was a warning to them rather than an example. Neither Walpole, Bute, North nor Chatham was a model to appeal to their increasing egalitarianism, and they were not likely to allow Louis XVI to secure a party of 'King's Friends' through the agency of the deputy for Aix.[138]

Other articles on the same theme appeared in October. The *Courrier* was attempting to prepare public opinion for a formal move in the Assembly. Mirabeau was pursuing two associated but distinct aims, to change the Ministry and to make it work in with the Assembly — a change of men and also a change of methods. In all the lobbying and negotiation which had to be undertaken it was the change of men which had to be presented as the main object, since the need for this was widely recognized while the need for a change of methods was not. One of Mirabeau's projects for a possible ministry has survived, and some points in it are of interest. Necker is still to be premier 'because it is necessary to render him as powerless as he is incapable, while retaining for the King the advantage of his popularity'; De Cicé is to be chancellor; Mirabeau himself is to be without portfolio since 'the government should advertise that its chief assistants will henceforth be men of principle, character and talent'; Talleyrand is to be minister of finance and Lafayette is to be in the Council, a Marshal of France with supreme powers to reconstitute the army.[139]

Lafayette was an indispensable ally, for his position as Commander of the National Guard gave him a powerful if unconstitutional pull over both Court and Ministry. He arranged for Necker to see Mirabeau on October 17th.

Since the interview which Malouet had arranged in May the Minister had learnt that the tribune was not a man to be ignored, and he now condescended to admit that he might, in the present circumstances, be useful to the King; he was sufficiently emphatic, however, that since his own influence was founded on his high moral reputation he must not be expected to accept Mirabeau as a colleague.

This being his attitude, Mirabeau's course was clear: he would seize every chance to attack the Ministry in the Assembly in the hope that its overthrow would be the chance for bringing its successor into working association with the legislature.

A chance of pressing this point occurred four days later. François, a Paris baker falsely suspected of hoarding flour, was lynched by a famished mob, and the municipality asked the Assembly for a law against riots. It so happened that only a week previously Mirabeau had himself proposed a riot act which the Assembly had not adopted, so now, on October 21st, he spoke at a certain advantage. He urged that it was with famine rather than with riots that the House should deal; the government was disclaiming responsibility for the food shortage on the not unreasonable ground that it lacked authority and means; very well then, let ministers explain what assistance they needed, let the Assembly instantly vote them the necessary powers and credits and, by doing so, make them responsible again. This would be a piece of practical collaboration by executive and legislative, more educative to the champions of the separation of powers than a dozen speeches or articles.

If the difficulty had simply been to convince the disciples of Montesquieu of their error the chances of overcoming it would have been reasonable. But the constitutional issue was never to be decided on its merits. Mirabeau's advocacy charged the whole business with the electricity of personal animosities. A cause which he championed always took colour from his personality;

this was part of his greatness and the whole ground of his fame. But though it could carry him to triumph in a popular cause, it could provoke bitter opposition when the matter was debatable. There had always been those whom his volcanic vehemence irritated and mortified, and the number of unfriendly deputies had increased of late, a thing which might not have mattered so much had not his low moral reputation exposed him to their malice. He laboured especially under the imputation of having conspired the October Days, which had been an outrage to the Assembly only less than to royalty, nor was he able to clear himself of this till a year had passed. His ill repute was a fatal weakness, for it put beyond his reach the steady estimation of reliant colleagues upon which alone a parliamentary statesman can build. Well-founded rumours that he might be included in a new ministry alarmed men of various types. Regarded as a venal careerist by most of the Left, as an unprincipled demagogue by most of the Right, he never gained the support of any dependable block in the chamber.

That his grand design for a reformed ministry would be opposed became evident on October 27th, when Pétion, the future Girondin, urged that ministers should be excluded from the Assembly. Mirabeau was able to get the discussion deferred, but it was warning of what resistance he might expect when he should move forward to his objective.

On November 5th, he believed he saw his opening. The authorities at Marseilles, in dealing with disturbances, had neglected some recent decrees of the Assembly. Mirabeau proposed that the ministers be called upon to *prove* that they had communicated these decrees to local authorities, and the proposal, with its suggestion of ministerial responsibility to the House, was carried. In high spirits he wrote the next morning to La Marck of his 'battle won yesterday against the ministers' and 'the great battle, the opening attack of which I make today, by a simple tactical evolution'. La Marck was perhaps less sanguine; he had received a note from Talon saying that a 'terrible cabal' was being formed against his friend.[140]

Mirabeau's tactic was the simple one of a holding attack in front to distract attention from the real blow to be delivered on the flank. The ever-present chaos of the bread supplies and the

235

disappearance of the metallic currency, which the fearful were hoarding, were to be the material for the frontal attack. He put three proposals to the Assembly: first that ships should at once be sent to the United States to bring back wheat in payment of the American war debt, secondly that the Finance Committee should draw up a plan for a national bank; the third proposal, slipped in to seem an innocuous corollary to the other two, was 'that His Majesty's ministers be invited to take a consultative part in the Assembly, until the constitution shall have fixed the rules to be followed regarding them'. There was a pretext for this in a recent act of the ministers who, by printing a note to the Assembly on the financial crisis, had caused public consternation which might have been avoided could they have presented the matter directly within the walls of the house. Mirabeau's hope was that this third and vital clause would pass without discussion under cover of the other two. It very nearly did. His speech was well received; a number of following speakers supported it, notably Clermont-Tonnerre. But Blin of Nantes got up and attacked Mirabeau's third clause, and De Noailles did likewise: only two dissentients, it is true; but they stood between Mirabeau and his victory; for, fatally, they caused the subject to be deferred, so that the hope of slipping the constitutional clause through before resistance could be concerted faded.

When the debate was resumed the following day Mirabeau's enemies on both sides of the house were on the alert. Yesterday it had been De Noailles, Lafayette's brother-in-law, who had checked him; now it was Lanjuinais (a future Girondin) who headed the counter-attack. He had been persuaded overnight by De Cicé, who was anxious for his own position, that Mirabeau must be excluded from the ministry at whatever cost. 'An eloquent genius,' Lanjuinais cried, 'is sweeping you away and overpowering you. What would he not do if he were a minister?' Then he proposed his decree; it was that *no member of the National Assembly should be capable of holding any ministerial post during the life of the present assembly or for three years afterwards.*

This motion would now be debated, and hours might pass before it came to a vote. There might be amendments; Blin, indeed, did secure the removal of the fatuous three-years disqualification. But Mirabeau felt the altered mood of the house,

and he knew that, on the central issue touching the Assembly
and the Ministry *now*, he was beaten.[141] Yet for the merits of
his case, and to answer the majority whom bilious suspicion of
himself was leading to commit a blunder which he knew to be a
public calamity, he spoke:

> I cannot believe that the author of the motion seriously wishes
> to have it declared that the *élite* of the nation cannot contain
> a good minister; that the nation's confidence given to a
> citizen should be a mark excluding him from the confidence
> of the monarch; that while proclaiming that all citizens are
> equally eligible for all employments it is necessary to except from
> this equality of rights the twelve hundred deputies whom the
> suffrage of a great people has honoured; that the National
> Assembly and the Ministry should be so opposed to each
> other that all measures which might secure greater unity
> of intentions and actions are to be discarded. No, Gentlemen,
> I do not believe that such can be the object of the motion,
> because it will never be in my power to believe an absurdity.
>
> No more can I believe that the idea is to insult the Ministry
> by suggesting that anyone who is a member of it ought, on
> that ground alone, to be suspect to the legislative assembly.
> Would anyone dare to say that the Minister on whom the
> nation had fixed all its hopes, and whom it recalled amid
> universal acclamation after the storm which had driven him
> away, should have been debarred from office if we had had
> the good fortune to see him seated amongst us?
>
> No, Gentlemen, I can believe none of these explanations,
> and I am therefore driven, out of respect for the proposer of the
> motion, to think that it is justified by some secret motive.
> This I shall now attempt to discover.
>
> I believe, Gentlemen, that it may possibly be expedient to
> exclude from the Ministry some particular deputy. But since
> it will not do to sacrifice a great principle in order to secure
> this particular advantage, I propose, as an amendment, the
> exclusion from the Ministry of the members of the Assembly
> whom the author of the motion appears to fear, and I under-
> take to tell you who they are.
>
> There are only two persons in the Assembly who might be
> the secret object of the motion. They are the proposer of
> the motion and myself.
>
> I say the proposer of the motion because it may be that his

237

modesty shrinks from some great mark of confidence, and that he wishes to ensure a way of refusing it by bringing about a general exclusion.

I say secondly myself, because widespread rumours concerning me have alarmed certain people, and because very possibly the author of the motion has credited these tales; because, moreover, it is quite possible that he has the same opinion of me that I have myself, in which case I am not surprised that he should think me incapable of filling a position which I regard as far above my abilities, especially if it were to deprive me of the lessons and the counsel which I have always received in this Assembly.

Here then, Gentlemen, is the amendment which I suggest: it is to limit the proposed exclusion to M. de Mirabeau, deputy of the Commons of Aix.[142]

5

The decree of November 7th, 1789, was a body-blow to Mirabeau. It destroyed what he knew to be the only hope of securing a government which could govern within the framework of the new constitution.

His personal chagrin was also intense. He was ambitious. On that at least his enemies were not wrong. He knew himself fitted for action at the highest level, nor could he be permanently content with triumphs which won nothing but applause. And he was desperate for money. Creditors would be less patient now that he could no longer calm them with hints of a ministerial salary soon to be his. He had to entertain (young Desmoulins had thought his republican purity in danger of corruption by the Thunderer's seductive hospitality, his choice Bordeaux and maraschino). He had a vast correspondence and needed Comps for secretarial work upon which Pellenc would be wasted. Then there was his *atelier*: Dumont and Duroveray, 'men of gold' he called them, were assiduous but not disinterested. They were backing him for the ministry, partly in the hope that, unlike Necker, he would help the democrats of Geneva, partly in the expectation of rising along with him. Neither was a French citizen and both had contacts in England which they might be tempted to resume if his prospects became dim. Dumont had always felt uncomfortable in his association with the raffish genius who, disgraced by his connection with such a woman as the Le Jay, allowed himself and his collaborators to be swindled by her over the accounts of the *Courrier de Provence*. As for Clavière, his affection for Mirabeau was not unruffled by fits of literary jealousy, and certainly included the hope of making the tribune's broad shoulders a step up to the ministry of finance.[143] The new decree wrecked Mirabeau's hopes of financial relief and threatened the cohesion of his workshop at the same time.

The sarcasm with which he ended his speech marks a change in his attitude to the Assembly. Hitherto he had felt himself partly incorporate with the house. Its authority was, in some part, his achievement, and within its walls one part, at least, of his talents had at last been recognized by all. He had felt for the chamber the affection of the athlete for the arena of his success. And now this assembly, his assembly, in order that it might vent its rancours against him had committed an act of criminal irresponsibility towards the commonwealth. A new note of scorn, not for this deputy or that group, but for the House as a whole now appears in his private correspondence.

Against one member, however, he did at the moment feel a special resentment, not for what he had done but for what he had failed to do. This was Lafayette.

The French Revolution is a tragedy of small men in great positions. By some jest of the ironic spirit the French people, in what was in some ways their greatest hour, showed a truly amazing instinct for bestowing their confidence on men of strictly limited capacities. The hard-dying popularity of Necker in 1789 and 1790, and the strange idolatry of Robespierre in 1793 and 1794 are examples. Both men were limited in everything except their vanity, which is why they come to mind in association with the honourable, gallant but faintly ridiculous figure of Marie Joseph Paul Yves Roch Gilbert de Motier, Marquis de Lafayette, Deputy for the Nobility of Auvergne, Commander of the National Guard.

Lionized since his return from the American War, his innate vanity, growing with nourishment, had combined with a narrow and inelastic intelligence to give this tall, serious man of thirty-two a personality impressive to the multitude but exasperating to intelligent men who tried to work with him. This was a pity since, in addition to many private virtues, he had three important virtues as a public man: integrity, complete sincerity in his political creed, and a manly sense of responsibility to the commonwealth.

He had found his faith once and for all in Washington's camp in his early twenties, and throughout the remainder of a long life, which witnessed six successive régimes in France and the transformation of Europe, he never modified it. He believed in government representative of, and responsible to, a republic of active and equal citizens. He did not love monarchy, but he was prepared to accept and loyally support a citizen-king.

In the opening phase of the Revolution the career of 'The Hero of the Two Worlds', as he liked his admirers to call him, had been strangely hesitant. In the Assembly of Notables he had caused a sensation by demanding the States-General, and when that cause triumphed he presented himself for election to the nobility of Auvergne. They imposed conditions which galled his republican sentiments but which he feared to refuse, and he left that noble gathering, to use his own words, 'elected but displeased', a phrase which would serve to describe him with some aptness in certain subsequent situations. Though the most famous man among the minority of liberal nobles, he played no part in the prolonged tussle for the formation of a single assembly, and even after that victory had been won by others his conduct as a deputy had been unimpressive. God-father to the infant United States, he might have been expected to make a declaration of rights his peculiar contribution to the regeneration of his own country, and he had, in fact, kept by him these last ten years a draft-declaration, only awaiting the moment to present it to his grateful fatherland. He produced it on July 11th. It was a Saturday. It was the day Necker was dismissed. A less opportune moment would have been hard to choose, and it fell flat.

Lafayette, in truth, was devoid of parliamentary gifts. But at this very moment the Bastille crisis and his election to command the National Guard saved him. Leaping from the benches of the *Menus plaisirs*, where so few had marked him, onto the back of his white charger, where he was splendidly conspicuous to all, he breathed with relief a larger air. Was he not, after all, a man of

Lafayette

action? American liberty had been won by deeds, not by words, and now the hour for deeds had struck in France.

In his new position he had great but ill-defined power, but he was never quite sure what he ought to do with it or to whom his final responsibility lay. Honourable and brave, he lacked the power to decide and to create, and needed either the support of trusted colleagues or the direction of a master; but the latter was denied him by the King's character, while the former was denied him by his own. An apostle of the brotherhood of men, he was doomed by temperament and circumstance to live in a sort of political vacuum. As Commander of the National Guard he became aloof from the Assembly of which he remained a member; as a provincial deputy and a noble he was aloof from the Parisian militia of which he was the head; as a democrat he was aloof from the Court to which birth and connections gave him entry, while as Lafayette he was always a little aloof from everybody. Yet for two years he enjoyed a general and immense popularity and he became a sort of symbol of what the average man meant by the revolution. He counted for more than any other single figure, with the doubtful exception of Mirabeau.

The ideas of the two men were not dissimilar. Both believed in liberty and equality, and both believed that the Crown should be preserved and could be strengthened by loyal acceptance of a revolution which had levelled society beneath it. Furthermore they both recognized the menace of anarchy. Yet their minds and tempers were so different that even when they said the same thing they seemed to disagree. What with Mirabeau was a matter of perception was with Lafayette a matter of doctrine. They spoke, as it were, in different moods, Mirabeau in the indicative, Lafayette with a somewhat confusing alternation of the imperative and the conditional. And they disliked each other. The profuse and exuberant Provençal was irritated by a man who always seemed afraid of giving himself away, while Lafayette's earnest and humourless mind mistook the other's reckless remarks for evidence of an incurable lack of principle. Mirabeau was mortified that a man whose ability he despised should have captured a position of such critical importance; he was envious of Lafayette's odd eminence and blameless reputation, and angered by the jealousy with which he guarded both. For, with unfailing

realism, he saw that he must come to terms with the man, whereas
the Hero of the Two Worlds never understood what the Tribune
of the People might bring him as a partner.

6

October was full of rumours of a new ministry, for the existing
Council inspired confidence in nobody. But in the absence of
any accepted parliamentary procedure for ending a discredited
government there took place countless confidential talks between
aspirants to office, who had to scheme for some sort of compact
with certain of the present holders, since the chance of the King
settling the matter on his own initiative was not worth considering.
Among those most active in making and comparing lists of
'possibles', in meeting for secret and abortive discussions, in
gauging each other's capabilities and in watching each other's
moves, were Mirabeau and the Bishop of Autun. Talleyrand
thought the former a scamp, but, having forgiven the old matter
of the Berlin letters, was coolly estimating which weighed heavier
in the balance, his ill-repute or his genius. Each respected the
other's talents and discounted his morals, and both knew the
limitations of Lafayette. But they both knew that he was, for all
that, the pivotal man, the one person so placed that he could when
necessary give a decisive shove to the Court or to the Ministry
or to both. The way in which he had brought about the exile of
Orleans was evidence of what he could do, and Mirabeau had on
that occasion been prepared to accuse Lafayette publicly of
exploiting his position to make himself Mayor of the Palace,
if only the Duke had had the nerve to stand his ground. But
if people imagined because of this that Mirabeau was one of
Orleans's men they were mistaken. 'They allege that I'm of his
party,' he said; 'I wouldn't have him as my valet.'

It was encouraging that Lafayette seemed as convinced as any
that some of the ministers must be replaced. Unfortunately he
could never make up his mind which, when or by whom. He
had sounded Mirabeau on the matter at least as early as October
8th, and a few days later was thinking of a ministry to include
him, Necker and the aged but respected Malesherbes. Perhaps

he had heard the story which Mme de Flahaut got from her reverend friend, the Bishop, and passed to her irreverent friend, Morris, that Mirabeau was to have a secret audience with the King. The story was false, but it illuminates momentarily the fog of intrigue and reciprocal over-reaching in which these clandestine negotiations proceeded, and it shows that while Mirabeau was still secretly at work on his Memorandum something was already in the wind suggesting obscure contacts between him and the Court.[144]

About the same time a meeting of anxious leaders took place in the home of Mirabeau's niece, Mme d'Aragon, Caroline's daughter. Alexandre Lameth, who was present with the inevitable Duport and Barnave, says that one object was to clear up misunderstandings between Mirabeau and Lafayette, and that another was to concert measures for a clean sweep of incompetents and secret reactionaries from all important public positions. If so, neither was achieved. Mirabeau sought to reassure the company by declaring that he himself could not be included in a new ministry because of the prejudice against him, but then the very presence of Lafayette seems to have roused in him a demon of mischief which drove him into making some shamelessly cynical remarks which shocked the Hero and made their misunderstanding worse. Lafayette said that anyone wishing to work with him must desist from attacks on the Queen. 'Very good, General!' replied Mirabeau; 'Since you wish it, let her live! A humiliated queen may be useful, but a murdered one is only fit to be the subject of a bad tragedy.'

As for the major object, everything depended on Lafayette pressing the agreed points on the Court; but he did nothing, and Lameth suggests that he was too intimate with Necker and Montmorin to act against them when it came to the point.[145] That was the trouble with Lafayette: no one ever really knew where he stood. He would have encouraging talks with Lameth and the leaders of the Left, with Talleyrand, the smooth opportunist, with the detached and cynical Morris, with the smug Necker and the pleasant Montmorin, with the slippery De Cicé and with the dull and distrustful King — and nothing would happen. It seemed impossible to pin him down.

Mirabeau tried hard to do so. He wooed Lafayette, not without signs of success. Within a few days of the meeting at his niece's house Morris reported him as being in a position to tell Talleyrand what the General's intentions were. The next day, October 19th, the Assembly held its first meeting in Paris, and Mirabeau took the opportunity to flatter Lafayette publicly in a speech proposing the Assembly's thanks to him and to Bailly for restoring calm in the capital (in which next day poor François was lynched). He was able to combine a compliment to the Commander with a reminder to his colleagues how valuable it had been to have a fellow deputy in a position of executive trust, for he was seeking Lafayette's favour both for himself and for his cherished scheme of a parliamentary ministry. The same day he wrote the Commander a flattering letter in which he dismissed Necker as 'a contemptible charlatan'.[146] The attempted suggestion was that they were two sensible and courageous men leagued to remove a minister who had become a public danger; the writer did not mention his own repulse by the minister two days previously.

Mirabeau unfortunately could not conceal that he was angling for a salary as much as for a place, and Lafayette, while ready to weigh the advantages of securing this dangerous man through his necessities, thought the less of him because of them. It was a weak position, for Lafayette was readier to buy his silence or absence than to help him to an office where he could be a rival. Montmorin suggested that Mirabeau might be given an embassy (Constantinople, a glittering prize of its sort, was mentioned) but when Lafayette put the suggestion it was not well received. La Marck agreed that it was unacceptable, reminding his friend that he would always have some money for him, so that there was no need to close with the first offer.

In the end Lafayette, with misgivings, agreed to 50,000 francs out of the secret service funds which he controlled. For this Mirabeau was to work with him against the Ministry; office, it was implied, would follow when the victory had been won. La Marck approved: 'Now you will really be what you are worth,' he wrote on October 26th, 'that is to say, superior to all.'

Thus it was in the confidence that Lafayette, having put money on him, would support him that Mirabeau advanced to assault the Ministry in the first week of November. When the critical moment came, however, Lafayette did nothing, 'equally incapable,' as Mirabeau complained, 'of breaking faith and of keeping his word *ad tempus*.' On Tuesday, the third, he was asking Talleyrand how great Mirabeau's influence was in the Assembly and being told that it was not enormous. On Wednesday Mirabeau found him 'furious' against the ministers. But on Thursday evening he was in conclave with them, and on Friday and Saturday Mirabeau was left to carry out his assault and his ill-starred 'tactical evolution' unsupported.[147]

Yet Lafayette was probably surprised to receive from him, on December 1st, a letter of reproach: 'How often, while acknowledging your qualities, have I not told you that your weakness for second-rate men would cause the finest of careers to miscarry and endanger the common weal by ruining you?' He blamed Lafayette for listening to the petty scandalous talk against him, and for imagining that his career was to be halted by slander and misrepresentation. 'If I am continually denied movement,' he ended, 'my only reply will be to go ahead.'[148]

As for the 50,000 francs, it was never paid. Twenty-three thousand was the sum which Mirabeau received, and which La Marck advised him to return.

CHAPTER XII

APPROACH TO THE COURT

'MY reply will be to go ahead.' That was bravely said, but in truth no clear road lay before him, and, as winter closed down, Mirabeau's temptation was towards dangerous and dubious schemes. 'War retempers men's souls and gives them back the energy they have lost through their immoral calculations.' He said this to La Marck when the latter reported Monsieur's apparent reluctance to press the October Memorandum on the King, and to the question how a bankrupt king could wage war he replied: 'Civil war is always made without money, and besides, in the present circumstances it wouldn't last long. Frenchmen all want jobs or money; they'd be given promises, and you'd soon see the King's party predominating everywhere.'[149]

The cynical note, the inclination to despair of a peaceful and constitutional solution of the country's problem is apparent; and for Mirabeau despair was a dangerous mood. With all his political insight, with all his prescience, he lacked the sobriety — even a certain stolidity — which are perhaps necessary to a statesman. Along with matured convictions, penetrating intellect and astounding vigour he brought to politics something of the artistic temperament, and the fatal decree barring deputies from the ministry enraged him as an artist scorned by his public is enraged. He allowed himself to be goaded into reckless courses.

When La Marck took his leave of the Count of Provence after their midnight conversation, Monsieur kept his copy of Mirabeau's Memorandum. He had, it will be remembered, been positive that the King would never adopt the bold policy it recommended, and La Marck had come away discouraged. Monsieur, however, seems to have shown the paper to the King and Queen, and it and he seem to have made a certain impression. At the close of October, at any rate, there was talk at Court of a ministry of which Monsieur would be the head and Mirabeau and Talleyrand members. It all came to nothing, breaking up, it seems, on the rock of the Queen's prejudices, onto which it was probably driven by an adverse wind from the direction of Lafayette.

For the General now enjoyed a begrudged measure of royal favour. Whereas the Queen thought that Mirabeau had been at least accessory to the vile attempt to murder her on the sixth, she had to credit Lafayette, whose personal angularities she found it hard to endure, with having been in some sort her protector ever since. And the General, in the late autumn, was deeply suspicious that Monsieur and Mirabeau were up to something. That they were in contact he knew; the comings and goings of De Lévis, Monsieur's Captain of the Guard, had been duly noted; but just what their contacts meant remained something of a mystery. It is something of a mystery still.

Yet above the shifting mists that shroud the politics of that autumn of 1789 one odd landmark protrudes. This is a conversation which took place between Mirabeau and Dumont. We have it on Dumont's authority. It is a recollection written down many years later. It is, by Dumont's own admission, an imperfect recollection. Yet the character of his narrative places the reality of the incident beyond doubt; and it is highly significant.[150]

What he tells us is this. In November or early in December, Mirabeau called on him one morning saying he had something of the greatest importance to tell him. They were alone. In the next room someone was playing the violin. Mirabeau began by describing the ghastly state of the country, the general anarchy, the uselessness of the Assembly as at present constituted. His manner was unusual; the familiar fire and energy were absent; he spoke slowly, weighing his words. After a while he drew from his portfolio some seven or eight pages in his own hand-writing. 'Here,' he said, 'is a plan by which France may yet be saved and her freedom secured. Read it through without interruption. I will then talk about the means of execution, and you will see that they are commensurate with the greatness of the measure. I cannot, however, tell you all, or the names of the parties concerned. It is a secret of honour — a solemn engagement.'

After the lapse of many years it is the general tone of a conversation which remains in the mind; trivial physical circumstances will often lodge in the memory as well. On the other hand things exact and schematic tend to become blurred if not effaced. Dumont recalls what, *as far as he remembers*, Mirabeau's paper contained. Its gist, as he recalls it, was roughly the gist of the

Memorandum of October 15th. That is to say, it was a plan to free the King from Paris and restore action to his government. But the scheme Dumont remembers differs from the October Memorandum in certain important particulars. For instance, Metz was *not* barred as a possible destination for the escaping monarch; again, the King, once free, was to cancel the Assembly's decrees as being contrary to law and founded upon a usurpation of power; further, he was to rally the nobility round him and call upon the clergy to support his action from their pulpits.

Now these are vital departures from the policy so carefully set out on October 15th, and if Dumont's memory was accurate then the document he saw was not a copy of the October Memorandum, but a travesty of it, showing all its audacity and none of its wisdom.

Dumont recollects that he objected strongly to the plan. 'You are labouring under a misconception,' Mirabeau answered. 'You imagine this plan to be a signal for civil war. No such thing. You know not to what extent the nation are still attached to their King and how exclusively monarchical we are. The instant the King is free the Assembly will be annihilated. There will be, doubtless, on the part of the Palais Royal some attempts hostile to the measure. If Lafayette should play the Washington he would deserve death and his fate would be sealed.'

Dumont poured on the scheme all the cold water he could. What hope, in the first place, was there that Louis would show the necessary energy?

'You do not know the Queen,' came the reply, 'she has prodigious strength of mind. She has the courage of a man.'

'But have you seen her?' persisted Dumont. 'Have you been consulted? Are you quite sure that full confidence is placed in you? Does not the Assembly command the power of public opinion? Would you establish freedom with Austrian soldiers?'

In his agitation he had raised his voice, and suddenly they both noticed that the violin in the next room had stopped. Fearing to be overheard they went into another room.

'I am certain,' Mirabeau resumed, 'that the court party are bent on making the experiment, and I think my co-operation necessary to its success and to direct it in favour of liberty . . . If it doesn't succeed the monarchy is lost.'

249

Dumont was unconvinced. It was a wild scheme, he said, nor would Mirabeau have contemplated it but for his rage at the decree of November 7th. He ought to remember that his power rested upon his position in the Assembly, and that he had no special claims or qualifications to be the minister of a king turned *frondeur*. He should remember, too, that there was a big difference between drawing up a plan and being one of the trusted inner circle who would put it into execution.

'This last consideration', Dumont writes, 'was decisive. He felt that he was employed only in a subordinate capacity — for he was not even acquainted with the names of the principal parties to the project of the King's escape . . . He therefore gave me his word of honour that he would withdraw from it, and urge Monsieur, who had induced him to join in it, to forego his purpose and advise the court party to turn their views towards the National Assembly . . . Two or three days later Mirabeau informed me that the court party, as well as he, had abandoned the plan. . . .'

What are we to make of all this? First, despite the discrepancies between the October Memorandum (the text of which we have) and the document which Dumont remembered Mirabeau showing him, it seems probable that they were substantially the same document. Dumont admits that his memory of the details is vague, and in the absence of other evidence we may, though not without hesitation, dismiss the notion that Mirabeau, a few weeks after drawing up the masterly October Memorandum composed a travesty of it, with its vital saving clauses left out.

But, if we assume that it was the October Memorandum, a question remains. Why did he show it to Dumont? It was a dangerous document, capable of destroying him if it became known, and a fresh confidant was an added risk. Was it not because Mirabeau had reason to believe that *action* more or less according to his plan was about to be taken? Duroveray was away at the moment; La Marck had either gone to Belgium or was on the point of going. If 'the experiment' was about to be made, was it not natural that he should wish to have one trusted counsellor of his own in the secret?

Who was going to make the experiment? Evidently Monsieur. But, equally evidently, Mirabeau was not in the centre of the plot. He had provided Monsieur with a scheme, but he had no control over the use he would make of it, or over the variations which he might introduce; and he only accepted such a position for himself because he was desperate.

Had he, perhaps, begun to have misgivings, and was that why he decided, while there was yet time, to consult the sober and judicious Dumont? It seems likely. For, a few days after his second talk with Dumont, in which he reported that 'the experiment' was off, a sensational event took place which sheds a measure of light on the whole business. This was the arrest of Favras.

This needy aristocrat was arrested on December 24th, on the order of Lafayette, who had been told that he was plotting to raise 30,000 royalists to protect the King's flight from Paris, to starve the capital into surrender, and to murder Bailly and himself. On Favras's person was found a compromising letter from Monsieur, which Lafayette chivalrously returned to its author, though he was not above mentioning it to the gossiping Morris a day or two later. Favras, however, was well known to be a client of the Comte de Provence, and the story was immediately spread that Monsieur had been plotting a counter-revolutionary *coup* which the good Lafayette had brought to naught.

Just how near this story was to the truth was never ascertained. If Favras held information implicating Monsieur he never revealed it, and he went to his hanging two months later with sealed lips, his death, according to Dumont, being no less comforting to his friends than to his enemies. But his arrest certainly scared Monsieur badly, and he proceeded publicly to exculpate himself with more haste and less dignity than might have been expected from the brother of the King. He at once sought out Lafayette and requested him, in the presence of others, to suppress a printed libel against him. Then he went to the Hôtel de Ville and made a speech to the Commune disclaiming all connection with Favras and professing his attachment to the new order of things; further, he sent a copy of the speech to the President of the Assembly, with a request that it should be read there too.

This prompt, unequivocal and, as it proved, effective reaction by Monsieur was Mirabeau's doing; indeed, he wrote the speech. Though royalty might allow him but partial confidence in its intrigues it seemed glad enough of his guidance in a crisis.

His own anxiety to clear Provence is easily explained. Even if the Favras affair carried no danger to himself he had good reason to assist Monsieur. Lafayette must not be allowed to profit by the occasion to make Monsieur 'a second Duke of Orleans'; it would be altogether too much if the Hero of Two Worlds were to add the scalp of a second prince of the blood to his trophies. Conversely, Provence must be cleared because Mirabeau was still hoping, though barred himself from the ministry by the November decree, to be the directing brain behind Monsieur's premiership. But if, as is more likely, he knew that Monsieur had indeed been at least partly cognisant of Favras's plot, and that the germ, at least, of that plot had been his own paper scheme, then his alarm at the arrest of Favras may well be imagined. Discovery of the true text of the October Memorandum would have been bad enough. Implication in a reactionary's travesty of that scheme would have been the end.

Mirabeau's courses in the winter of 1789 to 1790 resulted from a mood of bitter frustration combining with his congenital restlessness. From mid-December to mid-March he was unsoothed and unsteadied by the presence of La Marck, though they wrote often. Wherever he looked — to the Court, to the Ministry, to Lafayette, to the Assembly — he saw nothing to inspire confidence and he woefully compared himself to Cassandra, fated to predict the truth and never to be heeded in time.[151] Meanwhile his personal reputation was under merciless assault. From the rear he was pressed continually by his creditors; from his front came a nasty intermittent sniping at the scandals of his private life; from the right flank came fire whose ammunition was his supposed complicity in the March to Versailles, while from the left thundered a new cannonade from those who saw him leagued with Monsieur in suspect designs. Even his hard-driven body plagued him; in January his left eye was abominably inflamed and painful and he appeared in the Assembly terrific in his bandages.

It was in this mood that he attached himself in a sort of desperation to Monsieur, accepting terms of service which his better judgment cannot have approved, rather than endure total immobility. He never seems to have admired this patron much. In his many letters there is no word of frank praise such as he later used about the Queen. For beneath a crust of political astuteness Provence had a soft and pulpy nature, and Mirabeau knew it. Nevertheless he clung yet awhile to his patronage. In January he even lent himself to an agreement with the Court which Provence negotiated. The King promised a monthly payment of 50,000 *livres* and an embassy later, while Mirabeau promised to serve the King with his advice in private and his eloquence in public. But his direct relations were to be with Monsieur alone, and he undertook to refrain from any speech of which Monsieur did not approve. Only a fever to gain access to the government on almost any terms can explain his acceptance of such an arrangement.

This treaty remained a dead letter, and it was the very spine-lessness of Monsieur which caused it to. Mirabeau had tried hard to make him a powerful figure, exploiting for all it was worth the good impression made by his public declaration over the Favras plot. He believed he had given Provence a hand which, if played with courage, would make him prime minister. But the Queen's reserve and the hostility of Lafayette formed a barricade which Monsieur lacked the nerve to assault. Lafayette, indeed, was probably an insurmountable obstacle. It is not to be believed that, after the Favras affair, he would have tolerated Monsieur as premier, let alone Mirabeau as the power behind the scenes, and his popularity with his militia in the weeks following Favras's arrest was such that nothing which he resolutely opposed was practical politics.[152]

However that might be, by the end of January 1790, Mirabeau was through with his dishonouring and unprofitable flirtation with Provence. 'As for the Court,' he wrote to La Marck, 'what bales of cotton they are! What hesitation! What pusillanimity! What heedlessness! What a grotesque hotch-potch of old ideas and new projects, of petty dislikes and childish desires, of willy and nilly, of abortive loves and hates! But the lowest of all is Monsieur.'[153]

2

La Marck had gone to the Austrian Netherlands in December to attend to family interests likely to be affected by the Belgian revolt against the meddling reforms of the Emperor Joseph II. This insurrection was widely misinterpreted in Paris, where it was represented as a movement parallel to the French revolution. Mirabeau applauded it as an attack on Joseph II, for whom he never had a good word. But La Marck, though distressed at the Emperor's imprudences, was fundamentally loyal to the House of Austria and disliked his friend's attitude. During the winter months at Brussels he found the tenour of Mirabeau's letters less and less pleasing. Disappointment with Monsieur seemed to be sickening him of the Court, and, while his revolutionary convictions remained, his solicitude for the cause of authority seemed smothered by his angry contempt for its representatives. His rancour against Lafayette seemed to be growing immoderate too, for the General, for all his maddening limitations, was both loyal and brave. Indeed, before the spring of 1790 came in, La Marck's faith in Mirabeau had become seriously shaken.

But in the middle of March La Marck received a letter from Mercy Argenteau, Austrian ambassador to France, pressing him to return for important but unspecified discussions. Mercy was an old friend and, what mattered more, the Queen's most trusted adviser, so it was not a request which he could refuse. He reached Paris on March 16th, and the next morning called on Mirabeau.

The latter had also begged La Marck to return, and the warmth of his welcome quickly melted away the doubts and reserves which had grown during the last months. They spent the day together. Mirabeau's mood was much what his friend had expected. So misunderstood was he, so distrusted and slandered, that he was half inclined to wash his hands of politics altogether; already he was speaking less frequently from the tribune. La Marck knew him well enough not to take this kind of talk too seriously, and he left his friend with the old warmth between them quite revived, and with the conviction that if another and fairer chance were offered him to serve the Crown he would take it with both hands.

Two days later La Marck saw Mercy Argenteau. The Ambassador explained that the King and Queen had charged him to get La Marck's opinion of Mirabeau's present attitude. La Marck said that at the beginning of the States-General Mirabeau had expected the ministers to act somewhat like ministers in England,

and build up a government party in the Assembly. At that time the popular party had overwhelming public support, and Mirabeau had thrown himself onto that side with violence to make himself feared and sought-after by the government. His failure in the latter object had disappointed him bitterly.

That being the case, Mercy replied, the question now was whether he was still prepared to serve the Court, because, if he were, the King and Queen had definitely made up their minds to employ him. As for the conditions, they would leave those with complete confidence to La Marck, and all their dealings with Mirabeau would remain solely in his hands; they would depend upon him, of course, for the most complete secrecy; no hint of the business must reach Necker, with whom they were very dissatisfied.

La Marck, for his part, insisted on a condition: Mercy himself must meet Mirabeau and form his own independent judgment of him; only if he approved of him would La Marck accept the role of intermediary. The Ambassador boggled at this, fearing to compromise his diplomatic detachment, but La Marck remained adamant.

A fortnight passed. Then La Marck received a request to call on Mercy. He found him still reluctant to take any responsible part in the negotiations, but in the end he gave way. The question remained how he was to meet Mirabeau without it becoming known, for it would never do for the Tribune of the People to be seen hobnobbing with the representative of Austria. La Marck suggested his own house as a rendezvous. It fronted on to the Rue du Faubourg-Saint-Honoré but there was a garden-entrance at the back from the Champs-Élysées. Mercy could arrive in his coach at the front door in the usual way, while Mirabeau could come on foot, let himself in through the garden-gate with a key and come straight to La Marck's room without attracting notice.

At the meeting which followed the two men were able to size each other up. The impression was happy on both sides. Mirabeau repeated his conviction that the King must leave Paris, though not France, if the monarchy was to be saved, and he begged the Ambassador to press this upon the King if he should see him. Mercy told La Marck after Mirabeau had gone that he was very sorry their Majesties had so long put off having recourse to so eminent a man. Still, they seemed to realize their mistake, for he bore a message from the Queen: La Marck was to wait on her at one o'clock the next day.

Marie Antoinette's chief and still lingering objection to calling in Mirabeau was her belief that he had been connected with the horrors of the October Days, and she began with a shade of embarrassment by asking La Marck if he could reassure her on this point. Fortunately he was the one man able to do so and he told her what he knew. She expressed herself as satisfied.

At this moment the King entered the room.

'The Queen will have told you already that I wanted to employ the Comte de Mirabeau, if you think he desires and is able to be useful to me. What do you think about it?'

For answer La Marck gave the King a short lecture: it was a bit late to be thinking of enlisting men of talent; that should have been done as soon as the States-General met. Not only Mirabeau, but also many others would have been eager to co-operate then. Instead, they had been kept at a distance, and for lack of employment had become the leaders of revolutionary groups. The ministers had shown a conceit and presumption which had been scarcely justified by events.

'Oh! It's no good hoping for anything of that sort from M. Necker,' the King replied. 'Also, whatever M. de Mirabeau does must remain a profound secret from my ministers. I count on you for that.'

This was rather flabbergasting. Whose advice was Louis thinking of following — the ministers' or Mirabeau's? He couldn't follow the latter, not even partially, without his ministers knowing, for Mirabeau's counsel would be in such violent contrast to theirs. If he meant anything by this extraordinary remark, was it not that he wanted Mirabeau's advice but had no intention of acting on it?

'How do you think Mirabeau could serve me usefully at the moment?' asked the King.

La Marck said he would be better able to answer that when he had seen the Count.

'See him then, and let the Queen or me know what has been decided.'

'Would you not prefer me, Sire, to tell the Comte de Mirabeau, as from your Majesty, to put his views in writing?'

'Yes, better still; and you'll send me what he writes by way of the Queen. That's agreed, then.' With which King Louis, having nothing more to say, stumped heavily out of the room.

As La Marck took his leave the Queen said he must consider himself free to visit her as often as he judged necessary.

He went away with an uneasy mind. Might not the employment of Mirabeau merely add to the King's irresolution? Was it to be believed that the sort of furtive, backstairs consultations which he seemed to envisage could be of any avail for mastering a national crisis which threatened to overturn the throne? Or were Louis's intentions of another sort — was he hoping to entertain Mirabeau with a pretence of seeking his advice in order to neutralize him as an opponent? Either way, Louis's incomprehension of his own situation was nothing short of terrifying. One hope, nevertheless, remained: however confused or disingenuous the intentions of the royal pair might be at the moment, once they had exposed themselves to the persuasive force of Mirabeau's mind perhaps a new direction, a new determination, would transform their policy. They might even steel themselves to order the ministers to work with Mirabeau or get out.

But no good would be done by communicating these doubts and fears to his friend. If the arrangement was to succeed at all he must enter into it with enthusiasm and confidence, so La Marck confined himself to giving an account of what had been said. When he spoke of the Queen's fear that Mirabeau had been connected with a plot against her life the effect on the other was startling. His face changed, became yellow-green, hideous. He had known, of course, and scorned the vulgar rumour against him, but that the Queen herself had harboured the horrid suspicion — that was new, and it staggered him. It was a lightning-flash revealing sharp and clear in their sprawling extent the jagged ruins of his reputation. La Marck hastened to assure him that she now believed him innocent, and his horror abated. But later he would recur to the subject, shocked whenever he thought that She could have thought him capable of that.

But the rest of his friend's news was good, very good, and soon the depression of the last months was thrown off. His sovereign was calling him at last. For the moment that was all that mattered. No doubts as to the terms of service clouded the view ahead. He would serve at last; at long last he would be able to act. Indeed his new optimism was such that La Marck thought it well to warn him not to promise too much in his letter to the King.[154]

3

When Mirabeau reflected more soberly on his new prospects he saw that an effort must be made to gain the alliance of Lafayette. What the King had in mind as regards the ministers was uncertain. If he was prepared to order them to accept Mirabeau's guidance, well and good; if he were not, Mirabeau believed he could turn the Assembly onto them; the ministers, in short, could probably be dealt with. Not so Lafayette. Master of armed Paris, idol of the bourgeoisie, the Assembly would not dream of attacking him and the King would never dare. His National Guard was the revolutionaries' guarantee against reaction, the bourgeoisie's insurance against pillage and the Court's defence against the mob. He enjoyed free access to the Tuileries, and Louis was constrained to place at his disposal much of the sorry remains of crown patronage. Lafayette in fact already exerted an extra-constitutional leverage on the Court not unlike that for which Mirabeau was now hoping. Clearly, unless they could somehow pull together, an absurd tug-of-war might develop between them, with the King helpless in a loop of the rope.

Mirabeau wrote to the General on April 28th. It was a long letter and not over-tactful. The echoes of their former disagreement were too audible. Lafayette was again reproached for shunning too readily the collaboration of men whom he disliked personally, and he was treated to an exact though scarcely ingratiating description of how he stood as a result: 'There you are, then, M. le Marquis, I do not say isolated, but entirely surrounded by yourself . . .' He is warned again not to fancy that Mirabeau can be induced to sit idle; he is too well known for 'the impatience of talent' for that; but, equally, the writer sees the unwisdom of acting without Lafayette. Let them work together, then, and let the General either hold this letter as a pledge of good faith or, if he wishes to refuse the proffered alliance, return it as a man of honour and say no more about the matter. For the letter indeed held compromising matter in the form of a suggestion that Lafayette should, in the national interest of course, help to disencumber his new colleague of the debts which weighed him down.

Mirabeau's chronic money trouble was in nothing more unfortunate than in its effect on the General. Solvency is a matter of temperament, not of income, and Lafayette, one of the temperamentally solvent, regarded the needs of a man like Mirabeau with no sympathy whatever. He was unattracted by a partnership for which it would be necessary to pay, and Mirabeau would have been wiser not to have raised the question of money, especially as by now he must have known that he had a chance of a court-salary for which it would be unnecessary to embarrass Lafayette.

The latter characteristically neither accepted the proposed alliance nor declined it outright, though it seems that at some later date the letter was returned.[155] The General felt less need of the tribune's alliance because he believed himself secure in the King's support without it. In October 1789 he had professed to Louis a democratic monarchism very similar to Mirabeau's own, and now, in mid-April, about a fortnight, that is, after their Majesties had assured La Marck of their readiness to employ Mirabeau, Lafayette had addressed another note to the King on much the same lines, and had received in reply an assurance of his entire confidence.

La Marck had been anxious enough lest the King should divide his confidence between his ministers and Mirabeau and so reach only a more complete paralysis of the will. Had he known that Louis in his teetering inconsequence was dividing his confidence not between two parties but between three, he would probably have abandoned the whole business as past praying for. As it was, he stuck loyally to the task he had undertaken. The negotiation itself went smoothly — perhaps a little too smoothly. He had the sense that the royal pair did not understand the importance of the deal to themselves. Ought they not to be scrutinizing Mirabeau's intentions more narrowly? Their very readiness to strike the bargain suggested an alarming lightness of mind, a hint that though they were putting money on Mirabeau they had placed other bets as well.

Under the date May 10th, 1790, Mirabeau wrote his letter to the King. It was his second letter to that address. The first had been written twelve years ago when he was a prisoner in Vincennes. Now Louis XVI was a prisoner in the Tuileries.

Mirabeau declares his conviction that the restoration of the lawful authority of the King is France's primary need. For his part, he cannot bear to think that he may only have contributed to a vast demolition, or to see any head of the state other than the King. He undertakes to serve with all his power the true interests of the monarchy, but, to avoid misunderstanding, he insists that 'a counter-revolution would be as dangerous as it would be criminal'. He will need two months, he says, to build up a body of opinion supporting the Crown. Progress will be slow but sure, the work of a doctor and not of a quack.

> I am as deeply opposed to a counter-revolution as to the excesses into which the revolution has led the masses when left in the hands of clumsy or perverse persons. My conduct must never be judged piecemeal — by one act or by a single speech. It is not that I refuse to account for these separately, but that it is only the whole which can be judged and only the whole which can take effect. It is impossible to save the state from day to day.
> I promise the King loyalty, zeal, activity, energy, and a courage of which perhaps men have little idea. I promise everything, in short, except success, which never depends upon one man alone....[156]

The letter made an excellent impression, and when in a few days La Marck again saw the Queen it was clear that agreement would be reached. He took the opportunity to press upon her the futility of merely clandestine relations with Mirabeau: surely if his influence in the Assembly was to be turned to account he must have the confidence of the ministers whose policies he was ostensibly to defend. Her Majesty was explaining in reply that the present ministers could scarcely be induced to confide in Mirabeau, when her husband entered the room. He at once pooh-poohed the idea that Mirabeau would need the ministers' help; he was highly pleased with the letter, quite content, for his own part, to be a limited, constitutional monarch, quite confident that things would work out well enough in the end. Then he dealt briefly with the financial side of the agreement, and La Marck left the presence with bills for 1,000,000 *livres* in his pocket and pity and anxiety in his heart.

He explained the terms to his friend. They were generous enough. First he showed him four bills for 250,000 *livres* each. These were to be handed to Mirabeau at the dissolution of the Assembly if in the interval he should have served his sovereign faithfully and well; in the meantime La Marck was to hold them in trust, together with the original of the letter to the King. But what followed was perhaps best: the King would pay Mirabeau's debts up to 208,000 *livres* and, in addition, pay him a monthly salary of 6000.

Mirabeau's exaltation was immense. Freedom at last! Freedom from the dead weight of debt which had bent him down so long! Freedom from the mean shifts, the humiliating expedients, the mute reproaches in unpaid servants' eyes! To be able to move in the world unencumbered and unafraid! To be able to treat as an equal with Lafayette! To be able to radiate his influence over an expanding circle of admiring adherents, the constant guests at his table — and what a table it would now be! And the Kingdom and the King — what might not be hoped for now? Was it not — had he not always said that it was — the fatuity of Necker, Montmorin and the rest which had masked the fundamental goodness and wisdom of Louis XVI? What might not he achieve now, with Mirabeau to guide him?

La Marck did not damp his enthusiasm; it was not, perhaps, a bad spirit in which to embark upon the new venture. How desperate an adventure it was going to be he would learn soon enough, though it was less certain whether King Louis would learn too. From his recent conversations with their Majesties, which included two hours alone with the Queen, La Marck had brought away one profound and disquieting impression — that they were giving the Revolution only a part of their attention.

4

At the very moment of his bargain with the King, Mirabeau had a chance of demonstrating how he could perform his part of it.

Trouble had arisen between England and Spain. English merchants had made a settlement on Nootka Sound, Vancouver, an area hitherto uncolonized. The Spanish, claiming from of old the Pacific coast of America, seized English ships trading with the settlement. England, denying Spain's right over an area where she had made no effective occupation, demanded redress. This Spain refused and the countries came to the brink of war. On May 10th, the House of Commons voted a £1,000,000 for the navy, and Spain, with her weaker fleet, looked for help to France who, by the terms of the Bourbon Family Compact of 1761, was bound to assist her in such an emergency.

Montmorin, as foreign minister, reacted promptly; here, for once, was a situation he understood. Without awaiting a formal request from Spain, he sent a letter to the President of the Assembly informing the chamber that the King had ordered fourteen warships to be got ready as an answer to the English preparations. The government perhaps expected that a call to arms against the old and hated enemy across the Channel would rally the Assembly in patriotic unity around their King.

Never was hope more quickly disappointed. Patriotism, old national enmities, present national emergencies made no appeal to the deputies of the Left. On the other hand, the grand subject of peace and war in the new age of liberty and brotherhood — that was a topic after their own hearts. In the piecemeal business of decreeing the constitution, a process in which topics were dealt with much as they chanced to crop up, the question where the right of deciding on war or peace should reside had so far been overlooked. The Assembly rushed in with delight to repair the omission, and Montmorin found that he had started not a national rally but an ideologues' field-day.

It was Alexandre de Lameth who, on Saturday, May 15th, raised the question of constitutional principle. Barnave, his fellow 'triumvir' supported him, and a debate developed of a fury only paralleled by the veto discussions. It lasted eight days. For once the Right gave almost as good as they got, for on this issue they felt firm ground beneath their feet. But their defence of the King's immemorial prerogative only served to drive Left-wing idealists higher and higher into the empyrean of noble abstractions, and Robespierre enjoyed that day the unusual experience of holding the attention of the house. 'We must declare,' he said, 'that France renounces all ambitious projects and all conquests, and that she regards her limits as fixed by eternal destinies . . .' Mirabeau suggested that this was scarcely relevant to the Minister's message and that the subject might be adjourned. Menou spoke next: a king empowered to make war might drag the nation into unjust aggression; if the cause were just, then by all means let there be war; if England should offend against justice France ought to send out not fourteen warships but all her effectives by land and sea; in such a case the French, armed with justice, would attack the English on their own soil and show the world what a nation at war was like. This was greeted with crashing applause, and Mirabeau, remarking that fourteen warships were scarcely a menace to the constitution, proposed simply that the President should thank the King for the precautions he had taken. The house, momentarily deflated, agreed.

On the morrow the question of the right over war and peace was the order of the day. The public was becoming interested and the galleries filled up early. Charles de Lameth made a speech full of war-mongering kings, and included a reference to the gold of the enemies of the Revolution which the deputy for Aix may have thought possibly significant. He was followed by the Abbé Maury, a hard-hitter from the Right, who matched Lameth's wicked kings with a sufficient list of criminal republics. Then Pétion, from the Left, distinguished between offensive and defensive wars, and Maury asked mockingly what war was not defensive to the country making it. The next day Pétion was again equating democracy with the love of peace, and Malouet was pointing out that the one potentate who for a century had waged only defensive wars was the Grand Turk. And so it went on, from Saturday to Wednesday. The Left were in their element. 'Let all nations be free like us, and there will be no more war!' cried the Curé Rollet. 'You are about to deliberate for the universe!' declared Volney. 'You are about to convoke the assembly of the nations!' Representatives of the fighting services remained unconvinced, but the tide was running against them, and when Cazalès, indulging in a little Right-wing nonsense for a change, said the blood of one Frenchman was dearer to him than all the peoples of the world, he was hooted and hissed and had to apologize.

After his short intervention on Saturday Mirabeau held his peace while the Assembly blew off steam. By Wednesday he had decided upon the line he would take. It would lie somewhat left of centre, saving for the King the initiative over war and peace but ensuring a very strict accountability to the Assembly. Anxious for success he approached the formidable 'Triumvirate' that evening. It was no use. Their personal distrust of him was deep, while his project for a decree appeared to them a deviation from the new orthodoxy of popular sovereignty, and they parted knowing that a trial of strength was at hand.

It began the next day, Thursday May 20th, with a very long speech by Mirabeau. Its massive common sense was so well combined with respect for the fundamental principles of popular government that it is hard to see how deputies who attended to it could without perversity have found anything more to say. It was a masterpiece of persuasion, and the many-sided argument was unrolled with a majestic and unhesitating confidence. A certain affection of hesitation did, it is true, appear in the opening periods; that was often his way — to start quietly, even a shade diffidently, so as to tease his audience with suspense and capture their curiosity; but soon the 'forge-bellows' would begin to blow (the metaphor of a witness) and the cold arguments would be fused in the intensifying heat into a glorious oratorical whole.[157]

Previous speakers, he said, had wrongly assumed that the power over war and peace must be entrusted either to the King or to the legislative body. But it was a mistake to think that there was no middle way between paralysing the state by entrusting diplomatic action to an assembly never designed for action at all, and nullifying popular sovereignty by entrusting this power solely and exclusively to the executive which, though an instrument of the popular will, was not primarily designed to act as its expression.

Speakers had been hag-ridden by the fear that, if the monarch were to have the right of declaring war, the peace-loving people might be led into bloody conflicts to satisfy the private whim or dynastic ambition of the King. But the legislature could meet that danger in two effective ways, by refusing funds and by impeaching guilty ministers. Let them not, however, imagine that kings, courts and camarillas were necessarily more prone than parliaments to rash and criminal bellicosity:

We have heard one of our orators propose that, if England should make an unjust war on Spain, we should cross the sea at once, hurl one nation on another and have it out with these proud English in London itself, throwing in our last penny and our last man — and we all applauded. Yes, I caught myself applauding too. One passage of oratory sufficed to trick you for an instant out of your wisdom. Do you believe that similar feats of eloquence will not carry you into disastrous wars if ever the legislative body deliberates on the matter directly and exclusively? . . . You will not be deceived by ministers; will you never be deceived by yourselves? . . .
Look at political assemblies: it is always under the stress of emotion that they have voted for war. You all know the remark of the sailor who in 1740* precipitated the war between England and Spain. *When the Spaniards, having mutilated me, faced me with death, I commended my soul to God and my cause to my country.* A most eloquent fellow, that sailor, though the war which he set alight was neither just nor politic; neither the King of England nor his ministers wanted it, but the emotion of an assembly decided the matter.

It was a neatly topical example. The tactics of persuasion were neat too. On no point of theory were the ideologues more set than on the 'separation of powers'. They had used it against him with deadly effect on November 7th; he turned it against them now. A declaration of war was, theoretically, a motion of the will and therefore proper to the legislature; but *in practice* it was an *action* which, if performed by the legislature, would blur the line of demarcation between the powers.

He made a less subtle bid for the support of the theorists by a flattering allusion to the man whom he privately nick-named 'Mahomet'. He was nearing his close and preparing to read his proposed constitutional articles.

I will not seek to hide the feeling of deference with which I place them before you; still less shall I conceal my deep regret that the man who has laid the foundations of the constitution,

* The 'Jenkins' Ear War' began in 1739.

who has contributed most to your great work, that the man who has revealed to the world the true principles of representative government, that the Abbe Sieyès — I crave his pardon, but I must name him — should not come himself to place in his constitution one of the main springs of social order. . . .

But there were passages less pleasing to a Left-wing ear. Was the royal dignity, he demanded, no longer to be numbered among the nation's assets? Would not a king shorn of all authority have every temptation to become the enemy of the constitution which he ought to guard? Let them remember that it was to Carthage and Rome, states with no king at all, that citizens like Hannibal and Caesar had been dangerous: 'Make the monarch's magistracy what it ought to be; you will then no longer have to fear that a rebel king, himself abdicating his crown, may risk the race from victory to the scaffold.' (How could Barnave see himself, thirteen months later, riding in a coach with pitiful fallen royalty back to Paris from the east? How could Pétion see, two and a half years on, the Girondins voting for the death of Citizen Capet? Or by what light was Robespierre to foresee his republic grown pestiferous and fit to be blasted out of sight by the guns of Bonaparte?)

It was Barnave who replied. He was young, slim, elegant and very eloquent, the spoiled child of the Revolution. His head was all crowded with the truths and illusions of the hour, and his tongue gave them the kind of expression which won him the intoxicating admiration of his fellows. Weaker in voice and person than the great Provençal, he was, nevertheless, one of the very few deputies who could speak at length without a manuscript, and he was perhaps the ablest debater of them all. Between him and Mirabeau it was a match of champions.

The nation, he declared, would only will national wars; national wars were always defensive and consequently always just; therefore the nation's elected representatives ought to have the sole power of making war. It is some measure both of the mood of that assembly and of the eloquence of the speaker that a speech with this theme did for the moment efface the impression made by his rival's monumental realism.

On Friday, May 21st, after Cazalès's provocative speech, Barnave mounted the tribune again. Public excitement had

BARNAVE

become extreme; people had waited all night to be sure of gaining admission to the Manège and a crowd had gathered outside. It was the drama of personalities rather than the conflict of theories which had drawn them, for between the actual proposals of Mirabeau and Barnave the difference was not very great, certainly not irreconcilable. As a public personality there was still no one to be compared with Mirabeau, but the general idolatry of him had not survived the autumn leaves of 1789. The public was now divided into those for whom he was still an idol and those who preferred Barnave, not as an idol, for he had no magic, but as a symbol of their faith in the state reborn.

Mirabeau, with his friend Frochot beside him, sat listening to his adversary. Barnave was explaining that since the *Legislative Power* expressed the national *will*, and since a declaration of war was essentially an *act of will*, it was for the *Legislative Body* alone to make it. 'I've got him!' said Mirabeau, spotting the substituted term; he borrowed Frochot's pencil and wrote down a few words; 'That's enough to hear,' he said, 'I've got my reply. Let's go out.' They strolled in the Tuileries Gardens. Mirabeau, putting the debate out of mind, talked gaily of this and that, and made himself something more than agreeable to Mme de Staël when they encountered that intellectual but curvilinear lady.[158]

He returned to the Manège in time for Barnave's conclusion and to witness the ovation he received. The Left demanded that the discussion should be closed the next day. Scenting danger Mirabeau interposed: 'I demand an explanation of these words, "the discussion shall be closed". M. Barnave's friends either believe that his speech will triumph over all replies or else they do not believe so; if they do, surely we may trust that in the generosity of their admiration they will not fear an answer; if they do not, their duty is to accept further instruction.' The point was yielded and his chance to reply was saved.

But the crowd carried Barnave in triumph, and that evening the news-sellers were shouting in the streets: *Great treason of the Comte de Mirabeau exposed.*

Six thousand copies of this sheet, which was distributed free, had been hurriedly printed at the expense of the author, a certain Lacroix. That he was paid by the Triumvirate has not been proved, though his scurrilous violence was welcome to them: 'Your crimes are discovered at last, cunning imposter, and your genius will impose on us no longer . . . It was gold you wanted, it was for gold and honours that you declared yourself the supporter of the absolute veto . . . Beware lest the people pour into your viper's mouth this burning nectar to slake for ever the thirst by which you are consumed; beware lest the people parade your head as they carried that of Foulon, whose mouth was stuffed with hay. . . .'

Has something leaked out? Probably nothing definite. The libel was ferocious but quite vague.

On Saturday morning a vast crowd filled the Tuileries Gardens and all the streets and open places near the Manège. Nothing like it had been seen before. Some had secured perches by the windows, and from there let down on threads to the crowd below occasional bulletins of the course of the debate within. Rumours, hopes, fears passed in waves over that visible democracy like wind over the corn.[159]

All knew that Mirabeau was to speak. Many had read yesterday's murderous libel; many more had read shrewder criticisms like that in Marat's *Ami du peuple* which said 'Mirabeau has always declared for the good cause when it was a question of humbling the privileged orders; but can a single case be cited in which he has not fought against it when there was question of restraining the formidable power of the crown?'

'To the lamp-post with Mirabeau!' some voices cried as he made his way to the Assembly. Would the day's session cast him down from his pedestal, or would it seat him more firmly upon it? That, all men knew, was the issue.

Two speakers supported his middle way. One was Duquesnoy, who had thought him a madman with a tiger's face a year ago but had come now to think him the only man for saving the state; the other, Chapelier, moved an amendment securing to the King the exclusive right of *proposing* declaration of war, and Mirabeau, anxious for all possible support, accepted it with alacrity. But Duport, the triumvir, reiterated his group's conviction of the danger to the people of a strong executive, and then it was Mirabeau's turn to speak. 'They'll carry me out from here either in triumph or in little pieces,' he remarked.[160] As he went up to the tribune a deputy sneered: 'Yesterday the Capitol, Mirabeau, today the Tarpeian Rock!' A useful figure.

Groans and boos greeted his appearance on high. They were a long time subsiding, so he waited coolly with arms folded until he could be heard. Then he began:

> To bring opponents together it is useful to mark precisely the points on which they are agreed and those on which they differ. Friendly discussions do more for mutual understanding than slanderous insinuations, wild accusations, hatred, rivalry and intrigue . . . It is strange, this maniacal blindness of men who prefer their irascible self-conceit to the service of the fatherland, and who hand each other over to the prejudices and passions of the populace.[161]
>
> Only a few days ago it was I whom they wished to carry in triumph; and now they are shouting in the streets: *The Great Treason of the Comte de Mirabeau*. I had no need of this lesson to know that it is a short distance from the Capitol to the Tarpeian Rock, but the man who fights for reason does not admit he is beaten as easily as that. . . .

Now his eyes were fixed on the Lameths.

> Let those who at this moment vilify my case without having understood it, who accuse me of being the base stipendiary of men whom I have not ceased to combat — let them deliver to the fury of a deceived people the man who for twenty years has warred against all forms of oppression, who was speaking to the French of liberty and of a constitution while these vile calumniators were sucking the milk of the court and accepting all the prevailing prejudices —

this to teach the Lameths to descend to personalities; they had been educated at the Queen's expense —

> To these men I say: answer if you can; then slander me as much as you like.

Then he singled out Barnave and nailed him.

> In your speech you attributed the expression of the general will — to whom? To the legislative *power*. But to whom have you attributed it in your proposed decree? To the legislative *body*. I call you to order on that. You have violated the constitution. If you mean that the legislative body is the

legislative power you are upsetting all the laws we have made. If for expressing the general will on the subject of war the legislative *body* suffices, then by that the King is deprived of all that we have accorded to the executive power in our system —

The allusion to the veto was sufficiently daring at such a moment —

If, however, you are willing to substitute in your decree for the words *legislative body* the words *legislative power*, and to define this expression as an act of the National Assembly *sanctioned by the King*, we shall be at one on the question of principle.

Barnave had criticized his decree article by article; now article by article Mirabeau refuted the criticisms. It was a slow, inexorable demolition; and it was a complete triumph. As he came down from the tribune there was a great burst of applause, and when the cry went up for a vote Barnave, the Lameth brothers, Duport and their friends sat sour-faced and glum, with vengeance in their hearts but incapable of a reply.[162]

It only remained to decide in what order the competing proposals should be put to the vote, and here, for once, Lafayette threw in his weight and secured that Mirabeau's decree should be taken first. Even now a chance for amendments remained, and Alexandre de Lameth proposed that Article one should be altered so as to leave the actual declaration of war to the Assembly. Content with his triumph Mirabeau conceded the point.

How great in reality was his victory? On the constitutional issue it was, in truth, small: only the bare minimum of initiative had been saved for the crown. But the parliamentary triumph was resounding. He had wrestled with the champions of the Left on their own ground, on an issue of their own choosing, before a vast audience strongly inclining to their side; and he had given them a fall. The enemies of the executive had been checked and halted in full career, and his first service to the King had been rendered.

CHAPTER XIII

THE DESPERATE EXPERIMENT

IN the weeks preceding Mirabeau's engagement by the Court La Marck had been anxious as to the seriousness of the King and Queen. In the weeks which followed he became alarmed at the indiscretion of his friend. His sudden affluence seemed to have gone straight to his head. An unobtrusive expansion of his way of living was, of course, to be expected and even desired. Nothing had told more against him hitherto than his air of being an adventurer living on his wits, and that impression he would now be able to efface by paying his bills and living in the sober comfort of a decent gentleman's residence. But such prudential calculations never entered Mirabeau's head. Leaving the furnished apartment which had served him of late, he at once rented from Julie Carreau, the actress, her over-modish house in the Chaussée d'Antin, a place which, when he had done with it, gave the precisely wrong impression of ostentatious but ill-secured luxury.

To live grandly had been a craving ever since his first crazy plungings as a newly-wed. It was not the ease of luxury he needed, for he could live hard; it was magnificence, as the men of the Renaissance understood that word; and now, in this high summer of 1790, launched upon the greatest public things, he made haste to live to scale, magnificently.

A staff of servants was engaged, the faithful Legrain once more his valet-de-chambre. Horses were bought and a fine new coach painted a dashing blue — something for the populace to note and remember beside Lafayette's white charger. The hammer of the aristocracy put his servants into livery and had his arms painted on his coach. If the motto, IUVAT PIETAS, was oddly inappropriate, the moment for an heraldic display was chosen with a rollicking contempt for the decree of June 19th, whereby all use of titles, liveries and armorial bearings had been declared illegal. 'M. Riqueti' thought it a piece of transient egalitarian silliness, worthy of the Lameth brothers and Lafayette who, in a session that bordered on farce, had supported it. To destroy privileges was

one thing, but to decree for society a grey equailty was to flout
human nature. 'What you can never tear from the human heart,'
he commented to Mauvillon, 'is the power of ancient memories';
and when, one day, Frochot asked him if it was really possible
for the gentlemen of the Right to believe that they were of
different stuff from the rest of mankind, 'Not a doubt of it,' he
answered, 'and take it from me,' he added after a pause, 'it's an
error much harder to cure oneself of than you think.'

His feeling for historic continuity was offended by the attempt
to erase titles which were part of the vocabulary of the nation's
past, and it was this same feeling which caused him, when the
new departments were under discussion, to oppose any cantoniza-
tion which should cut across the boundaries of the historic
provinces.[163]

He filled his house with expensive things. His dinners became
famous. That the talk might flow freely each guest was provided
with a dumb-waiter laden with wines, glasses and silver, the
domestics appearing at intervals only to change the courses.
Against one wall stood a sideboard laden with costly plate;
valuable engravings were hung on another, pictures representing
the pleasures of the table on a third; on the fourth side gleamed
the tooled bindings of his books. The purchase of these was his
pet extravagance, and he spent on them no less than £7000 in
this last year of his life. He bought jewels, too, and Dumont, who
thought the whole house in bad taste, was surprised to see him show
his guests a casket of valuable gems. 'This was proclaiming the
civil list with a vengeance,' he commented, 'and I was astonished
it did not affect his popularity.'

That was also La Marck's worry, and he lectured his friend
on the folly of inviting curiosity about the cause of his sudden
prosperity. Mirabeau listened with the meekness which he
reserved for La Marck's reproaches, but he went on just as before.

His colossal energy was put forth now with no sort of brake or
reserve. He lived his life in public, like royalty, with little retire-
ment and no rest outside sleep. At seven each morning the house
began to fill with visitors, and from then till he left for the morning
session it was an uninterrupted levee. As he stepped to his coach
he would pass through a crowd waiting at his door to catch a
glimpse of him. His huge dynamic bonhomie must play upon

them all, building him up in men's imagination. No word, no gesture, no little act of personal consideration must be omitted which might help to establish him as the personality of the hour. Neglect of these arts of popularity had reduced the monarch to his present impotent isolation. What the King had lost, Mirabeau must win in unrivalled abundance to supply his need. He must magnetize himself to draw men after him into the vulgar monarchism which, in his plan, was to supersede the old chivalric royalism of the court and to swamp the rebellious envy of the factions. The Revolution was to be bitted and bridled, not stopped, and for this object Mirabeau was ready to be prodigal with life: the phrase is his own.[164]

His frequent and wide-ranging speeches in the Assembly were now almost the least part of his labours. There was a host of contacts to be maintained: for one man the persuasive, seemingly confidential chat in the corner, for another the merry badinage exchanged in passing, for another the good-fellow's slap on the back, for a trusted friend the earnest secret conclave. He worked in a world of men. His nights were otherwise employed, but it is to be remarked that, for all his notorious looseness with women — and the Le Jay kept no monopoly — we know of none who influenced appreciably his work.

A big part of this was his correspondence. It was immense, a part of the grand strategy of popularity. Comps, the passionate young Provençal who had given himself to Mirabeau as secretary in 1788, bore the drudgery, but we have his word that nothing escaped the great man's eye. Every letter, no matter how trivial, had to be answered, and the reply written, if possible, on one side of a single sheet so that he could read and sign it in one act. His memory was prodigious and he had the rare ability to attend to several matters at the same time. One day he was at work with Comps when the room, as often, was full of friends. Three or four conversations were going on at once, with Mirabeau taking a part in each. He was putting his signature to a letter when he stopped, then ran his pen across the page: 'I'm very sorry, my friend,' he said to Comps, 'but I don't repeat myself. Here's a phrase which is word-for-word what I wrote nearly three months ago. The idea is good and to the point; keep that, only put it in a fresh way.'

Forty years later Comps was to recall the hours when, at ease in the familiar circle of friends in his own house, Mirabeau let himself go: 'It was then indeed that he was magnificent; then indeed he was sublime!'[165]

2

There remained the problem of Lafayette. Despising him as a politician, but, as a politician, recognizing the head of armed Paris as a principal factor in the revolutionary situation, Mirabeau, at the King's instance, opened his new career by writing to him a famous appeal.

He reproached the General once again for his preference for mediocrities. 'I do not know of a single serious adviser or a single distinguished agent in your service. Not one of your trusted aides-de-camp lacks military merit; you might re-fight a capital American war with them. Not one of your friends lacks valour and virtue; they will all do honour to your reputation as a private citizen; but not one of the former has any knowledge of the people or the country, and not one of the latter has any knowledge of public affairs.' He complained that Lafayette moved in a world of busy and futile little committees: 'What I want to say to you is that I am more necessary to you than all your committees put together.' This might be true, but it was not the way to approach a man whose vanity he knew so well. Amends came tardily in the oft-quoted concluding passage:

> Oh, M. de Lafayette! Richelieu was Richelieu against the nation and for the court, and although Richelieu may have done a deal of harm to public liberty, he did a tolerable amount of good to the monarchy. Be Richelieu over the court and for the nation, and you will restore the monarchy while making public liberty more extensive and more solid. But Richelieu had his capuchin Joseph; have, therefore, a grey eminence of your own; otherwise you will ruin yourself while failing to save us. Your great qualities have need of my drive, and my drive has need of your great qualities. But you give your confidence to little men who, for petty reasons, by petty manœuvres and with petty views, wish to make us useless to each other. . . .

It was not a very winning letter. One does not gain an opponent by belittling his friends. It is hard, indeed, to believe that Mirabeau was wholly in earnest. The scorn for the General's associates was too wounding, the flattery of the man who had chosen them was too gross. Lafayette as a modern Richelieu — what an idea! The figure of the steel cardinal haunted Mirabeau's imagination often enough, to be sure, but it was not this stuffed dummy, this 'Cromwell-Grandison', this 'Clown-Caesar' (as he was beginning to call the Hero) whom he had cast for *that* part. The letter did not conceal the underlying contempt. He summoned Lafayette to an alliance, but, secure now through his contract with the Court, could not forego the satisfaction of speaking to the Hero as an equal and something more than an equal. But their relations to date had not been such as to make this tone of over-candid friend acceptable to one whose strength was that he did not realize his own limitations, and Lafayette, aware that he was, inexplicably, a figure of fun in his rival's table-talk, fortified his self-esteem with a frigid disdain for the public and private character of the tribune. Three weeks later, pressed by Frochot to support his rival's candidature for the presidency of the Assembly, he delivered himself of an almost incredible reply: 'I have vanquished the King of England in his power, the King of France in his authority and the people in its fury; I shall certainly not yield to M. de Mirabeau.'

'This,' Mirabeau commented, 'would be funny at the *Variétés Amusantes*, but, believe me, sooner or later he will pay for those words.'[166]

The letter evoked no response, and if Lafayette's deep repugnance for everything about Mirabeau was a public misfortune, his distrust of the sincerity of the overture was sufficiently justified. For on June 1st, the very day on which he wrote to the General, Mirabeau completed the first of his great series of Notes to the Court.

It began with a direct address to the Queen, for already he saw her character as the one patch of hard ground on which something might be built amid the mists and marshes of the Tuileries. It was a moving and dignified appeal for her confident support. But soon he came to the point, which was 'the Court's relations with the idol of the day, the so-called General of the Constitution, the rival of the monarch, in a word — M. de Lafayette'.

It was morally impossible, he insisted, to govern any longer with the present set of discredited ministers. Perhaps the decree barring deputies from office could be repealed, but, be that as it might, a new ministry must be chosen at all costs. The question then arose whether Lafayette should be consulted in the choice: could a ministry succeed to which he was opposed? What, in fact, was the exact measure of his power?

His power, the Note explained, depended upon the confidence he inspired in his army, and he inspired this confidence because he seemed to share the opinions of the masses. But those opinions were shaped not by him but by the horde of journalists and agitators; once let him oppose the popular current and he would soon be a general without soldiers. His future conduct could therefore be predicted. He would fear and flatter the populace out of self-interest, supporting the majority whether right or wrong; he would frighten the Court with popular disturbances for which he would be at least partly responsible, and then use them to show how indispensable he was. He would put the voice of Paris before that of France because it was from the capital, not the provinces, that his strength came. But since Paris was likely to be the last place in France to return to sanity, it followed that Lafayette was, of all citizens, the one upon whom the King could least rely.

To accept a Lafayette-nominated ministry would, Mirabeau continued, be to place the Kingdom under the dictatorship of Paris, whereas what was needful was for the country to bring the capital back to its senses; and for this there must be a ministry deriving its authority not from the commander of the Parisian militia but from the Assembly and the nation. Such a ministry would only have to snap its fingers at the General for his position to collapse. Deprived of the political influence which only the existing ministerial vacuum enabled him to exert, he would be thrown back upon 'the inertia of his own mind and the nullity of his talent'.

A ministry commanding respect in the Assembly — that was the vital thing. But it might be well to reduce the General's specifically military prestige as well. Why should he be allowed to appear as the sole military leader of the Revolution? Would it not be well to raise up a rival? Mirabeau suggested Bouillé, the commander at Metz, for the part: there was a man who enjoyed two things Lafayette lacked, the respect of the regular army and freedom from political contaminations. (Bouillé was not yet damned in progressive eyes with the unforgivable crime of quelling a mutiny.) Bouillé, however, would probably need a public relations officer, and there should be sent to him 'a man of talent who . . . while leaving military tactics to him, would be responsible on his behalf for the *tactics of popularity*'.

Mirabeau despised Lafayette as a noodle and resented him as a prig. Fires of envy and frustration tormented him when he contemplated the eminence of this man who had so many principles and so few ideas. Even so he was prepared to work with this rival provided — always provided — that they were to be on an equal footing, and that the General was forced to admit his need of him. That alone would compensate for the inconvenience of collaborating with such a man.

'The King', wrote Mirabeau in his second Note three weeks later, 'has by him only one man, and that is his wife . . . I like to think that she would have no use for life without the crown, but what I am certain of is that, if she does not save the crown, she will not save her life.' The secret adviser was using no courtier's arts or insinuations: 'The Queen must (*il faut que la reine . . .*) speak to Lafayette in the presence of the King (who must be prepared and resolute) and she must say to him: "You know and we know that M. de Mirabeau is the only statesman in this country. Understand that we are resigned or resolved to give him the confidence of despair. I ask you, I require you to couple yourself to M. de Mirabeau — completely, you understand, daily, publicly and in all matters." '

But Mirabeau's monopoly of statesmanship was less evident to his employers than to himself; he was their salaried secret correspondent whose ideas might sometimes be useful, that was all.

Great care was, however, taken to keep the correspondence secret. La Marck's relations with the Count were well known, and if the former had been seen frequently visiting the Tuileries the obvious inference would have been drawn by the hundreds whose patriotism took the form of a tireless snooping round the palace. The Notes must therefore be delivered by someone whose visits to the palace would arouse no comment, and the perfect go-between was found in François de Fontanges, Archbishop of Toulouse by favour of the Queen since Brienne's translation to Sens. He had been Marie Antoinette's almoner when she was Dauphine and he was of her intimate circle. A clerical deputy, he had hitherto been to La Marck but a nodding acquaintance, but henceforth he came frequently to his house and there, with due precautions, Mirabeau was able to talk with him. These contacts with a man who saw the Queen almost every day were precious. The Archbishop also handled the actual payment of Mirabeau and gave him, in addition to his monthly 6000 francs, something extra for Comps. Comps it was who copied out the secret Notes, and, though devoted, he was, it seems, a little deficient in nerve; 300 francs a month would act as a reward and also, perhaps, as an insurance.

Mirabeau and the Archbishop were careful to cut each other in public, but the prelate was soon transmitting notes at an average of two a week. It was natural, however, that the writer should seek a personal interview with the King and Queen; an hour of his physical presence would, he was confident, have more effect than a dozen memoranda. Mercy agreed and persuaded the Queen to give an appointment. The royal family were at Saint Cloud (that measure of personal liberty had not yet been denied them) and Mirabeau was told that the Queen would receive him there on July 3rd, at half past eight in the morning, an hour at which, it was hoped, there would be few about to mark his visit.[167]

Secrecy was vital. It was arranged that he should drive out to Passy the day before on an ostensible visit to his niece, Mme d'Aragon. From here it should be possible in the morning to make his way to Saint Cloud unnoticed. He would drive a two-horse cabriolet and, for greater security, only his nephew, young Du Saillant, should accompany him, dressed as a postillion. He had sometimes teased the boy for his simple ardour to serve his king; now, he explained, it was his wicked revolutionary uncle who was giving him his chance to do so. They drove off together through the freshness of that summer morning to St. Cloud, to an appointed door into the garden, and Mirabeau was at once admitted.[168]

Even now the Queen had to steel herself a little to receive with any cordiality the ugly fellow whom she had so recently regarded as the man of October. But of that Mirabeau saw nothing as he entered the room where those two were waiting for him. He saw the serene imperious brow, the rather long face, the small firm mouth and the fine eyes touched with new anxieties. She spoke: it would be out of place, she said, to grant an interview like the present to any common enemy of the crown, but when it was with a Mirabeau that one had to deal, then, indeed, the case was altered. . . .

What passed after this we can only surmise. Even this opening is recorded only by the prattling pen of her lady, Mme de Campan, who says she had it from her mistress's lips. It was not a long interview, and Mirabeau may have confined himself to professions of ardour and fidelity. The King seems to have declared his readiness to be a sovereign under the law. Only one thing is certain about it all and that is the impression made upon the visitor by the Queen. As a statesman he had already been disturbed by her peril; now as a man he was touched by her grace and dignity. But there was something else within him that was moved, something orbed and simple and half-forgotten amid the expedients of a muddied life, yet inherited and shared with the fine boy waiting beyond the garden gate with the horses — the spirit of mere loyalty. We need not doubt Mme de Campan's word that, as he kissed the Queen's hand at leave-taking, he cried 'Madame, the monarchy is saved!'

3

He returned to La Marck full of new zeal. 'Nothing shall stop me!' he said, 'I will perish rather than break my promises!' But if the monarchy was indeed to be saved there was everything to be done. Some of these things were outlined in his eighth Note, written that same day.

He compares the monarchy now with the monarchy of two years ago. Then the King was absolute in theory, but in practice baulked by a mass of obstructions — privileges of the clergy, privileges of the nobility, rights of the *parlements*, expectations of his courtiers and a vast tangle of anomalous franchises. All these things have now been swept away: 'The idea of creating only one class of citizens would have pleased Richelieu.' Formerly the whole odium of taxation fell upon the King; now, if he has somewhat less to give, he has nothing to demand; the Assembly decrees the taxes, but the King can still distribute rewards and gratifications. The chief items on the debit side are the foolish new atomization of administrative authority into countless elective local offices, and the irresponsibility of a legislature separated from the executive.

To set these matters right there is one sovereign remedy, and this is public opinion. The royal policy must be to watch public opinion, to influence it and to gain it, and no pains must be spared in maintaining constant touch with the provinces. There are ample signs of provincial discontent with the extravagances of the legislature, and divisions of opinion may lead to anarchy which, in its turn, may lead to civil war. In that event the important thing will be to deploy the armed forces only on behalf of the nation; they must never be used to defend sectional interests. It is the doctrine of the October Memorandum repeated in brief.

Mirabeau wanted to place the King where he belonged, that is, in the centre of the political stage. At all costs he must escape from the position into which he had drifted, a position where he appeared at best passive and acquiescent, at worst covertly hostile to the Revolution. Instead of being trailed ignominiously behind the revolutionary car, Louis should be seen sitting within it, benign and stately and as much at ease as in the state-coach of the old régime; he should also be heard from time to time giving directions to the driver.

At the moment two questions demanded immediate attention.

The first was the attitude to be adopted towards the Duke of Orleans. Exiled by Lafayette after the October days, he had just applied to the King for permission to present himself at court, but it looked as if his agents were preparing the ground for an act of defiance should permission be refused. On July 6th, Mirabeau warned the Court that bread was being distributed in Paris below the controlled price, that his brother, the Vicomte, had proof that in one week 67,000 francs had been handed out to the Regiment of Lorraine, and that certain journalists were enjoying incomes obviously never earned by legitimate sales. Would it not be wise to do a little counter-mining, to identify the 'bankers of anarchy' and discover their game? Desmoulins, for example, might be open to pecuniary persuasion and ought to be approached, especially as (and this must have caused the Queen to shudder with sick disgust as she recalled the Necklace scandal) Mme la Motte was rumoured to be in Paris.

Counter-mining was the more desirable because something, it seemed, had leaked out about the Saint Cloud interview. The *Orateur du peuple* had printed 'a letter found in the Park of Saint Cloud' full of cryptic references to Mirabeau and the Queen and a 'great day' approaching, and the Assembly's *Comité des recherches* was looking into the matter. Once more the cry of 'Great treason of the Comte de Mirabeau' was being heard in the streets, but he felt justly confident that his enemies had nothing solid to go on, and that he was giving adequate camouflage to his visit by going out frequently to Passy and riding about the country with his nephew. Still, since he was being spied upon, a bit of counter-espionage was called for: 'We must keep track hour by hour,' he told his employers, 'of the movement of MM. Lameth, Barnave, D'Aiguillon, Menou and Pétion.'

The essential thing, he argued, was to handle Orleans rightly. To forbid him to return would be a blunder: he would come just the same and his exploiters and hirelings would have their chance to make his return a humiliation for the Court. The old Orleanist party no longer existed; it was the Jacobins to whom the Duke might now be useful. The right course, therefore, was to receive him at court and speak him fair, since except in his role of aggrieved and persecuted prince he was negligible. Orleanism could now, in fact, be killed by kindness, and if the Duke at court should be one more embarrassment for Lafayette, so much the better.[169]

The King and Queen were persuaded, but an accident intervened and wrecked everything. For when the Duke entered the Tuileries, with at least half his mind resolved on peace with the Queen and her husband, he was affronted by a courtier who, ignorant of their wishes and seeing the smiling figure of treason before him in the flesh at last, thought the chance of giving the Duke a piece of his loyal mind too good to be missed. The result was that, after a stiff little interview, Orleans left the palace vowing to be revenged.

The second business demanding Mirabeau's attention was the forthcoming Festival of the Federation.

The Assembly had decreed that the anniversary of the taking of the Bastille should be a public holiday to be celebrated on the grandest scale. The idea caught the people's imagination and plans went quickly ahead. Nothing was to be spared which might make July the Fourteenth an occasion without precedent. Liberty and Equality had had plenty of advertisement; it was now Fraternity's turn, and the Fourteenth was to demonstrate visibly and triumphantly the new national unity and the brotherhood of all Frenchmen. The Champ de Mars was to be got ready for a monster parade of contingents of the National Guard drawn from every corner of the country. The focus of the vast ceremony would be an Altar of the Fatherland before which the Oath to the Constitution would be taken, and, so that everyone might witness the parade and its central acts, 'all classes of the people', Orleans's Scottish head-gardener recorded, 'went to work at the Champ de Mars where they hollowed out the Midle of this great inclossure and raised all arround a bank a Amphetheatre for the People; here was Ladys wheeling the barrow and loading allong with Shoeblacks and all promiscus'.[170]

Mirabeau saw in this unique national rally a supreme opportunity to popularize the monarchy. It would be an occasion for mass emotions, a day for profound yet simple feelings. It would be the perfect moment for Louis XVI to show himself to his people in his truest aspect, as a simple fellow, a kind father and their king. To miss such a chance would be a calamity, for concerning the Federation one thing was sure: if Louis did not take the centre of the stage Lafayette would.

Nothing, of course, could prevent the General's ordering the military part of the proceedings, but his role ought as far as possible to be confined to this. He must not be allowed to steal the political limelight as well. That should be reserved for the King in the first place, and, in the second, for the National Assembly.

But at the head of the Assembly would be its President, whose seat, it had been decided, was to be on the right of the throne.

His words and bearing could do much to stamp the occasion with the right emphasis, and Mirabeau set his heart on obtaining the chair for the fortnight in which the Fourteenth fell. He saw the possibilities: the Tribune of the People standing out there in the sunlight before the nation's representatives: there would not be wanting some moment for a speech, a phrase, a gesture even, towards the King — something to be remembered by the multitude and reported in the distant towns and villages by the *fédérés* when they got home, some picture in the vulgar eye of the monarchy rejuvenated and national.

Lafayette saw different possibilities, and when Talleyrand and others urged him to support the tribune for the next presidency he replied that so great an orator would doubtless obtain that honour in due course, but that on the present occasion it would be fitting for the Assembly to choose a man of irreproachable life. Since there was a general feeling that the Fête was Lafayette's special concern, it was not Mirabeau who was elected President on July 5th, but a certain De Bonnai.

Part of Mirabeau's dream for the Fourteenth would therefore remain a dream. But it might still be possible to place the King in his proper place, and he urged Louis to take the initiative and summon a committee of the Assembly to draw up the oath and settle ceremonial details. Lafayette should be summoned simply as one member of the committee, which should include Sieyès, Talleyrand and, of course, himself. The King ought to invite the ambassadors to the Fête: it would show the importance he attached to it and make him popular.[171]

It was no use. Louis could not be galvanized into even a semblance of initiative. The great day came closer and closer, yet he seemed resigned to the minimum part intended for him by Lafayette; he would, that is, be content with swearing to defend the constitution. Mirabeau hoped for something better than that; he wanted the King to arrive on horseback as the commander-in-chief and to make a speech which should be the high point of the day: 'Frenchmen, citizens, brothers, friends . . .' such were the terms he should use.[172] But with only two days to go nothing was agreed. The Archbishop urged upon the Queen the desirability of a royal speech and was ready with a draft from Mirabeau's pen. The Queen herself favoured the idea but, early on the thirteenth, confessed that she could in no wise prevail upon her husband to speak in public the following day. All he would do was to receive that afternoon at the Tuileries a deputation of *fédérés* who wanted to present an address; he would say a few words then. Later in the morning the Queen told the Archbishop what he proposed to say: there was to be a hint of his desire to visit the provinces before long. Perhaps it would make up a little for the absence of a speech at the parade next day, for it was to be printed and distributed freely. 'You see,' the Archbishop observed to La Marck, 'that they are far from attaching importance to the things which deserve most attention. We must expect often to experience this sort of difficulty from the man with whom we have to deal.'[173]

The great day arrived, and it poured. But rain could not damp the warm enthusiasm of the multitudes who were abroad, of the parading *fédérés* waiting, soaked but fraternal, for their turn to move in the big parade, of the spectators cheering all along the processional route from the empty site of the Bastille to the Champ de Mars, or massed around that amphitheatre where 10,000 men could drill together.

When a signal-gun was fired the central solemnities began. On the raised Altar of the Fatherland Mass was offered by the somewhat unhabituated hands of Talleyrand, and when it was over he blessed the flags of the eighty-three departments.

Then Lafayette went up to the altar. With a fine gesture he laid his sword upon it. Then, phrase by phrase, he pronounced the oath which, with drums and cannon for punctuation, the serried thousands repeated after him. After that majestic thunder the Assembly, repeating the oath in its turn, was but a feeble voice. Then it was the turn of the King. He did not approach the altar, where all could have seen him, but took his special oath from his canopied throne. He spoke loud, but his single voice was lost in that great space, and he was so hard to see that some thought (and certain papers wickedly suggested) that he had disdained to take the oath at all.

But Lafayette's gesture had been seen and applauded by everybody. Scarcely had he come down from the platform than the *fédérés* broke ranks and rushed upon him. They kissed his face, his hands, his clothes; he could scarcely mount, and when he was in the saddle they kissed whatever they could — his breeches, his boots, his bridle, even (it is said) the horse itself. It was his hour.

The fact that Orleans had been ignored was poor comfort for Mirabeau. The Federation, he lamented to the Court three days later, had compromised the King without benefit to his authority. The whole affair had played into Lafayette's hands, enabling him to appear as 'the man of the Federation, the unique man, the man of the provinces'. He had been allowed to steal the position which the vast majority of the provincials present had wished and expected the King to occupy. A golden opportunity had been lost, a chance of restoring the prestige of the monarchy, of reducing Lafayette to his proper dimension of servant, the Assembly to its proper dimension of legislative body and all the factious and envenomed scribblers and republican agitators of Paris to the impotence which their true proportion to the nation ought to impose. It had been a chance of moral escape from the hideous position into which the monarchy had drifted. It had been let slip. Physical escape must therefore be discussed afresh. The King, Mirabeau thinks, should go at least as far as Fontaine-bleau; no need for the move to be surreptitious; let him be escorted by the National Guard to the boundary of the Department of Paris and by regular troops from there; let him appear *on horseback* to inspect both regulars and militia; let him chat with other ranks as well as officers; let him be national and military while giving no shadow of excuse for 'orgies similar to that which served as a pretext for the October business'.

4

Spain's dispute with Britain over Nootka Sound, and the prospect of France being drawn in under the Family Compact of 1761, had precipitated the violent but not strictly relevant debates on the right of declaring war. There remained the question of the Family Compact itself and how the National Assembly would regard it. 'Family compact' — the very words were redolent of the bad old days when dynasts had treated their dominions as so many private estates to be bought, sold, ceded or swopped without so much as a by-your-leave to the peoples concerned.

Was the now-sovereign nation to be bound by the dynastic arrangements made between the two Bourbon houses in 1761? The compact was offensive as well as defensive, and the National Assembly had just decreed that France renounced all wars of aggression. That was one difficulty. There was also the wider question whether national sovereignty was compatible with external obligations incurred in the days of despotism. It seemed that the Assembly's answer was likely to be an emphatic negative. The idealists, shuddering at the idea of an offensive war, would combine with the demagogues, who could think of no enemy but the Court, to call not only the Family Compact but also all existing treaty obligations into question.

On June 16th, Spain formally and a little tartly required France to fulfil her obligations and to let Britain know that she stood by her ally. Montmorin was acutely embarrassed. On the one hand France's duty was clear; on the other he knew the temper of the Assembly, and meanwhile Britain with her overwhelming fleet was putting the screw on Spain. Montmorin hesitated unhappily, and it was not till August 2nd that he plucked up courage to put the matter before the Assembly. But Mirabeau had been working on the problem in secret for over a month.

His solution, reached well before the end of June, was realistic. To throw away the Spanish alliance would, he was sure, be folly. Since Holland, through France's failure to support the anti-Orange party, was now signed up with England and Prussia, Spain remained for France the one ally who combined proven loyalty with an interest in withstanding British imperialism. On the other hand it was certain that the Assembly would never endorse the Family Compact in its present form. The right thing, therefore, was to change the form and keep the substance, to recast the alliance in new terms and make it a *national* compact. He urged the King and Queen to send at once a special envoy to Madrid to negotiate the revised treaty; in this way they would be able to face the Assembly with the *fait accompli* of a fully national and unimpeachably defensive instrument, and so disappoint Jacobins itching for a new opportunity to revile the Court.

In this plan of action the Foreign Minister featured hardly at

all. Mirabeau and La Marck discussed the desirability of Montmorin being consulted as if it were quite an open question, though
they agreed in the end that His Majesty's Minister of Foreign
Affairs had better be informed of what was afoot. Their correspondence is some indication of the pernicious anaemia from which
the official ministry suffered at this time.[174]

A special envoy was sent to Madrid, but the negotiations hung
fire. Florida Blanca, the Spanish minister, viewed the French
Revolution with wholehearted detestation, and had pretty well
come to the conclusion that, between the ravings of the Assembly
and the impotence of the foreign office, there was no one in France
with whom genuine negotiations could be conducted; even if he
agreed to a revised compact, the instrument would be useless
until it had been ratified by what seemed to him a parliament of
criminal lunatics. His mind was turning, therefore, to making the
best terms with England that he could get; they would doubtless
be hard, for the confusion in Paris was as evident to London as to
Madrid.

On July 29th, there was a belated movement on the French
side. The Assembly awoke to the truth that revolutions have
diplomatic consequences and decided to appoint a Diplomatic
Committee. On August 1st, Mirabeau was nominated a member
and easily dominated his colleagues (including Barnave) by the
weight of his knowledge of foreign affairs. It was on the next
day that Montmorin put the Spanish question before the Assembly,
and, as they immediately referred it to the new committee, Mirabeau found himself continuing, though now in a public capacity,
to do the Foreign Minister's work. That he, if anyone, was for
the moment the *de facto* manager of foreign policy was recognized
by Pitt, who, a little later, sent Hugh Elliot on a special mission
to talk to his old friend.

Mirabeau reported the committee's recommendations on
August 25th. After pouring his libation to the new god of international brotherhood he came to the business in hand. France
should declare that her existing treaties stood, unless or until they
should have been modified by the National Assembly; on the other
hand any offensive commitments should henceforth be considered
null and void; as for the Family Compact, the Assembly should
pray His Majesty to negotiate with Spain a *national* bond, and

meanwhile to order the number of ships-of-the-line in commission to be raised to thirty. The next day Pétion protested against even a provisional recognition of treaties — even defensive treaties — made in the unregenerate past, but Mirabeau was able to brush this nonsense aside and, seizing upon the suggestion of another deputy, to raise the suggested number of ships to forty-five — not a ship too many if England was to be encountered.

But England was not to be encountered. Florida Blanca, having waited over two months for France to declare herself, had finally despaired of help from a country that seemed to have no government, and he had opened negotiations with England. In October he agreed to abandon Nootka Sound. Pitt had won and France had lost her ally through the inability of her ministers to act with any authority or dispatch. Unable either to carry the parliament with him or to act without its approval, Montmorin had hesitated and the Spanish alliance had been lost.

5

This sorry fiasco underlined more than ever the need of a ministry with parliamentary authority, and Mirabeau now pressed the King boldly to demand the repeal of the fatal decree disqualifying deputies from office. If the Assembly complied, then it would be possible to have a government capable of confident action; if they refused, their responsibility for governmental futility would be plain to all reasonable men: 'When one cannot obtain what is good, there is something to be said for making one's opponents commit a blunder.'[175]

Mirabeau's opinion of the Assembly was hardening rapidly. He was convinced that the trouble lay with a faction of some thirty deputies whose suspicion of the Court and, indeed, of anything savouring of an authority not their own had become pathological. These 'thirty voices' were able again and again to dominate the chamber because they were learning to act as a party and because they were the group in closest sympathy with much wilder elements outside. They were discovering the advantages of having no enemies to the Left and the technique of silencing their opponents by fear. The bloody-minded were assiduous spectators in the galleries of the Manège and the thirty seldom scrupled to play to them, while in the streets there was now an unremitting propaganda which, if unmoderated, must lead to murder on an appalling scale. Desmoulins was guilty of this sort of thing, but his *Revolutions de France et de Brabant* was out-distanced by a pamphlet entitled *C'en est fait de nous* and signed *Marat, l'ami du peuple*. After suggesting that the King — 'this "good king" who disdained to swear fidelity to you on the Altar of the Fatherland' — was about to fly to the Austrians, and that Lafayette was planning to blast honest citizens with artillery, it shrieked: 'It is all up with you unless you rush to arms, unless you find again that heroic valour which twice — on July 14th and October 5th — saved France . . . Lock up the Austrian Woman . . . lay hands on all the ministers and their subordinates . . . Five or six hundred heads would have assured you peace, liberty and welfare; a false humanity has held your hands. . . .'

This was a bit too much even for deputies of the Left, and for very shame they had to yield to Malouet and the moderates and agree that Marat should be prosecuted. But even so Pétion and Alexandre de Lameth did all they could to remove teeth from the decree against seditious libel, and Marat, in the upshot, went scot free.

Mirabeau saw that only a bench of minister-deputies (led by himself) could destroy the Thirty's monopoly of power by providing an alternative pole of attraction within the chamber. It might, he thought, be good policy to pick some ministers boldly from the turbulent left: Jacobins in the ministry, he said, would soon cease to be Jacobin ministers. So he urged Louis to demand the repeal of the disqualifying decree, and Louis thought it would doubtless be an excellent thing, and did nothing whatever about it. Meanwhile Marat was urging citizens to 'set up 800 gibbets and hang on them all the traitors, with the infamous elder Riqueti at their head'.[176]

If he must abandon hope of leading the chamber as a minister Mirabeau must at least be able to guide the ministers as an accredited adviser. At present he could not do even that. Mercy Argenteau, whose regard for him had steadily increased, now fully agreed that a ministry prepared to work with him was imperative, and Mercy, if anyone, was the man to convince the Queen. In this, indeed, he succeeded; it was the King with whom nothing could be done; he listened to other advice and, thinking the more opinions he heard the better, never came to the point of action at all.

Then, at the very end of September, Mercy was ordered by Leopold II to go to the Hague on a special mission. He never returned, and his disappearance gravely weakened Mirabeau's influence at the Tuileries. It was compensated only a little by the recent departure of Necker.

In the last year the banker had been reduced to his 'stature of an ordinary mortal'. Once a symbol of reform, later a revolutionary mascot, he had, after the delirium of his reinstatement in July 1789, dwindled into a nerveless and depressing little minister of whom nobody any longer expected anything in particular. He distrusted the new paper money which Clavière had invented and Mirabeau had supported, and Mirabeau was pressing Clavière on the Court as his successor. Necker's health was deteriorating and, while there was nothing left in France to gratify his prosy vanity, there was a great deal to upset his nerves. In August disorder in the army had culminated in a most alarming mutiny at Nancy, and on September 2nd an ugly anti-ministerial riot at the Tuileries, in protest against Bouillé's effective measures of repression, frightened him badly. A warning word from Lafayette settled the matter; he handed in his resignation and took coach for Geneva. Not a dog barked, except at Arcis-sur-Aube where the municipality held him till advised by a message from the Assembly to let him proceed in peace.

Though Clavière did not get his place, Necker's exit was of some advantage to Mirabeau because he had retained to the end an odd ascendancy over Montmorin. Freed from the Banker's prejudices, Montmorin, with some help from the Queen, began to view Mirabeau with new eyes. Unlike Necker, he knew his own limitations and was pathetically anxious for guidance.

Meanwhile Mirabeau continued to bombard the King with Notes. Four themes recurred with variations. There was the escape-theme, the appeal to France against Paris and the risk — a risk to be run — of civil war. There was the ministerial theme: a parliamentary ministry if possible, but a ministry open to Mirabeau's advice at any rate. Then there was what may be called the propaganda theme: a new government-inspired newspaper and a whole network of agents in the provinces should build up a body of articulate opinion supporting the crown and demanding a revision of the constitution. Finally there was the Lafayette theme.

Mirabeau's bitterness towards the General was becoming something like an obsession. He was ready to deflate and discredit the man by any means available. On no account, he urged the Court, must Lafayette be allowed to go to Nancy and pose as the restorer of military discipline, for he would make himself a sort of Lieutenant-General of the Kingdom. No, he must be kept in Paris by appeals to his vanity as protector of the royal family; sooner or later something would force him to fire on the people, and on that day he would be finished.

Mirabeau soon had a fresh grievance. At the end of September the Châtelet held its long-awaited inquiry into the March to Versailles. Mirabeau, by an able speech and with La Marck's testimony, cleared himself of complicity. Orleans was also acquitted for lack of conclusive evidence. Since both were deputies it remained for the Assembly to endorse these findings, and since Mirabeau's enemies were even now by no means satisfied, he thought a timely word from Lafayette might tip the balance in his favour. The floating vote of the centre was the danger, for the centre distrusted him but were grateful to Lafayette for public order. In La Marck's presence the General promised to speak for Mirabeau, but when the appointed day, October 2nd, arrived he was not in the house. Mirabeau, who was enduring a painful attack of intestinal inflammation, sent him an angry message: 'Let M. de Lafayette cite a single occasion on which I have not done more for him than I promised: *let him cite a single occasion when he had not broken his word to me, and I agree to let bygones be bygones.*' But even now, he added, if only the General would acknowledge the impossibility of disregarding his enmity, he for his part was ready to swallow his 'deep and supremely just resentment' and work with him.[177]

It soon became known that the Assembly was going to move for a new ministry capable of executing its decrees. Mirabeau immediately pressed the King to be beforehand in the matter, and boldly to announce the names of a parliamentary ministry which would necessitate the immediate repeal of the disqualifying decree. But it was not in Louis XVI to act like that, and Mirabeau asked La Marck what use there was in his sending volumes of advice to people who took no notice of it. He had begged for another personal interview, in vain; Lafayette might see Their Majesties whenever he chose, but not Mirabeau; and then, on October 18th, he made a discovery: it was that they were taking advice in another quarter. A barrister called Bergasse, an eloquent but timid liberal-royalist who, like Mounier, had lost his nerve after the October Days and abandoned his seat in the Assembly, a man absorbed in mesmerism and innocent of political action — this man, it seemed, was giving advice — and very stupid advice — to the Court.

In his anger Mirabeau wrote to the shocked La Marck of the 'dementia' of the 'royal cattle'. Half from pique, half from policy, he decided to show that he was not to be trifled with. A little playing to the Left might freshen his fading popularity and remind royalty of his demagogic power at the same time. The next day the expected vote of censure was moved against the ministers. It was defeated by a chance majority of forty-three, but the occasion of the vote was another matter which gave him a timely chance for Jacobinical posturings.

Mutiny had occurred in the Brest fleet, which had hauled down the Lilies and hoisted the Tricolor, and in the Assembly Foucault condemned this insult to the old flag and suggested that the new three-coloured plaything should be left to children. Mirabeau had had a considerable success at the Jacobins the night before; he now mounted the tribune, once more the tiger of 1789.

'At the first words spoken in this strange debate,' he began, 'I felt patriotic rage rising to white heat within me' — applause from the Left, laughter from the Right — 'Before I have done, gentlemen, you will have, I swear, no temptation to laugh. . . .

'Everybody knows how the whole nation rejoiced when the monarch ordered the troops to carry, and himself carried, these glorious colours, this rallying sign of the children of liberty; everybody knows that only a few months ago the rash man who dared to show any disrespect for this ensign of patriotism would have paid for the crime with his head!' — angry murmurs from the Right, resounding cheers from the Left. The volcano continued to pour molten lava down its right flank: these royalist deputies were, in effect, saying 'we think ourselves strong enough to hoist the White, the colour of counter-revolution' — growing hubbub, but above the din the orator could be heard '. . . indulge no such dangerous dreams, for the awakening would be prompt and terrible.' Renewed cheers and one voice heard shouting 'This is the language of a rebel!' Then he swept to his conclusion proposing that the sailors should not only fly the Tricolor but also replace the customary three shouts of *Vive le roi!* by the single shout of *Vive la nation, la loi et le roi!*

It was an inexpensive triumph, but as the applause died down a royalist shouted 'Mirabeau is a scoundrel!' His arrest was instantly proposed. 'I suggest that we pass to the order of the day,' put in Mirabeau. 'We ask that M. de Mirabeau be called to order,' cried the enthusiasts, 'an insult to him is an insult to us all!'

Though the ministry had escaped the vote of no confidence, it was discredited beyond recovery and crumbled away. The ministries of Marine and War changed hands, Champion de Cicé very reluctantly surrendered the Seals and, of the old set, only Montmorin, who had been excepted from the motion of censure, remained. Of the new ministers two were Lafayette's men. Again and again Mirabeau had warned the King not to let the General meddle in the choice of ministers, and this was the result; just as well, then, since he carried so little weight with the Court, to recover his influence with the Jacobins. That he aimed to gain leverage over the latter for the ultimate service of the former was something about which even La Marck had moments of doubt, and which the Queen never really believed at all. She thought of him as a man whose opinions might be picked at, never as one to whom the destinies of her family could be entrusted. Had Mirabeau known that, at this very moment, the Bishop of Pamiers was on his way to Metz with a letter from the King in order to put before Bouillé a plan for the forcible rescue of the royal family, a plan of mere reaction, resting in part on the prospect of foreign intervention and devised by that embodiment of pre-Bastille royalism, Breteuil, he would have had less choler to spare for the trivial intervention of Bergasse.

Although Burke lamented the failure of ten thousand swords to leap from their scabbards to avenge the least look threatening the Queen with insult, there remained nobles of the sword who thought that three inches of steel in the vitals of a political opponent had no fellow. Mirabeau received numerous challenges. His way was to enter them in his notebook and promise satisfaction after the Assembly had been dissolved. 'It is not fair,' he remarked when challenged by an obscure and valiant country squire, 'that I should risk a man of brains like myself against a fool like him.' Mme de Staël, who tells the anecdote, adds that no one ever suspected his courage, so bold and martial was his bearing.

Charles de Lameth lacked Mirabeau's self-assurance, and, though doubting his right to hazard a life which belonged to his constituents, allowed himself to be provoked by the Duc de Castries. They met in the Bois de Boulogne on November 12th, and Lameth received a thrust in the arm which gave him a high fever and convulsions.

Those Parisians who were usually ready to excuse the episodes which ended with the exhibition of undemocratic heads on pikes, were not prepared to tolerate as a political instrument that symbol of a barbaric past, the gentleman's rapier. The story had begun to circulate that there was a plot by royalist swordsmen to pick off one by one the people's champions, and Mirabeau repeated it that night at the Jacobins. Lameth's wound, he was glad to report, was not dangerous, but it would be best, he thought, for deputies henceforth to show their courage by refusing challenges to single combat; meanwhile let the Society at once send a deputation to the wounded patriot to express their sympathy and admiration.[178]

Early the next morning he was writing to La Marck: 'The Lameths, very perversely, are making the Castries affair fizz in public, and if there is not a disturbance it's a great sign that most of their influence is lost; but what is particularly blackguardly is that they are connecting it directly with the Queen.'

There was a disturbance all right. Lameth supporters, gesticulating on tables and even asserting that Castries's point had been poisoned, worked up their hearers to the necessary pitch of indignation; whereupon these — no chance mob, but the regular newspaper-reading, plot-detecting, court-suspecting loungers of the Palais Royal cafés — went off to the Hôtel de Castries and, scrupulously abstaining from loot, systematically smashed its contents to smithereens and hurled the debris out of the windows. Only a portrait of the King was spared, so it was said.

It was not till they had been at it for over an hour that Lafayette arrived with reinforcements for the entirely complacent guards already in the neighbourhood. Saluting the crowd most graciously, he ordered bayonets to be fixed. 'We are not at Nancy, comrade,' a spectator shouted, 'don't resist the justice of the people!' He need not have worried.

That evening a deputation demanded at the bar of the Assembly a law against duelling and the punishment of Castries. When a royalist deputy demanded the punishment not of Castries but of those who had sacked his residence, tempers rose on both sides of the house. Malouet and Mirabeau both made for the tribune but Malouet got there first and went up. As he waited for the din to subside Mirabeau said to him: 'I came to speak on the same side as you; you know I'm more popular with the house; let me have your place!' Malouet hesitated: would Mirabeau promise to demand justice against the rioters? He promised and Malouet stepped down. This conversation was, of course, inaudible to others, and the Right, seeing only the worthy Malouet yielding the tribune to the overbearing demagogue, began to shout 'Down with the scoundrel!' Mirabeau's blood mounted instantly. Forgetting the moderating speech he had intended, forgetting his duty to condemn lawlessness, forgetting even his opportunity to hold Lafayette up to derision, he let fly with a reckless defence of those who had sacked Castries's house, and hurled at the royalists gibes which nearly provoked some to physical violence.

'You've broken your word!' said Malouet as, amid cheers from the Left, he returned to the floor.

'You're right,' answered Mirabeau, 'and I'm ashamed of it; but you can blame your gentlemen over there; you heard them!'[179]

Two days earlier he had written urgently to his employers.

It was now quite certain, he told them, that the La Motte was in Paris. He had even discovered one of her addresses — a house next to that of Orleans's chancellor. He discussed anxiously the significance of the news. Who had brought the woman back to Paris and what was their dirty game? Why had not Lafayette done his duty and arrested her at once as an outlaw? Was she a marionette in the hands of the Lameths and was Lafayette afraid to challenge them? It was all at present very obscure, but Mirabeau's anxiety was real. He saw the danger of the Necklace affair being dug up again, of a re-trial and of endless filth flung at a queen now ten times more defenceless; he saw her this time charged openly with adultery, the possibility of a divorce and of a bewildered, broken-hearted Louis putting off the crown which hurt so much. Alone with La Marck, Mirabeau was shaken with rage: 'I'll snatch this unhappy queen from her executioners,' he swore, 'or I'll perish in the attempt!' [180]

Marie Antoinette was pleased by his solicitude, but what was she to think when her champion condoned the lawlessness of her declared enemies and reviled loyal gentlemen, her friends? Was she to notice that he had made it a mitigation of the rioters' behaviour that they had religiously respected a portrait of the King? How could she distinguish between the nobility of the sword, which Mirabeau always attacked, and the monarchy, to which they were the background ordained in the whole world she had known? He sent her, it is true, an apology for his Castries speech. It was an over-ingenious defence of his methods of keeping the popularity without which he could not serve the crown, and it ended with an outburst against Lafayette for not preventing the riot which Mirabeau was now excusing himself for having excused. It would have been better to admit that he had lost his temper; that the Queen could have understood. Marie Antoinette could understand a royalist and she could recognize a rebel, but Mirabeau's democratic monarchism and the precarious double game he was playing were things she could never like or truly comprehend. The Archbishop was so shocked at the Castries outburst that he nearly advised her to refuse further communications from the demagogue. Only La Marck, after explanations, remained confident in the ultimate loyalty of his friend, who, at this moment, enjoyed another and very public triumph. [181]

By 1790 the Paris stage had become less the mirror held up to nature than a sounding-board to reverberate political passions. Audiences listened for lines which echoed partisan convictions, and plays were punctuated by bursts of alternating applause as sentences patient of royalist or republican interpretations were spoken on the stage. Nor were these competing demonstrations always confined to noise, which is why, when the Theatre de la Nation put on Voltaire's old piece *Brutus*, the police prudently insisted that patrons should surrender not only their swords but even their canes before entering the auditorium. Mirabeau decided to attend the first night, if he could get a seat. It would, he thought, be fun. It was. The house was packed and expectant and when he appeared in his box he was greeted with thunderous applause. 'Up in the gallery, Mirabeau!' they shouted, and soon a deputation came to him saying: 'The French people demand their Brutus.' Then they laid warm hands upon him and practically carried him to sit in triumph among them. They might well have hissed the Queen.[182]

A fortnight later, on November 30th, he delivered an address, albeit a moderate address, to inaugurate his first term as President of the Jacobin Club.

CHAPTER XIV

FAILURE

THE constituent Assembly made two blunders which, together, threw the locomotive of revolution off the rails leading to an agreed, if drastic, reformation of the common-wealth, and sent it down the incline into war, insurrection, terror and dictatorship.

The first blunder was the decree of November 7th, 1789, which, by disqualifying deputies for the ministry, doomed the legislature to irresponsibility and the executive to impotence. The second was the decree establishing what was called the Civil Constitution of the Clergy. Wiser than his colleagues, Mirabeau recognized and incessantly condemned the first; he was as blind as the majority to the second.

Like the November decree this was a gratuitous blunder. There had been a case for the confiscation of church property and the substitution of state-salaries for the clergy. Some levelling-down of clerical incomes was an overdue reform, and if the substitution of a salaried for an endowed priesthood was a more questionable change, it might at least be excused by the over-riding economic crisis. These things having been accomplished, however, there was really no need to do anything more. 'We are concerning ourselves too much with the clergy; they should be paid and left in peace,' Mirabeau remarked casually in May. An adjustment of diocesan and parish boundaries to fit the new administrative map was doubtless desirable, but it was not an urgent matter and could have been achieved through temperate arrangements with the bishops and with Rome. Conservative clerics would not have liked the new order, but no questions of conscience would have arisen for anyone. And this should have pleased revolutionary deputies, for in April 1790, when Dom Gerle, the Carthusian, moved that the Catholic religion alone should be authorized by the state, they had refused even to discuss his motion and, after hearing from Mirabeau an extravagantly histrionic citation of the Saint Bartholomew massacre as a sample of what came of mixing politics with religion, had declared that the state had no power over consciences.

Nevertheless in February the Assembly had charged its ecclesiastical committee with the task of considering what should be the relations of church and state in the new France, and on May 29th the committee produced its plan — the Civil Constitution of the Clergy.

The ancient dioceses were to be swept away; in their place each of the new departments was to have a bishop, who was to be elected by all the voters, lay as well as clerical, Catholic or otherwise; similar arrangements were to be made for the parishes; every ten departments were to be under a metropolitan who should give canonical institution. No suggestion whatever was made that these sweeping changes, creating and destroying spiritual jurisdiction at a thousand points, should be submitted to the authority whom French Catholics regarded as their spiritual head, the Pope. On the contrary, bishops were to be forbidden to apply to Rome for any sort of confirmation. Furthermore, not only papal authority but spiritual authority as such was to be disregarded; for when, in the ensuing debates, a bishop proposed that a council of the national church should consider the whole matter, he was told plainly that the church was part of the state; and when negotiations with Rome were suggested the idea was rejected on the same ground. After this proof that the state intended to arrogate to itself what was in effect spiritual jurisdiction all the bishops (except Talleyrand) withdrew from the debates, and the Civil Constitution was passed on July 12th.

How is this apparently wanton attack upon Catholicism to be explained? It is not sufficient to remark that those who supported the scheme were largely avowed free-thinkers hostile to the Church, caesarian lawyers jealous of the sovereignty of the State, Protestants with bitter memories of Catholic intolerance and disgruntled churchmen of sectarian tendencies and Jansenistic sympathies. For these facts do not explain why the Assembly did not adopt another course more consonant with its avowed principles, to wit the *separation* of the church from a state which had become theologically neutral.

The explanation is to be found less in principles than in prejudices. The Gallican hierarchy was part of the old régime. The bishops owed their sees to the patronage of the old monarchy and had, till yesterday, derived their incomes from ancient feudal properties. They would not have been human if they had not resented the Revolution more or less openly, and the Assembly was therefore anxious to replace a hierarchy representing the old régime by one devoted to the new society. The old Gallican spirit was, as it were, to be democratized, and if the process should involve the disappearance of most of the present bishops, so much the better. It was a calculation which left out of account just one fact, the fact that the French Church was not only Gallican but also Catholic. The revolutionaries, blind to what even Louis XIV had recognized, had tripped headlong over an object not very conspicuous in the age of enlightenment, the rock of Peter.

They were prepared for a schism. They viewed with equanimity the prospect of a minority of the clergy refusing the Civil Constitution and accepting the status of sectarian pastors. What they were not prepared for was what took place, refusal by the majority of clergy high and low, and also by a considerable mass of the laity, to touch the Civil Constitution at any price: a refusal which reduced not the French Catholics but the State church to the dimensions of a sect. These nominal representatives of the people had not only lost hold of the Catholic idea, but were also quite unaware of its hold on many people whom they were supposed to represent; and Mirabeau shared in their gross miscalculation.

He never for a moment doubted that Catholicism was as much a thing of the past as feudalism. 'What are you afraid of?' he asked some anti-clericals one day. 'The rich benefices no longer exist; indifference is universal. Leave things alone, and within thirty years there'll be no more priests.' He had taken a leading part in the secularization of church property, but, apart from advocating that priests should be free to marry, he had scarcely any hand in the Civil Constitution of the Clergy. He did not think it particularly important. Not till it had begun to split France in two did he realize his mistake. Then his very indifference made him able to approach the subject with a certain detachment; but detachment closed to him the heart of the matter, so that he could have heard nothing more than rhetoric when Montlosier cried: 'Drive the bishops from their palaces and they will retreat to the cottages of the poor whom they have fed; take from them their gold crosses and they will carry wooden ones; it was a wooden cross that saved the world!'

On August 24th, Louis XVI, under great pressure and with misgivings, sanctioned the decree and the Civil Constitution became law. On October 3rd, the Archbishop of Aix published a reasoned protest on behalf of the clergy, and at once the strength and extent of Catholic resistance became apparent. The decree required the clergy to take a 'civil oath' which, by implication, involved them in renouncing their beliefs concerning spiritual jurisdiction, and the great majority assumed an attitude of passive resistance, pending such time as the Church might sanction with spiritual authority the new arrangements proposed by the state. Such authorization was, however, highly improbable. Not only had the state made a point of not seeking it, but it is unlikely that Pius VI would have been ready for a concordat at this time. Like the other rulers of Europe he regarded the Revolution as a virulent but transient fever, not as the arrival of a new kind of state.

Surprised and angered by the clergy's resistance the Assembly proceeded to apply the screw, and on November 26th, the deputy Voidel proposed a code of penalties against the non-jurors. All who failed to take the oath within a week were to be regarded as having resigned their cures; any priests who, having refused the oath, should continue to perform their functions were to be prosecuted as disturbers of the peace and deprived of full civic rights, and any persons who should concert or encourage resistance to laws 'accepted or sanctioned by the King' were to be treated likewise.

That day the King wrote secretly to Breteuil in Switzerland authorizing him to sound the friendly courts of Germany. 'I have chosen you to entrust you with the interests of my crown. You know my intentions. . . .'

Mirabeau did not know his intentions, and he had in his own nature no measure by which to gauge the awful crisis of conscience through which the King was passing. He did not realize that horror at the false position in which he found himself had finally disgusted Louis with the Revolution and all its works. So long as it had seemed only a political affair Louis had been at least half-resigned to the Revolution, prepared, so far as his sentiments went, at least to entertain Mirabeau's incessant doctrine of monarchy under the Tricolor. His own political ideas had never amounted to much more than a hazy benevolence. But there was nothing hazy about his religious faith, and this business of the Civil Constitution and the Oath had convinced him that his whole policy of concessions to the Revolution had been mistaken from the start. His good nature, his love for his people had been shamefully abused; each concession had led only to fresh demands, and the end of it had been that he was so shorn of authority that they had been able to force him into acting against his conscience. He was oppressed by a sense of sin, and that was something which Mirabeau had perhaps never known. It became suddenly evident to Louis that the Tricolor was the emblem of Satan. The Enemy had been unmasked late in the day; on plausible pretexts and under a humanitarian disguise he had occupied every strategic point; direct resistance to him was no longer possible for the moment; but if he could not be withstood he might be outwitted. The Revolution had deceived the King; he would do the same to it. Compromise with it was no longer to be thought of.

If Mirabeau did not yet realize how little credit his doctrine now enjoyed at Court, he was at least awakening to the public consequences of the Civil Constitution. He had no objection to the plan as such, but to persist with it when that meant splitting the nation in two offended his sense of the politic. He wrote strongly to Mauvillon in this sense. Yet when, on November 27th, Voidel's proposals were debated, he proposed a decree which, except in one particular, was no less ferocious than Voidel's; he would even have made it an offence for any non-juror to hear confessions; but his bill did provide a loop-hole, for it named no time-limit for taking the Oath and thereby left a way open for second thoughts and negotiations. Yet his tactics that day were all wrong. Determined as ever to keep in with the revolutionaries, he spoke in violent terms. His bill may have been secretly aimed at peace but his speech was a war-speech. Even had the Court trusted him thus far, this exhibition would have destroyed their trust; and it did not even achieve its purpose; for though it was Mirabeau's speech which chiefly inflamed the debate and was afterwards remembered, it was Voidel's bill which was decreed.

But it was not merely Mirabeau's tactics which were mistaken. His strategy was totally at fault. Over this business of the Church he had no surer guide than the Abbé Lamourette, soon to be State-bishop of Lyon and later a victim of the Terror. His own judgment failed him. He groped uncertainly for a policy, uneasily aware that he had miscalculated the shape and size of the business.[188]

He should have met the bigots who were about to launch a persecution of the nation's religion with frank defiance. It was an issue of conscience for all, and the finesse of his double policy was a useless instrument for handling it. It was an issue on which, had he taken firm ground, he could have rallied behind him both anxious Catholics and worried liberals. It was his supreme chance to stand forth as the champion of the nation against the intelligentsia, of France against Paris and of the King as the representative Frenchman. His own irreligion and revolutionary reputation would have been positive assets in making such a stand, for thousands, who dismissed protests by royalists and churchmen as mere reaction and sacerdotalism, would have listened if the Tribune of the People had denounced Voidel's decree in the sacred name of freedom of conscience. And who was better placed to oppose the whole idea of a state church supported by discriminatory oaths than the man who, in July 1789, had protested against the use of the term 'dominant cult'? 'I don't like that word "dominant",' he told the house, 'and I need a definition. Is it an *oppressive* cult which is meant? But you have banished that word, and the men who have assured the right of liberty do not claim that of oppression.'

Beyond voting for the Civil Constitution he had had no hand in it. He could, therefore, without inconsistency, have demanded its repeal or at least its suspension and revision in the name of religious liberty. He could have shown how the refusal of the majority of priests to take the oath would make useless to the state the minority who swore it, and he could have asked what use a clergy would be whom Catholics did not want and philosophers did not need.

Had Mirabeau taken this stand it is unlikely that he would have swayed the house. Anti-clericals of all sorts were in full cry, and in the arena of Parisian politics he would have lost ground. But his protest would have gone on record, and it is that which would have mattered. Catholics with no other reason to like him would have been grateful to him, liberals accustomed to admire him would have been shaken in their support of the extreme Left, and the King and Queen would have received what they were beginning to require — some tangible proof that he was really prepared to challenge the Leftists whom, whatever he might say of them in secret, he seemed monotonously ready to gratify in public. He could not perhaps have stopped the persecuting decree, but he could have promoted a situation in which Louis, once out of Paris, could have been a symbol (if no more) of clemency and sanity. Finally he would have established a *claim* to his sovereign's confidence, and would have had a chance to steer him clear of the merely reactionary conspiracies to which he was now leaning in his distress.

He did not see his opportunity. It is true that, as Catholic resistance became so widespread that something like a religious war seemed likely, his secret correspondence was full of cunning suggestions that the Assembly should be allowed, even encouraged, to 'entrap itself'. He even explained his own conduct as being, in reality, a machiavellian *politique du pire*. But such ingenuities were less than convincing, and were no help or comfort whatever to Louis, who was now required to sanction a persecution of the Church which he had sworn at his coronation to protect and of which he remained a devout and loyal son.

Louis hesitated in agonizing perplexity. His delay was denounced as the prelude to the counter-revolution which the *émigrés* were incessantly prophesying from the safety of Coblenz and Mainz. To exercise his veto would be to provoke, quite certainly, immediate insurrection, an uprising which would scarcely stop till the throne had been overturned and the Queen butchered. He sent a last desperate appeal to the Pope to make possible some sort of provisional submission by the clergy. He was not given time to receive the reply before the preparations for insurrection became unmistakable. Advised that further delay might result in a massacre of priests in the streets, Louis sanctioned the decree. 'I would rather be King of Metz than remain King of France in such a position,' he said, 'but it will soon be over.' It was December 26th, the feast of St. Stephen.

Three days earlier Mirabeau completed the most massive of all his memoranda to the Court, his famous Forty-seventh Note. It began with a very careful analysis of the existing position and ended with schemes of the greatest complexity for mastering it. But to the matter which for three months had occupied the soul of the King it made no reference at all.

Exactly a week before Louis sanctioned the enforcement of the Oath, Mirabeau was elected President of the Jacobins for a second term.

2

Mercy Argenteau, as ambassador, had had ample opportunity of sizing up Montmorin, and saw in him a man who, for all his timidity and indecision, was intelligent enough to recognize the dangerous drift of things, humble enough to welcome advice and loyal enough to guard dangerous secrets for the Court. Almost the last act of Mercy before leaving France was to persuade the Queen to employ La Marck to bring the Foreign Minister and Mirabeau together. Montmorin, sole survivor of the old ministers, felt a stranger among his new, Lafayette-approved colleagues, and was pathetically anxious for La Marck's guidance, but the first move seems to have come from a different quarter.[184]

Two men, Talon and Sémonville, opportunists and intriguers, had once been numbered among Lafayette's clientèle. Latterly, however, their role of Rosencrantz and Guildenstern had drawn them into uncertain relations with Mirabeau, while they had also taken secret salaries from the Foreign Minister. Their noses were keen for a profitable intrigue, and it was a visit by Talon to La Marck which actually brought about the first *rapprochement*. Talon was emphatic that not a breath of the matter should reach Lafayette. La Marck, Mirabeau and Montmorin treated Talon and Sémonville with merited reserve, and their function was little more than catalytic. But Mirabeau saw the chance of strengthening his weakening hold upon the Court and eagerly agreed to meet the Foreign Minister on December 5th.

It was a chastened Montmorin who received the sometime publisher of the Berlin Letters. Gone was all pretence of condescension, all suggestion that he had more to give than to receive.

Not that he was, even now, at his wit's end; he had ideas, especially as to the profitable expenditure of secret service money; but he desperately needed help and impulsion. Lonely, discouraged, apprehensive and a victim of indigestion, the little man was feeling for the support of a stronger brain and a more resilient will.

He traced for his visitor some general lines of policy: would M. de Mirabeau take these vague suggestions and elaborate them into an applicable plan of action? Mirabeau was very willing and set himself at once to his task. It took him over a fortnight, and, since the resultant memorandum ran to over 21,000 words and was composed just when there was added to his other cares the presidency of the Jacobin Club, the wonder is that he got it done in the time.

3

Entitled *Survey of the condition of France and of the means of reconciling public liberty with the royal authority*, this Forty-seventh Note to the Court* is the last great document of Mirabeau's career. More than all his other writings it has determined men's judgment on him, for it provides, as it were, a magnificent cross-section of his mind within fifteen weeks of his death. If we compare it with the October Memorandum, written fourteen months earlier, we are able to measure what in the interval the Revolution has done to France, and what it has done to Mirabeau.

His basic convictions remain unaltered. Though the crown has slipped into ever increasing impotence, though the characters of the royal pair have been shown ever more clearly to be unequal to their responsibilities (he says quite bluntly that the King's indecision is a principal difficulty), though their reluctance to trust him has been proved again and again, yet he is unshaken in his monarchism. He is equally unshaken in his belief in the foundation work of the Revolution. The fears he expressed in October 1789 that the movement, when captured by Paris, would take an anarchical turn have been only too well justified. The envy and rancour of the demagogues has driven them into courses

* Known thus because this is its number in Bacourt, *Correspondence de Mirabeau* (Brussels, 1851).

which they cannot abandon with safety to themselves or pursue without disaster to the kingdom. On the site cleared by the revolution of the summer of 1789 they have reared a gimcrack edifice of political folly, but Mirabeau will not allow that the original work of clearance was anything but a blessing. He distinguishes between the early destructive work of the National Assembly and its later constituent legislation, and he insists, as ever, that the former was necessary and just. He is as set against reaction as ever. Counter-revolution he will not hear of; but 'counter-constitution' is another matter.

The big change since October 1789 is in his attitude to the National Assembly — not to the idea of a representative sovereign legislature, but to the actual Assembly of the moment. He thinks it has become the supreme menace to the safety of the state and that it is beyond reformation. Arrogant in exercising an authority for which it possesses a dubious electoral mandate, poisoned by the spirit of faction within and intimidated by demagogic pressure from without, disorderly in its procedure yet morbidly jealous of its dignity, unfitted itself to rule yet unwilling to let anyone else do so, excluding ministers from its body in the name of the separation of powers while arrogating to its committees increasing powers of inquisition and police, the Assembly is a body with which nothing can be done. Its sober members, despised and distrusted by the extremists, remain unheard, while between the extremes of Right and Left there is little to choose. The nobility and clergy angrily oppose what is genuinely desired by the people, and their support of the crown is a positive liability. The 'patriots' have pushed their campaign against monarchy so far that they dare not go back; they are committed men, fearful lest any recession of the revolutionary tide should rob them of their new importance and expose them to the vengeance of the gentlemen opposite. In such a chamber sane legislation has become an impossibility, yet a sane and judicious revision of the constitution is imperative if France is to survive.

What, then, is to be done with this parliament of bigots and fanatics? It must be given enough rope to hang itself, it must be allowed and even assisted to dig its own grave. The revision of the constitution is, at the moment, a task psychologically impossible for the Assembly and politically impossible for the King.

A royal proclamation of reforms failed ignominiously on June 23rd, 1789; it is quite unthinkable now, for the nation would at once rally to support the sovereignty of a body of whose pretentious incompetence it is in reality weary. Similarly, any open threat to the Assembly's work would drive the 'patriots' into declared republicanism while giving them the plausible excuse that only thus could the Revolution be saved. The only safe procedure is to let this present Assembly die in public estimation of its own self-engendered maladies, and to hasten the process by the secret administration of toxic doses.

To ruin the Assembly and replace it by a successor which will revise the constitution and restore some authority to the crown Mirabeau recommends methods of machiavellian duplicity. The Assembly is to be tempted or provoked into passing unpopular decrees and rejecting sensible bills. It should be induced to pass laws favouring the city of Paris so that it may arouse the resentment of the provinces. It must be bombarded with popular petitions which for one reason or another it will refuse. It must be led into wasting its time and the public's patience in debating trivialities. Ministers must incessantly complain of the practical difficulties of enforcing the new laws and embarrass the legislature by asking for elucidations. Motions threatening the royal power must be combated for purposes of propaganda, but other stupid motions must be allowed to pass, and the stupider the better. A good way of promoting idiotic legislation is to have it demanded by men influential in the Paris sections and opposed in the chamber by notoriously unpopular members of the Right. Mirabeau's mind teems with ruses of this description.

Such a policy will demand agents, and it is in his plans to secure these that his machiavellianism is most unblushing. Only a few parliamentary agents will be required: three or four from the Right, a handful from the centre and another handful from the Left. The plan is to have *agents provocateurs* planted in each camp. These are to have no knowledge of each other's doings; each is to be in touch with Montmorin and to fancy himself the one deputy honoured with the Minister's confidence. Montmorin, in his turn, will meet Mirabeau daily to discuss progress and decide on each fresh step. Only the Minister and Mirabeau are to know the whole plan and the ultimate object. The agents will be told no more than is necessary for each of them to know. They are to be induced to compass limited objectives only, and their several principles, prejudices and weaknesses will suggest in each case the kind of inducement to be offered.

The cynicism of the scheme is breathtaking. Mirabeau was loyal to the Monarchy and loyal to the Revolution as most Frenchmen understood and desired those things. But he was disloyal — perfidiously disloyal — to the Assembly of which he was a member and had once been a champion. It was his way to forget that the means employed determine the end achieved, and the means he now proposed to use would have debased the currency of public life only less than the methods of intimidation so increasingly and disgracefully employed by the committed men of the Left. Only one excuse can be advanced for his lack of scruple, and he himself would have thought it a justification. It is that, beneath the forms of constitutional procedure and beneath all the solemn plausibilities of the hour, a deadly though undeclared war was in progress between the forces of order and those of chaos. He advocated employing deceit and corruption on a vast scale to alter the current trend of things because he was convinced that, if that trend continued, the end would be either an anarchy or a tyranny in which political freedom would perish altogether. Before condemning him we should remember the Terror and the Empire.

The policy of sapping and mining the present Assembly is only one part of the plan unfolded in this Forty-seventh Note. It is equally important to popularize the persons of the King and Queen and to ensure that the next Assembly shall be of a better complexion. He urges that their Majesties should show themselves frequently in public, that they should walk about the streets, attend reviews of the National Guard and occasional sessions of the Assembly, and visit hospitals and factories. It is the recipe for citizen-monarchy which might haved save the legitimate dynasty if they had adopted it, as it would have saved Louis Philippe if only he had been a legitimate dynast. As for the next assembly, Mirabeau thinks it should meet in some city other than Paris. To prevent its resembling the present chamber a decree should be obtained from the latter making its members ineligible to its successor; failing this, a law must be passed imposing a residential qualification on candidates; otherwise 'there is not a demagogue nor a pamphleteer not a conspirator in Paris who may not hope to be nominated in some part of the kingdom. We shall see the Desmoulins, the Marats, the Linguets and the Dantons triumphing over the worthiest citizens. There is a man of that sort available for every department, though he might well fail to obtain nomination in his own. Furthermore, if the Paris Jacobins choose to make use of the Club's formidable branches, it would be easy for them . . . to make themselves masters of all the elections in the kingdom. What (asks the President of the Jacobin Club) could then be hoped from the next legislature?'

We have here an example of that penetration to the marrow of politics which was Mirabeau's greatest gift. He saw the as-yet unrevealed power of a disciplined political party, how it could cut through the unsolidified sentiments of the national mass like a hot knife through butter. Indeed, as one reads this Forty-seventh Note one gets the impression that he felt the coming tragedy of 1792 — the war, the massacres, and dictatorship of a party — in his bones.

The King and his ministers, Mirabeau insists, have neither control over nor knowledge of the country, whereas the Jacobins, now a nation-wide network, are rapidly acquiring both. It is his urgent concern to challenge their tightening grip on the nerves and arteries of the nation's life, and he outlines a great system for the secret collection of intelligence and the exercise of covert influence. Here again there is a scheme for the employment of secret agents, each to know only his immediate superior and his limited task. Mirabeau's plans bear, indeed, a resemblance to the underground movements of our own day, and they are repellent for the same reasons. But it is easier to condemn such methods than to be sure what others could have succeeded against 'the frantic demagogy' of Paris and the movement of the Club which was so soon to hold France in a grip of iron. For the truth is that the seeds of the Terror had already been sown and were germinating fast. The fear and the hope of counter-revolution were forcing them into a malignant tropical growth. The *émigrés* aristocrats believed in counter-revolution and hoped for it; the Jacobins believed in it and feared it. Only Mirabeau disbelieved in it. The ground-work of the Revolution could not in his opinion be obliterated even by a successful armed reaction. Counter-revolution was, he thought, a bogey. But he knew the power of bogeys in politics, and he feared that, if things went on as they were, this one would stampede the nation into self-mutilation. To prevent that he was prepared to stop at nothing.

'In revolutions a petty morality kills the greater,' he used to say. It was his greatest error, the expression of his worst defect — a lack of principle. 'Mirabeau, Mirabeau, less brilliance and more virtue, *ou gare la lanterne!*' The warning appeared in Fréron's *Orateur du Peuple* in May 1790, and a year earlier his father had forecast that he would fail to make his way because he was weak in his moral foundations; even La Marck, who loved him, was to confide in Mercy, in January 1791, his uneasiness at Mirabeau's preference for devious methods, for covering his tracks, for securing political alibis.[185]

There was, indeed, too much cleverness about the schemes in the Forty-seventh Note for them to be really practical. They would have required the cool and resolute co-operation of the King with an inner cabinet of nerve-hardened conspirators, when, in reality, the only instruments available were the listless irresolution of Louis and Montmorin's jumpy nerves. Furthermore, the requisite subordinate machinery had all to be made, and there was insufficient allowance for the inevitable hitches and indiscretions attending the enlistment and calculated hoodwinking of so many agents of different types.[186] Finally, the Note itself was too long. La Marck took it to Marie Antoinette and read her the concluding passage, a very moving peroration. But she was easily fatigued by mental concentration, and it is quite uncertain whether she ever waded through the *chef d'œuvre* of the only man of genius the gods had sent her. Mirabeau had always overrated the Queen's capacity for sustained thought; he forgot the inevitable preference of such a woman for the quiet and undemanding chivalry of a Fersen. But, even if his programme had not suffered from all these defects, it is certain that by now no plan of his stood any chance of being adopted by his employers. For they no longer accepted what to him was axiomatic — that the achievements of 1789 were irreversible. He had failed them on the vital matter of religious freedom, and his voice was that of an alien in their ears.

That the church question was vital does not seem to have entered his head. He thought it a topic like other topics, something over which he could safely shout with the Left. Three times in January he spoke with gratuitous violence against the non-juring clergy. On the second occasion his speech was so immoderate as to displease even the Left and to bring down a rebuke from the Jansenist Camus; yet a week later he was writing coolly to the Court:

> It would have been impossible to find a more favourable opportunity for bringing together a great number of malcontents . . . and of increasing the King's popularity at the expense of the Assembly's. For this it is necessary (1) to encourage the largest possible number of ecclesiastics to refuse the oath (2) to encourage active citizens in the parishes who are devoted to their priests to refuse to re-elect . . . (4) to prevent the Assembly adopting palliative measures which might enable it to retreat cautiously and preserve its popularity.

The persecution, it seems, does not matter; the spying and delation that invariably accompany it do not matter; the consciences of multitudes to be put on the rack do not matter; nothing, it seems, matters except the supposed requirements of tactics. Equipped with at least two of the gifts that make for great statesmanship — superabundant energy and intellectual power — he dwindles at times in these last months into something depressingly like a politician for lack of a much commoner resource: simply the sound conscience which tells the good man at what point he must turn and fight for justice regardless of consequences.

4

Mirabeau's failure to fasten on the issue of liberty raised by the Assembly's religious policy was the great mistake of his last year. But it was not his only one. In his Forty-seventh Note he refers to what he calls the 'useful malcontents', by which he means the moderates or constitutional royalists, men who, like himself, are equally opposed to despotism and to anarchy. He laments that, between the rival bigotries of Left and Right, these sober and upright deputies are dwindling steadily in numbers and influence.

Why, one may ask, had he never put himself boldly at their head? They were the only group with whom he saw eye to eye, and he was the one man who could have supplied what they lacked — force, fire and leadership. In revolutionary times moderate men are usually immobilized by their best qualities; they are dismissed as fainthearts, shufflers and traitors by the enthusiasts on the wings. Their very qualities — their ability to see two sides of a question, their sense of the importance of gradualness — go with a cool and accommodating temper. They are fitted to generate light rather than heat, and the weakness of their fire puts them at a crippling disadvantage when, to right and left of them, the opposing benches are aflame.

This was the situation of the moderates in the Constituent Assembly, and Mirabeau alone could have rescued them from it. Only he could have made these moderates a fighting force; only he could have put fire into their bellies and led them to the offensive; while only among these men could he have found a party. They distrusted him deeply, it is true, but he could have worn down their distrust. His brief contact with Malouet in May 1789 provided an opening which could have been widened. But he did nothing about it, and the moderates, hearing from him sometimes the echo of their own beliefs but just as often the jarring note of Jacobin fury, remained distrustful.

Mirabeau failed to ally himself with these men of the centre. He believed that he could do more as a moderate in disguise among the extremists. He believed that his force lay in his popularity, and that only by appearing among the 'patriots' could he preserve that popularity. If this was a mistake it was a mistake primarily of tactics. But, as in the matter of the Church, his pursuit of tactics led him to burke a moral issue. Too cunning to make a bold stand for liberty of conscience where the Church was concerned, he failed to stand for liberty of assembly when that right was denied to the constitutional royalists.

Rejecting the short-sighted folly of over a hundred deputies who abandoned their seats in shocked disgust after the October Days, Malouet, La Tour Maubourg, Liancourt, Rochefoucauld and others had, with the blessing of Lafayette, formed a club with the colourless name of *Les Impartiaux*. It was not a robust foundation and it soon petered out. But in December Malouet and Clermont-Tonnerre revived it under the name of *Société des amis de la Constitution monarchique*. This was a singularly unfortunate name because, since only the final adjective distinguished it from the proper style of the Jacobins, it became known for short simply as the *Club monarchique*, and such was the distraction of the times that its blameless intentions counted for less than its invidious distinguishing label. When its membership showed signs of increasing, the Jacobins felt it was time to take notice and, without a shadow of evidence, denounced it in speech and press as a reactionary conspiracy. When it organized a modest distribution of food to the needy, Barnave accused it in the Assembly of seeking to corrupt honest citizens with 'poisoned bread'. Nor was this all. Two day later Clermont-Tonnerre's house was attacked, and the attitude of the mob became so threatening that it soon became almost impossible to find a proprietor willing to risk his furniture by letting his premises to so unpopular a society. When one was at last found his place was besieged by an angry crowd whom Bailly, putting in a tardy appearance, assured that measures would be taken to suspend the sessions of 'a society which disturbed the public peace'. Denied the right of free association which the Jacobins were always so prompt to claim for themselves, the Monarchist club was forced to suspend its activities.

The affair was scandalous. Nothing better illustrates how little the 'patriot party' now cared for the conditions of a free society, and how right Mirabeau was to regard current politics as in reality a war in which all was fair. But what were the outraged constitutional monarchists to think of the tribune who stood by without protest while they suffered such injustice? These men were his potential allies. All his future schemes aimed at putting just such men in control. Would it not have been worth his while, to say the least, to champion their right as citizens to free association — even at the risk of angering the Jacobins? Had not Mirabeau talent enough to make a Barnave or a Lameth blush in such a dispute? He judged otherwise. He had eschewed the Monarchist Club because, secretly bound to the Court, he could afford no ground to his watchful colleagues in the Rue Saint

Honoré for an accusation of royalism. Nevertheless, when they were so shamelessly persecuted he should have chosen their case to speak for the right of free association to which he, they and the Jacobins were formally committed.

5

He had a special reason for avoiding a step which might have shaken even momentarily his popularity in the chamber; for, just when the intimidation of the Monarchist Club was reaching its height, the fortnightly election of a president of the Assembly was impending. He had long coveted this honour, yet it had eluded him repeatedly. Lafayette had prevented his election at the time of the Federation, and had forgotten what Mirabeau regarded as an implied promise to support it at a later date. On January 3rd, he missed the presidency by only three votes, but on the next occasion he failed by a wide margin. The Assembly, shocked by that violent speech of his on the church question, chose the Abbé Grégoire. It should have been a warning that his precious tactics might fail to achieve even their immediate purposes. However he more than recovered the ground lost by a brilliant report on foreign affairs for the military and diplomatic committees. Dumont, back in France after some months' absence, helped him, but his success was his own and was won in what had always been his chosen field. The result was that on the following day, Saturday, January 29th, he was elected to be the forty-fourth President of the National Assembly.

If the Assembly's long refusal to choose him shows how much less was his personal credit than his forensic ascendancy, his fortnight's occupancy of the Chair proved how justified his ambition had been. No sooner was he installed than the House recognized a change, as an ill-schooled colt knows at a touch the confident seat and firm but gentle hands of a great horseman.

Never had the office of President been so well filled. This was the unanimous verdict. The habitual hubbub, the farcical disorders in which a score of deputies would be on their feet simultaneously shouting and gesticulating, while the ushers strove vainly to make them sit down and the President's hand-bell rang high and unattended above the din; the aggravating and profit-less cross-purposes in debate; the immoderate interruptions of interesting speeches and the unremitting buzz of conversation which drowned dull ones — for a memorable fortnight these chronic excesses were curbed. An incomparable chairman, Mirabeau could still a yammering outburst with a word of authority perfectly timed, closure a vexatious controversy with a concise and acceptable summing-up, and — most precious gift — freshen the proceedings with the touch of humour. One day an esteemed but long-winded deputy, being the object of an unjust accusation, demanded leave to defend himself. 'Pray, Sir,' came the President's reply, 'do not deprive us of the pleasure of doing you justice without having heard you!' For once the timid and the less robust had a chance of a hearing. When the venerable Tronchet was engaged in reading a long and rather dull report there was so much chatter that his voice was being drowned. The hand-bell rang. 'Gentlemen,' the President interposed, 'please remember that M. Tronchet's lungs are not as strong as his head.'

It was the President's duty to reply to the numerous deputations which presented petitions at the bar of the Assembly. During Mirabeau's term deputations were received from the lyric poets, from the Quinze-Vingts (the ancient hospital for the blind), from the society of inventors, from the doctors of law and from the Quakers. Mirabeau's replies, short, apt and gracious, were universally admired. The Assembly felt itself magnified in the person of this President who put so much into his task. Indeed, the extra strain in this fortnight told upon him, and his old enemy, ophthalmia, rose up and attacked him and forced him to absent himself for two days. Increasingly in these early months of 1791 his body groaned and protested at the mounting tax upon it.

On February 8th, a deputation of the Paris municipality pleaded for an advance to help it meet the debts which the Revolution had obliged it to incur. The President's reply was superb: 'Do not be alarmed at the cost of your efforts; it is an advance made to liberty. You have sown in a fertile soil which will repay you all the treasure you have entrusted to it. Only one source of prosperity is still wanting to this metropolis, and that is the union of its citizens, the public tranquility which is so incessantly disturbed by false alarms, and which a mob of intriguers would like to imperil . . . Vice itself can be a despot; is it to be the only one too strong for the city of Paris to overthrow?' The rebuke was so beautifully woven into the context of praise that there was much applause. That same day La Marck left Paris for Metz to discuss with Bouillé certain schemes of Mirabeau's for the removal of the King from the capital.

Mirabeau's presidency ended on Monday, February 14th. That day he received his last deputation. It was from the Paris commune and it expressed the anxiety felt in the city at the intended departure of the King's aunts for Rome. The purpose of these two pious old ladies was simple enough: they wanted to be able to receive the Sacraments from Catholic priests without subterfuge or danger, and it is a measure of the power of the counter-revolutionary bogey that their journey was regarded by 'patriots' with the darkest suspicion. Were the royal aunts, it was asked, going away to plot with foreign powers, or was the King himself planning to emigrate and anxious to leave no hostages in his enemies' hands? No one knew, but it was widely feared that the old ladies were up to no good.

Mirabeau replied to the deputation in guarded terms. He recognized the premonitory rustle of a storm from which he would be unable to seek shelter.

6

Though the somnambulant mind of Louis XVI had turned against the Revolution, it was as incapable as ever of retaining a plan of action. He read with interest all he could find about Charles I of England, yet Montmorin found that he listened to warnings about his own situation as if they concerned the Emperor of China. He was fatigued by the very idea of pursuing Mirabeau's grand design, and La Marck's discouragement was only prevented from becoming absolute by his feeling for the Queen and his knowledge that she was at least capable of resolution. But he overestimated her confidence in himself and her willingness to accept without reserve a plan proceeding from Mirabeau. He did not fully realize how purely experimental her attitude was or that she would always keep other plans in hand as well. Yet it was an uneasy suspicion that the idea of escape was now uppermost in her mind which determined him to try to prevent such an undertaking from becoming an irreparable calamity.

He and Mirabeau were now convinced that removal to Fontainebleau would give insufficient security. So gravely had the general position deteriorated that no place nearer than Compiègne would give the necessary protection against a Parisian *coup-de-main*. Though the object of escape was ever the same — to enable the King to appeal to the nation at large — the forces of republicanism were by now so much extended that it would be necessary at first to pass behind the cover of loyal troops. But where, by now, were loyal troops to be found? The revolutionary spirit had left very few regiments unaffected. Soldiers' councils (to use a modern term) were undermining discipline at an alarming rate. The two chief military areas were, as ever, the North and the East. But the northern command was under Lafayette's friend and fellow 'American', Rochambeau, so that there remained only the eastern command of Bouillé. 'To retire to Metz or any other frontier would be to declare war on the nation and to abdicate the throne', Mirabeau had written in October 1789. Now there was no choice. Bouillé was loyal without being a reactionary, and he was the one general who retained some authority over his troops. Mirabeau remained insistent that the King's journey should not be surreptitious, that he should give out some colourable pretext and go to Compiègne in broad daylight, and that Bouillé should simply move troops westwards to meet and ensure the safety of the royal family.

La Marck's sister was on the point of returning to Vienna. It would be possible for him to visit Bouillé and discuss things with him under cover of accompanying his sister as far as Strasbourg. Montmorin and the Archbishop persuaded the Queen that this was a good plan, and, in due course, her husband gave his limp assent and wrote a note for La Marck to present to Bouillé; it told the general that he might put the most complete confidence in the bearer.

Confidence, however, was the last thing Bouillé felt when La Marck arrived at Metz. Bouillé was a puzzled and worried man. Three months ago he had received a similar royal recommenda-

tion for the émigré Baron de Breteuil, and he knew something of
the covert knight-errantry of Axel Fersen; he knew that La Marck
represented Mirabeau and that Mirabeau and Breteuil were at
opposite points of the political compass. But this was not all.
He had lately received inquiries from the Count of Artois, as well
as a letter from Lafayette, putting him on his guard against La
Marck and Mirabeau. This he might have disregarded; he thought
Lafayette an enthusiast drunk with vanity; but it was not all. He
had been warned of La Marck's coming visit in a letter from the
King himself in which His Majesty had explained that, although
Mirabeau was not very estimable and had been very well paid,
Bouillé might *perhaps* find useful suggestions in his plan: 'Listen
to him [La Marck],' the King had written, 'without committing
yourself too much, and let me have your observations.'

At first, therefore, Bouillé was on his guard with La Marck,
but the latter was not discouraged. He explained that there was
no question of a counter-revolution in his proposals, and proceeded to enlighten the general as to the popular nature of Mirabeau's monarchism. To capture Bouillé's confidence he told
him something of Mirabeau's employment by the Court and more
about his feud with Lafayette, and thereafter the conversation
ran more freely. La Marck laid before Bouillé Mirabeau's ideas
on the royal escape, explaining that in essence it would be a
political move, a step preliminary to an appeal to the nation;
the military measures required would be merely precautionary —
sufficient to place the royal family beyond the physical reach of
their enemies, but no more.

Relieved to be shown at last a project of escape and restoration which was neither counter-revolution nor obvious folly,
Bouillé gave the plan his hearty approval and wrote in the same
sense to the King. To La Marck he added a parting observation:
what was to be done should be done quickly; the subordination
of his own troops was becoming every day more uncertain.

La Marck got back to Paris on the seventeenth. He made his
report to the King and Queen and, of course, to Mirabeau.
The latter was much encouraged; it was a real gain to have got
the support of Bouillé; perhaps now something would really be
done, and he began to consider the details of the great move,
especially the proclamations which the King would make to the

319

nation as soon as he was free. He believed that the effect of these would be overwhelming, but, should Jacobin propaganda in the provinces prove more potent than he anticipated, then there would be nothing for it but civil war.[187] With the best general and the one statesman of genius at his side, why should the King shrink from that arbitrament?

7

Mirabeau needed the tonic of hope at this moment, for the strain of his life was telling on his giant constitution in a way which even he could not ignore. While La Marck had been away he and Montmorin had been busy with a task outlined in his grand design — the enlistment of agents. Sémonville and Talon were already busy in the capital, and had made contacts with Danton which were at least highly profitable to that patriot.[188] The parallel scheme for influencing the Assembly also needed to be set in motion. It was agreed that Malouet should be enlisted, and during the session of February 11th the President gave a note to an usher to hand to the deputy for Riom. It read: 'I have been of your opinion for a long time, longer than you think. Now I want to prove it to you. Have you any objection to meeting me at the house of a friend of yours, M. de Montmorin, tomorrow at six o'clock?' — 'I shall be there,' was Malouet's pencilled reply.[189]

He called on Montmorin that same evening. The Minister revealed the secret of Mirabeau's relations with the Court (not the whole secret; that was more than he knew himself), and he explained something of the plan of action upon which Mirabeau and he were working. Malouet reminded him how much better it would have been if he had listened to his advice in May 1789. 'That was really your fault,' replied Montmorin, recalling how Malouet had stayed away from Mirabeau's ill-starred interview with Necker and himself. Ironically it was now Malouet who was doubtful of the tribune's intentions and Montmorin who was eager to remove his doubts. The little minister was optimistic: 'This isn't the moment for discouragement,' he said, 'and you mustn't think that all is lost because you've been unable to keep your Monarchist Club going.'

Montmorin handed Malouet a paper of Mirabeau's for him to study before the three of them met the next evening. It seems to have been a version of the Forty-seventh Note edited for consumption by a chosen inner circle of assistants. Malouet saw nothing to shock him in what he read, and was much encouraged to discover that, even at this late hour, the Court had a plan of action.[190]

It was not till ten the following night that the meeting with Mirabeau took place. Malouet was shocked at his ravaged appearance; he was obviously in pain; with his enflamed and bloodshot eyes starting from their sockets he was horrible to see, a man with the mark of death on him. But he was electrifying. Malouet began with some practical objections to the plan he had just studied. 'There is no time left for weighing objections,' Mirabeau replied; 'if you have doubts about my proposals produce something better, but do it quickly, for we have not long to live. While we wait we shall die of consumption or by violence. The more you insist on the reality of the evil, the more urgent is the remedy. You question my means? Name the man who, having the same will to act as I, is better placed to do so. All sensible people and even a part of the rabble are on my side. What matter if I am suspected, if I'm accused of being sold to the Court? Nobody will believe that I have sold the liberty of my country, that I am planning to put it in chains. This is what I'll say to them: "You have seen me in your ranks," I'll say, "fighting against tyranny, and it's tyranny that I'm fighting still. But I have always reserved the right and duty to defend lawful government, constitutional monarchy and the protective authority of the monarch." Make no mistake, I am the only man in this patriotic horde who can speak thus without eating his words. I have never adopted their romantic illusions nor their metaphysic nor their useless crimes!'

Malouet was overwhelmed. He said that Mirabeau would splendidly undo the harm he had done. 'No!' came the fierce rejoinder, 'I have never done harm willingly; I have bowed to the circumstances in which I have found myself. The great harm which has been done is the work of all, except for the crimes, which are the work of individuals.'

Exhaustion was gaining on him; he was bathed in sweat; but

he went on: 'You moderates who have not been moderate enough
to appreciate me; you ministers who have not taken a single step
which was not a blunder, and you, fool of an Assembly, who
know not what you are saying nor what you are doing — you are
the people who have done the harm!'

They talked on into the night. They concerted plans. Malouet
said he could answer for fifty deputies. By two o'clock Mirabeau
was so feverish and exhausted that he could no longer speak, and
they separated.[191]

8

No single thing bedevilled the first two years of the Revolution
more than the emigration of princes of the blood and grandees
of the old régime after the Bastille crisis. Though the incitements
to terrorism of Marat and his sort are never to be excused, it was
the shameless caste-selfishness of the *émigrés* — their boasts, their
threats, their hobnobbing with foreign courts — which gave such
men their audience.

The fact that the King's brother, Artois, had headed the emigration, and that so many of the Queen's friends had followed him,
cast over Louis and Marie Antoinette a cloud of suspicion which
was the emotional cause of that paralysis of the monarchy which it
was Mirabeau's supreme purpose to cure. But so long as they
could be represented as having any understanding with the princes
across the Rhine he knew that his task would be hopeless.

On February 19th, after indiscreetly elaborate preparations,
the King's aunts, Mesdames Adelaide and Victoire, set off for
Rome. Rumours of their intention had caused a radical outcry
and a deputation to the King urging him to refuse them permission to depart; but Louis had stood firm on their right to go
wherever they chose like ordinary citizens and had given them
passports. The *Mercure de France* wrote: 'The Royal Family is
only a family of ordinary citizens when it is a question of refusing
them the deference due to their birth; but distinctions are made
against them when it is necessary to deny them the natural rights
of the citizen. Hurrah for the Casuists of the democratic religion!'
Yet patriotic suspicions were not entirely unjustified. The aunts'

journey *had* political significance. If Louis had adopted Mirabeau's advice of an unconcealed departure for a published destination inside France, it would have been practicable to take his aunts with him. But he was leaning more and more towards schemes of furtive evasion, and he would have one worry the less if the old ladies could be got safely out of France before it.

Mirabeau thought the aunts' journey would compromise the King and perhaps be dangerous to themselves, and he had advised Louis how to act. He should tell the Assembly that he was opposed to Mesdames leaving Paris when so many tradesmen were feeling the loss of *émigré* patronage, but should explain that he was unsure whether he had any constitutional authority to interfere. If the Assembly made no ruling, then at least the King would have shown that Mesdames' departure was none of his doing; if the Assembly declared that royal personages were subject only to the ordinary law, then the King would stand acquitted of responsibility for the *émigrés* princes; if, on the other hand, the Assembly accorded to the King the right to order the movements of his family, then Louis could recall the absent princes and clear himself before the nation of complicity in their designs.[192]

It was excellent advice and it was, of course, neglected. It was Mirabeau's last Note to the Court.

As he had foreseen, the aunts had an eventful journey. On their first day out, Saturday 19th, they were held up near Fontainebleau. The local officials were in doubt about their passports, but the commander of their cavalry escort lost patience and cleared the road by force. The news of this kindled fresh alarm in patriotic breasts, and on Tuesday the inevitable Barnave rose to protest at Mesdames' adventure and to suggest that Monsieur would be the next to go; whereupon a mob went off to the Luxembourg and forced Provence to promise not to emigrate and to move his residence at once to the Tuileries, where they could more easily keep an eye on him.

On Wednesday morning a crowd led by members of the *Société fraternelle* — an inexpensive club for both sexes affiliated to the more exclusive Jacobins, and meeting on the floor beneath the famous Dominican library — went to the Tuileries to demand the recall of Mesdames. When Bailly tried to explain to them that Mesdames had the same right to travel as anyone else, they made a rush at their pedantic Mayor, who was only saved from injury by some National Guards.

That evening both the Jacobins and the Fraternal Society were in a nervous state. The former were exchanging opinions as to the wicked intentions and ubiquitous activity of the Monarchist Club (which had not dared to meet for a month) when a deputation from downstairs made their flesh creep with tales of underground passages from the Luxembourg in which a thousand armed men could be concealed, and with circumstantial details of a plot to smuggle the Dauphin out of France by substituting at the palace a little boy from the Faubourg Saint-Antoine who was his double.[193] The Jacobins then discussed what punishment they should demand for the cuirassiers who had cleared the way for Mesdames Tantes, but the subject was dropped when Laclos, Orleans's chief agent, rose to propose something more serious. This was a decree, to be forced through the Assembly at once, against 'all *émigrés* of whatsoever rank they might be'. It would impose on those who refused to return mounting penalties, culminating in death, while offering a pardon to any *émigré* returning to France with the head of a fellow expatriate in his luggage.

The next morning a demand was raised in the Assembly that the officer commanding the escort should be called to account for overpowering a local authority in the exercise of its duty. Mirabeau shrewdly upheld this view; but he had scarcely sat down when news arrived that the aunts had been stopped again.

The municipality of Arnay-le-Duc in Burgundy was holding them and awaiting the Assembly's instructions. Mesdames, for their part, had written a note to the Assembly and dispatched a courier to the King for his orders.

A violent debate at once arose. Some censured the municipality for exceeding its powers; others commended it for having acted to the best of its belief in the national interest. This was the opinion of Barnave, and the house looked like going on to vote that the Arnay-le-Duc officials had in fact served the national interest when Mirabeau moved that, since no existing law forbad the free passage of the princesses, there was nothing to discuss and the matter should be referrred to the executive. He had taken his stand firmly and precisely on the point of law, and he was at once challenged. A deputy broke in with the assertion that there *was* a law justifying the detention of Mesdames: 'I will cite it,' he cried, '*It is the law of the public safety.*' All the Terror was implicit in his words. Mirabeau at once seized on the deadly phrase, and reminded the house that the safety of the people demanded above all things that the laws should be respected. The debate dragged on into weariness. At last Menou seized a pause to remark that Europe would be astonished to hear that the National Assembly had devoted four hours to discussing the departure of two ladies who preferred to hear Mass in Rome rather than in Paris. There was a blessed burst of laughter and Mirabeau's motion was carried almost unanimously.

The relief of tension was only momentary. While the debate had been going on some women from the Fraternal Society had attracted a crowd to the Terrasse des Feuillants, between the Assembly Hall and the Tuileries Gardens. When they heard the result of the vote they swarmed up to the palace railings and demanded to see the King. From behind the railings the officer commanding the National Guard was unable to soothe them. He sent word to the King, who replied that he would receive a deputation the next day, but the women screamed that by then the courier would be on his way with the orders for the passage of Mesdames. The crowd became ugly, but at this point Lafayette arrived. He ordered his men to load and fix bayonets, brought up a couple of cannon and, without firing a shot, dispersed the mob. He was loudly hooted, but he had the city patrolled throughout the night.

The next day the Assembly discussed a bill concerning *the residence of public functionaries*. It named the King as 'the first public functionary', so that, if it were passed, Louis would be unable to leave Paris without breaking the law. Mirabeau saw that he must strike at once, and when he declared roundly that he would oppose all factious persons threatening the principles of monarchy by whatever arguments, he was powerfully applauded. He was fighting in the open at last — and he was carrying the house. Had yesterday's scene outside the Tuileries conceivably marked high tide for the 'patriots'? The thirty or so deputies for the Left were uneasily aware of a change in the wind: Lafayette showing resolution in the streets; Mirabeau facing them squarely in the house with numbers at his back — these were new things.

The Jacobins had been content that such bodies as the Fraternal Society and Danton's Cordeliers Club should, like irregular troops, skirmish far out on their Left wing; but were they, perhaps, advancing too fast and too far? Were they exposing the main body to a counter-stroke?

Just at this moment placards were stuck up by the Directory of the Department of Paris, a body to which Mirabeau had recently been elected. These bills warned the public against disorders and hinted discreetly that the Jacobins were trouble-makers. Their authorship was scarcely in doubt. Mirabeau had thrown down the glove. 'I hear the seething of a patriotic wrath about to burst over your head, unworthy Jacobin,' wrote Des-moulins of his fallen idol. The Jacobins had accepted the challenge.[194]

The real battle began on Monday, February 28th, when the project for a decree against the *émigrés* came before the Assembly. The debate was fierce. The galleries cheered, booed and inter-rupted incessantly. Mirabeau opposed the bill with all his force. No one had less cause than he to love the *émigrés*, but he calculated that the proposed decree would envenom a situation which was already compromising the Court, and that it would heighten a national neurosis which could help only the republicans.

He spoke three times. He read the house the passage from his Address to Frederick William II in which he had exhorted that despot to allow freedom of emigration to his subjects, and he asked the Assembly to refuse even to discuss the present bill as being incompatible with the constitution of liberated France. His plea nearly succeeded, but not quite, and the argument from national emergency was reiterated. In his second speech he warned the Assembly not to confuse a measure of police security with a law. He said that the law proposed was barbarous as well as uncon-stitutional; it would set up a committee of three with dictatorial powers to forbid exit from the kingdom and enforce the return of travellers: 'If you make a law against emigrants,' he ended, 'I swear never to obey it!'

There were indignant cries from the Left. The debate con-tinued. When Mirabeau mounted the tribune for the third time

Jacobin interruptions amounted to systematic barracking. Yet the house, in truth, was at last growing a little impatient with the factious Thirty, and he, with his orator's instinct, sensed where the weight of sympathy lay, what the house would take and what it would not take. Suddenly he was no longer addressing the chamber; he was turned sideways, looking full at the Jacobin deputies. *Silence aux trente voix!* he thundered. He completed what he had to say without further interruption.

The bill against emigrants was not thrown out, as he would have wished; but it was referred back to the committees, that is, shelved; and in fact no such law was made till after his death.

The silencing of thirty of the vainest and most talkative men who have ever plagued a legislature by a simple command was a feat so astonishing that, presented with the bare fact, we are at a loss fully to explain it. From all we know of their temper we should expect them to have rioted at such impudence from their fellow deputy and Jacobin, the more so because, only a minute earlier, one of them had asked angrily by what right Mirabeau exercised a dictatorship over the chamber. There, however, the incident stands, a strange monument to the authority which he could, at times, exert over an audience.

But it was a declaration of war, and he knew his enemies. He had a dinner-appointment that evening with D'Aiguillon and other Jacobins. He presented himself — and he was refused admittance.[195] And the determination of the Thirty to overthrow him would be all the more desperate because of what had happened elsewhere that day.

A mob had gone out to Vincennes to make of it a second Bastille. There was a silly story current that it was connected with the Tuileries by underground passages which might be used by the Court for their escape. At the same time some hundreds of loyal gentlemen, fearing that, if July 14th was to be re-enacted at Vincennes, October 5th-6th would thereafter be re-enacted at the Tuileries, armed themselves and formed a voluntary bodyguard at the palace. Lafayette had a busy day, but he acted with praiseworthy speed and decision, and was as successful in mastering the mob at Vincennes as in the easier task of disarming the gallants at the Tuileries. But the disturbance might provide Mirabeau with ammunition for use against the more fanatical Jacobins unless they could pull him down first.

The Club met as usual that night and Duport got up to denounce Mirabeau's insolent dictatorship. He was warming to his theme when, to the surprise of all present, the dictator entered the room and sat down. Mirabeau was infuriated to hear Duport bracketing him with Lafayette, and as soon as the Triumvir had finished he demanded leave to reply. Something like hell was let loose at him for a few minutes, but in the end they heard him. A witness says that 'he shook from his breast the darts of his adversary, who was not of his stature, and pelted him with fragments of rock'. Then Alexandre de Lameth was given the floor, and he made against his old adversary what was probably the most damaging attack he had ever suffered. His audience was rocking with delight and his victim appeared, for once, to be seriously shaken. Mirabeau had not come to face the music as a mere act of bravado: he had come with a purpose — to parry the attack upon him. He was anxious to prevent the whole great Club being turned against him. Not only did it contain many estimable men, but it was now an organization so influential and so widely ramified that loss of membership would have been loss of a useful strategic position. He was fighting not the Jacobins but the Thirty and, at their head, the old Triumvirate. Nevertheless his attendance that night was a nice example of his 'art of daring'.

In a supreme effort he answered Lameth. From a witness we get the impression of a fighting bull at bay, visibly tiring but still terrible, still able with a contemptuous toss of the great head to maul his foes and throw them back. His courage, indeed, succeeded. He commanded too much admiration and enforced too much hesitation for the assault against him to be pressed to an immediate conclusion. But after he had left that meeting he said to a friend: 'I have just signed my death warrant. It is all up with me. They will kill me.'

They had received a check; but they were still the leaders of the only organized party in France.[196]

CHAPTER XV

CONCLUSION

Sa mort fut, comme sa vie, un malheur public
MALOUET.

I T is the judgment of some historians, particularly of the great
Aulard, that the deeper significance of the Revolution escaped
the mind of Mirabeau.[197] They are repelled by his cynicism, by
his contempt for the theoretic idealism which stirred so many of
his contemporaries, and imparted to the movement a nobility
which is some offset to its follies and its crimes. They incline to
see in him a man of vast but perverted talents, who mistook the
popular movement and who, by seeking to divert it from its proper
end, succeeded only in troubling its passage.

The present book has been written under the impulse of an
opposite belief.

There is in many historians a determinist habit of mind which
predisposes them to regard that which actually happened as what,
in the nature of things, was bound to happen. It is a prejudice
which deprives the failures of history of their proper significance.
It represents them as standing for causes predestined to be lost
and therefore moribund before they were defeated, and it removes
the nerve from history.

It is certainly true that the Revolution which took place was
not the one which Mirabeau desired and believed possible. But
the fact of his defeat does not settle the question whether his
revolution was desirable for, and desired by, France, or the further
question whether it was, in the circumstances of the time, possible.

Mirabeau's revolution would have preserved the Monarchy
as an integral part of the French state, and by doing so it would
have preserved the continuity of the nation's growth. The
destruction of the Monarchy meant for France a breach with the
past far more damaging than would have been the case in many
other lands, for the French nation was, in a very special sense,
the creation of its kings. The French Monarchy was more than
the symbol of national unity; it was its form. That form the
Revolution smashed, and France ever since, like a crustacean that

has lost its shell, has been searching for a new form in which to exist. The search was, for at least four generations, quite unsuccessful, and never more so than in the attempt to restore the Monarchy in 1815. For this experiment failed precisely because, though the House of Bourbon had survived, the Monarchy had not; it had become the perquisite of a party and had ceased to be the property of the people. The Revolution had left France for royalists and Bonapartists and republicans to quarrel over, and patriotism no longer carried with it, as a matter of course, any particular loyalty to the form of the state. This was a source of weakness to the nation, especially in times of strain.

Mirabeau's attachment to monarchy had little of sentiment and nothing of mysticism in it. He defended the crown because he believed it to be the only institution which could guarantee to France in the future the unity it had given her in the past. If an alternative centre of unity had existed, he would have been ready to consider it on its merits; but it did not exist, and he clung to the monarchy because he had a passionate faith in the unity of the nation. In this he was a most representative Frenchman. The 'patriots', too, desired the unity of the nation, but, unlike Mirabeau, they lost sight of its governing condition. The 'patriots' loved Man and gave him a 'first public functionary' to respect; Mirabeau understood Frenchmen and tried to give them a king to love. He failed and his doctrine was thrown aside; but this was not because it was alien or unattuned to the temper of the nation, but because of certain accidental circumstances; and of these the first was the character of Louis XVI.

Patriotic and, in his own way, remarkably brave, Louis was utterly incapable either of thinking out a policy of his own or of sticking to the policy of an adviser. This irresolution was his only serious fault, but it was so serious as to amount to a kind of mental incapacity. Fragments of policies and residual prejudices lay about in the chamber of his mind in a confusion which he was never able to clear up. His leaning towards the new conceptions of limited and responsible monarchy was unaffected, but it was a leaning and no more; pulling him the opposite way was an untidy bundle of prejudices derived from his environment and his ancestors. Fragmentary and unrelated ideas — bits of Turgot, of Necker, of Breteuil and of Mirabeau — floated about in the thick fog of his vague optimism and rendered him incapable of consistent action, often of any action at all. The only chance of escape from this fog lay in the constant influence of someone so placed as to be able to exert a sustained pressure upon him. But the only person so placed was his wife, and it was his final misfortune that she, though a great deal more resolute, was politically less intelligent than her husband. At least his deepest instincts were national; hers were merely maternal and dynastic. Mirabeau had thought at first that she would open a way for him to the confidence of the King. He was mistaken; she constituted in reality an impenetrable barrier. There was in Louis a string which could vibrate, albeit feebly, to the keynote of Mirabeau's admonitions; from the Queen his doctrine of democratic monarchism could evoke no answering note at all. Mirabeau was a monarchist without a monarch.

He was also a politician without a party. Here the fault lay in himself. In so far as his failure to win the confidence of his fellow-deputies was due to the evil reputation with which he had come among them, he admitted his own responsibility. Again and again he would exclaim to friends like La Marck and Dumont that he was expiating cruelly the misdeeds of his youth. 'There were moments', wrote Dumont, 'when he would have consented to pass seven times through the fiery furnace to purify the name of Mirabeau.' But they were only moments; the misdeeds did not all belong to his youth, and it was not in him to repair the damage. He remained to the end a person of whom men of moral refinement were apt to be chary.

Furthermore he never went about to attract a coherent party of regular supporters. He indulged a certain contempt for his fellow-deputies and was too prone to seek for short cuts to the power which he coveted. It was always his instinct to use his force as a speaker rather to convince the Court and the ministers that he was to be reckoned with than to inspire the reliance of his colleagues, and the final result was that he inspired confidence in neither quarter. Yet the concentration of the confidence of both king and legislative assembly in one man was the very keystone of the constitutional arch which he had designed. It was not his fault that the formation of a responsible parliamentary ministry was frustrated by the fatal November Decree, but it was his error to snatch at a position of backstairs influence thereafter, instead of working patiently to win the leadership of the sensible but unorganized majority of the Assembly.

Not that there was, as is often suggested, any dishonour in his compact with the Court.[198] Even Lafayette later admitted that Mirabeau only accepted pay to be of his own opinion. The accusation that he was 'sold to the Court' came from men who suspected the King and Queen of precisely those anti-popular designs from which he never ceased to dissuade them. 'A sorry time indeed,' commented La Marck after the Saint-Cloud interview, 'when a man could be accused of treason for having had an interview with his sovereign.' The very fact that the cry of treason could be raised at all is a measure of the need that someone should restore Louis XVI to the national and popular position which he had lost.

The flight to Varennes, a little over two months after Mirabeau's death, was the true death-blow to the Monarchy. That fatal and foolish journey bore all the marks of a furtive emigration and of an appeal to alien force against the Revolution. It was different in kind from the sort of move which Mirabeau had intermittently advocated. But it is fair to ask whether he was not in some measure to blame for the disastrous event through having encouraged in the royal pair an escape psychosis. In judging of this the first thing to remember is that escape from Paris was by no means the dominant theme in his Notes to the Court; the King is advised how to grapple with the Revolution; not how to escape from it, and removal from Paris is never advocated except as a means to that end. Secondly, it must be remembered that the idea of flight had floated in the Queen's mind ever since the October Days — for seven months, that is, before Mirabeau became a regular adviser. Throughout 1790 the idea was never absent from the Austrian Queen, for it was kept before her by the constant pressure of her adoring Swedish knight, Fersen. The Civil Constitution and the Oath, presenting Louis with a simple question of conscience which he could understand, clinched the matter. From that point it was as certain as anything could be that the attempt to get away from Paris would be made. But only Mirabeau could have given the right aspect to the move; for he alone saw that it must be, and appear to be, an escape from Paris *to France*.

332

CONCLUSION

The question whether Mirabeau understood the Revolution or whether the heart of the matter was closed to him may perhaps be answered by posing and answering two further questions.

What did the Revolution ultimately achieve? For what part of their heritage do Frenchmen today regard it with gratitude? Surely for the establishment of a common and equal citizenship. The Revolution proclaimed the principle and went some way to realize it, and its work endures in France today. It is the abiding thing which dictatorships, reactions, disasters and even parliamentary politics have failed to wash away; and it is an idea which Mirabeau held with unwavering tenacity.

Again, to what aspects of their post-revolutionary history do Frenchmen look back with least pride and with most inclination to mutual recriminations? Surely to the political instability and the cleavages of party and class from which their country has suffered ever since 1793. In a century and a half at least eight distinct régimes, all of which have collapsed and died quite suddenly, none of which has found any significant body of mourners — it is an uninspiring record and one in striking contrast to the majestic continuity which France enjoyed for centuries under her kings. It is the paradox of the Revolution that it gave France a greatly heightened sense of national unity while robbing her of a visible object of habitual and general loyalty. The Republic had its enthusiasts, Bonaparte had his grateful admirers and the Bourbons had their passionate but diminishing partisans; but, after the fall of Louis XVI, no dynasty and no system was able to rely on the instinctive loyalty of the nation as a whole. That was the unhappy condition from which Mirabeau might have saved his country, and it is because he fought for an equal citizenship under the historic monarchy that, despite a moral obliquity which tarnished his fame and contributed to his failure, an undeniable splendour surrounds his memory.

2

He mounted the tribune for the last time on March 27th, and the speech he delivered was in two ways characteristic of the man. It was on a subject of which he knew next to nothing, and the effort it required, which was heroic, was made in the cause of friendship. The subject before the house was the ownership of mines, and few topics can have held less intrinsic interest for him. But La Marck was an important mine-owner and a great part of his fortune was at stake. So La Marck had briefed the invaluable Pellenc with facts and figures, Pellenc had written two long and impressive speeches, and Mirabeau, having delivered the first a week earlier, took the second with him on what he may have guessed might be his last drive to the Salle du Manège.

All his life he had been a prodigal, spending money, virility and his cerebral and nervous energies with a sort of exultant abandonment. For the last two years, and above all during the last ten months, his profusion of vital powers had been utterly unchecked. Yet he had not even been fit to start with. Not only had his old kidney trouble always remained and the ophthalmia contracted in Vincennes never been cured, but also, just after the opening of the States-General, he had had an attack of jaundice. He had neglected to nurse it properly, and his constitution, allowed no rest for recuperation, probably suffered from the after-effects so common with that disease. Tortured intermittently by nephritic colics and by an inflammation of the left eye which threatened to destroy that organ, he began to show symptoms of some more deep-seated disorder. He suffered at times from an inflammation of the intestines which prostrated him with atrocious agony. Yet, when only half-recovered from such attacks, he would return to his labours and his pleasures unsobered and unafraid, and the expense of his vitality would continue.

On March 21st and 22nd, he took part in the debates on the constitutional laws governing the regency: the matter touched the hereditary character of the monarchy and could not be neglected. But his speeches were the efforts of a sick man. He grew worse, but on Friday, the twenty-fifth, being a little recovered, he had two dancers from the *Opéra* to supper. The next night he was seized by violent internal pains, but on the following day, by an effort of will which approached the sublime, he spoke in the decisive debate on the mining industry. When it was over he made his way in pain to La Marck's house. 'Your case is won,' he gasped, 'and I am a dead man.'

He spent the next day in bed. Dr. Cabanis, his close friend, attended him. His illness, which combined sharp rheumatic spasms in the diaphragm with intestinal inflammation, pursued an uneven course. Excruciating torments would pass, leaving the sufferer exhausted but calm. Then the tide of pain would well up again, rising higher at each return, engulfing him. Cabanis, a physician with a distinguished future, used all his skill and was at first hopeful of saving his friend. But the recurrent paroxysms alarmed him and he suggested calling in a second opinion. Loyal to his friend, Mirabeau scouted the idea.

Outside in the street a press of people, silent and anxious, had collected. As soon as the rumour had spread that Mirabeau's life was in danger this crowd had gathered, and it hung about continuously for the five days of his agony, so that visitors found it hard to reach his door. Among these was Talleyrand, a suitable confessor for such a penitent, as someone unkindly remarked. 'It is very difficult to get to you,' he said as he entered the sick-room; 'like the people of Paris, I've come to your door three times a day, and I've waited with them for news of you.' Mirabeau was pleased and flattered: 'Yes,' he said, 'the day one dies is always a great one for the people.' Never was his actor's sense of a situation more acute than in this, his last. The old friends, their later coolness forgotten, talked together for over two hours; and it was perhaps to Talleyrand that the dying man spoke the famous words which Frochot, who was constantly at his bedside, recorded: 'I carry with me the pall of the Monarchy; after my death the factions will fight over its remains.'

At parting he handed the Bishop the text of a speech, with a last request that he would read it for him in the Assembly. 'Mirabeau is dramatizing his death,' Talleyrand remarked after leaving the house. But on the day of the orator's death he read the speech in the chamber, where the deputies listened in mournful silence, thinking of the glorious voice which they would hear no more. The subject was the law governing inheritances, and, though the text was mainly the work of Reybaz, it had been worked over in the usual way by Mirabeau. One passage must surely have been the latter's own, a passage containing this sentence: 'Tell all fathers that their true power should reside in the authority of their virtues, in the wisdom of their lessons and in the marks of their tender affection. . . .'[199]

The King and Queen sent regularly to inquire after the man whom they had never brought themselves to trust, feeling at his approaching end some dim apprehension of loss. The Jacobin Club, more surprisingly, showed a generous and respectful concern, and it is pleasant to record that it was Barnave who proposed and himself headed a deputation to No. 69 Chaussée d'Antin. Charles de Lameth refused to be of the party; he had, he explained, accused Mirabeau of being the mortal enemy of their Club, and his illness could not alter his opinion. But many remembered how, when Lameth had lain wounded after his encounter with Castries, it was Mirabeau who had proposed and himself accompanied the Jacobin deputation to his bedside.

La Marck did not at first press himself upon the sick-room, thinking it best to give nature and Dr. Cabanis a chance. But when, on the evening of Tuesday the twenty-ninth, he learnt that Cabanis had abandoned hope, he came at once and stayed most of the time until the end.

There were certain practical matters which could not be put aside, in particular the question of Mirabeau's papers. It was imperative that the records of his secret correspondence should not fall into the wrong hands, and the imminent danger of this was evident from the presence outside the house and even within it of people attracted by something other than sympathy. Agents of the Jacobins and also of Lafayette were visibly on the prowl, but the most disturbing presence was that of Sémonville. The man hung about the place like a private detective, watching everyone who entered and left and even questioning the servants. Perhaps he only wanted to get hold of papers compromising himself, but perhaps his motives were less purely defensive; anyway he was a warning that no further time should be lost in taking measures of security.

On Wednesday La Marck resolved to risk disturbing the patient by broaching the question, but the voice from the bed forestalled him: 'My friend, I have here many papers which might compromise a lot of people — you, for instance, and, above all, those whom I would so gladly have rescued from the dangers threatening them. It would perhaps be wisest to burn them all, but I confess that I cannot bring myself to it. It is in these papers that posterity, I hope, will find the best justification of my conduct;

it is in them that the honour of my memory lies. Couldn't you take them away? Couldn't you put them out of reach of our enemies, who at the present moment could make such dangerous use of them to mislead public opinion? But promise me that one day these papers shall be known, and that your friendship will find a way to vindicate my memory by having them published.'[200]

La Marck gave the promise with all his heart and, in the fullness of time, fulfilled it.*

At the moment, though, there was no time to waste. Pellenc was summoned and the two of them got to work. They worked fast, burning papers they thought unimportant and, in their haste, inevitably destroying some that should have been saved. But by the evening the job was done and La Marck, taking every care not to meet anybody on his way, carried the chief documents of Mirabeau's political career away to his own house. After stowing them away safely he returned to the bedside.

Some time previously the two of them, in an idle hour, had discussed what was the finest way for a man to die. La Marck had forgotten that conversation, but, as he sat by the fireplace of the sick-room, the voice from the bed, weaker now, called him. He went over. Mirabeau took his hand and pressed it: 'Well, my dear connoisseur of fine deaths,' he said, 'are you satisfied?'

Perhaps it was a gleam of the old affectionate mockery in the pain-worn eyes which undermined La Marck, for now, for the first time, he wept. Mirabeau saw it, and then it was he who gave comfort to his friend, for in the quiet of that room on the night of Wednesday, March 30th, he made a confession of gratitude and love which La Marck was to treasure through the rest of his many years. Not for nothing did the ancients make of the gift of speech a god.[201]

'He carried with him to the tomb the consolation of having many friends.' La Marck, who wrote this, soon received letters from Lord Minto and Sir Hugh Elliot full of an affection for their old school-friend which surprised him coming from two undemonstrative Britons; and the grudging and censorious Dumont was to write to Romilly: 'I felt, from the grief I experienced at his loss, that he had acquired a stronger hold on my affections than I had myself been aware of.'[202]

* See the note on Authorites, p. 341.

This man, who had so great a talent for friendship, was not lonely at the end. In addition to La Marck and to Frochot, who did much of the nursing with his own hands and was praised by the sufferer for his gentleness, Caroline du Saillant came often — the one member of his family with whom he had never quarrelled. And there were humbler assistants. There was Comps, who, when he believed — prematurely, as it proved — that his master was dead, made a most unsuccessful attempt to cut his own throat and added considerably thereby to the anxieties of the household. And there was always the devoted Legrain. He had settled down at last and had taken a wife, once chambermaid to Henriette de Nehra. She was devoted to her master and, though herself pregnant, watched over him unceasingly during this last week.

Mirabeau was troubled about his will. He was as vague as ever about his true financial position, but there were certain persons, he explained to La Marck, to whom he wished to leave mementoes and to do a little good. La Marck promised to see that his wishes were carried out, and Mirabeau, who had never ceased to be a bankrupt at law, made his will.

Caroline's boy was to be his heir in chief, but he made a list of legacies which were to be paid first. To La Marck he left 'all his papers, letters and writings relating to public events' as well as his silver plate and his rings with their caskets, the value of the latter to be employed at his discretion in charitable works. To Cabanis he left his manuscripts 'touching legislation, literature and politics', together with a box bearing his portrait and books to the value of £240. Among numerous other bequests two in particular may be noticed: £1200 to be used by La Marck for the purchase of an annuity for little 'Coco'; and £1000 to be invested in the same way for the benefit of Madame de Nehra.

When the claims of the dead man's creditors were presented it was found that the estate could pay only a little over ten shillings in the pound. But La Marck had made his friend a promise, and the particular legacies were in due course paid out of his own pocket.

The night which followed was one of great pain, but when the light returned Mirabeau asked to be moved over to the window. Outside in the spring morning the young leaves were showing on the trees. He was moved by the sight. 'You are a great physician,' he said to Cabanis, 'but there is a physician greater than you: the author of the wind which lays all things low, of the water which penetrates and fertilizes all things, of the fire by which all things are revived or decomposed.' Cabanis was a materialist, and these words to him are the only evidence we have that, in the hour of death, Mirabeau had any thoughts beyond the world he was about to leave. He faced death with no visible sign either of fear or of repentance.

Legrain and his wife were at hand, and he told her that, in her condition, she should be looking after her family; but she would not go. La Marck came early, but the pains that had racked and wrecked the patient during the night began to return, and soon he could not speak. The pains were giving him no respite now and soon they rose up triumphing within him, clawing and rending in a supreme malignancy. Legrain's wife was supporting him, but he was just able to sign to her to turn away that she might not see what was coming. La Marck took him in his arms. The tortured body drove forth great shouts, and twisted suddenly in a horrible convulsion. Then the eyes were staring up, through the window, into the spring sky; for Mirabeau was dead.

It was half-past eight in the morning of April 2nd, 1791.

3

The demonstrations of public grief could scarcely have been greater if France had lost a beloved sovereign dying full of years and honour. Even while Mirabeau was still alive the people had insisted on the closing of certain places of entertainment, and now that he was dead all theatres were shut, all balls and festivities were prohibited. Not only the Department of Paris and the Municipality but also many provincial departments went into public mourning.

The capital had recently seen the erection of Soufflot's magnificent new church of Sainte-Geneviève, and on the day after Mirabeau's death a deputation from the Department made to the grieving Assembly the following proposal: that the new edifice should be reserved for the reception of the remains of the nation's great men, dating from the epoch of its liberty; that Honoré

Riqueti de Mirabeau should be judged worthy of this new honour; and that above the classical portals of the new temple of civic piety should be inscribed the words: AUX GRANDS HOMMES LA PATRIE RECONNAISSANTE.

The proposal was decreed with an unusual unanimity; Robespierre, Chapelier and, it is again pleasant to record, Barnave were particularly enthusiastic in their support. As the new church was not quite ready for an entombment it was decided that the Tribune of the People should rest for the time being in the crypt of the old Ste.-Geneviève, beside the remains of Descartes.

The funeral took place on Monday, April 4th. The huge cortège began to form at five o'clock. A detachment of cavalry of the metropolitan National Guard led the column. After the horsemen came sappers and gunners of the sixty Parisian battalions; then came Lafayette, riding with his staff at the head of infantry drawn from all the sixty battalions; then the military band: 'A mournful rolling of drums and the harrowing strains of funeral music filled all hearts with a religious terror', reported the *Moniteur*. Behind the band the clergy walked, and then, born aloft on the shoulders of sixteen men of the dead man's own battalion of Grange-Batelière, came the coffin. It was draped in the battalion's colours, and upon it, where with his ancestors the insignia of feudal rank would have been placed, there lay a civic crown.

Behind walked the National Assembly, ministers of the King and representatives of all the civic bodies of the metropolis. Finally came the clubs and the patriotic societies, most conspicuous of all the Jacobins, who had voted to attend in a body. But one society was absent — the Monarchist Club. It had been formally closed down by the Municipality on the day on which Mirabeau had taken to his bed.

The procession, some three miles long, moved at a solemn pace between two continuous lines of the National Guard and along streets packed with a silent crowd, many of whom were in tears. It was not till midnight that the place of commitment was reached.

Paris was not to see again so great a concourse of her people until a day, still twelve weeks distant, when they would stand again, in silence of another sort, to watch a large and dust-smothered berline complete the last stage of its journey back to the Tuileries from Varennes.

AUTHORITIES AND NOTES

MIRABEAU'S SPEECHES — There have been numerous collections of these. That which has been used here is the original edition of Etienne Méjan, 1791-92. It is in five volumes, and the first two were printed by the Widow Le Jay.

Thirteen of the most famous speeches are in vol. I of Morse Stephens: *The Principal Speeches of the Statesmen and Orators of the French Revolution* (Oxford 1892), which also contains useful critical matter.

THE NOTES which follow indicate the other principal authorities upon which the text has been based. Unless otherwise indicated, Roman numerals refer to volumes, Arabic numerals to pages.

The following abbreviations have been used:

BACOURT—*Correspondance entre Le Comte de Mirabeau et le Comte de La Marck* pendant les années, 1789, 1790 et 1791, recueillie, mise en ordre et publiée par Ad. de Bacourt (2 vols., Brussels 1851; 3 vols., Paris 1851). The Brussels edition has been used, but since there are two editions, references are given where possible to the dates of letters.

This collection, which includes the famous Notes to the Court, is the principal authority for Mirabeau's last two years. It consists mainly of the papers which La Marck, shortly before his death, entrusted to Bacourt for publication, in fulfilment of his promise to the dying Mirabeau.

Hardly less important than the documents is the long *Introduction*, which is, in effect, La Marck's own memoir of his relations with Mirabeau and with the Court.

BRISSOT — J. P. Brissot: *Mémoires*, 3 vols. (1830).

COTTIN — Paul Cottin: *Sophie de Monnier et Mirabeau* (Paris, Plon, 1903).

DUMONT — Etienne Dumont: *Recollections of Mirabeau* (London 1832. A French edition was published in the same year).

FERRIÈRES — Marquis de Ferrières: *Correspondance inédite, 1789, 1790, 1791*, pub. Henri Carré (Paris, Colin, 1932).

HALEM: *Paris en 1790, voyage de Halem*, traduction, introduction et notes par Arthur Chuquet (Paris, Plon, 1896).

LEGG — L. G. Wickham Legg: *Select Documents illustrative of the History of the French Revolution*, 2 vols. (Oxford 1905).

LOMÉNIE — Louis de Loménie: *Les Mirabeau, nouvelles études sur la société française au XVIIIᵉ siècle* (Paris, Dentu, 1889-91).

MALOUET: *Mémoires de Malouet*, publiés par son petit-fils, le baron de Malouet, 2 vols. (Paris, Plon, 1874).

D.-MEUNIER: *Comtesse* — Dauphin Meunier: *La Comtesse de Mirabeau* (Paris, Perrin, 1908).

MONTIGNY: *Mémoires biographiques, politiques et littéraires de Mirabeau*, 8 vols. (Paris 1833-35). An English translation, covering the first four volumes of the French work, appeared in 1835.

This is the massive and compendious monument to Mirabeau's memory compiled by his 'adopted' son, Lucas de Montigny, who withheld his own name from the title-page. A work of filial piety rather than of critical scholarship, it contains masses of original material. It is best taken in conjunction with the highly critical volumes of De Loménie.

ROMILLY: *The Life of Sir Samuel Romilly*, written by himself, 2 vols. (London, Murray, 1842).

WELSCHINGER — Henri Welschinger: *La Mission secrète de Mirabeau à Berlin* (Paris, Plon, 1900).

NOTES

[1] Loménie, III, 1-2; D.-Meunier: *Comtesse*, 124-7.
[2] Loménie, III, 9-19.
[3] Lady Minto: *A Memoir of the Rt. Hon. Hugh Elliot* (1868).
[4] Loménie, II, 454.
[5] Ibid., III, 28-38.
[6] Ibid., 39-45.
[7] Ibid., 43-50.
[8] Ibid., 59-64.
[9] Ibid., 77.
[10] Dumont, 219; D.-Meunier: *Comtesse*, 33-5.
[11] Ibid., 48.
[12] *Lettres de Vincennes*: Mémoire to the Marquis de Mirabeau (*see* note 23); D.-Meunier: *Comtesse*, 20-1.
[13] *Lettres de Vincennes*, as note 12.
[14] D.-Meunier: *Comtesse*, 73.
[15] The letters are printed in Ibid., 96-8.
[16] Ibid., 129-35 (Letters of Emilie to M., 3, 5, 6, 13.ix.1774).
[17] Ibid., 129-93.
[18] Ibid., 196.

[19] Cottin: pp. xi-xxix, and letters pp. 71, 78.
[20] *Des lettres de cachet et des prisons d'état*; D.-Meunier: *Autour de Mirabeau* (Paris, Plon, 1926) 27-8.
[21] *Lettres de Vincennes*; D.-Meunier: *Autour de Mirabeau*, 23-30.
[22] Ibid., 42-4.
[23] These letters were kept by the Lieutenant of Police and were duly stored in the Bastille, where the police records were kept. When the Bastille was destroyed great quantities of such papers were burnt, but much was saved and carted away, including the 'official' Mirabeau-Sophie 'correspondence'. Manuel, Procureur-syndic of the municipality of Paris, published the correspondence in 1792. There have been subsequent editions.
[24] Cottin, p. lxxxii.
[25] *Ma Conversion* eventually found an appropriate publisher. After a first edition in London in 1783 it reappeared as *Le Libertin de qualité, ou confidences d'un prisonnier au château de Vincennes*, écrites par lui-même. A Stamboul, de l'imprimerie des Odalisques, 1784, avec huit figures.
[26] D.-Meunier: *Autour de Mirabeau*, 40.
[27] *Lettres de Vincennes*: M. to Le Noir, 29.ix.77 and 26.xii.77.
[28] D.-Meunier: *Comtesse*, 231.
[29] Dumont, 17.
[30] Loménie, III, 657.
[31] *Lettres de Vincennes*: M. to Dupont, vii.79.
[32] Ibid., M. to Sophie, 9.v.79.
[33] Ibid., Sophie to Boucher, 7.viii.79; D.-Meunier: *Comtesse*, 220.
[34] Loménie, III, 353.
[35] D.-Meunier: *Comtesse*, 237.
[36] Loménie, III, 362.
[37] Ibid., 391-2.
[38] Cottin.
[39] Loménie, III, 396-9.
[40] D.-Meunier: *Autour de Mirabeau* (M. vu par son valet de chambre).
[41] Cottin, pp. ccxlv-vi.
[42] Romilly, I, 179-80, 191.
[43] Brissot, II, 149-53, 348-9; Loménie, III, 442-5.
[44] Romilly, I, 192; Dumont, 42.
[45] D.-Meunier: *Autour de Mirabeau*, 238.
[46] Ibid., 239-40.
[47] D.-Meunier: *Comtesse*, 239, 255.
[48] Full text in Ibid., 243-9.
[49] Ibid., 255-6.
[50] Loménie, III, 499; D.-Meunier: *Comtesse*, 261-2.
[51] Ibid., 240; Loménie, III, 502.
[52] Full text printed as an appendix to Loménie, III.
[53] D.-Meunier: *Comtesse*, 239.
[54] Ibid., 272-3.
[55] Ibid., 232, 273; Brissot, II, Letter from M. to Brissot, 2.viii.83.
[56] Loménie, III, 547-54.
[57] Lady Minto, op. cit., Appendix.
[58] Ibid.; Loménie, III, 562-4; Brissot, II, 369.
[59] Lady Minto: op. cit., 285.
[60] Loménie, III, 570.
[61] Romilly, I, 57-8.
[62] Dumont, 22-3.
[63] Romilly, I, 236.
[64] Brissot, II, 175-93.
[65] Romilly, I, 196.
[66] D.-Meunier: *Autour de Mirabeau*, 144-59.
[67] Romilly, I, 222, 228, 242.

[68] Loménie, III, 579-80.
[69] Ibid., 559-61.
[70] *Dénonciation de l'agiotage* (1787), 69-70.
[71] J. Droz: *Histoire du règne de Louis XVI* (Paris, 1839), I, 401; Loménie, III, 624-38.
[72] Ibid., 638-48.
[73] Welschinger, 8-10.
[74] Ibid., 11-5, 499.
[75] D.-Meunier: *Autour de Mirabeau*, 161-2.
[76] Welschinger, 235 (M. to Périgord, 21.ix.86).
[77] Ibid., 25 (*Situation actuelle de l'Europe*).
[78] *Lettre sur l'invasion des Provinces-Unies à M. le comte de Mirabeau et sa réponse* (published in Brussels, 1787, by Dutch republicans in exile for resisting the Stadholder who, to Mirabeau's indignation, had been supported by a Prussian army).
[79] Welschinger, 173, M. to Périgord, 17.viii.86.
[80] Ibid., M. to Périgord, 13.i.87.
[81] Brissot, II, 370f.; Welschinger, 150; Loménie, III, 637.
[82] Ibid., 644-58.
[83] D.-Meunier: *Autour de Mirabeau*, 178-9.
[84] Loménie, IV, 87-8.
[85] Montigny, VII, 214.
[86] Dumont, 15; Romilly, I, 71.
[87] Montigny, VII, 115, 121; Brissot, III, chap. III.
[88] Loménie, IV, 67, 69.
[89] Talleyrand: *Mémoires* (1891) 192-3; Droz (*see* note 71), II, 38-47.
[90] Loménie, IV, 111-21.
[91] Dumont, 44.
[92] *Dénonciation de l'agiotage* (1787), 72-5; *Lettres du Comte de M. sur l'administration de M. Necker* (1787); Loménie, III, 683f., IV, 124.
[93] Malouet, I, 220-1.
[94] Bacourt, I, 237.
[95] The precise details of how the *Histoire secrète* came to be published are uncertain. I have given what seems to me the most plausible account. *See* Welschinger, 43-5; Bacourt, I, 242; Loménie, IV, 163f.
[96] Bacourt, I, 239-42; Malouet, I, 278; D.-Meunier: *Autour de Mirabeau*, 214.
[97] D.-Meunier: *Comtesse*, 278.
[98] Dumont, 38; Loménie, IV, 270.
[99] Montigny, VI, 39-42; *États-généraux No. 2.*
[100] Loménie, IV, 272-4; Bacourt, I, 244.
[101] *Lettres à ses commettants*, II.
[102] Dumont, 53n.
[103] The speech is in Méjan and other collections. Arthur Young, who was present, says Mirabeau spoke without notes for nearly one hour.
[104] Dumont says that this peroration was based on a hurried pencilled suggestion by himself.
[105] The precise order of events after the King's withdrawal from the Menus plaisirs is not quite certain. I have followed that favoured by Wickham Legg, *Select Documents of the French Revolution*, I, 33.
There is also uncertainty as to the exact words spoken by Mirabeau to Dreux-Brézé. The only certain thing is that they were sufficiently bold and striking to become instantly famous. The version given here is that which Mirabeau published three days later in his Thirteenth Letter to his Constituents. It is by no means the most striking version (he is credited by many with having said 'Go, tell your master that we are here by the will of the people . . .') but, for that very reason, it is likely to be as accurate as it is possible for the report of an impromptu apostrophe, made at an exciting moment, to be. The question is treated carefully in Legg, op. cit., and in Loménie, IV, 328-36.
[106] Malouet, I, 221, 245, 257.
[107] Ibid., 275.
[108] Ibid., 276-81; *see also* Dumont, 44.

[109] Bacourt, Introduction.

[110] Ibid.

[111] Ibid.

[112] Montigny, VI, 107; Ferrières, 83, 84.

[113] The speech is printed in full in Morse Stephens: *Orators of the French Revolution*, vol. I.

[114] Dumont, 86-7; Montigny, VI, 117; Loménie, IV, 346.

[115] Montigny, VI, 131. Full details of the elder Mirabeau's later years are in Loménie, esp. vol., II.

[116] *Dix-neuvième lettre du. C. de M. à ses commettants (see Legg, I, 43-7).*

[117] Ibid. This is the only version of what Mirabeau said. It was an impromptu outburst and was doubtless improved for publication. The story about the supplies for Paris being intercepted was widely believed, but may well be false.

[118] Bacourt, Introduction; Montigny, VI, 132; Loménie, IV, 361-72.

[119] Montigny, VI, 168-9; Bacourt, Introduction.

[120] For a very full account of *Les Impartiaux* and the later *Club monarchique*, see Malouet, II.

[121] Bacourt, Introduction; Morse Stephens, I; Brissot, II, esp., 149-53, 343-50 for Clavière. Mirabeau's debt to his collaborators is fully discussed in Barthou: *Mirabeau*, chap. XVII.

[122] The speech and Dumont's account of it are printed in full in Morse Stephens, I.

[123] For Desmoulins's early admiration for Mirabeau *see* Labracherie: *Camille Desmoulins* (Hachette 1946).

[124] Cottin, pp. ccxlviii-cclx. The exact date of the receipt of Ysabeau's letter is uncertain. It would have taken two days to reach Versailles from Gien, so 11.ix. is the earliest possible date. Mirabeau spoke in the Assembly on 15.ix. so can scarcely have received it later than 12.ix.

[125] The speech is in Morse Stephens.

[126] Bacourt, Introduction.

[127] Loménie, IV, 461-6.

[128] Bacourt, Introduction. On the question of Mirabeau's alleged relations with Orleans *see also* Dumont, 137-42.

[129] Bacourt, letters between M. and La Marck, 13.x.89.

[130] Ibid., I.

[131] Ibid., I, Mme du Saillant to Comtesse de Mirabeau.

[132] Speech in Assembly, 22.vii.89.

[133] *Doutes sur la liberté de l'Escaut, quatrième lettre* (London 1784); Montigny, VII, 9-10.

[134] Bacourt, Introduction.

[135] Ibid., La Marck to M., 10.xi.89.

[136] Malouet, II, beginning of chap. XIII.

[137] Legg, I, 131.

[138] Ibid., 167; Romilly, I, 270.

[139] Bacourt, I.

[140] Ibid.

[141] Loménie, V, 53.

[142] In order to give some idea of the ironic sweep of this impromptu speech I have, while abridging it, dispensed with the customary trailers to mark omissions. The text is in Morse Stephens, I.

[143] Dumont, 98-102, 188-91; Romilly, I, 294.

[144] Morris: Diary, 8-11.x.89.

[145] Bacourt, Note 12 to the Introduction.

[146] Ibid., M. to Lafayette, 19.x.89.

[147] Morris: Diary, 3.xi.89; Bacourt, M. to La Marck, 6.xi.89.

[148] Bacourt.

[149] Ibid., Introduction.

[150] Dumont, 166-73.

[151] Bacourt, M. to La Marck, 23, 29, 31.xii.89; 4, 10, 18, 20, 27.i.1790; Romilly I, 290.

[152] Bacourt, M. to La Marck, 29.xii.89.

[153] Bacourt, M. to La Marck, 27.i.90; Loménie (V, 60-79) takes the view that a treaty between Mirabeau and Monsieur was drafted but never signed.

[154] Bacourt, Introduction.

[155] Ibid., *see* explanatory note attached to Mirabeau's letter of 28.iv.90.

[156] Ibid.

[157] The speech of 20.v.90 is printed in full in Morse Stephens. Pellenc probably worked on the draft, but of all Mirabeau's prepared speeches it is probably the most wholly his own.

[158] Montigny, VII, 257-60.

[159] A. de Lameth's account, quoted in Montigny, VII, 257-8.

[160] Montigny (VII, 260-4) disputes this remark, refusing to admit that his hero could have shown any sign of fear. But was it not simply a touch of grim humour? Humour was not Montigny's strong point.

[161] I have translated somewhat freely and made abridgments in the passages quoted in order to suggest the temper and fluency of the original. This is printed in full in Morse Stephens, I, 165-80.

[162] Ferrières: *Mémoires* (1821), II, 36-7.

[163] Speech of 3.xi.89; Dumont, 210-11.

[164] Montigny, VII, 214.

[165] D.-Meunier: *Autour de Mirabeau*, 206-7.

[166] Bacourt, M. to La Marck, 26.vi.90.

[167] Ibid., Toulouse to La Marck, 1.vii.90.

[168] Loménie, V, 128-30; Bacourt, M. to Toulouse, 1.vii.90 and note to letter of La Marck to Mirabeau of 4.vii.90.

[169] Ibid., sixth and seventh Notes to the Court.

[170] Quoted in J. M. Thompson: *English Witnesses of the French Revolution.*

[171] Bacourt, ninth Note to the Court; M. to La Marck, 7.vii.90.

[172] Ibid., fourteenth Note to the Court.

[173] Ibid., Toulouse to La Marck, 12 and 13.vii.90.

[174] Ibid., La Marck to M., 26.vii.90.

[175] Ibid., twenty-sixth Note to the Court, 12.ix.90.

[176] Ibid., thirtieth Note to the Court, 14.x.90; also Introduction.

[177] Ferrières, 294; Bacourt, letters between M. and Louis de Ségur, x.90.

[178] Halem, 338.

[179] Malouet, II, 98-9.

[180] Bacourt, Introduction and forty-first Note to the Court.

[181] Ibid., Toulouse to La Marck, 15.xi.90; La Marck to M., 16.xi.90.

[182] Halem, 308-10.

[183] Dumont, 212-13.

[184] Bacourt, Introduction.

[185] Ibid., La Marck to Mercy, 26.i.91.

[186] Ibid.

[187] Ibid., Introduction.

[188] Ibid., M. to La Marck, 10.ii.91; Loménie, V, 286-7.

[189] Bacourt, Montmorin to M. 9.ii.91; Malouet, II, 100.

[190] Ibid., 100-9.

[191] Ibid., 108-10.

[192] Bacourt, fiftieth Note to the Court, 2.ii.91.

[193] D.-Meunier: *Autour de Mirabeau*, 254.

[194] Ibid., 266.

[195] Ibid., 267.

[196] Ibid., 268-9.

[197] Aulard: *Les grands orateurs de la révolution* (1914), p. 19.

[198] For an opposite view, put with great cogency, see Barthou: *Mirabeau.*

[199] Welschinger, 79-82.

[200] Bacourt, Introduction.

[201] Ibid.

[202] Romilly, I, 323.

INDEX

INDEX

INDEX

INDEX

351

INDEX

Mirabeau, Comte de: *(contd.)*

141-3; returns to Paris and obtains through Talleyrand a mission to Berlin, 143-4; the Letters from Berlin, 145-8; Letter to Frederick-William II, 148-9; scandal over Dupont's essay, 150-2; end of the Berlin mission, 154, 155; hope of a mission to Holland, 155-6; *Dénonciation de l'agiotage*, 157-8; *Adresse aux Bataves*, 159; sees Romilly in Paris (1788) and meets Dumont, 159-60; opposes Slave Trade, 160-1; deserts Mme de Nehra for Mme Le Jay, 161-3; attitude to Brienne and the *parlements*, 165-7; solicits Montmorin for employment, 165-6; his opinion of Necker, 167-8; vainly seeks Montmorin's support for his election to States-General, 168-9; scandal of the *Secret History of the Court of Berlin*, 169-72; election campaign at Aix and Marseilles, 172-5, 188; position in States-General at its opening, 176, 177, 180; remarks on inaugural ceremonies in *États-généraux*, 176-7; criticism of Necker's speech, 179-80; suppression of *États-généraux* and publication of *Lettres à ses commettants*, 181; share in struggle for a single chamber, 181-7; monarchist sympathies, 185, 189; contributions to the Great Debate of June 15-17th, 1789, 187-91; defiance of Dreux-Brézé and motion for inviolability of deputies, June 23rd, 1789, 193-4; reputation, May-June, 1789, 195-6; reveals his monarchism to Malouet, 196-7; first interview with Necker, 198; beginning of relations with La Marck, 198-201; proposes Address for removal of troops, July 8th, 1789, 202-3; attends his father's funeral, July 14th, 1789, 204; July 15th: speech to deputation to demand removal of troops, 205-6; supports demand for dismissal of Breteuil, etc., 207; misses election as Mayor of Paris, 208; attitude to abolition of feudalism on August 4th, 1789, and to Declaration of the Rights of Man, 209-210; attitude to the moderate royalists and to the Left, 210, 312-3; speech defending the royal veto, 210-4; his collaborators and the *Courrier de Provence*, 211-2; popularity in Paris, 213-4; hears of Sophie's death, 214-5; supports Necker's 'patriotic gift' in a famous speech, 215-6; growth of friendship with La Marck, who recommends him to the Queen, 216-9; anger at the royalist banquet at Versailles and his threatening speech on October 5th, 1789, 219-20; concern for the monarchy after the October Days, 221-2; Memorandum of October 15th, 222, 223, 224-228, 231-2; promotes nationalization of Church property, 229-31; plans for a reformed and parliamentary ministry, 232-4; second interview with Necker, 234; campaign for a parliamentary ministry and its failure, 233-8; dismay at the decree of November 7th, 1789, 238-9; resentment against Lafayette; their mutual dislike, 239, 242-6, 291-2; intrigues with the Comte de Provence, 247-53; brought by Mercy Argenteau and La Marck into relations with King and Queen, March-April, 1790, 253-8; overture to Lafayette, 258; secret employment by the Court begins, May 1790, 260-1; defends royal prerogative of declaring war and peace, 261-70; extravagant living and intense activity after engagement by the Court, 271-4; last effort to win over Lafayette, whom he criticizes to the Court, 274-7; secrecy of his correspondence with the Court, 277-8; interview with the King and Queen, July 3rd, 1790, 278-9; advice concerning Orleans, 280-2; and as to how the Festival of the Federation should be used by the King, 282-5; urges revision of the Family Compact to save Spanish alliance, 285-8; urges King to demand repeal of law barring deputies from ministry, 288-9; themes of his Notes to the Court, 290-1; growing impatience with the Court, 291-2, 293; speech on the question of the Flag, 292-3; refusal to fight duels, 294; equivocal conduct over the Lameth-Castries affair, November 1790, 294-5; the Queen's distrust of him, 295-6, 317-318; triumph at first night of *Brutus*, 297; President of the Jacobin Club, 297, 305, 310; blindness over the Civil Constitution of the Clergy, 298-305, 311, 312; help sought by Montmorin, 305-6; Forty-seventh Note to the Court, 305, 306-11, 312-3; estimates the growing power of the Jacobins, 310; failure to lead the constitutional royalists or to protest at intimidation of Monarchist Club, 312-5; President of the Assembly, February 1791, 315; makes contact with Bouillé through La Marck to concert plan for King's escape, 317-20; calls Malouet into conference; latter's

353

INDEX

355

INDEX

Thonon, 63

Toulon, 21, 22, 174, 196

Toulouse, Achbp. of (*see* Brienne *and* Fontanges)

Troyes, 164

Tuileries, 226, 231, 258, 260, 267, 268, 277, 281, 284, 290, 323, 325, 327

Turgot, 17, 28, 56, 75, 90, 124, 135, 136, 137, 150, 151, 152

VALDHAON, MME DE, 55, 66, 92, 100

Valette, de la, 28

Vallet, Curé, 214

Vancouver, 262

Varennes, 332, 340

Vassan, Marie Geneviève de (*see* Mirabeau, Marquise de)

Vassan, Marquis de, 12

Vaucluse, 115

Vaughan, Benjamin, 129, 131

Vence, Comtesse de, 46-7, 91, 110

Vergennes, 101, 102, 128, 129, 140, 143-144, 147, 156, 161

Vermont, Abbé, 136

Verrières, Les, 63, 64, 65, 100, 103

Versailles, 16, 17, 34, 94, 113, 132-3, 155, 176, 199, 201-3, 213-4, 219-21

Veto, the royal, 189, 210-4, 220

Vienne, Achbp. of, 187

Villeneuve-Mouans, 48-9, 62, 63, 108

Vincennes, 18, 71, 72-4, 75, 76, 77, 81, 87, 94, 101, 327

Voidel, 301-3

Volney, 263

Voltaire, 43, 55, 128, 130, 297

WASHINGTON, 207, 240

Waterford, 102, 121

Wilkes, 125

YORKTOWN, 124

Ysabeau, Dr., 95-6, 214